ASEAN-JAPAN
RELATIONS

The **Institute of Southeast Asian Studies (ISEAS)** was established as an autonomous organization in 1968. It is a regional centre dedicated to the study of socio-political, security and economic trends and developments in Southeast Asia and its wider geostrategic and economic environment. The Institute's research programmes are the Regional Economic Studies (RES, including ASEAN and APEC), Regional Strategic and Political Studies (RSPS), and Regional Social and Cultural Studies (RSCS).

ISEAS Publishing, an established academic press, has issued more than 2,000 books and journals. It is the largest scholarly publisher of research about Southeast Asia from within the region. ISEAS Publishing works with many other academic and trade publishers and distributors to disseminate important research and analyses from and about Southeast Asia to the rest of the world.

ASEAN-JAPAN
RELATIONS

Edited by
TAKASHI SHIRAISHI
and
TAKAAKI KOJIMA

INSTITUTE OF SOUTHEAST ASIAN STUDIES
Singapore

First published in Singapore in 2014 by
ISEAS Publications
Institute of Southeast Asian Studies
30 Heng Mui Keng Terrace, Pasir Panjang
Singapore 119614

E-mail: publish@iseas.edu.sg   *Website*: bookshop.iseas.edu.sg

The responsibility for facts and opinions in this publication rests exclusively with the authors and their interpretations do not necessarily reflect the views or the policy of the publisher or its supporters.

ISEAS Library Cataloguing-in-Publication Data

ASEAN-Japan relations / edited by Takashi Shiraishi and Takaaki Kojima.
   1. Southeast Asia—Foreign relations—Japan.
   2. Japan— Foreign relations—Southeast Asia.
   3. Southeast Asia—Foreign economic relations—Japan.
   4. Japan—Foreign economic relations—Southeast Asia.
   5. East Asia—Economic integration.
   I. Kojima, Takaaki
DS525.9 J3A811   2014

ISBN 978-981-4519-21-2 (soft cover)
ISBN 978-981-4519-22-9 (E-book PDF)

Typeset by International Typesetters Pte Ltd
Printed in Singapore by Mainland Press Pte Ltd

CONTENTS

PREFACE

In the autumn of 2011 I proposed a joint study on ASEAN-Japan relations to Ambassador K. Kesavapany, then director of the Institute of Southeast Asian Studies (ISEAS), and Professor Takashi Shiraishi, president of the Graduate Institute of Policy Studies (GRIPS). They gave their consent to my proposal. Ambassador Tan Chin Tiong, director of ISEAS, added his support to the project.

The objectives of the proposed joint study were to re-examine and critically analyze relations between ASEAN and Japan and to give future perspectives and directions. I was of the view that despite its importance, the ASEAN-Japan relationship had been undervalued and overlooked on both sides in recent years. In this respect, however, I am happy to observe that there has been a favorable change, especially since Shinzo Abe came back to power as prime minister of Japan in December 2012. He is focusing on ASEAN as one of the pillars in his foreign policy.

To implement the joint study, Professor Shiraishi and I tried to recruit competent contributors not only academics but also practioners from ASEAN and Japan to cover various fields such as foreign policy, security, business, development assistance, and fiscal cooperation and to shed light from different angles. We are grateful that Professor Tommy Koh, ambassador-at-large at Singapore's Ministry of Foreign Affairs, Professor Kishore Mahbubani, dean of the Lee Kuan Yew School of Public Policy, and Rodolfo Severino, former ASEAN secretary-general, accepted our request to contribute.

I acknowledge the support of the Japan Foundation, which provided the grant for the publication of this monograph. I would like to express my appreciation also to six generous donors to the project: Mitsubishi Corporation, Mitsui, Sumitomo Corporation, Itochu Corporation, Marubeni, and Sojitz Corporation.

I am indebted to Sunandini Arora Lal, Wee Wong, and Dr. Motoko Kawano of GRIPS for their painstaking efforts at editing this monograph.

Last but not least, I thank Professor Shiraishi, co-editor of this monograph. Without his distinguished expertise and extensive network, this publication would not have been possible.

ABOUT THE CONTRIBUTORS

Takashi Shiraishi, President, GRIPS

Takaaki Kojima, Visiting Senior Fellow, ISEAS, Former Ambassador to Singapore

Rodolfo C. Severino, Head, ASEAN Studies Center ISEAS

Pavin Chachavalpongpun, Associate Professor, CSEAS, Kyoto University

Mie Oba, Associate Professor, Tokyo University of Science

Moe Thuzar, Fellow, ISEAS

Jun Honna, Professor, Ritsumeikan University

Ian Storey, Senior Fellow, ISEAS

Yoshihiro Otsuji, Vice Chairman of Institute for International Economic Studies; Adjunct Professor, GRIPS

Kunihiko Shinoda, General Manager, Beijing Office, Japan Oil, Gas and Metals National Corporation

Yose Rizal Damuri, Head of Economic Department, Center for Strategic and International Studies, Indonesia

Yoichi Nemoto, Director, ASEAN+3 Macroeconomic Research Office (AMRO)

Satoshi Nakagawa, Senior Coordination Officer, ASEAN+3 Macroeconomic Research Office (AMRO)

Naohiro Kitano, Deputy Director, JICA Research Institute

G. Sivalingam, Visiting Senior Fellow, ISEAS

Kishore Mahbubani, Dean, Lee Kuan Yew School of Public Policies

Tommy Koh, Ambassador-at-Large, Ministry of Foreign Affairs, Singapore and Chairman, Institute of Policy Studies, Lee Kuan Yew School of Public Policy, Singapore

1

AN OVERVIEW OF JAPAN-ASEAN RELATIONS

Takashi Shiraishi and Takaaki Kojima

Something interesting has happened to the Japan-ASEAN (Association of Southeast Asian Nations) relationship over the past 15 years.

Things had begun on a hopeful note. Japan took a series of initiatives in regional cooperation up to the 1997–98 East Asian economic crisis and did everything it could to help the crisis-hit countries. The ASEAN-Japan Summit was held for the first time in 1997 at the initiative of Prime Minister Hashimoto Ryutaro (1996–98), who announced that Japan would work closely with ASEAN to stabilize Asian currencies and the Asian financial market. Japan, under his leadership, also proposed to establish an Asian Monetary Fund to provide liquidity support for the crisis-hit countries. In 1998, Finance Minister Miyazawa Kiichi spearheaded an initiative to provide funds to reflate the crisis-hit economies, which led to the establishment of the Chiang Mai Initiative in 1999. The ASEAN-Japan Summit, which was institutionalized along with the ASEAN Plus Three (APT) in 1999, has been held every year since. In 2002, Prime Minister Koizumi Junichiro (2001–06) called for a Japan-ASEAN economic partnership agreement as a first step to building an East Asia community. The Japan-ASEAN Commemorative Summit was held in Tokyo in 2003 when Japan signed the Treaty of Amity and Cooperation (TAC). Japan, together with Indonesia and Singapore, played a crucial role in establishing the East Asia Summit (EAS) in 2005, which extended its membership beyond APT to India, Australia, and New Zealand. In the wake of the 1997–98 crisis, ASEAN

Plus processes thus emerged as a major framework for regional cooperation, with ASEAN as the hub.

Subsequently Japan-ASEAN collaboration stagnated and Japan's profile declined in the region. There were domestic and regional reasons for the stagnation. With prime ministers changing practically every year from 2006–12 after Koizumi stepped down, Japan hardly took any important diplomatic initiatives concerning ASEAN. Japan's economic stagnation also led to the decline in its Official Development Assistance (ODA) and Foreign Direct Investment (FDI) to ASEAN. On the other hand, China has risen economically and hence in its power and profile in ASEAN. It has also taken its own initiatives in shaping the region, such as its FTA proposal, accession to TAC, and the Declaration on the South China Sea.

During these years, something curious happened. After the 1997–98 crisis, ASEAN Plus processes appeared as the primary framework for regional cooperation, often in the name of East Asia community-building, and ASEAN served as a hub for all these processes. But this project is now clearly under question and the future of East Asia no longer looks stable. In light of this change, Japan has once again started to treat ASEAN as a regional group in its own right and with its own weight. This is demonstrated by the fact that Prime Minister Abe Shinzo, who came to power in December 2012, visited Vietnam, Thailand, and Indonesia in his first overseas visit in January, and Malaysia, Singapore, and the Philippines in July 2013. The question is why these changes took place. We argue that the shifts in the Japan-ASEAN relationship can best be understood if they are analyzed in relation to changes in the regional framework in East Asia, Asia-Pacific, and Indo-Pacific.

BRIEF HISTORICAL SURVEY

Since the early history of Japan-ASEAN relations has been thoroughly explored, it suffices for us to note a few important points and limit our historical survey of the Japan-ASEAN relationship to the last 15 years.

ASEAN and Japan have enjoyed a close relationship ever since the establishment of ASEAN in 1967. Japan became the first dialogue partner of ASEAN in 1977 under Prime Minister Fukuda Takeo, who is remembered for the Fukuda Doctrine. Japan was also the largest donor of development assistance to ASEAN for many years. Japanese business invested heavily in the ASEAN region and established extensive production networks and supply chains in the region and beyond. In the early post-Cold War years, Japan also worked closely with ASEAN in the Cambodian peace process.[1]

In retrospect, however, it is Japan's economic cooperation that has had the most lasting impact on ASEAN countries, and it arguably forms the bedrock of the Japan-ASEAN relationship. Japan has given high priority to ASEAN in development assistance. Japan provided development assistance for economic and social infrastructure such as roads, ports, power stations, water and sewerage systems, and human resources development. It also contributed to the creation of a better environment for private sector investment and trade promotion. Japan's FDI surged in the wake of the 1985 Plaza Accord, which saw the swift and substantial appreciation of the yen. ASEAN countries such as Malaysia and Thailand made remarkable progress in the development of manufacturing — export expanded, jobs were created, middle classes increased, and domestic markets expanded. Just as important, the concept of the "developmental state", which began as a heuristic description of Japan's postwar emergence as an economic power, became both an analytical model and a grand strategic prescription, as seen, for example, in Malaysian Prime Minister Dr Mahathir's "Malaysia Inc." for East Asian/Southeast Asian state-building and economic development.

The 1997–98 economic crisis hit some of the ASEAN countries, especially Thailand, Indonesia, and Malaysia, very hard and threatened the developmental state model. As mentioned above, Japan did all it could to help the crisis-hit countries to overcome the crisis. It proposed the establishment of the Asian Monetary Fund and provided funds to reflate the economies through the Miyazawa Initiative, which amounted to US$80 billion in total (in comparison with US$8 billion from the United States and US$4 billion from China). While not a few foreign firms withdrew, Japanese business kept their operations in the region.[2]

Japan also provided emergency humanitarian assistance for food supply and medical care. In those critical years, the Chiang Mai Initiative (CMI) was institutionalized along with the APT, as Nemoto and Nakagawa show in their chapter. The CMI has since been expanded and updated: in 2010, the CMI Multilateralization Agreement took effect and the total fund available has increased to US$240 billion. In addition, in 2006, membership of the East Asia Summit (EAS) was extended to include India, Australia, and New Zealand, in addition to APT.

Confronted with the stalemate at the World Trade Organization meeting in Doha, Japan also changed gear, as Otsuji and Shinoda demonstrate in their chapter, pushing for trade liberalization with a Japan-Singapore Economic Partnership Agreement (EPA) in 2002 (negotiated in 2000–01, signed in January 2002, and ratified in December 2002). Prime Minister Koizumi also called for a Japan-ASEAN EPA in 2002. The Japan-Singapore

EPA, along with China's call for a China-ASEAN FTA, set the momentum for EPAs and FTAs in East Asia. Japan concluded EPAs with Thailand in 2005; Malaysia, the Philippines, and Indonesia in 2006; and Brunei in 2007. Japan also signed a framework agreement with ASEAN in 2007. The Economic Research Institute for ASEAN and East Asia (ERIA) was also established in Jakarta in 2007, mainly with Japanese funding.

Security cooperation also expanded, albeit quietly.[3] Stretching across the Indian Ocean and the South and East China Seas, Southeast Asia is geopolitically crucial for Japan's security, as seen in the fact that more than 80 per cent of Japan's oil import comes through Southeast Asia from the Middle East to Japan. Though memories of war and Japanese atrocities in the 1940s linger on, Southeast Asian fear of the resurgence of Japanese militarism has receded and few these days question Japan's security role in East Asia and Asia-Pacific. The Cambodian Peace Settlement process marked the turning point. Working closely with ASEAN states, especially Indonesia and Thailand, Japan dispatched military personnel and civilians to the UN Transitional Authority in Cambodia (UNTAC). Japan also dispatched SDF personnel to East Timor for the transport of relief goods and provided other logistics support to UNHCR and to UNTAET for peacekeeping operations (PKO). In addition, Japan provided financial support to ASEAN for its PKO missions in East Timor.

At the end of the Cold War, Japan also took the initiative at the 1992 ASEAN Post-Ministerial Meeting to put political and security dialogue on the senior officials' meeting agenda. This initiative, among others, led to the establishment of the ASEAN Regional Forum (ARF) in 1994. Japan also took initiatives in maritime security in Southeast Asia, with a special focus on the Malacca Straits. Japan had already been collaborating with the littoral states of Indonesia, Malaysia, and Singapore over decades in maritime security, but faced with increased piracy in the region's waters, Japan strengthened antipiracy cooperation with such measures as the provision of vessels and equipment, joint research, joint patrolling exercises, and training of law enforcement officials. Japan also extended financial assistance to IMO and the Antipiracy Centre in Kuala Lumpur. An international conference on antipiracy was held in 1999, with the participation of 16 countries including all the ASEAN member states. In his Singapore speech in 2002, Prime Minister Koizumi pushed for cooperation between Japan's coast guard and its ASEAN counterparts. As a result, the Regional Cooperation Agreement on Combatting Piracy and Armed Robbery against Ships in Asia (ReCAAP) was concluded, though its effectiveness is limited because, unhappy with the decision to house the ReCAAP

Information Sharing Center in Singapore, Indonesia and Malaysia have not joined it.

LOCATING JAPAN-ASEAN RELATIONS IN THE REGIONAL SYSTEM

The question, then, is how to make sense of Japan's ASEAN initiatives and the changing Japan-ASEAN relationship. The answer to this lies in locating Japan-ASEAN relations within the broader context of dynamics specific to the region we now call "East Asia".

In the concluding chapter of *Network Power: Japan and Asia*, Takashi Shiraishi and Peter J. Katzenstein (1997) examined the historical trajectory of the East Asian regional system up to the mid-1990s. Fashioned under American hegemony in the early Cold War years in a way that was comparable to, but different from, the Western European regional system, the organization of the East Asian regional system was informed by two strategic decisions. One was double containment: containing the Soviet Union and communist China on the one hand, and Japan on the other hand. This was achieved by integrating Japan's military power into the U.S.-led regional security system, and by U.S. control over Japan's energy supply. The regional hub-and-spokes security system was built on this strategic decision. The other was the fashioning of a triangular trade system of the U.S., Japan, and Southeast Asia (and later Taiwan and South Korea). Japan's two most important prewar trading partners were the United States and China. Although Japanese business wanted to trade with China in the early years of the Cold War, there were issues with undermining U.S. containment of China. The U.S. encouraged Japan to go south, eventually leading to the creation of a system of triangular trade among the U.S., Japan, and Free Asia (minus Japan).

China was not part of this trade system. But a series of developments in the 1970s paved the way for China's integration with the evolving triangular trade system. China normalized its diplomatic relationship with the United States and Japan in the early 1970s, and embarked on modernization from 1978 onwards. It has posted high economic growth rates since then. Domestic political and economic factors have no doubt been indispensable for this transformation, but it was also a product of the politics of integration — part of the invitation for China to develop, as Mark Selden (1997) argued — supported by the U.S. and Japan. Regional economic development from the mid-1980s to the late 1990s, which was crucial for East Asian regionalization, also helped China's transformation and development and led to the integration of China into the regional economy.

That China successfully transformed itself from socialism to a socialist market economy turned out to be crucial for the survival of other socialist states in its vicinity. Both the dynastic party state in North Korea and the military junta in Burma/Myanmar survived while becoming increasingly dependent on China. Vietnam followed in China's footsteps and transformed itself from socialism to a socialist market economy. The region, once bifurcated along communism versus Free Asia ideological and political lines, became increasingly integrated in economic terms in the 1980s and 1990s.

These developments led to the evolution of an East Asian regional system that is structurally different from the European one. Toward the end of the 1980s, democratic revolutions took place in Eastern Europe, culminating in the collapse of the Berlin Wall, the unification of Germany, and the disintegration of the Soviet Union. These changes soon led to the expansion of NATO, as well as to the deepening and expansion of European integration, and the bloody civil wars in the former Yugoslavia in the 1990s. Nothing of this sort took place in East Asia. Democratic transformations did occur in the 1980s — not in socialist countries, but in the Philippines, South Korea, and Taiwan. No socialist states in East Asia collapsed.

In the post-Cold War era, China and Vietnam, if not Myanmar and North Korea, have thus come to be integrated into the regional and global economy, while remaining outside the U.S.-led hub-and-spokes regional security system. This development has created a tension in the regional system that will mount structurally as China rises. Yet, until recently, the system had been stable for three reasons. First, the United States remained engaged in the region, with the U.S.-Japan security alliance, the backbone of the U.S.-led regional security system, redefining its mission not only for Japan's security but also for the region's security and stability. Second, China — its party and state — set economic development as its highest priority, following Deng Xiaoping's dictum of "hide and bide", opting to change the regional system from within. And finally, a regional political project of building an East Asia community has emerged in the wake of the 1997–98 East Asian economic crisis. This happened in part to create a mechanism for regional cooperation, especially in currency, as a hedge to the kind of U.S. intervention that Indonesia, Malaysia, South Korea, and Thailand had experienced; and in part to promote trade and investment in the region in view of the stalling of WTO negotiations and the transformation of the regional triangular trade.[4]

Crucially, China's emergence as an economic powerhouse has brought about an important change in the triangular trade system. In the aftermath of the East Asian economic crisis, Japanese, South Korean, Taiwanese, and other firms reorganized their regional production systems. Capital and intermediate goods were produced in their home countries and production bases in Southeast Asia, while final products were assembled in China for export to the United States and other markets. As a result, the triangular trade system, which had consisted of Japan, Asia (minus Japan), and the U.S., came to be organized with China, Asia (minus China), and the U.S. as its three pillars. This change led to the expansion of Chinese exports to the U.S. and the EU, while the intra-regional trade in capital and intermediate goods expanded between China and the rest of Asia.

The Chinese government also embarked on engaging neighboring states in the wake of the East Asian economic crisis. China normalized its diplomatic relations with its neighbors in two waves: with the U.S., Japan, Thailand, Malaysia, and the Philippines in the 1970s, and with Brunei, Indonesia, Singapore, South Korea, and Vietnam in the early 1990s. The 1990s, however, saw the emergence of two thorny security issues between China and its East Asian neighbors. One concerns Taiwan. Tension between China and Taiwan mounted in the mid-1990s with the first Taiwanese presidential election. China organized military exercises in Taiwan's vicinity and exerted pressure in the hope of influencing the election outcome, while the U.S. and Japan redefined and expanded the mission of their alliance. These developments marked the beginning of China's anti-access strategy.

There also emerged the issue of territorial disputes with China's neighboring states. China occupied the Paracel Islands in 1974 but had no physical presence further south until 1988, when its navy took South Johnson Reef. In 1992, China enacted the Law on the Territorial Sea and the Contiguous Zone, in which its "territorial land" was defined to include "the mainland and its offshore islands, Taiwan and the various affiliated islands including Diaoyu Island, Penghu Islands, Dongsha Islands, Xisha Islands, Nansha (Spratly) Islands and other islands". China also embarked on its military modernization and redefined the PLA mission as the maintenance of the maritime environment and defense of maritime interests.

The enactment of the Law on the Territorial Sea and the Contiguous Zone instantly created territorial disputes in the South China Sea between China, on the one hand, and Vietnam, Brunei, Malaysia, and the Philippines, on the other. Vietnam and China scrambled to occupy as many features in the South China Sea as they could in the same year. Tensions mounted between China and Vietnam over oil exploration, prompting ASEAN to issue a declaration of concern urging the parties involved to exercise restraint and settle their disputes peacefully. In 1995, however, while advocating a bilateral approach in settling the disputes, China occupied Mischief Reef, which is claimed by the Philippines. This development again prompted ASEAN foreign ministers to issue a joint declaration urging all the parties involved to refrain from actions that may threaten peace and safety in the South China Sea.

The ASEAN Regional Forum (ARF) was established in 1994, in part to engage China in a multilateral framework. Initially, China was not an active participant. It did not want the Taiwanese question to be raised there; it chose to deal with territorial disputes in the South China Sea bilaterally and did not want its freedom of action to be constrained multilaterally. Toward the end of the 1990s, however, China adopted a new security concept that led to multilateral engagement of its neighbors in East Asia. In 1999 it proposed the institutionalization of financial cooperation, with the APT as framework. China also agreed to hold a summit meeting with Japan and South Korea in the same year, and to institutionalize the summit the following year. In 2002, China and ASEAN concluded the Framework Agreement on Comprehensive Economic Cooperation and the Joint Declaration on Cooperation in the Field of Nontraditional Security Issues. China and ASEAN also signed the Declaration on the Conduct of Parties in the South China Sea in 2002, as a guideline for interstate behavior until agreement could be reached on a more formal code of conduct. The situation in the South China Sea stabilized. In 2005 the national oil companies of China, the Philippines, and Vietnam signed a three-year joint marine seismic project to explore waters off the Philippines. In the meantime, China signed the Treaty of Amity and Cooperation (TAC) in Southeast Asia — ASEAN's signature pact of association — in 2003. In 2004 China and ASEAN upgraded their relations to an enhanced strategic relationship.

Against this backdrop, China — its party and state leadership — adopted the policy of building good relations with its neighbors and making them its partners (与鄰為善以鄰為伴). The APT emerged as a major mechanism for China to address regional issues and to engage ASEAN and other neighboring states in regional architecture-building without U.S. participation. This policy also informed the Chinese approach to Japan.

China's new policy initiatives, combined with its remarkable economic rise, have largely succeeded in calming fears of China as a threat and have enhanced its presence in the region impressively. Some in ASEAN have jumped on the bandwagon. China's trade with its neighbors has been expanding steadily. Its tourists are visiting neighboring countries in ever increasing numbers. China also actively promotes economic cooperation in infrastructure developments such as highway construction, power plant building, and power grid construction, especially in the Greater Mekong sub-region (GMS). China's rise beckons with all the opportunities it offers for neighboring states, industries, firms, and individuals to benefit economically.

At the same time, China's effort to safeguard its security by developing what it considers a reasonable force structure to deter the U.S. has created insecurity among neighboring states. We have also witnessed since 2008 a major shift in China's policy toward its neighbors. China has revised the "hide and bide" dictum and opted for a more assertive external policy. Territorial disputes have intensified in the South China Sea with the Philippines and Vietnam as well as over Senkaku/Daioyu islands with Japan.[5] There is no sign of a change in China's position on what it defines as "core" issues; on the contrary, issues defined as such have increased in recent years. China's military buildup, including its project to transform its navy into a blue water navy, has progressed significantly. Chinese popular nationalism, which has been cultivated by the CCP since the 1990s to buttress the party-state regime, calls for aggressive and assertive actions on its territorial claims. All of these manifestations of China's rise raise questions on whether China is intent on creating a Sino-centric sphere in East Asia and whether China envisions a multipolar world in which this Sino-centric regional sphere exists side by side with the U.S.-led sphere and the EU.

In this context, China's neighbors have come to be increasingly concerned about China's assertiveness. Although China-watchers disagree about its causes, the fact remains that China has become assertive in the South and East China Seas. Carl Thayer (2010) documents well the development in the South China Sea. Suffice it to note here that China's increasing advances in maritime territorial claims in the South China Sea have led to frictions with Vietnam and the Philippines, and made it a source of "serious concern" in the words of Indonesian President Susilo Bambang Yudhoyono. China's National People's Congress decided to create a county-level town in Hainan province, with administrative responsibility over the Paracel and Spratly islands. The Vietnamese government announced that, in 2009 alone, China had seized 33 Vietnamese fishing boats and 433 crew members in the maritime area both states claim. All of the claimant states except Brunei have built structures and garrisoned the features they occupy. Tensions over territorial disputes have also mounted in recent years in the East China Sea between China and Japan.

The U.S. — whose high-handed intervention during the Asian financial crisis of 1997–98 had generated a backlash on the part of ASEAN, South Korea, and Japan, and which, in the wake of 9/11, had focused its foreign and security policy on the war on terror in the Middle East and neglected Southeast Asia — has now become more actively reengaged in East Asia as an "ally" to countries that want to hedge the risks posed by an assertive China. In his November 2009 speech in Tokyo, President Barack Obama reconfirmed U.S. engagement in East Asia as a Pacific nation. At the July 2010 ARF meeting in Hanoi, U.S. Secretary of State Hillary Clinton stated that the U.S., "like every nation, has a national interest in freedom of navigation, open access to Asia's maritime commons. The United States supports a collaborative diplomatic process involving all claimants for resolving the various territorial disputes without coercion. We oppose the use or threat of force by any claimant".[6] When China sent warships to disputed waters and staged massive naval exercises in a show of force, the U.S. dispatched an aircraft carrier to the South China Sea off Da Nang. And most recently President Obama, in his Australian parliament speech in November 2011, reconfirmed the U.S. as a Pacific power, reaffirmed its determination to maintain its military presence in the region, announced its engagement with ASEAN as a regional organization, and called for the creation of a free, fair, and open trade system with the Trans-Pacific Partnership (TPP) as a model.

A series of developments on the ground have also confirmed U.S. reengagement in East Asia: the resumption of military exchanges with Indonesia as well as U.S. provision of patrol boats to the newly established Indonesian coast guard; the launch of Vietnam-U.S. defense policy dialogues at the deputy ministerial level; the second U.S.-ASEAN Leaders Meeting; the U.S. agreement to provide India with sensitive missile and civilian nuclear technology; and security policy dialogues at the deputy ministerial level between the U.S. and the Philippines. It should also be noted that the U.S. is not only reengaging with Southeast Asia, but is also more willing than the previous administration to participate through multilateral channels.

The region of East Asia thus finds itself between two superpowers. The global financial crisis has accelerated China's rise, military modernization, and influence in regional affairs, while the U.S. has responded by beefing up its military presence and reengaging with East Asia. These forces have led to friction in the maritime domain and strategic competition for influence.

In the face of these assertive superpowers, however, ASEAN has not been passive. It has, in fact, successfully emerged as the hub of region-making, whether through ASEAN Plus FTAs and EPAs, or APT and EAS. ASEAN decided to expand the EAS to include the U.S. and Russia, in addition to the previous ASEAN Plus Six. ASEAN has also sought to develop regional security architecture, such as the ARF and more recently the ASEAN Defence Ministers Meeting (ADMM)-Plus process, which puts ASEAN in a position to set the agenda and make decisions (Thayer 2010, 30).[7] Key Southeast Asian states have reacted by adopting self-help measures to shore up their defense capabilities, while aligning themselves with the U.S. and its allies to pursue hedging strategies as a response to the geopolitical transformation now unfolding in Asia-Pacific.

Japan has also reaffirmed its alliance with the U.S., after Prime Minister Yukio Hatoyama briefly flirted with the idea of an East Asia community as a way to make the triangular relations among Japan, China, and the U.S. "equilateral". This is clear from policy speeches delivered by Prime Ministers Kan Naoto, Noda Yoshihiko, and Abe Shinzo. Prime Minister Abe, for instance, underlined the importance of the Japan-U.S. alliance in his policy speech at the beginning of 2013: "Of course, it is the Japan-U.S. alliance that serves as the cornerstone of Japan's diplomacy."[8] He also confirmed that Japan and the U.S. share a common strategic vision and face similar challenges in the Asia-Pacific region and beyond.

All of these developments have led to a recent shift in the framework for regional cooperation from East Asia back to Asia-Pacific. The APT started in 1997 to promote regional cooperation in response to the currency crisis and heavy-handed U.S. intervention. Persisting memories of this intervention may explain why the CMI retains the APT framework for liquidity support. However, China's recent assertiveness has caused a stir among many states in the region, leading them to align themselves with the U.S. and its allies while expanding the framework for regional cooperation back to Asia-Pacific, of which the U.S. is a part. This explains the emergence of the Regional Comprehensive Economic Partnership (RCEP), ASEAN Plus Six FTA, and TPP as two pathways to the FTAAP and ASEAN Plus DMM and EAS processes for security dialogues. Above all, there was the extension of EAS membership to the U.S. and Russia, a highly symbolic move.

Things may change if China redefines its position on territorial issues. For now, however, there is no sign of a shift in its policy, and tension has mounted between the regional security and the regional trade systems — not only because China has become more assertive in territorial issues, but also because it is not above deploying trade as a foreign policy instrument to impose its will on its neighbors on territorial sovereignty issues. Moreover, as the episode at the ASEAN foreign ministers' meeting in July 2012 in Cambodia demonstrates, China does not hesitate in undermining ASEAN unity to defend its territorial position. As tension mounts, not only the U.S. allies but others too have aligned themselves with the U.S., while engaging China multilaterally and seizing opportunities offered by China for economic gains. The regional framework for cooperation is flexible enough to swing back and forth between East Asia, where the U.S. is excluded, and Asia-Pacific, where it is included. East Asian regionalism has been shaped by a history of small and middle powers having to negotiate between at least two great powers. The regional system, despite its inherent structural tension, has much staying power in the region of East Asia/Asia-Pacific.

Japan-ASEAN relations have evolved in tandem with the regional dynamics sketched out above. Admittedly Japanese government leaders have not been able to articulate Japan's ASEAN policy as did, for instance, President Obama in 2012 at the Australian Parliament. But there was and still is a broad consensus that ASEAN is a strategic partner for building a stable and prosperous Asia/Asia-Pacific. This explains why Japan opted for East Asia community-building with ASEAN as the hub, then engaged ASEAN as a strategic partner in regional cooperation with East Asia and Asia-Pacific, in a partly overlapping and partly in-tension framework. After he came to power in December 2012, Prime Minister Abe announced five principles of diplomacy toward ASEAN during a visit to Vietnam, Thailand, and Indonesia: "Strengthening Japan's relations with ASEAN will be indispensable for the peace and prosperity of the region while also being in Japan's interest."[9]

Deeply unhappy with the U.S. intervention in the 1997–98 East Asian economic crisis and the way IMF handled it, Japan embarked on the APT and CMI with ASEAN as the hub. This was reinforced by the change in Japan's trade policy to promote FTAs/EPAs first with Singapore, then with other individual ASEAN countries and ASEAN as a whole. As is often pointed out, the competition and rivalry between Japan and China was a factor in Japan's engagement with ASEAN. China's call for a China-ASEAN FTA was instrumental in persuading the Japanese public that a Japan-ASEAN EPA was necessary. China's signing of the TAC with Southeast Asia also prompted Japan to sign one. But it is far from the case that Sino-Japanese rivalry drives Japan's ASEAN policy. APT, as well as the East Asia community, was aimed at regional cooperation and, at least in part, as a risk hedge, with the high-handed intervention of the U.S. during the 1997–98 crisis still fresh in memories.

But those days are gone. It is China, rather than the U.S., that looms large as an assertive putative superpower, if not hegemon, in the region now. Recoiling from the prospect of a revolutionary change in the regional order that would disrupt the stability and prosperity of the region, Japan has sought to play its part in strengthening the U.S.-led hub-and-spokes regional security system and in building a network of security cooperation from its base. Japan has embarked on security dialogues with some of the ASEAN countries as well as other players in the region. More recently, Japan and U.S. have been implementing an informal division of labor in which the U.S. will maintain military presence in the region and provide military cooperation, while Japan will provide law enforcement cooperation, especially in coast guard capacity building — as attested by the maritime security cooperation announced at the Japan-ASEAN Summit in 2012. As the current Sino-Japanese conflict over the Senkaku/Diaoyu islands demonstrates, territorial and sovereignty issues both in the South China Sea and the East China Sea will increase in importance in the future. Japan and ASEAN share common concerns and interests to secure safe and free navigation in the seas and address territorial and sovereignty issues peacefully, in accordance with international law, including the United Nations Convention on the Law of the Sea (UNCLOS) and TAC, as well as the UN Charter and the ICJ Statutes.

At the same time, a stable Asia means little if it is economically stagnant and/or if part of it comes under China's sphere of influence and is closed off to the outside world. Deepening ASEAN integration, in this context, not only promises to create a common market and manufacturing bases with a 600-million population, but also to better integrate the region with the world and East Asia/Asia-Pacific. As one of the largest trading partners and investors, Japan definitely has a major stake.

This also explains Japan's strategic interests in the development of CLMV countries (Cambodia, Laos, Myanmar, and Vietnam). Japan has been active in providing development assistance to CLMV, especially in the field of infrastructure building. This is because developing infrastructure is of crucial importance in order for Japanese business to expand and deepen production networks and supply chains. Developing highways and power grids horizontally from Vietnam to Myanmar via Laos, Cambodia, and Thailand will also be instrumental in keeping the GMS open to the global and regional economy, in light of China's attempt to build a hub-and-spokes system with Kunming as the center. This is the intent of the ASEAN Connectivity Master Plan, adopted at the ASEAN Summit in 2010, which is shared by other donors, the ADB, and the World Bank.

Arguably the most important strategic question in the region now is how to engage with a rising China while hedging the risk it poses. This is a challenge faced by both Japan and ASEAN. The crucial question is how to persuade China to commit itself to the joint endeavor of rule- and norm-making, together with all the other parties. All the network modules in which East Asia/Asia-Pacific integration manifests itself — APT, EAS, and other ASEAN Plus processes, as well as ARF and Asia-Pacific Economic Cooperation (APEC) — are useful and have to be deployed for this purpose. In this endeavor, it is important for ASEAN to remain in the driver's seat, precisely because it is not in a position to impose its will on any other party. Although ASEAN is in crisis — as attested by the failure of the ASEAN foreign ministers' meeting in July 2012 to issue a joint communiqué on the South China Sea question — the crisis also provides an opportunity for Japan and ASEAN to develop a new joint project to enable ASEAN to regain its hub status in rule- and norm-making in this region.

It was once a given that regional integration in East Asia was market-driven, without any common political will. Those days are gone. The 1997–98 East Asian economic crisis gave rise to the project to build an East Asia community for cooperation in such fields as currency and trade. East Asia community-building proceeded in a network style with ASEAN as the hub. The more Japan and China competed for regional influence, the more pronounced ASEAN's status as a hub became. China's effort to undermine ASEAN unity is precisely a backhanded recognition of ASEAN's importance as a hub for region-making. Faced with a China intent on advancing its territorial claims in the South China Sea and preventing the internationalization of the issue, ASEAN is clearly at the crossroads. Unable to gain a united position on the South China Sea issue, it may shy away from playing the role of a hub for security cooperation and focus more on economic community-building. On the other hand, it may opt for empowering ASEAN itself, in order to prevent the member-state that happens to be Chair of the Year from imposing its own priorities on ASEAN, while striving to overcome economic divisions among its members and promote economic integration.

Japan's stake in strengthening ASEAN as an institution and a regional hub is beyond question.[10] Supporting the ASEAN economic community and security community is an important objective in itself, but it is also crucial to Japan's strategic interests to ensure that the regional order evolves in a peaceful and steady manner. At the same time, strengthening ASEAN is a means of making ASEAN Plus processes the main mechanism for rule- and norm-making in the region. Superpower rivalry tends to delimit the arena for regional cooperation; strengthening ASEAN is, above all, a way of ensuring that no superpower can dictate the relations among the member countries, what shape the region will take, and how the region will evolve.

Notes

[1] For Prime Minister Fukuda Takeo's initiatives, see Shiraishi, 1997, pp. 185–86.

[2] For Japanese moves in the 1997–98 crisis, see Shiraishi, 2005, pp. 17–40.

[3] For Japan's Southeast Asia initiatives in the immediate post-Cold War years (before the 1997–98 crisis), see Yamakage, 1997, pp. 275–305.

[4] See Pempel, 2010.

[5] For the territorial disputes in the South China Sea, see Ian Storey's chapter as well as Thayer, 2010.

[6] For the policy process leading to Secretary of State Hillary Clinton's statement at the 2010 ARF, see Bader, 2013.

[7] ASEAN defense ministers met for the first time in 2006 to start the process of institutionalizing defense cooperation on a regular basis. The ADMM brought under its umbrella separate meetings of the ASEAN service chiefs (army, navy, and air) and military intelligence that had been meeting informally outside the official ASEAN framework. The third ADMM, held in Thailand in 2009, adopted the Joint Declaration on Strengthening ASEAN Defense Establishments to Meet the Challenges of Non-Traditional Security Threats. ASEAN held its first ADMM Plus meeting in Hanoi in 2010 with the participation of defense ministers from eight of their dialogue partners, which included, among others, Australia, China, Japan, and the U.S. (Thayer 2010, 25–26).

[8] See Abe's speech, "Shoshin Hyomei Enzatsu". Available at <http://www.tokyo-np.co.jp/s/article/2013012801001630.html>.

[9] See Abe's speech, "Hirakareta Umi No Megumi: Five New principles of Japanese Diplomacy", Ministry of Foreign Affairs of Japan. Available at <http://www.mofa.go.jp/mofaj/press/enzetsu/25/abe_0118j.html>.

[10] See, for instance, Shiraishi, 2013.

References

Bader, Jeffrey A. *Obama and China's Rise: An Insider's Account of America's Asia Strategy*. Washington D.C.: The Brookings Institution, 2013.

Katzenstein, Peter J. and Takashi Shiraishi. *Network Power*. Ithaca: Cornell University Press, 1997.

Ministry of Foreign Affairs of Japan. Available at <http://www.mofa.go.jp/mofaj/press/enzetsu/25/abe_0118j.html>.

Pempel, T.J. "More Pax, Less Americana in Asia". *International Relations of the Asia-Pacific*, no. 10 (2010): 465–90.

Selden, Mark. "China, Japan, and the Regional Political Economy of East Asia". In *Network Power*, edited by Peter J. Katzenstein and Takashi Shiraishi. Ithaca: Cornell University Press, 1997.

Shiraishi, Takashi. "Japan and Southeast Asia". In *Network Power*, edited by Peter J. Katzenstein and Takashi Shiraishi. Ithaca: Cornell University Press, 1997.

———. "The Asian Crisis Reconsidered". In *Dislocating Nation-States: Globalization in Asia and Africa*, edited by Patricio N. Abinales *et al*. Kyoto: Kyoto University Press, 2005.

———. "Japan Must Boost Its ASEAN Ties Strategically". *The Japan News*, 15 July 2013.

Shoshin Hyomei Enzatsu. Available at <http://www.tokyo-np.co.jp/s/article/2013012801001630.html> (accessed 28 January 2013).

Thayer, Carlyle A. *Southeast Asia: Patterns of Security Cooperation*. Canberra: Australian Strategic Policy Institute, 2010.

Yamakage, Susumu. "Japan's National Security and Asia-Pacific's Regional Institutions in the Post-Cold War Era". In *Network Power*, edited by Peter J. Katzenstein and Takashi Shiraishi. Ithaca: Cornell University Press, 1997.

2

JAPAN'S RELATIONS WITH ASEAN

Rodolfo C. Severino

Japan has, for many years, held a position of transcendental importance for the Association of Southeast Asian Nations, or ASEAN, as well as for its member countries.

INSTITUTIONAL LINKAGES

In December 2003, the leaders and foreign ministers of Japan and the ten-nation ASEAN gathered in Tokyo to "commemorate" 30 years of ASEAN-Japan relations. It was the first time that ASEAN leaders had met outside of Southeast Asia. At that "Commemorative Summit", according to a Japanese government summary, Japanese "Prime Minister Junichiro Koizumi clearly stated that Japan would continue to regard its relationship with ASEAN as very important and confirmed that Japan and ASEAN should further develop their relations as sincere and open partners that 'act together, advance together.'"[1]

Indonesia's President Megawati Soekarnoputri, speaking for all of ASEAN, pointed out:

> In the past three decades, ASEAN and Japan have developed a mutually beneficial partnership and cooperation which continue to deepen and widen. Let me reaffirm that the ASEAN-Japan long-standing relations and cooperation have contributed significantly to the peace and prosperity of the people in Southeast Asia as well as in the wider region of East Asia and the Asia-Pacific.

Although our relationship is in a good state, nevertheless the dynamic global and regional environments require ASEAN and Japan to work together even more closely. Globalization and greater interdependence among countries in the world presented ASEAN and Japan with new opportunities and new challenges.

Megawati continued:

Japan has been and will continue to be the most important economic partner of ASEAN. We therefore agreed to develop a broad-based economic partnership underpinned by the ASEAN-Japan Comprehensive Economic Partnership Agreement to develop deeper understanding among our people.[2]

At their summit meeting in Phnom Penh in November 2012, the ASEAN states agreed to Japan's proposal for another Commemorative Summit in December 2013, or ten years after the first one. At their summit in November 2002, also in Phnom Penh, the Japanese and ASEAN leaders had declared their intention to conclude a "framework" for an ASEAN-Japan Comprehensive Economic Partnership (AJCEP) agreement, which they concluded in October 2003 in Bali. In April 2008 Japan and all ten ASEAN member-states completed the signing of the AJCEP agreement, which covered trade in goods, trade in services, investments, economic cooperation, and dispute settlement.

Although both Japan and ASEAN have continued to deny any relationship between the AJCEP and developments elsewhere in the world, their announcement of their intention to conclude an AJCEP framework agreement came after then Premier Zhu Rongji of China proposed in 2000 an ASEAN-China free trade agreement (FTA), which was signed in November 2002. While the report of the high-level task force on the AFTA-CER[3] FTA antedated the Chinese and Japanese announcements, it was, for political reasons, not signed until February 2009. The start of negotiations of two other ASEAN FTA agreements with external partners was announced well before 2009 — negotiations with India began in 2003 and with the Republic of Korea in 2004.

The 2003 ASEAN-Japan Commemorative Summit in Tokyo, however, was followed by similar ASEAN Summits with China (2006, in Nanning, capital of the Guangxi Zhuang Autonomous Region, southern China, to "commemorate" the 15th anniversary of China's "Consultative Partnership"[4] with ASEAN), the Republic of Korea (2009, Jeju Island, the 20th anniversary of the ROK's admission as ASEAN's "Sectoral", not full, Dialogue Partner), and India (2012, New Delhi, the 20th anniversary of India's "Sectoral" Dialogue Partnership with ASEAN).[5]

What happened in 1973 that ASEAN and Japan were commemorating in 2003? Certainly it was not Japan's becoming ASEAN's first Dialogue Partner. Australia and the European Economic Community (EEC), later the European Union, each claim to have been the first ASEAN Dialogue Partner and date the start of the Dialogue system to an event that supports its claim. The Europeans reckon that start as having taken place with the establishment in 1972 of the Special Coordinating Committee of ASEAN Nations, or SCCAN, a body that ASEAN had set up especially to conduct its interaction with the EEC. The Australians, on the other hand, date the founding of the system of ASEAN Dialogue Partners to 1974, when ASEAN and Australia started their Dialogue relations, with Australia being generally recognized as the first individual country to be a Dialogue Partner of ASEAN. To commemorate this, the Australian and New Zealand prime ministers were invited to Vientiane for a summit meeting with ASEAN in 2004. (New Zealand joined the system in 1975, Canada and the United States in 1977, and the Republic of Korea as a full Dialogue Partner in 1991. China, India, and Russia took part in the ASEAN Post-Ministerial Conferences for the first time in 1996. Other countries have pressed to join in, notably Pakistan, currently a Sectoral Dialogue Partner.)

What ASEAN and Japan were apparently observing in December 2003 was the 30th anniversary of the start in 1973 of their close, albeit "informal", consultations. The ASEAN foreign ministers (the foreign ministers had been taking care of ASEAN trade matters before 1976) had called for those consultations in April of that year in order to raise with their Japanese counterpart Japan's production and export of synthetic rubber, something that threatened the economy of Malaysia, which was, then as now, one of the world's leading exporters of natural rubber, together with those of Indonesia and Thailand. ASEAN's reaction in the next few years to Japan's response to the ASEAN countries' concerns about rubber alternated between welcome for and dissatisfaction with the Japanese government's interventions in the global rubber market.

The start in 1973 of ASEAN-Japan ministerial consultations could thus be considered as a milestone both in ASEAN-Japan relations and in ASEAN's system of Dialogue Partnerships. In 1978 the ASEAN foreign ministers invited their Japanese counterpart to join them in Pattaya, Thailand, on the occasion of ASEAN's annual ministerial meeting, the 12th formal one. The meeting with Japan was called the Post-Ministerial Conference, or PMC. The ASEAN PMC with the foreign ministers of ASEAN's Dialogue

Partners, held immediately after the annual ASEAN foreign ministers'
meeting, has since 1980 become an annual affair. In any case, Japan was
clearly a pioneer in the process.

Until 1996, when China, India, and Russia began to take part in them
— a time when those countries had not yet been recognized as economic
powers — the Dialogue Partnerships were, from ASEAN's point of view,
focused on market access. In the early years the focus was on commodities
such as rubber, tin, and vegetable oils; later it was on foreign direct
investment; and, throughout — especially with the entry into ASEAN of the
four newer and less-developed members — it was on official development
assistance. It therefore comes as no surprise that until the mid-1990s,
when China, India, and Russia — which then had little to contribute
economically to Southeast Asia — were finally admitted into the Dialogue
system, ASEAN's Dialogue Partners consisted exclusively of developed
countries.[6] Those countries were, for a long time, ASEAN's leading actual
or potential export markets and sources of investment, technology, tourists,
and development aid. At the same time, the Southeast Asian countries
were aware of their own strategic importance to the world's major powers,
particularly in terms of location and natural and other resources.

Partly because of the perception that it was fundamentally Washington's
political and security ward, and the strictures that were imposed on its
security and military capabilities by its own U.S.-written but popularly
supported constitution, and partly also because, most likely as a result,
it had a propensity to respond to international developments with cash
handouts, Japan used to be viewed by the international community,
including Southeast Asia, as a mainly economic animal. Nevertheless, like
those of other major powers, Japan's economic purposes had their own
strategic dimension.

As I pointed out in the book that I wrote and the Institute of Southeast
Asian Studies in Singapore published in 2006, Japan has conducted its
relations with ASEAN in three principal, mutually reinforcing ways —
trade and investments, development assistance, and political and symbolic
gestures. As it emerged from the Pacific War and its occupation by the
United States, Japan saw Southeast Asia once again as a source of needed
raw materials, including fossil fuels, certain minerals, and timber, as well
as an export market and, later, as a site for some Japanese manufacturing
industries. "To be able to perform these functions, Southeast Asia had to
have its purchasing power raised, its people trained, and its infrastructure
built," I wrote. "Development assistance was meant not only to promote
Japanese exports to Southeast Asia but also to increase the region's capacity

to absorb Japanese investments, as well as strengthen political links with individual countries in the neighbouring area. In any case, Japanese overseas development assistance (ODA) was highly concentrated in Southeast Asia. Even in the 1990s and beyond, Southeast Asia accounted for around 30 per cent of Japan's ODA."[7]

As a leading market, source of investments and technology, and financier of cultural and people-to-people exchanges, Japan reinforced political ties with Southeast Asia, while the bonds between the Japanese and Southeast Asian states fashioned the political framework for trade, investments, and development aid, as well as for cultural exchanges.

As for the Southeast Asians, there was some apprehension about Japanese economic domination, even as they appreciated the market opening up, especially for their manufactured exports, the jobs created, and the benefits bestowed by the cultural exchanges. Although, in their pragmatism, they had largely gotten over the bitter memories of invasion, occupation, and atrocities, and although their governments did not go so far as to fan anti-Japanese sentiments for political gain, many Southeast Asians harbored a resentment of what the Japanese had done to them and their fellow nationals during the Japanese occupation of their countries during the Pacific War.

This was the situation in which Japan's prime minister, then Kakuei Tanaka, embarked on a round of ASEAN capitals — then five — at the beginning of 1974. In that round, Tanaka and Japan's political elite were apparently surprised by the overtly anti-Japanese manifestations of the riots that greeted Tanaka in Jakarta and, to a lesser extent, in Bangkok. These anti-Japanese sentiments were particularly alarming for Tokyo in the light of the sharp rise in the price of crude oil as a result of the hostilities in the Middle East in 1973. A reexamination of Japan's relations with Southeast Asia, one of its main sources of energy and other raw materials, for which it had fought a war just a few decades before, was clearly called for.

Part of this reassessment was evidently the greater attention that Japan devoted to Southeast Asia. It is perhaps no coincidence that the Japan International Cooperation Agency, or JICA, was established in 1974 in the Ministry of Foreign Affairs as the country's leading conduit for official development aid. Nor perhaps was it a coincidence that the Ship for Southeast Asian Youth was set up the same year. The ship is a Japanese luxury liner that brings together every year 300 to 350 young people from Japan and the ASEAN member countries for a congenial cruise, calls at Southeast Asian and Japanese ports, and family stays.

More than three years after the Tanaka swing in Southeast Asia, Prime Minister Takeo Fukuda and his colleagues from Australia and New Zealand met with the ASEAN leaders — still five — on the occasion of the second ASEAN Summit. After the meeting, in August 1977 in Kuala Lumpur, Fukuda embarked on his own round of ASEAN capitals, at the end of which, in Manila, he enunciated what has become known as the Fukuda Doctrine — a peaceful, nonmilitary Japan, consolidation of Japan's "heart-to-heart" relationship of mutual confidence with Southeast Asia, equal partnership with ASEAN and its member countries, and mutual understanding with the nations of Indochina. The significance of the fourth and last plank of this "doctrine" arises from the fact that it was pronounced shortly after the end of the "American War" in Vietnam and the rest of the former French Indochina and amid the domestic controversy that it had been arousing in the United States.

Since then, Japanese prime ministers followed in Fukuda's footsteps in visiting ASEAN capitals early in their tenures — Zenko Suzuki in 1981, Yasuhiro Nakasone in 1983, Noboru Takeshita in 1989 (having met with ASEAN's leaders, together with those of Australia and New Zealand, on the occasion of the third ASEAN Summit, in December 1987 in Manila), Toshiki Kaifu in 1991, Kiichi Miyazawa in 1993, Tomiichi Murayama in 1994, and Ryutaro Hashimoto at the beginning of 1997.[8] With the enlargement of ASEAN from six — the original five plus Brunei Darussalam — to ten, a process that started with the admission of Vietnam into ASEAN in 1995, the round of ASEAN visits by every new Japanese political leader became more selective but remained *de rigueur*.

In 1981 the Japanese government, with nominal financial contributions from the ASEAN member states, set up the ASEAN Promotion Centre on Trade, Investment and Tourism (later renamed the ASEAN-Japan Centre) in Tokyo, the first of only four such governmental centers in state capitals. The ASEAN-Japan Centre is devoted to the promotion of Japanese imports from, investments in, and tourism to the ASEAN countries. It has served as a reliable source of information on ASEAN and its member countries, thus helping the ASEAN embassies in Tokyo with their information and promotions work, if not doing that work for them. It was not until the 21st century that similar centers were founded in Seoul, Beijing, New Delhi and Moscow, with structures and modes of financing different from their predecessor in Tokyo. In keeping with the Commemorative Summit's directive to "reform" the ASEAN-Japan Centre, an Eminent Persons Committee was formed in 2005 to recommend steps for such a reform. The committee submitted its final report to the ASEAN-Japan Summit meeting in Cebu in 2007. This led to amendments to the agreement establishing the center.[9]

Toward the end of 1997, Prime Minister Mahathir Mohamad of Malaysia, exercising his right and privilege as host and chair of that year's ASEAN Summit, invited his counterparts from China, Japan, and South Korea to Kuala Lumpur for the first top-level meeting of what has come to be known as ASEAN+3. Before many years had passed, it became evident that the new ASEAN+3 scheme, with the Chiang Mai Initiative in the finance sector as its centerpiece, was growing speedily both as a concept and in terms of forums and mechanisms. The perception was also gaining headway that ASEAN+3 was being increasingly dominated by a rapidly rising and seemingly well-coordinated China. To those who held this perception, a hedge was needed to counterbalance ASEAN+3.

Intentionally or not, the East Asia Summit, or EAS, although originally conceived as the institutionalization of the ASEAN+3 summit-level forum, would serve this purpose. ASEAN seized its reins and laid down three criteria for states other than the ASEAN+3 countries to be included in it — full Dialogue Partnership with ASEAN, accession to the 1976 Treaty of Amity and Cooperation in Southeast Asia (TAC), and "substantive relations" with ASEAN. The first two criteria were matters of fact. The third was clearly a matter of political calculation.

According to these criteria, it was decided that Australia, India, and New Zealand — all ASEAN Dialogue Partners, all signatories to the TAC (in fact, it appears that Australia felt compelled to accede to the TAC, which it had been reluctant to do, in order to be allowed to take part in the EAS), and all judged to have "substantive relations" with the association — would participate in the new "leaders-led" forum. Publicly supported primarily by Indonesia, Japan, and Singapore, the EAS was first convened in 2005 in Malaysia, whose turn it was to chair and host the ASEAN Summit. True to its practice of yielding to ASEAN on matters that Beijing did not deem to be in its vital interest, China apparently had to give up its ambition to host the first or second EAS, ASEAN having insisted that each EAS be held in the ASEAN country hosting and chairing the ASEAN and ASEAN+3 Summits.

Before long, in 2009, the EAS, with its 16 participants, invited Russia, which had desperately wanted to take part in the inaugural EAS, and the United States to join it, mainly on account of ASEAN's desire to keep the United States engaged in the region. Accordingly, President Barack Obama and Foreign Minister Sergey Viktorovich Lavrov (representing the Russian leader) attended the EAS in 2011 in Bali and in 2012 in Phnom Penh. Both Russia and the United States had apparently expressed their interest in taking part in the EAS in order to have a voice in the affairs of East

Asia. Evidently, Japan and several ASEAN states thought that such a voice for Russia and the United States would be in their interest too.

JAPAN AND ASEAN — AND EAST ASIAN — INTEGRATION

Meanwhile, the 1985 Plaza Accord was having an enormous impact in both Japan and Southeast Asia. One of the important elements of the Plaza Accord was the substantial appreciation of the Japanese yen against the U.S. dollar, particularly between 1985 and 1987. An effect of the appreciation was the economic incentive for Japanese companies, with the encouragement of their government, to invest in production facilities in Southeast Asia (China, Taiwan, and South Korea were not yet manufacturing powerhouses) and elsewhere in the world. As a result, it can truly be said that the industrialization of much of Southeast Asia started with the appreciation of the Japanese yen.

In 1996, ASEAN agreed to set up the ASEAN Industrial Cooperation (AICO) scheme, which would allow production facilities of the same conglomerate in two or more ASEAN countries to trade products at the CEPT/AFTA tariff end-rate. It is highly significant that most of the firms that participated in the AICO scheme were well-known Japanese automotive and electronics companies, such as Toyota, Nissan, Honda, Isuzu, Denso, and Sony. (However, only four ASEAN countries — Indonesia, Malaysia, the Philippines, and Thailand — were involved substantially in the scheme.) With the CEPT/AFTA tariff rate of ASEAN's leading trading nations dropping to zero, the ASEAN economic ministers decided to terminate AICO in 2011.

According to the Japan External Trade Organization (JETRO), investments by Japanese companies in ASEAN were overtaken by those that they made in China only in 2012 and have far outstripped those that they placed in India. In this and other ways, Japan and its companies have shown that they recognize their interest in the integration of ASEAN as a regional economy. An integrated Southeast Asian economy would make it easier and more profitable for goods produced by Japanese firms in the region to move around within that region and to be bought and consumed in it or exported elsewhere. Japanese ODA makes this possible, mainly through its financial support for the construction of infrastructure and the development of human resources.

In addition to its humanitarian impulses, this is one of the reasons why Japan's technical cooperation program is increasingly devoted to projects, some of which are undertaken in collaboration with more-advanced ASEAN members, aimed at narrowing the income and development gaps among and within ASEAN countries. In terms of narrowing the development divide between the six older and the four newer ASEAN member states (the four newer ones include three "least-developed nations," as designated by the United Nations), which has become a mantra in ASEAN circles, what this means for Japan is more focused Japanese attention to the economic development of the newer ASEAN member states. For example, of the 47 projects funded by non-ASEAN partners in the first work plan (2002–08) of the Initiative for ASEAN Integration, a program aimed at facilitating the economic integration of the four newer members into ASEAN, more than half had Japan's support. (It is not generally known that 186 projects were supported by the six ASEAN member states considered as being more advanced than the other four.) Whether these projects are effective or not is another issue.

Issued by the ASEAN leaders in October 2010, the Master Plan on ASEAN Connectivity is meant to tie the ASEAN countries, including the four newer ones (all located on mainland Southeast Asia), closer together through infrastructure, trade and investment facilitation and promotion measures, and people-to-people exchanges.[10] Japan is at the forefront of support for the Master Plan, which was put together mainly by the Japanese-led and -funded Economic Research Institute for ASEAN and East Asia, or ERIA,[11] and whose projects are largely financed by the Japan ASEAN Integration Fund (JAIF). Part of Japan's involvement is its support for the development of ports and the improvement of logistics. As a measure toward promoting better coordination and a manifestation of the earnestness of its support, Japan has set up a Task Force on Connectivity. Japanese government ministries and agencies and business organizations belong to the task force, which also interacts with the ASEAN Connectivity Coordinating Committee. JAIF was set up specifically to support ASEAN's community-building efforts, including the three blueprints in the ASEAN Community Roadmap.[12]

Japan is also involved, particularly in the form of financing and the presence of Japanese "experts", in several subregional development schemes in Southeast Asia. These encompass the Greater Mekong Subregion (GMS) and its economic corridors, the Indonesia-Malaysia-Thailand Growth Triangle (IMT-GT) among Sumatra, eight states of Peninsular Malaysia and southern Thailand, and the Brunei-Indonesia-Malaysia-Philippines East ASEAN Growth Area (BIMP EAGA) among Brunei Darussalam, eastern Indonesia, East Malaysia, and the southern Philippines. Japan's contribution to the GMS is focused primarily on improving the investment climate in the subregion, mainly through the financing of infrastructure construction, including that of the second international bridge across the Mekong, and support for policy reform. Although the subregional schemes are technically outside ASEAN, the regional association often takes note of their development. All the states involved in them are ASEAN members, plus, in the case of the GMS, China. Now, Japan has pledged its support for the Master Plan on ASEAN Connectivity, support that includes financing for the development of the required human resources and infrastructure.

Despite the money and efforts of Japan's government and firms, and despite economic integration's patent benefits to the region and its individual nations, ASEAN is not yet fully integrated as a regional economy. Japan, therefore, has had to strike separate deals with individual countries. Even before the completion in April 2008 of the signing of the Comprehensive Economic Partnership agreement with ASEAN as a group, for example, Japan had concluded "comprehensive" bilateral agreements with Singapore (2002), Malaysia (2005), the Philippines (2006), Thailand (2007), and Indonesia (2007) embodying the specific interests of each of the parties.

Soon after the 1997–98 East Asian financial crisis struck, particularly in South Korea and the ASEAN countries of Thailand, Indonesia, the Philippines, and Malaysia, Japan gained points in East Asian eyes with its proposal, made by some Japanese officials, for an Asian Monetary Fund in apparent rivalry with the International Monetary Fund. Tokyo lost goodwill and esteem when it seemed to cave in to U.S. pressure and withdrew the proposal. At the same time, China won points and goodwill simply by refraining from engaging in "competitive devaluations" with East Asian countries that were seeing their currencies losing their value. However, the Japanese proposal for an Asian Monetary Fund has seemed to find new life in the evolving Chiang Mai Initiative Multilateralization, in which Japan has played a leading role.

Under a program called the New Miyazawa Initiative (the late Kiichi Miyazawa was then minister of finance), Japan offered in October 1998 the equivalent of US$30 billion to "assist Asian countries in overcoming their economic difficulties and to contribute to the stability of international financial markets".[13]

It is a safe guess that although both states are, deliberately, officially coy about admitting it in public, China and Japan see themselves as rivals for global leadership, especially in East Asia. This rivalry is evident in the tension between the East Asia Free Trade Area (EAFTA) and the Comprehensive Economic Partnership for East Asia (CEPEA).

EAFTA was originally conceived of as being based on ASEAN+3. It was proposed in 2001 by the East Asia Vision Group (EAVG) of "eminent intellectuals" from the ASEAN+3 countries. The EAVG had been formed at the instance of then South Korean President Kim Dae-jung and led by his government in Seoul. Its report was endorsed by the intergovernmental East Asia Study Group (EASG) at the ASEAN+3 Summit of November 2002, with the creation of an EAFTA as one of the nine "Medium-term and Long-term Measures" (as distinct from the 17 Short-term Measures) that the EASG recommended for implementation.[14] Again at the proposal of the South Korean president, the ASEAN+3 leaders had formed the EASG of senior foreign-ministry officials and the ASEAN secretary-general. According to its own terms of reference, the EASG saw itself as "part of the ASEAN+3 process". Invoking "the Joint Statement on East Asia Cooperation of the ASEAN+3 Summit in Manila in 1999 and the discussions of the Leaders at their various ASEAN+3 Summits", the EASG's November 2002 "Final Report" to the ASEAN+3 leaders said that the EASG was to "assess the recommendations of the EAVG" and "explore the idea and implications of an East Asian Summit."[15]

ASEAN+3 had apparently not reached consensus on the EAFTA-CEPEA tension. The press statement of the Cambodian chairman of the November 2002 ASEAN Summit and related meetings had this to say: "The (ASEAN Plus Three) leaders expressed willingness to explore the phased evolution of the ASEAN+3 summit into an East Asian summit. ... Leaders agreed with the Republic of Korea's vision for ASEAN+3 summits to evolve in the long term into East Asian summits and eventually an East Asian Free Trade Area."[16] The formulation was evidently the result of many compromises. In any case, the statement does not define the nature of the "phased evolution" or set the duration of the "long term" or, indeed, address the all-important question of participation.

Even as China favors ASEAN+3, Japan patently prefers CEPEA — which is based on the East Asia Summit — whether it is an East Asia of ASEAN+3+3 (Australia, India, and New Zealand) or an East Asia of ASEAN+3+5 (with Russia and the United States) or more. The Japanese preference is clearly reflected not only in the fact that Japan proposed CEPEA, but also in the work of ERIA. Led by Japanese nationals, funded largely by Japanese money, and supported by Japan's Ministry of Economy, Trade and Industry (METI) and the METI-directed JETRO, ERIA was proposed by Japan and is evidently supportive of economic cooperation among ASEAN+3+3 or more. In the words of its chairman's statement, the January 2007 EAS "welcomed Japan's proposal for an Economic Research Institute for ASEAN and East Asia (ERIA)".[17]

At the same time, a small ASEAN+3 Macroeconomic Research Office (AMRO) has been set up in Singapore.[18] Established in 2011, it is headed by a Japanese national, on a two-year term, after the one-year tenure of his predecessor and first head of AMRO, a former Chinese official. The office is supposed to undertake some of the regional economic surveillance functions of the Chiang Mai Initiative Multilateralization, generally regarded as the core of ASEAN+3 economic cooperation. These functions used to be performed by the ASEAN Secretariat with the support of the Asian Development Bank. AMRO is basically supported by Japan's Ministry of Finance.

Thus, the Japanese government, through its enormous financial and human resources, is at the heart of all regional economic cooperation institutions and mechanisms. Basically supported by METI, CEPEA and ERIA indicate Japan's preference for the EAS and its schemes, while the Ministry of Finance's backing for AMRO has Japan's foot also in ASEAN+3 and its financial-cooperation initiative. Both are headed by Japanese nationals.

According to their chairman's statement of October 2009, almost four years after they or their predecessors first met, the then-16 East Asia Summit leaders, welcoming the decision of the ASEAN economic ministers to ask the ASEAN Senior Economic Officials Meeting (SEOM) "to discuss and consider the recommendations" of the working group set up to study CEPEA, observed that "CEPEA and East Asia Free Trade Area (EAFTA) could be examined and considered in parallel".[19] If this was a directive for SEOM to reconcile EAFTA and CEPEA, it was obviously an attempt to pass on to the senior officials an impossible task, since the two schemes involve different, if overlapping, participants and are promoted by different sets of states with divergent national interests.

However, a compromise may have been reached with the adoption by the ASEAN leaders in November 2011 of an ASEAN "Framework" for a new Regional Comprehensive Economic Partnership (RCEP), a set of "principles under which ASEAN will engage interested ASEAN FTA partners in establishing a regional comprehensive economic partnership agreement and, subsequently, with other external economic partners". It later emerged that the RCEP agreement would be among the ASEAN members and those countries that had free-trade, Comprehensive Economic

Cooperation, or Comprehensive Economic Partnership agreements with ASEAN as a whole — China, Japan, India, the Republic of Korea, and Australia and New Zealand. These would be the EAS participants, but, at least initially, without Russia and the United States. The ASEAN Summit meeting announced in April 2013 that the negotiations on the RCEP would start in May 2013 "with a view to completing them by 2015."[20] The initial round of those negotiations did take place in May.

The idea is to consolidate the FTA, CEC, or CEP agreements that ASEAN as a group has with external partners, thus, among other things, avoiding the "noodle- or spaghetti-bowl" effect[21] with which exporters and importers are presumably confronted when navigating the disparate rules of origin embedded in the agreements. The RCEP would also, again presumably, seek to update these agreements, some of which are over 20 years old. With the U.S.-promoted Trans-Pacific Partnership, or TPP, very much alive, the RCEP is apparently acceptable to the proponents of both EAFTA and CEPEA.

A similarly open-ended trade scheme is the TPP, which antedated the RCEP and is now being pushed by the United States. The original parties to the TPP were Brunei Darussalam, Chile, New Zealand, and Singapore (since June 2005). Now, several other countries are engaged in negotiations with the original four participants and among themselves — Australia, Canada, Malaysia, Mexico, Peru, and Vietnam, as well as Japan and the United States. From March 2010 to August 2013, 19 rounds of formal negotiations were held, five of them in the United States. The participation of Australia, Brunei Darussalam, Malaysia, New Zealand, Singapore, and Vietnam in both the TPP and RCEP negotiations supposedly indicates the inclusive nature of the two proposed free-trade schemes.

Despite its explicitly and technically open-ended character and the repeated assurances by American officials that the TPP is meant not to exclude China but, indeed, to prevent the Pacific from being "split down the middle", those officials and others insist that the TPP should contain provisions that would make it a "high-quality" trade agreement and, presumably, require certain domestic reforms of some participants in order to indicate and make possible the height of its quality. While making it easier for members of the U.S. Congress to support the agreement and giving reform-minded persons in putative participant countries something to invoke, such provisions would make it difficult for the Chinese government, for example, to join the negotiations, unless one or the other — China or the United States — "gave" or the two somehow reached a compromise to the satisfaction of both. Nor has China been "invited" to take part in the negotiations, in contrast to the way that Japan has been pressured to do so. It is not only China that seems to be outside the ambit of the TPP. Other large economies, like those of Indonesia, South Korea, India, Russia, Brazil, and South Africa, are too.

The Democratic Party of Japan (DPJ) was quite ambivalent about the TPP, probably concerned about the lobbying power of the agricultural and medical sectors and, at the same time, about Japan's relations with the United States. Then Prime Minister Yoshihiko Noda of the DPJ expressed Japan's desire to join the TPP negotiations at the APEC Economic Leaders Meeting in Honolulu and on the occasion of the ASEAN-related summit meetings in Bali, both in November 2011. However, he was, at least publicly, unheard from on the subject at the APEC meeting in Vladivostok the next year.

Having taken over Japan's political leadership after the Liberal Democratic Party's sweeping December 2012 electoral victory, the new prime minister, Shinzo Abe, visited Washington, D.C., in February 2013. With the United States having agreed that Japan could seek exemptions for rice and other "key products" from tariff reduction and tariff elimination, Abe was able to announce on 15 March 2013 that Japan would seek to join the TPP negotiations. He vigorously defended the Japanese decision against the vocal criticisms of the politically powerful agriculture sector. The United States and the other TPP states approved Japan's participation in April 2013.

I expect the RCEP to be much looser, more general, and less economically "serious" than the TPP. It is also reasonable to expect that both agreements will eventually be concluded, since the two schemes so far are not mutually exclusive, and that the RCEP will be signed first, since it seems to be easier to negotiate than the TPP.

The Keidanren, Japan's Federation of Economic Organizations, has been both a pillar of support and a catalyst for Japanese economic and business policy toward Southeast Asia, particularly for regional economic integration through ASEAN. Counting the country's leading business corporations as its members, the Keidanren has been sending high-level missions almost every year to several ASEAN countries, assessing the climate for Japanese exports, investments, and tourism in each of them, and demonstrating the solid nature of ASEAN-Japan business links.

Japan's relations with Southeast Asia, however, go beyond markets, investments, financial arrangements, tourism, and economic aid. They include culture and other forms of Japanese "soft power". Japan contributed the equivalent of some US$20 million to the ASEAN Cultural

Fund, over which the ASEAN Committee on Culture and Information has almost complete discretion. Japan has turned over to the ASEAN Foundation, set up in 1997, another US$20 million, to support ASEAN's people-to-people, regional consciousness-raising, and other ASEAN-related activities. It is called the Japan-ASEAN Solidarity Fund, but it is financed entirely by Japan. In addition to the Ship for Southeast Asian Youth, alumni of which have formed regional and national networks, young people from ASEAN countries take part in the Japan-conceived and -funded JENESYS, the Japan-East Asia Network of Exchange for Students and Youth. In 2009 the Japanese government established the Japan Creative Centre, in Singapore.

JAIF was set up, in March 2006, to encourage and fund the transfer of Japanese technology to ASEAN member countries, as well as the inflow of Japanese investments into them. At the ASEAN-Japan Summit meeting of November 1999, Prime Minister Keizo Obuchi announced the establishment of the Japan-ASEAN General Exchange Fund, or JAGEF, to support the government agencies in Cambodia, Laos, Myanmar, and Vietnam handling ASEAN matters. Replacing the Japan-ASEAN Cooperation Promotion Programme (JACPP), which had been around since 1983 and which JAGEF seeks to update, it would also help strengthen the functioning of the ASEAN Secretariat. JAGEF and JACPP have received more than US$15 million from the Japanese government. They have funded a number of Initiative for ASEAN Integration and other "capacity-building" ASEAN projects.

Founded in 1972, the Japan Foundation is the only Japanese government agency devoted to artistic and cultural exchange between Japan and the rest of the world, including Southeast Asia, where it has facilities in five ASEAN capitals (Jakarta, Kuala Lumpur, Manila, Bangkok, and Hanoi). It conducts numerous activities designed to make the Japanese language and culture known throughout the world.

JAPAN'S POLITICAL AND SECURITY ACTIVISM

By the time the late 1980s and early 1990s came around, the configuration of global power and security, including in Asia-Pacific, had been transformed. The Cold War, with its simplicities, had ended in favor of more traditional — and more complex — arrangements of international relations. The Soviet Union had disintegrated, although the influence of Russia, the USSR's successor state, on the "near abroad", to some extent and in some ways, remained. Both the Warsaw Pact and the Comecon[22] had dissolved. The Berlin Wall had crumbled, and Germany had been reunited. The European Union enlarged itself to include states that had been part of the former Soviet empire or even of the Soviet Union itself. The American-led North Atlantic Treaty Organization, or NATO, expanded up to the very doorstep of a truncated Russia. Meanwhile, the world's new states were dealing with the consequences of decolonization and seeking to build their nations within the artificial boundaries drawn by their former colonial masters.

The transformation of global power and security was taking place, in specific ways, in Asia-Pacific. The United States had withdrawn its forces from Vietnam and the rest of the former French Indochina. It was forced to leave the military bases that it had used in the Philippines since colonial times. The Soviet Union had pulled out its presence from Afghanistan. The economic and political reforms that India had been instituting, leaving the economic door slightly ajar, were gaining some traction.

Perhaps more significantly, the death of Mao Zedong, the arrest of the Gang of Four,[23] and the ascendancy of Deng Xiaoping led to the adoption and implementation in China of "reform and opening-up" economic policies, the four "modernizations",[24] and a greater pluralism in Chinese society. These developments, in turn, were resulting in the rise of China's economic and military power and its political and diplomatic influence.

The Tian An Men Square "incident" in early June 1989 caused a political upheaval in Beijing and led to some expectation that the Chinese political system would change in a way commensurate with the Chinese people's economic aspirations. However, although the Tian An Men events may have resulted in hastening the opening to some extent of Chinese society, the Chinese people's yearning for social stability and economic prosperity seems to have prevailed. China remains a one-party state today.

In Southeast Asia, the ASEAN countries kept their economies open and plugged into the rest of the global economy (all belonged or were eventually to belong to the World Trade Organization) and were economically growing quite rapidly. The impact of the political and economic turnaround in Indonesia, ASEAN's largest economy and country, was taking hold. The initiative in instituting changes in Indonesia's economic policies, including those in foreign economic relations, had been seized by the "Berkeley mafia." The Indonesia-conceived, -organized, and -led "informal workshops on managing potential conflict in the South China Sea" had been inaugurated and were a going concern.[25] Vietnamese forces had withdrawn from Cambodia, and a political settlement had been achieved, at least temporarily, in that unhappy country. The main divisions in Southeast Asia were starting to heal.

Thus it was that, at their summit meeting in 1992, their fourth, the ASEAN leaders, then six, called on their ministers and other officials to "intensify (ASEAN's) external dialogues in political and security matters by using the ASEAN Post-Ministerial Conferences (PMC)".[26] The use of economic, social, educational, and cultural cooperation as a disguise for ASEAN's political-security purposes had been dropped.

In May 1993, senior officials of ASEAN and its Dialogue Partners gathered in Singapore, the then ASEAN chair, to determine how best to carry out the ASEAN leaders' directive. They agreed that political and security issues in Asia-Pacific could not be properly discussed in the changed political and security configuration in the region and in the world without the participation of China and Russia, then not yet ASEAN Dialogue Partners, and of Vietnam, then not yet an ASEAN member. A new ASEAN forum had to be created, with the officials recommending that it be called the ASEAN Regional Forum.

"ASEAN" had to be in its name. The idea of using the ASEAN PMC for political and security discussions had publicly come from ASEAN's leaders. The ARF's ministerial meetings would take place on the occasion of the annual ASEAN foreign ministers' meeting, with the ASEAN chair presiding over the ARF meetings. Moreover, ASEAN "centrality", to which there was no plausible alternative, had to be maintained. A retired Australian diplomat also pointed to the difficulties of starting an entirely new organization of states, even as ASEAN ministers and officials and others in the region frowned on any proposal for a non-ASEAN association to discuss Asia-Pacific political and security issues. As early as the middle of 1991, Japan's then foreign minister, Taro Nakayama, had proposed using the PMC for "political dialogue" in the face of what was reported as opposition from the United States and misgivings on the part of some ASEAN members.[27]

In view of Japan's active involvement in the ARF's founding, it is not surprising that Tokyo co-chaired with Jakarta the first meeting, in 1996, of the Inter-sessional Support Group on Confidence Building Measures, or ISG on CBM. The growing number of networking, confidence-building, and other cooperative activities — Inter-sessional Support Groups of more or less permanent bodies and Inter-sessional Meetings for one-time events — that take place throughout each year, with activities ranging from joint exercises on search-and-rescue and disaster relief to gatherings of heads of defense educational institutions, are called "inter-sessional", because they take place between foreign ministers' sessions. Each of them is chaired jointly by an ASEAN country and a non-ASEAN participant.[28]

In 2005 the ISG on CBM was renamed the Inter-sessional Support Group on Confidence Building Measures and Preventive Diplomacy, or ISG on CBM and PD. There had been growing disagreements over the notion of preventive diplomacy, the second stage of the ARF, as outlined in the forum's concept paper,[29] with some suspecting that preventive diplomacy would be used as a pretext for interfering in a participant state's internal affairs. The ISG on CBM and PD serves as the working group for the meetings of ministers, with senior foreign-ministry and national-security officials usually taking part in its gatherings. The forum's positions on international and regional issues, inevitably the results of compromises, are normally negotiated in the group. Four days after a tsunami (a Japanese word) hit northeastern Japan in March 2011, Japan, together with host Indonesia, led an ARF disaster-relief exercise in Manado, with about 4,000 participants from 25 countries. The exercise received much media attention on this account.

It is quite significant that it was in a Southeast Asian country, Cambodia, that Japan's armed forces first ventured out of their homeland, even if only to man a UN peacekeeping operation. Two Japanese officers lost their lives in that endeavor. Tokyo provided a Japanese diplomat, Yasushi Akashi, to head the UN Transitional Authority in Cambodia of 1992–93. Japan also contributed some imaginative ideas for the resolution of the political crisis that erupted in Cambodia in 1997. Cambodia's entry, in 1999, resulted in ASEAN's expansion to its present membership of ten.

It is obvious that ASEAN and Japan, both dependent in various degrees on foreign trade, share national interests in regional and global peace and stability; the prevalence of the rule of law, including international law; economic openness; and freedom and safety of navigation and overflight. This is why the territorial and jurisdictional issues underlying the conflicting claims in the East and South China Seas and the use of military force in the pursuit of those claims tend to erode the efforts in building a political and security community in East Asia.

CONCLUSION

The reason why I have devoted so much space and time, relatively speaking, to the historical background of ASEAN-Japan relations and to their substance over the years is to show both the long-standing nature and the continuing magnitude of those relations. These characteristics of ASEAN-Japan relations tend to be forgotten in the face of the recent experience of Japan's economic difficulties and the common perception that neighboring China, much larger in population and land area, is a nation on the rise, while Japan is on the decline. Much has been made of China having overtaken Japan as the world's second-largest economy in terms of GDP. As I stated above, "The perception was also gaining headway that ASEAN+3 was being increasingly dominated by a rapidly rising and seemingly well-coordinated China."

There are many explanations for this perception, possibly a wrong one, of Japan as a country in the doldrums or even in decline, a perception, however, that may change after the Japanese economy's apparent recovery. One is the lack of coordination among government, semi-government, and nongovernment agencies, especially on the part of those charged with managing foreign aid and relating to the ASEAN region. Another is the short duration in leadership positions of most of Japan's political leaders. Still another is the relative slowness of the way decisions are made for the country. And then there is the propensity of Japanese political leaders to recycle ongoing programs with ASEAN and other regions and name the repackaged programs after themselves or label them with new names. All of this may, in turn, be attributed to the complications of the Japanese political system and to the need of leaders for the support of the faction, the party, and the people.

Whether it is worth changing that system for the sake of a better perception of Japan on the part of Southeast Asia and the rest of the world, a critical perception, is something for the Japanese people to decide.

A former ASEAN secretary-general, Rodolfo C. Severino is the head of the ASEAN Studies Centre at the Institute of Southeast Asian Studies, Singapore. The views expressed here are his own. Catherine Rose James and Pham Thi Phuong Thao, research assistants at the ASEAN Studies Centre, contributed to research for this piece.

Notes

[1]   Ministry of Foreign Affairs of Japan, *Japan-ASEAN Commemorative Summit (Meetings of Leaders and Foreign Ministers): Overview*, December 2003.

[2]   Transcript provided by Japan's Ministry of Foreign Affairs of the Joint Press Conference following the Japan-ASEAN Commemorative Summit, 12 December 2003.

3   AFTA is the ASEAN Free Trade Area. CER is the Closer Economic Relations between Australia and New Zealand. CEPT stands for Common Effective Preferential Tariff (for AFTA).

4   "Consultative Partner" was the name given by ASEAN to China and Russia in recognition of those countries' important roles in the affairs of East Asia but before consensus was reached within ASEAN on bestowing full Dialogue Partnership on them.

5   Being designated as a "Sectoral Dialogue Partner" means the relations with ASEAN of the country so designated are limited, at least in theory, to trade, investments, and tourism.

6   The Republic of Korea became a party to the Paris-based Organisation for Economic Co-operation and Development (OECD), and thus was perceived to have joined the ranks of developed countries, in December 1996. However, in ASEAN it had become a "Sectoral Dialogue Partner" in 1989 and a full Dialogue Partner in 1991.

7   Rodolfo C. Severino, *Southeast Asia in Search of an ASEAN Community* (Singapore: Institute of Southeast Asian Studies, 2006), p. 294. The book was launched at the ASEAN-Japan Centre in Tokyo, among other places.

8   Ibid., pp. 295–97. In this paper, the surnames go last in Japanese names.

9   See the Web site of the ASEAN-Japan Centre in Tokyo. Available at <http://old. asean.or.jp/eng/>.

10 The Master Plan has been published by the ASEAN Secretariat.

11 See below.

12 The road map, with its three blueprints — for the ASEAN Political-Security Community, the ASEAN Economic Community, and the ASEAN Socio-Cultural Community — has been published by the ASEAN Secretariat.

13 "A New Initiative to Overcome the Asian Currency Crisis (New Miyazawa Initiative)", Japan Ministry of Finance. Available at <http://www.mof.go.jp/ english/international_policy/financial_cooperation_in_asia/new_miyazawa_ initiative/e1e042.htm>.

14 The *Final Report of the East Asia Study Group*, as submitted to the ASEAN+3 Summit in November 2002, can be found on the Web page of Japan's Ministry of Foreign Affairs. Available at <http://www.mofa.go.jp>.

15 Ibid., pp. 63–65.

16 *Press Statement by the Chairman of the 8th ASEAN Summit, the 6th ASEAN+3 Summit and the ASEAN-China Summit*, Phnom Penh, Cambodia, 4 November 2002.

17 *Chairman's Statement of the Second East Asia Summit*, Cebu, Philippines, 15 January 2007.

18 See Web page of AMRO.

19 *Chairman's Statement of the 4th East Asia Summit*, Cha-am Hua Hin, Thailand, 25 October 2009, para. 19.

[20] *Chairman's Statement of the 22nd ASEAN Summit*, Bandar Seri Begawan, 24–25 April 2013, para. 30.

[21] Columbia University Professor Jagdish Bhagwati coined the term "spaghetti bowl" in reference to the proliferation of regional preferential trading arrangements bearing disparate rules of origin.

[22] Like the Warsaw Pact in the military sphere, Comecon, the Council for Mutual Economic Assistance, was an organization led by the Soviet Union and consisting of socialist countries mainly in Eastern Europe. It lasted from 1949 to 1991.

[23] The Gang of Four comprised Jiang Qing (Mao Zedong's wife, who has been reported as having committed suicide in prison), Wang Hongwen (a young "model worker"), Yao Wenyuan (chief propagandist and ideologue of the Mao regime), and Zhang Chunqiao (government and party boss of Shanghai). The quartet were accused of calling many of the shots in China during the Great Proletarian Cultural Revolution in that country and were detained less than a month after Mao died.

[24] The "four modernizations" refer to agriculture, industry, science and technology, and national defense. Although, as understood today, the term is associated mainly with Deng Xiaoping, it was actually formulated by then Premier Zhou Enlai in 1975, shortly before his death.

[25] The "informal workshops" have continued, even after Canadian funding was ended in 2001.

[26] *Singapore Declaration of 1992*, 28 January 1992, para. 3.

[27] Rodolfo C. Severino, *The ASEAN Regional Forum* (Singapore: Institute of Southeast Asian Studies, 2009), pp. 6–14.

[28] *ASEAN Regional Forum Documents Series 1994–2006* (Jakarta: ASEAN Secretariat, March 2007).

[29] Severino, *ASEAN Regional Forum*, pp. 141–45; *ASEAN Regional Forum Documents Series 1994–2006*, pp. 12–19.

3

APPROACHES TOWARD REGIONALISM: JAPAN, CHINA, AND THE IMPLICATIONS ON ASEAN

Pavin Chachavalpongpun

Japan has enjoyed amicable relations with the Association of Southeast Asian Nations (ASEAN) since it was granted Dialogue Partner status in 1977. But like other key partners of ASEAN, Japan has been from time to time constrained by other equally important foreign policy issues that might have obstructed the development of their bilateral relationship. Japan has undoubtedly invested its diplomatic energy overwhelmingly in its alliance with the United States, a foreign policy choice deemed imperative from Japan's strategic perspective. Japan lives side by side with historical enemies, China and South Korea, with China now emerging as a rising power. Its relationship with them is today shaped in part by renewed friendship as much as embittered historical memories. Japan has recently intensified territorial claims in the East China Sea against China and South Korea, even though the latter countries' leaders attempted to strengthen relations with Japan. At one point, protests against Japan in various parts of China further deteriorated bilateral ties. Meanwhile, China's close ties with North Korea have affected the region's security outlook and at times worried Japan and South Korea. The March 2013 meeting between the vice ministers of defense of Japan and ASEAN disclosed a real concern over the tension on the Korean Peninsula, particularly after

North Korea undertook its third nuclear test. In part, security concerns on the Korean Peninsula have dictated Japan's strategic considerations and thus legitimized the country's close cooperation with the United States.[1] Such conditions have formed a certain viewpoint within Japan in regard to its approach toward regionalism, and in particular to its relations with ASEAN. Yet, it is imperative to note here that those conditions are not the only factors that explain the current state of ASEAN-Japanese relations. After all, ASEAN has remained important in Japan's Asia policy.

Japan's relations with ASEAN have been solid mainly because there were no outstanding disputes between the two sides, neither political nor economic. Successive Japanese governments have offered generous financial aid and technical assistance to a number of ASEAN countries as well as supporting Japanese conglomerates investing in ASEAN's markets. In retrospect, Japan's diplomatic activism toward Southeast Asia was seen in the mid-1960s but was more evident in 1977 following the announcement of the Fukuda Doctrine.[2] Prime Minister Takeo Fukuda, while paying an official visit to Manila, made a famous speech in which he articulated his country's new foreign policy. Fukuda's initiatives were intended to deal with the new reality in which Southeast Asia was divided between ASEAN and communist Indochina. In essence, his speech indicated that for the first time in the post-World War II era, Japan was willing to play an active role in both economic and political affairs in Southeast Asia without depending on military imperatives and in such a way as to make military considerations less prominent. The doctrine consisted of three key points: rejection of the role of a military power; promotion of a relationship of mutual confidence and trust, or "heart-to-heart" diplomacy; and equal partnership with ASEAN for building peace and prosperity throughout Southeast Asia.[3] In 2008, Prime Minister Yasuo Fukuda upgraded his father's doctrine through the declaration of the "Inland Sea" vision.[4] Therefore, while the Fukuda Doctrine has served as the bedrock of Japan's diplomacy toward Southeast Asia, subsequent leaders of Japan have continued to reinvent new initiatives toward ASEAN so as to be able to catch up with the changing regional environment. Prime Ministers Ryutaro Hashimoto (1996–98) and Keizo Obuchi (1998–2000), for example, were active during 1997–98 and took a series of initiatives toward ASEAN now remembered as the Asian Monetary Fund (AMF) and Miyazawa initiatives.[5] At the same time, China has emerged as a major force in the past decades. China opposed the AMF, but it was the United States that was mainly responsible for shooting it down. Despite the tension between the two countries over Prime Minister Junichiro Koizumi's Yasukuni visit and Japan's attempt to become a permanent member of the UN Security Council, Japan and China worked in harmony in the wake of the 1997 financial crisis and helped greatly to strengthen the ASEAN Plus processes. The creation of ASEAN Plus 6 was probably the first occasion on which Japan and China diverged about the direction in which ASEAN Plus processes should develop.

The proposed creation of the East Asian Community (EAC) apparently unveiled the different approaches taken by Japan and China toward Asian regionalism. The EAC was initially suggested by South Korean President Kim Dae Jung in 1998.[6] But the Korean initiative was not the first endeavor to integrate East and Southeast Asia. In 1990, Malaysian Prime Minister Mahathir Mohamad suggested the establishment of the East Asia Economic Group, later renamed the East Asia Economic Caucus (EAEC), which was to include the ASEAN member states, China, Japan, and South Korea. Baogang He (2004) argued that Mahathir's proposal was the boldest and most assertive attempt to build exclusive Asian regionalism. It provided an "Asian-only" alternative to the Asia-Pacific Economic Cooperation (APEC), favoring a return to the notion of a distinctive "Asian Community".[7] The EAEC was, however, never seen through officially. EAEC's Asian exclusivity was possibly responsible for its failure. And in terms of trade structure, APEC seemed to have made far more sense than the EAEC, at least from a Japanese perspective.

Not until 1997 did ASEAN express its serious interest in developing a more concrete structure that would incorporate East Asian neighbors. Several factors, such as the Asian Financial Crisis (with US intervention, which posed a risk and the need to create a mechanism for regional cooperation while keeping the United States out) and expanding regional integration in Europe and the Americas compelled ASEAN to redefine the concept of regionalism and strengthen its position on the global stage. For example, in the aftermath of the financial crisis, ASEAN countries established the Chiang Mai Initiative to manage regional short-term liquidity problems and to facilitate the working of other international financial arrangements and organizations such as the International Monetary Fund. This initiative brought Southeast Asia into direct contact with Northeast Asia. Eventually, ASEAN decided to launch the ASEAN+3 forum as a coordinator of cooperation between ASEAN and the three East Asian nations of China, Japan, and South Korea. The first ASEAN+3 leaders' meeting was held in 1997, and the ASEAN+3 has since served as a lynchpin institution in the formation of the larger EAC.[8] In 2002, during his visit to Singapore, Koizumi made the first public speech supporting the idea of an EAC.

This paper seeks to make a number of arguments and highlight certain perceptions about Japan's modern relations with ASEAN and, in particular, the nation's vision of regionalism in the context of the EAC. First, it argues that the changing regional landscape, which includes the rise of China, has been a significant factor behind Japan's renewed enthusiasm in ASEAN and Asian regionalism. But it must be made clear that Japan's Asia policy is not to dilute China's influence on the region. On the contrary, Japan understands the need for the evolution of the regional order. The question is how to make it happen, in what direction, and with what principles. Other countries, including Japan, do not want China to impose its rule on others. The Japanese government, under both the Democratic Party of Japan and the Liberal Democratic Party, has come to realize the usefulness of ASEAN as a hub for regional cooperation. Overcoming the Chinese influence has not been the ultimate objective, although keeping the right balance of power has always been in Japan's interest. And in this process, political alignments and partnerships have proven useful for Japan. As evident, Japan has underlined the ASEAN hub status while continuing to engage China. Ultimately, what matters most to members of the region is rule making and norm building.

Second, Japan's approach toward an EAC is greatly different from that of China. The differences must not be construed as Japan and China adopting different views regarding regionalism. Instead, they expose the extent to which the two countries have taken advantage of regionalism differently to fulfill their national interests vis-à-vis ASEAN. For example, while China prefers closed regionalism as it allows Beijing to better maneuver its relations with ASEAN, Japan promotes open regionalism in order to maintain a balance of power in the region. Third, this situation has led to the perception of a fierce rivalry between Japan and China, which has generated both positive and negative repercussions in the region, specifically on the pace of regionalism. Positively, it has stimulated other regional players — such as ASEAN and South Korea — to step up their game. Moreover, it has encouraged ASEAN to reinforce its own organization, in the face of the supposed Sino-Japanese competition, by taking a lead role where different opinions persist. Negatively, it could derail regional cooperation efforts. And in reality, member countries may put too much emphasis on defending their national gains rather than gains to the region.

SINO-JAPANESE DYNAMICS IN ASEAN

Although Japan has maintained a strong relationship with ASEAN, the relationship has faced several challenges over the years, particularly those stemming from Japan's Asia policy. Japan's official development assistance (ODA) to Southeast Asia has been in decline in recent years, and this will negatively impact Japan's foothold in the region. From 2000 to 2007 the share of Japan's ODA in total ODA commitments to four main ASEAN recipients — Indonesia, Malaysia, the Philippines, and Thailand — decreased significantly, from 78.1 per cent to 38.1 per cent.[9] On the contrary, China has been more aggressive in its approach to forging solid ties with ASEAN. In the words of Singaporean Minister Mentor Lee Kuan Yew, "It has become the norm in Southeast Asia for China to take the lead and Japan to tag along. Since Japan is unable to recover its economy, it has been left in a rather inconvenient position as compared to that of China."[10] China-ASEAN official relations commenced only in the mid-1990s. China was accorded full Dialogue Partner status at the 29th ASEAN Ministerial Meeting in July 1996 in Jakarta, 19 years after Japan acquired the same status. However, China was the first Dialogue Partner to accede to the Treaty of Amity and Cooperation in Southeast Asia — which it did at the seventh ASEAN-China Summit in October 2003 in Bali, one year before Japan decided to sign the same document. Table 3.1 illustrates features of Japan's diplomacy vis-à-vis ASEAN in comparison to China's.

Unlike Japan, China has long regarded Southeast Asia as its sphere of influence, both in the historical context (with China perceiving itself as the Middle Kingdom and its relations with Southeast Asia being based on a tributary system) and in the contemporary period, and has attempted to maintain that level of influence through developing closer links with the region. But China's inroads into Southeast Asia have not always been smooth. During the Cold War, noncommunist states in Southeast Asia were suspicious of China because it supported communist insurgency in the region. Today, some Southeast Asian countries still regard Beijing as a potential threat. As China has risen economically, it has modernized its army. The modernization of the People's Liberation Army and the remaining territorial disputes over the Spratly Islands have revived Southeast Asia's fear of China's growing military threat. Among other disputes, the one in the strategically important South China Sea proved so contentious that an annual ASEAN gathering held in Cambodia in July 2012 ended without even a basic diplomatic communiqué, which appeared to have

TABLE 3.1
Japan's and China's Activities with ASEAN11

Political Cooperation with ASEAN	China	Political Cooperation with ASEAN	Japan
Full Dialogue Partner status	1996	Full Dialogue Partner status	1977
ASEAN-China Cooperative Operations in Response to Dangerous Drugs (ACCORD)	2001		
Signing of Joint Declaration on Strategic Partnership for Peace and Prosperity	October 2003	Signing of Tokyo Declaration for the Dynamic and Enduring ASEAN-Japan Partnership in the New Millennium, together with the ASEAN-Japan Plan of Action	December 2003
Signing of the Treaty of Amity and Cooperation	2003 (First Dialogue Partner to do so)	Signing of the Treaty of Amity and Cooperation	2004
MOU for Cooperation in Non-traditional Security Issues	2004	Joint Declaration for Cooperation on the Fight against International Terrorism	2004
Appointment of ASEAN ambassador: Xue Hanqin	December 2008	Appointment of ASEAN ambassador: Katori Yoshinori	October 2008

Table 3.1 (Cont'd)

Economic Cooperation with ASEAN[12]	China	Economic Cooperation with ASEAN	Japan
Signing of the Framework Agreement on Comprehensive Economic Cooperation to establish the ASEAN-China Free Trade Area (ACFTA)	2002	signing of the ASEAN-Japan Comprehensive Economic Partnership	2008
• Signing of the Agreement on Trade in Goods & Dispute Settlement Mechanism	2004		
• Signing of the Agreement on Trade in Services	2007		
Plan of action to implement the Beijing Declaration on ASEAN-China ICT Cooperative Partnership for Common Development (2007–12)	2007		
ASEAN-China Investment Agreement	2009 (The ACFTA was realized on 1 January 2010.)		
Two-way trade	China emerged as ASEAN's largest trading partner, accounting for 11.6% of ASEAN's total trade in 2009.	Two-way trade	Japan accounted for 10.5% of total ASEAN trade in 2009.

Memorandum of Understanding (MOU) on Establishing the ASEAN-China Centre	2009	ASEAN-Japan Centre	1981
MOU on Cooperation on Intellectual Property and MOU on Strengthening Cooperation in the Field of Standards, Technical Regulations and Conformity Assessment	2009		
Launch of ASEAN-China FTA Business Portal (BIZ Portal)	2010		

Sociocultural Cooperation with ASEAN	China	**Sociocultural Cooperation with ASEAN**	Japan
Beijing Declaration on ASEAN-China Cooperation on Youth	2004	Japan-East Asia Network of Exchange for Students and Youths	2007
MOU on Cultural Cooperation	2005		
Signing of ASEAN-China MOU on Information and Media Cooperation	2008		

been rejected by China. Ironically, Chinese diplomats working in Southeast Asia take every opportunity to stress their country's peaceful coexistence principle and keenness to become a part of ASEAN's regionalization process.[13] To demonstrate this, China initiated a free trade agreement (FTA) negotiation with ASEAN in 2002, after realizing the usefulness of a Japanese-Singaporean FTA (the Japan-Singapore Economic Partnership Agreement) initiated earlier in the year. The same year, at the end of the sixth China-ASEAN Summit, the two parties also signed a Declaration on Code of Conduct in the South China Sea with the aim of maintaining peace and stability in the South China region, as a way to alleviate the region's threat perception of China. In parallel, China has firmed up its ties with individual members of ASEAN on a bilateral basis. Thailand became the first country in ASEAN to have concluded a bilateral FTA with China, which came into effect in 2003. China has also begun conducting annual military exercises with Thailand, to emulate Cobra Gold but on a much smaller scale. Cobra Gold represents the largest military exercise in Asia, which is between Thailand and the United States.[14]

It is evident that the extent of interaction between Japan and China has heightened over the years. After the first ASEAN+3 summit in 1997, there were efforts from all key countries in the region to construct a new platform that would help consolidate an East Asian regionalism. In 2000, ASEAN commenced a feasibility study on the establishment of the EAS. The EAS was to perform as a key forum for materializing an ASEAN-centric community. The EAS, which had its first meeting in 2005 in Kuala Lumpur, consists of the ASEAN+3 members plus India, Australia, and New Zealand. The five-year gap between the EAS's initial idea and its first summit offered an opportunity for Japan to develop its approach of a regional community and claim its ownership, as unveiled in Koizumi's speech in 2002. Accordingly, the Japanese government recommended a commemorative summit with all ASEAN members to mark the 30th anniversary of ASEAN-Japan diplomatic relations; it became the first summit between ten ASEAN countries and Japan outside the Southeast Asian region. The commemorative summit was eventually organized in December 2003 in Tokyo despite initial disagreements from some ASEAN members about the rationale behind the event. They thought that another meeting in Tokyo would be redundant since ASEAN and Japanese leaders had held a similar meeting a few months earlier in Indonesia. In order not to spoil the mood of cooperation and jeopardize Japan's goodwill, ASEAN went along with Tokyo's idea. The success of the commemorative summit increased Japan's strategic position vis-à-vis ASEAN.

China responded to Japan's increasingly assertive diplomacy vis-à-vis ASEAN by offering to host the first EAS on Chinese soil as a symbol of its genuine commitment to the East Asian regionalization process. But the offer was declined — not only by Japan but also by some ASEAN members who insisted on ASEAN maintaining its centrality in the EAS. Instead, Malaysia played host to the first EAS in 2005, followed by the Philippines in 2006, Singapore in 2007, Thailand in 2009, and Vietnam in 2010.[15] As China's offer was stalled, Japan came up with a new proposition to co-host the EAS with Malaysia. Simultaneously, Japan produced its Concept Paper on the EAC in 2004 to elaborate on its vision of Asian regionalism. China immediately rebuffed Japan's proposition and insisted on allowing a single host of the EAS. In 2005 Beijing also distributed the Modality Paper, the Chinese version of an EAC, to counter Japan's Concept Paper. The seeming diplomatic settling of scores between Japan and China put a great deal of pressure on ASEAN, at the same time as ASEAN wanted to direct its own regionalization. This undoubtedly put the spotlight on the different approaches toward regionalism between Japan and China even when their actions seemed to recognize ASEAN as the chief driver of regional integration.

IMPACTS ON THE REGION

The roles played by China and Japan have had strategic implications — both positive and negative — for their relations with ASEAN and the EAC process. In the relatively least developed region, the Greater Mekong Subregion (GMS), both China and Japan have evidently stepped up their diplomatic game in cultivating their influence. But they have cooperated in the promotion of GMS development too. For ASEAN, this regionalization process has continued alongside its own aspiration to lead the region, as evident in the vigorous debates involving Indonesia, Singapore, and Malaysia in the search for the kind of regional integration they needed. The major tasks for the organization, as part of preserving its centrality in Asian regionalism, are to take advantage of the Sino-Japanese dynamics and to minimize their unconstructive impact.

Building a Healthy Community

There are at least three benefits stemming from the Sino-Japanese dynamics that can enhance the community-building process. First, the seeming competition between the two countries for leadership has set a new precedent for other countries in the neighborhood to revise their strategic positions and to take a leading role in regional cooperation for the sake of their own interests as well as those of the region. One has to admit that not all countries in the East Asian region are excited about regional integration, particularly if they have to surrender a certain degree of their sovereign rights. New initiatives from China and Japan designed to influence the shape and form of an EAC allowed ASEAN to find the most appropriate modality for a future cooperative framework. For example, ASEAN had a chance to compare Japan's Concept Paper on the EAC with China's Modality Paper, and picked what it thought was best for the region. This could serve as a good example for smaller countries, such as South Korea or New Zealand, to stand up and claim their share of regional prosperity through their vision, initiatives, and recommendations regarding an EAC. Taking South Korea as an example, it has begun to step up its game by increasing its involvement and familiarization with ASEAN as well as with individual members. Currently, South Korea is ASEAN's fifth-largest trading partner; its total two-way trade with ASEAN amounted to $US74.7 billion in 2009, trailing only China, Japan, the United States, and the European Union.[16] It enthusiastically takes part in the ARF and the ASEAN+3 framework. In fact, the idea and concept of the EAS were originally from the reports of the East Asia Vision Group and the East Asia Study Group, which were spearheaded by the initiative of South Korea. Additionally, the Korea-ASEAN Free Trade Agreement was concluded in 2007. The commitment on the part of Japan and China, demonstrated through their relentless competition, has to a certain level increased South Korea's incentive to pursue the same role in using an EAC concept to increase its regional role and deepen its regional presence.

Second, the different approaches of Beijing and Tokyo presented an opportunity for ASEAN to cement its central role in an EAC effort. ASEAN has insisted on remaining at the center of all regional cooperative frameworks and has claimed that no other organizations or individual countries in the region can do a better job because ASEAN is neutral and trusted by all regional powers.[17] The perceived competition between Japan and China has molded certain bonds in their relationship with ASEAN. In an attempt to increase their influence in the region, both China and Japan, to various degrees, have been willing to support ASEAN's centrality in regional integration. They are content to accommodate ASEAN even when they realize that the group may not be capable of tackling certain issues. The competition has so far led to a sharp division among members of the EAS — those who lend their support to Japan tend to disagree with China's view on regionalism, and vice versa. Some of these views are fiercely in conflict with each other. ASEAN has stepped in and tried to close that division, performing as a bridge between the two Asian powers and thus bolstering its status as the key driver of regional cooperation. The existence of different opinions also permits ASEAN to exercise its leadership and authority to make decisions where agreements between China and Japan cannot be reached, particularly on the modality and future direction of an EAC. Besides, with support from both China and Japan, ASEAN can strengthen its leadership in APEC; all the ASEAN countries except Cambodia, Laos, and Myanmar are members of APEC. Some countries are particularly active in the promotion of APEC, such as Singapore and non-ASEAN members such as the United States. Some ASEAN members also take part in the Trans-Pacific Partnership (TPP), which is a multilateral free trade agreement designed to integrate the economies of the Asia-Pacific region. Members of the TPP from ASEAN include Brunei, Singapore, Malaysia, and Vietnam (the former two are original members, while the latter two are currently in negotiations to join the TPP).[18] The dynamics between China and Japan will certainly contribute to the progress of many FTA cooperation frameworks in the region — such as the TPP — and, as a result, to the region's overall economic growth.

The third benefit of the Sino-Japanese dynamics is that the rise of China has in many ways brought ASEAN and Japan together, even closer than before. ASEAN needs China for its own economic growth, but it is also wary of China's growing influence in the region. ASEAN thus shares with Japan a concern over the influence of China in Southeast Asia. For ASEAN, working with Japan could help alleviate the level of concern, since both parties understand the reality in which any unilateral attempt to restrain the Chinese influence would be difficult, if not impossible. As Japan and ASEAN have found a common interest in the face of China's rising power, their relationship has progressed further. It is evident that the mission to balance China's power has reinvigorated Japan's diplomacy toward ASEAN. And strategically speaking, Japan and ASEAN are not alone in this game of balancing regional power. The United States and Australia have had solid relations with Japan and maintained their firm ties with key ASEAN members. These factors are imperative for Japan and ASEAN in generating a balance of power in the face of China's rise. The success of the EAS in admitting the United States (and Russia) in 2010 may be perceived as a triumph for Japan and ASEAN. For example, the EAS could provide another important venue for the United States, Japan, and India to consolidate their alliance to counter China's rise. In 2011, the three countries launched a trilateral strategic dialogue on security and economic issues, including measures to deal with China's expansion of its naval power.[19]

Celebrating the EAC?

It is too soon to celebrate the success of the EAC just because the seeming competition between Japan and China may have produced some benefits for the region. If the tension between China and Japan escalates, it may well destabilize the region. After all, too much emphasis on the supposed rivalry would only highlight the importance of national interests on the part of Japan and China over the ultimate goal of achieving genuine regional integration. Moreover, it may sway the ASEAN agenda at the EAS. Since the concentration is on maintaining their dominant position in the region, both China and Japan have been trying to influence the EAS agenda so as to satisfy their own national interests. Ironically, while such an attempt on the part of China and Japan may encourage ASEAN to act as a united organization that could bridge the differences, it could also break up its own unity. As the *Congressional Research Service (CRS) Report for Congress* summarizes, there are a range of perspectives within ASEAN on the EAS and China's evolving role in a potential EAC. Singapore has taken a leading role in articulating the benefits of an open regional framework for Southeast Asia. Prime Minister Lee Hsien Loong stated, "ASEAN does not want to be exclusively dependent on China, and does not want to be forced to choose sides between China and the United States or China and Japan." He also reportedly stated, "If the world is split up into closed blocs or exclusive spheres of influence, rivalry, antagonism and conflict are inevitable." Singapore has supported India's inclusion in the EAS and sought continued US engagement in the region. Burma and Laos are often viewed as already significantly under China's influence in Southeast Asia.[20] The polarization within ASEAN could be deepened if the seeming competition between China and Japan continues.

Finally, if history is any indication, ASEAN must realize that too much outside interference could harm regional integration efforts. In the past 60 years, almost all attempts to create regional groupings in Asia have failed miserably. At the end of the Bandung Conference in 1955, China revealed its intention to establish some sort of regional grouping in order to reinstall its sphere of influence in Southeast Asia. The Union of Soviet Socialist Republics (USSR) also came up with a similar idea of reuniting communist states in this region. To contain both China and the USSR, the United States launched its own regional initiative through the setting up of the Southeast Asian Treaty Organization, an Asian version of the North Atlantic Treaty Organization. All of these regional alliances either failed to take off or did not live up to their original purposes. But the idea of regionalism became more tangible when ASEAN was founded in 1967. Arguably, unbridled Sino-Japanese competition poses a challenge to ASEAN's role as the driver of East Asian regionalism, including the EAC, since the agenda could be influenced by the interests of China and Japan.

CONCLUSION

The relationship among the three key actors in East Asia — ASEAN, China, and Japan — has been complicated, even more so since they embarked on the EAC-building process. The sense of competition that seems to exist will not vanish anytime soon: this has become the character of power politics in East Asia. It can be argued that Japan is shifting its stance from pacifism after several encounters with China, such as their maritime feuds stirred by a collision incident off Diaoyu/Senkaku Islands in 2010 and again in 2012. Japan, while searching to work with China to find a solution, has also seemingly stepped up activities to curb China's expanding clout and picked up the pace to find friends to achieve that goal, indeed through the process of EAC building at the same time. Strategies have been developed, mainly to achieve Japan's interests that reflect its realist thinking. China, in the meantime, has adopted similar strategies, employing its intimate ties with certain ASEAN members to further strengthen its position in the region, and often taking a lead in regional initiatives.

This paper has sought to explain the current stage of the EAC through a series of arguments. But one point must be made here in this final paragraph: intra-regional conflicts and legitimacy crises are also responsible for delays in ASEAN community building, which is now due to commence in 2015, such as the current territorial dispute between Thailand and Cambodia and the continued political violence in Thailand. Therefore, problems for a united community do not derive merely from the dynamics between China and Japan. As has been shown throughout the text, both countries have unveiled the different paths they take as they support ASEAN's efforts in building an EAC. While China opposed the inclusion of non-Asian members, Japan was in search of more friends in the region to shore up its position to challenge the growing Chinese influence. In this process, the seeming competition has been perceived as a boon, as much as a bane, for ASEAN. Positively, it has provoked ASEAN and other states to sharpen their diplomatic skills in multilateralism, as shown in the case of China and Japan, and to grasp any advantages that arrive with an EAC. For ASEAN in particular, the seeming competition has assigned the grouping a special responsibility: to reiterate its importance as the engine in the region's community-building process.

Notes

1   For further discussion, see Christensen, 1999, pp. 49–80.
2   Shiraishi, 1997, pp. 182–86.
3   Hirata, 2001, p. 85.
4   In his speech titled "When the Pacific Ocean Becomes an Inland Sea," Prime Minister Yasuo Fukuda pledged that Japan would (1) resolutely support the integration and development of ASEAN, (2) reinforce its alliance with the United States and discharge its responsibilities as a peace-fostering nation, (3) develop infrastructure for intellectual and youth exchanges in Asia to underpin the future of the region, and (4) address through a universal effort the challenge of achieving economic growth while simultaneously protecting the environment and fighting climate change (Shiraishi 2008).
5   See Lipscy, 2003, pp. 93–104.
6   Stubbs, 2002, p. 443.
7   He, 2004, p. 112.
8   Terada, 2006, p. 5.
9   Blaise, 2009, p. 6.
10 *Asahi Shimbun*, 28 October 2003. Cited in Terada, 2006, p. 6.
11 Source: ASEAN Secretariat, 2011*a*.
12 ASEAN trade with the Plus Three countries remained robust. Trade with these countries reached US$413.8 billion in 2009, declining by only 15.5 per cent compared to the US$489.5 billion reported in 2008, and registered a 27 per cent share of total ASEAN trade in 2010. The 2009 value of total trade between ASEAN and its Plus Three Dialogue Partners was still higher than its pre-crisis level of US$405.4 billion in 2007. Source: ASEAN Secretariat, 2011*b*.
13 Private discussion with Chinese Ambassador to Singapore Wei Wei, 11 October 2010, Singapore.
14 Chachavalpongpun, 2010, pp. 196–97.
15 Thailand was initially scheduled to host the EAS in 2008, but it was forced to postpone it to 2009 due to its domestic crisis.
16 Source: ASEAN Secretariat, 2011*a*. (Also see Lee, 2010.)

[17]   Chachavalpongpun, 2009.
[18]   The original agreement on the TPP among Brunei, Chile, New Zealand, and Singapore was signed on 3 June 2005 and entered into force on 28 May 2006. Eight additional countries — Australia, Malaysia, Peru, the United States, Vietnam, Canada, Japan, and Mexico — are currently negotiating to join the group.
[19]   *People's Daily Online*, 2011.
[20]   Vaughn, 2005, p. 5.

References

ASEAN Secretariat. 17 January 2011*a*. Available at <http://www.aseansec.org/7672.htm>.

————. 22 February 2011*b*. Available at <http://www.aseansec.org/16580.htm>.

Blaise, Séverine. "Japanese Aid as a Prerequisite for FDI: The Case of Southeast Asian Countries". Asia-Pacific Economic Papers, Australia-Japan Research Centre, ANU College of Asia and the Pacific, Crawford School of Economics and Government, no. 385, 2009.

Chachavalpongpun, Pavin. "ASEAN Summit: Superstructure Versus Infrastructure." *Bangkok Post*, 20 October 2009.

————. *Reinventing Thailand: Thaksin and His Foreign Policy*. Singapore: Institute of Southeast Asian Studies, 2010.

Chongkittavorn, Kavi. "(10+3)+(1+2)+(?+?)=Asian Identity?" Paper presented at the fourth High-Level Conference on "Asian Economic Integration: Toward an Asian Economic Community", organized by India's Research and Information System for Developing Country and Singapore's Institute of Southeast Asian Studies, New Delhi, India, 18–19 November 2005.

Christensen, Thomas J. "China, the U.S.-Japan Alliance, and the Security Dilemma in East Asia". *International Security* 23, no. 4 (Spring 1999).

Emmerson, Donald K. "Asian Regionalism and U.S. Policy: The Case for Creative Adaptation." RSIS Working Paper no. 193, 19 March 2010.

He, Baogang. "East Asian Idea of Regionalism: A Normative Critique". *Australian Journal of International Affairs* 58, no. 1 (March 2004).

Hirata, Keiko. "Cautious Proactivism and Reluctant Reactivism: Analysing Japan's Foreign Policy toward Indochina". In *Japanese Foreign Policy in Asia and the Pacific: Domestic Interests, American Pressure, and Regional Integration*, edited by Akitoshi Miyashita and Yoichiro Sato. New York: Palgrave, 2001.

Lee, Chi-dong. "South Korea, ASEAN Agree to Upgrade Ties to Strategic Partnership. *Yonhap*". 29 October 2010. Available at <http://leavefreedom.blogspot.com/2010/10/lead-s-korea-asean-agree-to-upgrade.html>.

Lipscy, Phillip Y. "Japan's Asian Monetary Fund Proposal". *Stanford Journal of East Asian Affairs* 3, no. 1 (Spring 2003).

Malkin, Bonnie, and Malcolm Moore. "WikiLeaks: Kevin Rudd Warned of Need to Be Ready to Use Force against China". *The Telegraph*, 6 December 2010.

Nair, Deepak. "Regionalism in the Asia-Pacific/East Asia: A Frustrated Regionalism". *Contemporary Southeast Asia* 31, no. 1 (April 2009).

People's Daily Online. "Japan, India, U.S. to Team up to Counter China's Naval Power", 6 January 2011. Available at <http://www.peopleforum.cn/viewthread.php?tid=59434>.

Peou, Sorpong. *Peace and Security in the Asia-Pacific: Theory and Practice*. Santa Barbara, Denver, and Oxford: Praeger, 2010.

Prasirtsuk, Kitti. "Japan's Vision of an East Asian Community: A Perspective from Thailand". *Japanese Studies* 26, no. 2 (September 2006).

Rajan, D.S., and Raakhee Suryaprakash. "East Asia Summit: An Appraisal". *ISAS Insight* 10 (30 December 2005).

Severino, Rodolfo C. *Southeast Asia in Search of an ASEAN Community: Insights from the Former Secretary-General*. Singapore: Institute of Southeast Asian Studies, 2006.

Shiraishi, Takashi. "Japan and Southeast Asia". In *Network Power: Japan and Japan and Asia*, edited by Peter J. Katzenstein and Takashi Shiraishi. Ithaca: Cornell University Press, 1997.

———. "Renewing Fukuda Doctrine". *Yomiuri Shimbun*, 21 July 2008.

Soeya, Yoshihide. "An East Asian Community and Japan-China Relations". *East Asia Forum*, 17 May 2010. Available at <http://www.eastasiaforum.org/2010/05/17/an-east-asian-community-and-japan-china-relations/>.

Stubbs, Richard. "ASEAN Plus Three: Emerging East Asian Regionalism". *Asian Survey* 42, no. 3 (May–June 2002).

Terada, Takashi. "Forming an East Asian Community: A Site for Japan-China Power Struggles". *Japanese Studies* 26, no. 1 (May 2006).

Thayer, Carlyle A. "China-ASEAN Relations: ASEAN Plus Three: An Evolving East Asian Community?" Unpublished paper. Available at <http://csis.org/files/media/csis/pubs/0004qchina_seasia.pdf>.

Vaughn, Bruce. "East Asia Summit: Issues for Congress". *CRS Report for Congress*, 9 December 2005. Available at <http://www.au.af.mil/au/awc/awcgate/crs/rs22346.pdf>.

4

THE NEW JAPAN-ASEAN PARTNERSHIP: CHALLENGES IN THE TRANSFORMATION OF THE REGIONAL CONTEXT IN EAST ASIA

Mie Oba

INTRODUCTION

The Japan-ASEAN (Association of Southeast Asian Nations) partnership has a long history, beginning in the early 1970s. Japan began to have an informal dialogue with ASEAN in 1973 in order to resolve trade frictions over synthetic rubber. Prime Minister Takeo Fukuda proposed the Fukuda Doctrine and stressed the necessity of "heart-to-heart", "person-to-person" understanding when he was invited to the second ASEAN Summit in Kuala Lumpur in August 1977.[1] Japan played an important role in the process of trying to find a resolution to the prolonged internal conflict in Cambodia, and contributed to reconstructing the country. After the 1997–98 Asian Financial Crisis, Japan's presence was evident in the various projects and plans to help crisis-hit countries overcome their problems as well as revitalize their economies. For example, the New Miyazawa Plan (1998), which was a package of financial assistance directed toward Thailand, Malaysia, the Philippines, the Republic of Korea (ROK), and Indonesia, was financed by Japan. In the early 1990s, Japan and ASEAN institutionalized the Meeting of ASEAN Economic Ministers and Minister

55

for International Trade and Industry (AEM-MITI). AEM-MITI focused on economic cooperation between ASEAN and Japan, including assistance for Indochina (Vietnam, Cambodia, and Lao PDR) and Myanmar, with the aim of supporting these countries' aspirations to be members of ASEAN.[2] In addition, economic ministers of ASEAN countries and Japan agreed to establish the Cambodia-Laos-Myanmar Working Group, which aimed at narrowing the developmental gap in Southeast Asia, at the AEM-MITI meeting held in September 1994. ASEAN economic cooperation actually began with an agreement between ASEAN economic ministers in 1992 to establish the ASEAN Free Trade Area (AFTA). After this, Japan-ASEAN industrial cooperation started encouraging greater integration and development in Southeast Asia. The Japan-ASEAN partnership carried a heavy weight for ASEAN countries because of Japan's position as the second-largest economic power in the world.

However, several new trends in East Asia since the beginning of the 21st century led Japan to rethink and reconstruct the Japan-ASEAN partnership. The rise of China, the acceleration of ASEAN integration, and the rapid development of ASEAN-centered regional architecture transformed economic circumstances in East Asia. These trends are interconnected with each other and have transformed the regional economic landscape of East Asia, significantly changing the character of the Japan-ASEAN partnership. The relative weight of the Japan-ASEAN partnership has declined. The partnership now places great emphasis on the necessity of Japanese support for ASEAN integration and development beyond bilateral support to each ASEAN member state. The partnership is also clearly placed in the context of broader regional integration in East Asia and in community building, namely, an East Asian community. Furthermore, in the security field, ASEAN's crisis because of China's unilateral and sometimes offensive activities over the South China Sea created a new dynamism in this region. Since the end of the first decade of the 21st century, the United States' "return to Asia" policy, which is obviously a response to the rise of China, is another other key factor that has given the regional power balance a new shape.

This paper examines the trajectory and development of the Japan-ASEAN partnership since the early part of the 21st century from a Japanese perspective. It outlines the future prospects of this partnership, and suggests some recommendations for enhancing the Japan-ASEAN partnership, which seeks to maintain and enhance regional stability, peace, and prosperity. The next section reviews several new trends that are transforming the Japan-ASEAN partnership. The third section focuses on the process of advancement of ASEAN-centered regional integration in East Asia and how Japan can contribute. The fourth section looks at China's offensive and unharmonious diplomacy, which has not only created fear among neighboring countries but also brought about a fluctuation in the ASEAN-centered regional architecture, as well as regional instability. This section also points out the implication of the United States' return to Asia and stresses the importance of collaboration between Japan, ASEAN, and the United States in maintaining regional stability. Finally, this paper introduces some tentative recommendations for the ASEAN-Japan partnership in the changing regional context.

NEW TRENDS IN EAST ASIA SINCE THE BEGINNING OF THE 21ST CENTURY

The Rise of China

Changes in the balance of power in East Asia have become obvious since the early years of the 21st century. The main factor in this change is the rising power of China. The expansion of China's presence was more discernible during the beginning of the 21st century than in previous eras. The country's growth rate was about 8 per cent from 2000 to 2002 and above 10 per cent from 2003 to 2007.[3] China's entry into the World Trade Organization in 2001 accelerated the expansion of its trade. China's share in global trade increased by 8 per cent for exports and 6.4 per cent for imports in 2006.[4] The presence of the Chinese economy in the deepening East Asian production network expanded,[5] and the increase of China's economic presence translated into an increased political presence in East Asia.

In addition to their country's economic success, the Chinese began to take a more positive attitude toward contributing to the development of regional frameworks and were no longer averse to engaging in regional arrangements. The Chinese government began to conclude an ASEAN-China Free Trade Agreement and bilateral free trade agreements (FTAs) with some ASEAN countries. In addition, it actively began to engage with the Greater Mekong Subregion and proposed various projects in the area. In October 2003 China signed the Treaty of Amity and Cooperation (TAC) with India, both countries' first time as Dialogue Partners. It also contributed to the effort to upgrade the Shanghai Five to the more formal Shanghai Cooperation Organization. China's positive attitude to regional arrangements is reflected in its strategy to mitigate any fear of the country on the part of its neighbors. This strategy has also created sensitivity among Japanese elites in relation to the rise of China and led them to reconstruct policies toward ASEAN that incorporate a comprehensive East Asia policy supporting their own interests.

The Acceleration of ASEAN Integration and Its Economic Development

The second trend in East Asia in the 21st century is that ASEAN countries have intensified their efforts to advance economic integration among their own economies. They have reinforced various attempts to promote ASEAN economic integration for achieving further economic development, as well as efforts to narrow the developmental gap in Southeast Asia since the early years of the 21st century. The Initiative for ASEAN Integration was launched in 2000, with the objective of narrowing the development gap and accelerating economic integration in ASEAN, particularly among Cambodia, Lao PDR, Myanmar, and Vietnam (CLMV). AFTA, which had been promoted since the early 1990s, was almost realized in 2003. The Bali Concord II (2003) saw the realization of the ASEAN Community. It was to be composed of an ASEAN Security Community, an Economic Community, and a Socio-Cultural Community by 2020; later the target year for community building was changed to 2015.

It should also be mentioned that the ASEAN countries increased their presence in the region during the first decade of the 21st century. The weight of ASEAN economies expanded during this decade in spite of the setbacks related to the 1997–98 Asian Financial Crisis. Data on the growth rate of GDP show that the economies of the ASEAN advanced countries (Indonesia, Malaysia, Philippines, Thailand, and Singapore) recovered steadily and sustained sufficient growth to advance their economic development following the crisis.[6] The Global Financial Crisis in 2007–09 hit ASEAN economies, but the extent of the damage was relatively light compared to that during the Asian Financial Crisis.

Construction of ASEAN-Centered East Asian Regional Architecture

The third trend in the 21st century is that the institutionalization of East Asia has advanced and ASEAN-centered East Asian regional architecture has become apparent. Signs of ASEAN-centered East Asian regional architecture could already be found in the establishment of the ASEAN Regional Forum (ARF) in 1994 and ASEAN+3 in 1997. In the first decade of the 21st century, the ASEAN countries made further efforts to position

ASEAN as the institutional center of the East Asian regional architecture. They strengthened bilateral ties with all Dialogue Partners through the conclusion of FTAs as well as through their signing of the TAC. In addition, they cooperated through the East Asian Summit (EAS), which in 2005 established the ASEAN-centered regional framework. The concept of "ASEAN centrality" developed not only because it was convenient for Dialogue Partners, especially China and Japan, to avoid serious competition over initiatives in the region, but also because the ASEAN countries themselves were eager to put themselves in a position that would allow them to influence emerging regional structures.

East Asian regional architecture is a mixture of several multilateral forums and bilateral ties that ASEAN has developed with Dialogue Partners. ASEAN-centered characteristics of East Asian regional architecture derive from the latter's institutional structure mentioned above as well as the fact that the support and assistance of Dialogue Partners to the ASEAN are indispensable for achievement of ASEAN integration. ASEAN-centered regional integration has also been promoted through the concept of the Regional Comprehensive Economic Partnership (RCEP), which aims to promote regional integration among ASEAN member states and ASEAN FTA partners. The concept of ASEAN connectivity is set to be extended to the concept of "connectivity plus", to include ASEAN as well as Dialogue Partners.

Toward a Horizontal Relationship

Despite Japan's strong role in shaping regional integration, the overall weight of Japan's presence decreased during the first decade of the 21st century. Some economic indicators show this trend. For example, the amount of Japan's nominal GDP was about US$4.141 trillion, which was five times that of China's and eight times that of the ASEAN economies in 2001. In 2006, China's nominal GDP was half that of Japan's, while the nominal GDP of the ASEAN economies was one-fifth that of China. China's GDP exceeded that of Japan in 2010, and the nominal GDP of the ASEAN economies became about one-third that of Japan. The same trend can be found in the amount of GDP per capita. These facts indicate that the economic predominance of Japan in East Asia, which had been sustained throughout the postwar period, quickly eroded in the first decade of the 21st century. The power structure of East Asia, within which Japan had held a predominant position for several decades, changed rapidly during this decade, with China establishing its superiority in the region; and the power balance between Japan and the ASEAN countries rapidly became more horizontal.

Japan had been the only great power in Asia in the modern era. After its collapse due to its defeat in World War II, Japan revived as the predominant economic power. The predominance of the country's position in the region shaped the Japanese national identity that Japan was the only advanced power in Asia. Such a national identity affected the postures of Japanese political and economic elites toward Asia. From their point of view, Japan should have been able to lead other Asian countries as an economic power as well as to have a role in providing them with economic and technological assistance. However, the change in the power balance among East Asian countries shook the Japanese identity, and Japanese elites were forced to search for a new stance in their approach toward the rest of Asia, including ASEAN.

ASEAN-CENTERED REGIONAL INTEGRATION AND THE JAPAN-ASEAN PARTNERSHIP

Japanese elites began to take seriously the rise of China and to reconstruct new directions for the country's policies toward East Asia. They also began to consider the fact that the relationship between Japan and ASEAN had shifted from being a vertical to a relatively horizontal one. The process of regional economic integration in East Asia indicates a trajectory of further transformation within the Japan-ASEAN partnership. Japanese elites had to tighten the ASEAN-Japan partnership keeping in mind ASEAN centrality, in order to construct a favorable regional climate in East Asia.

Implications of AJCEP for Japan-ASEAN Partnership

Prime Minister Junichiro Koizumi's speech titled "Japan and ASEAN in East Asia: A Sincere and Open Partnership" was the first document that indicated the new direction of Japan's policy toward ASEAN in the 21st century.[7] Koizumi gave this speech when he visited Singapore in January 2002, and in it he proposed several specific ideas including the Initiative for Japan-ASEAN Comprehensive Economic Partnership (AJCEP), commonly called the Japan-ASEAN FTA, and the establishment of an "extended" East Asian community composed of Australia and New Zealand in addition to the ASEAN+3 member states.

The Japanese government began to take a positive stance toward an FTA at the end of the 1990s, though it had been cautious about the spread of FTAs up to that point and had refrained from entering into an FTA with any country.[8] The negotiation of the Japan-Singapore Economic Partnership Agreement, which was signed during Koizumi's visit, had already started before the agreement between China and ASEAN to form their FTA. However, it was obvious that several proposals, such as the AJCEP and an "extended" East Asian community, in Koizumi's speech were a reaction by Japan to China's approach toward ASEAN and the formation of a China-ASEAN FTA, which could also be directly linked to Japan's proposal of the AJCEP. ASEAN and Japan adopted the Framework for Comprehensive Economic Partnership in Bali in October 2003, and they signed the Agreement on Comprehensive Economic Partnership (AJCEP) in April 2008.[9] The AJCEP between Japan and every ASEAN country except Indonesia came into force in March 2012.[10]

The Japanese government regarded the AJCEP as a tool to extend its political leverage to ASEAN. "The Strategy of Japan's FTA Policy", published by Japan's Ministry of Foreign Affairs in October 2002, stressed that the FTA contained political implications and stated that Japan should give priority to the negotiation of FTAs with ASEAN as well as the Republic of Korea in order to construct a regional system in which Japan could take the initiative in East Asia.[11] The AJCEP was expected to provide the Japanese economy with opportunities to further access the developing East Asian economies. For example, Japan's Ministry of Economy, Trade, and Industry (METI) placed the AJCEP as a measure to construct the "East Asian Business Area".[12] In other words, Japan began to depict a regional vision for an integrated East Asia that would be favorable for its own country, and its partnership with ASEAN was critical to the achievement of this vision, especially in the face of China's rising significance.

RCEP: Beyond ASEAN Integration and ASEAN+X Linkages

Japan's strategy to advance regional economic integration beyond a bilateral FTA with ASEAN stimulated a surge of arguments on the establishment of a regional economic area in East Asia. The idea of an "East Asian Business Area" provided the basis for the proposal of an East Asian Economic Partnership Agreement (EAEPA) in April 2006 by the METI. The EAEPA aimed to encourage trade liberalization, outlining rules on investment, intellectual property rights, and economic cooperation on environmental protection and human resource development. Later, the EAEPA was renamed the Comprehensive Economic Partnership in East Asia (CEPEA) and was composed of EAS members.

By contrast, the Chinese government strongly supported the idea of an East Asian Free Trade Area (EAFTA) comprising only the ASEAN+3 countries, which also aimed to realize the goals outlined by the CEPEA. Both the CEPEA and EAFTA were examined by working groups at the nongovernmental level, and these working groups submitted final reports. The confrontation between advocates of the EAFTA and those of the CEPEA lasted for about five years and reflected the opposing interests of Japan and China and their regional visions of East Asia, following the establishment of the EAS.

The confrontation between two models of ASEAN-centered regional integration eventually ended due to the Sino-Japan "compromise", indicated through the Japan-China Joint initiative on "Speeding Up the Establishment of EAFTA and CEPEA" proposed in August 2011.[13] In this proposal, Japan and China jointly proposed establishing three new working groups (on trade in goods, trade in services, and investment) for trade and investment liberalization.[14] The Sino-Japan joint initiative was welcomed by ASEAN countries, and in November 2011 ASEAN leaders endorsed a framework for RCEP, replacing references to CEPEA and EAFTA with references to the ASEAN FTA Partner. At the seventh EAS in November 2012, leading members of RCEP, ASEAN, and ASEAN's FTA partners officially launched the RCEP negotiation.

The RCEP concept was endorsed by several documents adopted at the first Economic Ministers' Meeting and at the ASEAN FTA Partners Consultation in August 2012. Furthermore, the direction of regional economic integration in East Asia was outlined during the 19th ASEAN Summit and leaders meeting in November 2012. First, the leaders implied East Asian regional integration would be advanced along the lines of the CEPEA, which Japan had strongly supported. "ASEAN's FTA partners" were composed of "+6", not "+3". Second, those documents reiterated the view that regional integration should be promoted by recognizing "ASEAN centrality". From the viewpoint of economic scale, ASEAN could not provide the central role in the process of advancing substantial regional integration and cooperation. However, "ASEAN centrality" was indispensable in promoting regional integration in East Asia, and China and Japan competed to drive the initiative.

Establishment of ERIA

The strong initiative of the Japanese government to establish the Economic Research Institute for ASEAN and East Asia (ERIA) stemmed from the

Japanese strategy to contribute to promoting economic integration in East Asia as well as to keeping and expanding Japanese presence in this region. The origin of the ERIA was the "Global Economic Strategy", which was announced by the METI in April 2006. The Global Economic Strategy attempted to answer the questions of how Japan contributed to East Asian regional integration in order to construct an appropriate regional order, and how Japan kept its presence in the region.[15] Along these lines, it proposed the establishment of an East Asian OECD to promote regional integration in East Asia.

Based on this idea, Minister of Economy, Trade, and Industry Nikai Toshihiro proposed the establishment of the ERIA at the 13th ASEAN-Japan Economic Ministers' Meeting in April 2006. The Expert Group on the ERIA, which was composed of specialists from 16 member states of EAS and representatives from the ASEAN Secretariat, began to discuss the basic concepts, guidelines, and organizational structure of the ERIA as well as research themes and capacity-building projects that should be promoted in the ERIA. Japanese representatives also led the discussion in the expert group. Japan again proposed the establishment of the ERIA at the second ASEAN Summit in January 2007, taking into consideration the discussions of the expert group, and other participants welcomed it. The ERIA began to promote some pilot projects in May 2007, and the third EAS formally decided on the establishment of the ERIA. The ERIA inaugural governing board meeting was held in June 2008 and adopted the Statement on the Establishment of ERIA.

The objectives of the ERIA are to intellectually contribute to the efforts for regional integration in East Asia while conducting policy research under three pillars: "deepening economic integration", "narrowing development gaps", and "sustainable development", with the announcement of policy research results through seminars and symposia, and with policy recommendations to EAS and ASEAN summits and other meetings.[16] The activities of the ERIA actually have an influence in shaping the promotion of East Asian economic integration, such as the examination of ASEAN connectivity, which is mentioned in the next section.

ASEAN Connectivity and Connectivity+: Implications for Japan-ASEAN Partnership

The Global Financial Crisis provided further impetus for advancing regional economic integration in East Asia. The ERIA submitted a Comprehensive Asian Development Plan (CADP) to the fifth EAS in October 2010. On the other hand, the concept of "ASEAN connectivity" was proposed at the 15th ASEAN Summit in Cha-am Hua Hin in October 2009, and one year later ASEAN leaders adopted the Master Plan ASEAN Connectivity (MPAC) at the 16th ASEAN Summit. The concept of ASEAN connectivity aimed at strengthening intra-regional connectivity within ASEAN and its subregional group, which meant CLMV.[17] This proposal also showed ASEAN's intention to keep its central position in East Asian regional integration in spite of its relatively small economic scale. The MPAC presented the three key elements of ASEAN connectivity, namely, physical connectivity, institutional connectivity, and people-to-people connectivity.[18] The specific plans and projects that were examined and finally included in CADP affected the plans and projects in the MPAC.

Japan has demonstrated its strong support for the promotion of ASEAN connectivity on a number of occasions. In addition to the "Initial Plan for Cooperation on ASEAN Connectivity" in 2010, Prime Minister Yoshihiko Noda gave an assurance that Japan would extend assistance for the "Formation of the Vital Artery for East-West and Southern Economic Corridor" and the "Maritime Economic Corridor" and announced a "List of flagship projects for enhancing ASEAN connectivity"[19] at the 14th ASEAN-Japan Summit in November 2011. Leaders of the EAS member countries adopted the "Declaration of the 6th East Asia Summit on ASEAN Connectivity" in November 2011, showing their commitment to reinforcing ASEAN connectivity, and discussed the possibility of extending connectivity beyond ASEAN.[20]

The promotion of ASEAN connectivity lays the foundation for the realization of the AEC. One of the significant aims of ASEAN connectivity is to build up a strong infrastructure that interconnects ASEAN countries, in order to narrow the gap between CLMV and the more advanced ASEAN countries. The development of the Indochina region has been the focal point for reinforcing integration, regional stability, and prosperity in ASEAN. From the ASEAN side, ASEAN connectivity requires financial and technical support from Dialogue Partners, including Japan. From Japan's point of view, its contribution to ASEAN connectivity has been to respond to ASEAN's needs. However, Japan has also sought to take political advantage in East Asia through its important role in this process.

Regional Financial Cooperation and Japan

The Asian Financial Crisis in 1997 significantly altered Japanese elites' beliefs about the general regional situation as well as regionalism in

Asia. Japan, which had apparently been reluctant to take the initiative in promoting regionalism in Asia, changed its attitude toward regionalism in East Asia and played a leading role in financial cooperation for assistance and revitalization of Asian economies. Although Japan's proposal of an Asian Monetary Fund in August 1997 suffered a setback because of strong U.S. opposition and China's reluctance, Japan announced the New Miyazawa Initiative, which would make available US$30 billion to crisis-hit countries in Asia. The implementation of the New Miyazawa Initiative led to the establishment of a regional network of foreign currency swaps: the Chiang Mai Initiative (CMI), which was agreed upon at the ASEAN+3 financial ministers' meeting in May 2000.

The CMI under ASEAN+3 encouraged further communication among policy makers in the financial field in member countries so that an informal network in terms of financial cooperation could be constructed in East Asia. This informal network sometimes allowed policy makers to share perspectives on the risks for financial stability in East Asia. For example, with information captured in this informal network, Japan decided to double the maximum amount of assistance to Indonesia from US$6 billion to US$12 billion in April 2009 in order to mitigate Indonesia's economic damage from the Global Financial Crisis.

Furthermore, at the 11th ASEAN+3 Finance Ministers' Meeting in Madrid in May 2008, CMI Multilateralization (CMIM) was agreed upon.[21] The Special ASEAN+3 Finance Ministers' Meeting in Phuket in February 2009 seriously considered the contagion of the economic crisis and agreed to adopt concrete policy measures in order to ensure regional market stability and to foster confidence in the market. In this regard, it decided to increase the size of the CMIM from US$80 billion to US$120 billion.[22] The CMIM agreement came into effect in March 2010. Japan and China were the biggest donors: they each donated US$38.4 billion, accounting for 32 per cent of the entire contribution by members of CMIM.

To specify the activities of the CMIM, the ASEAN+3 Macroeconomic Research Office (AMRO) was established in Singapore in April 2011. The AMRO's job is to "monitor and analyze regional economies in order to contribute to early detection of risks, swift implementation of remedial actions and effective decision-making of the CMIM".

REBALANCING OF POWER AND
NEW DIRECTION OF PARTNERSHIP

In addition to the rise of China, the country's unilateral actions in the South China Sea and its intervention in the ASEAN decision-making process have eroded ASEAN's unity as well as created a new dynamism in peace and security in the region. The United States' rebalancing policy can be understood as an effort to counterbalance the increased presence of China, but it also has the potential to make clear the split among ASEAN countries. In the face of this trend, a new ASEAN-Japan strategy is required in order to preserve and promote peace and stability.

China's Virtual "Veto" Power in the Architecture

China's tough diplomacy toward neighboring countries — for example, its attitude toward territorial issues in the South China as well as East China Seas — has caused fear among East Asian countries, including Japan, over its intentions since early 2010. The conflict between China and Japan over maritime interests around Senkaku Island was intensified after the Chinese fishing boat collision incident in September 2010. The territorial dispute over the Spratly Islands between China and some Southeast Asian countries, including Vietnam and the Philippines, has worsened.

ASEAN member states are facing difficulties in preserving the unity and cohesion of ASEAN, due to China's rise as well as its tough attitude toward maritime and territorial issues in the South China Sea. ASEAN and Chinese foreign ministers agreed to start working on a Code of Conduct (COC) for the South China Sea, which would be legally binding. Japanese Foreign Minister Koichiro Genba said Japan would support finalizing the COC with collaboration from the United States.[23] Japan's anxiety over conflict with China over Senkaku Island led to an increased interest in issues relating to the South China Sea, as well as its support for the COC.

Territorial conflict over the Spratly Islands obstructed negotiations over the COC and split opinion among ASEAN member states. The ASEAN Ministerial Meeting (AMM) held in July 2012 could not adopt a joint statement. At the eighth EAS, held in November 2012, the Cambodian chairman did not take up the proposal by Vietnam and the Philippines that territorial conflict in the South China Sea should be dealt with as an international issue. The Cambodian position within the ASEAN meetings probably followed the Chinese diplomatic preference regarding maritime territorial conflicts. China was clearly opposed to internationalizing maritime territorial issues at the summit. The diplomatic stances of Cambodia, Laos, and Myanmar tend to be close to those of China due to their similarity with China's political regime as well as their economic dependence on the Chinese. In other words, China seems to have a "virtual" veto in ASEAN meetings by means of its strong influence over these countries.

The Implication of the United States' Return to Asia

While China's leverage is growing, the U.S. presence in the region is also increasing. The United States began to demonstrate its diplomatic stance that it was going to "return" to Asia after the Obama administration took over in 2009. This can be interpreted as a response to the Bush administration's policies, which were often criticized for overlooking Asian affairs. The United States signed the TAC and the convention of the first U.S.-ASEAN leaders' meeting in 2009. Further, the United States' participation in the ASEAN Defense Ministers' meeting plus (ADMM+) and its affiliation with the EAS were indicative of the stronger support shown by the Obama administration to multilateralism in East Asia than the previous administration. According to Jeffrey A. Bader, who served in the Obama administration as senior director for East Asian affairs on the National Security Council from 2009 to 2011, the Obama administration staff "believed that an America embedded in emerging multilateral institutions would give comfort to countries uncertain about the impact of China's rise and provide important balance and leadership".[24]

While deliberately avoiding the surge of tension with China, the Obama administration expressed its concern about maritime issues through its involvement in maintaining stability in the region. For example, at the National Convention Center in Hanoi, just after her attendance at the ASEAN Regional Forum meeting in July 2010, U.S. Secretary of State Hillary Clinton stressed concerns about freedom of navigation and open access to Asia's maritime commons; she also called for respect of international law in the South China Sea.[25] In addition, President Barack Obama announced that 2,500 U.S. Marines would be stationed in Darwin.

As mentioned before, China has conducted unilateral actions in the South China Sea and has sometimes intervened in the ASEAN process, as was seen in the result of the AMM in July 2012 in Cambodia. The presence of the United States is expected to counterbalance China's rising presence. Even though its relative position in global politics has declined after the Global Financial Crisis, the United States is still a superpower; and its resolute attitude could restrain China's offensive diplomatic manner. On the other hand, it is also possible that the intensification of U.S. presence would not be welcomed by the ASEAN countries because traditionally they have not wanted one external power to have a predominant influence.

China's unilateral actions as well as intervention in the ASEAN process have shaken ASEAN's unity and split ASEAN countries into two camps: those that are pro-China and the rest. The U.S. presence in the region might make clearer such a split. Such a split would also reflect a clash of values and norms. The realization of "universal values" comprising democratization, protection of human rights, and rule of law were specified as the common aims of ASEAN in the ASEAN Charter. However, to what extent each ASEAN member state realizes and accepts them is unclear; and the countries, specifically Cambodia and Laos, that have not fully introduced "universal values" into their internal political and social systems tend to be positioned close to China politically.

On the other hand, ASEAN member states recognize the necessity of democratization, protection of human rights, and rule of law across the region in order to improve the investment environment and attract more inflows of foreign direct investment from developed countries. Authoritarian regimes are newcomers to ASEAN, especially Myanmar's military junta, which was recognized by ASEAN countries as a serious obstacle to achieving regional stability and prosperity. Now, the process of democratization in Myanmar, which began in 2010, seems to be succeeding in making Myanmar's political decision-making process more transparent, and in allowing Myanmar nationals to enjoy political freedom. The result of the democratization of Myanmar will serve as a test of the prospects in the ASEAN region to promote democracy, protection of human rights, and the rule of law.

New Approach of ASEAN-Japan Partnership

The U.S. presence will probably prevent China from taking further unilateral and offensive actions. Besides, Japan and ASEAN have been having a hard time mitigating the tension over territorial issues with China. Considering such a situation, the new ASEAN-Japan partnership should continue to support links with the United States in order to develop a favorable regional climate and to help achieve common interests in the face of the inevitable restructuring of power due to the rising importance of China. It would be prudent to judge whether this rise is a threat or not. In failing to find a clear answer to this question, Japan and ASEAN should attempt to maximize the chances that China's rise will become a stabilizing and constructive force rather than a threat to peace and stability in East Asia. To achieve this goal, Japan and ASEAN should cooperate more with the United States through the strategic coordination of Japan-ASEAN and U.S.-ASEAN linkages.

Japan under the Abe administration, which started at the end of 2012, has expressed a positive engagement in ASEAN since early 2013. For example, Prime Minister Shinzo Abe has already visited seven ASEAN countries — Vietnam, Thailand, and Indonesia (January 2013); Myanmar (May 2013); Malaysia, Singapore, and the Philippines (July 2013) — and has reiterated Japan's commitment to ASEAN peace and prosperity. Japan's enhanced engagement with ASEAN is a response to the new regional dynamism caused by the rise of China as well as the rebalancing by the United States. It is intended to push ASEAN countries toward "universal values" rather than the principles promoted by China, which is opposed to democracy, human rights, and the rule of law.

CONCLUSION

Efforts to enhance the Japan-ASEAN partnership continued after the turn of the millennium, and reflected many of the changes in the regional landscape mentioned above. In the first decade of the 21st century, Japan and ASEAN adopted various documents to indicate the new direction of their partnership. The Tokyo Declaration in October 2003 indicated the common strategies for action and listed seven areas: (1) reinforcing comprehensive economic partnership and monetary and financial cooperation, (2) consolidating the foundation for economic development and prosperity, (3) strengthening political and security cooperation and partnership, (4) facilitating and promoting exchange of people and human resource development, (5) enhancing cooperation in culture and public relations, (6) deepening East Asian cooperation for an East Asian community, and (7) cooperation in addressing global issues. The plan of action enumerated specific programs for each area.

In addition, in November 2011 Japan and the ASEAN countries adopted the "Joint Declaration for Enhancing ASEAN-Japan Strategic Partnership for Prospering Together," also known as the Bali Declaration, at the 14th Japan-ASEAN Summit. It identified five strategies "to further enhance peace, stability, and prosperity in the region." The five strategies were: (1) strengthening political-security cooperation in the region, (2) intensifying cooperation toward ASEAN community building, (3) enhancing ASEAN-Japan connectivity for consolidating ties between ASEAN and Japan, (4) cooperating to create a more disaster-resilient society, and (5) cooperating to address common regional and global challenges.[26] This declaration comprehensively covered the goals of the Japan-ASEAN partnership.

Between the announcements of the Tokyo Declaration and the Bali Declaration, regional circumstances changed due to various trends that have been mentioned in this paper. Activities under the Japan-ASEAN partnership were affected by these regional circumstances while in some instances contributing to shape them. While the Bali Declaration maintains the basic premises of Japan's policies toward ASEAN, which were indicated in the Koizumi speech and the Tokyo Declaration, it also contains a number of departures, caused by developments in the Japan-ASEAN partnership and regional situation. First, it focused more attention on political-security cooperation than the Tokyo Declaration did. For instance, it referred to the requirement of deepening cooperation between Japan and ASEAN over maritime security and maritime safety. It also mentioned the issue of the South China Sea. Second, it expressed clearly Japan's enthusiastic support for ASEAN, for example, for ASEAN connectivity and for the construction of the ASEAN community. Third, it more specifically stated the expected role of the regional framework in the various areas, including political-security, economic, and social-cultural. It reaffirmed Japan's and ASEAN's commitment to further intensifying regional cooperation in East Asia and building a regional architecture, as well as Japan's support for ASEAN's centrality.

Japan's policies toward ASEAN in the new millennium are strongly related to policies concerning how Japan should construct a new regional structure that would be favorable to its own interests under the new trends in this region. Japan has attempted to retain, and if possible extend, its influence in Southeast Asia in order to realize favorable regional circumstances for itself. With such a broad vision, Japan should contribute to the promotion of specific projects to stabilize the regional order as well as to provide further prosperity in East Asia. Achievement of the RCEP, reinforcement of ASEAN connectivity, and connectivity plus will continue to be critical agendas for the Japan-ASEAN partnership and will determine the specific character of an integrated regional economy. The development of CLMV and its role in narrowing the economic gap among ASEAN member states alongside the U.S. commitment to East Asia ought to counterbalance the rise of China. There is a risk that U.S. commitment will fluctuate according to regional circumstances. However, it is important that Japan and ASEAN try to keep the United States committed to East Asia.

Notes

1   Speech by Prime Minister Takeo Fukuda, Manila, 18 August 1977.
2   For details on the development of Japan-ASEAN economic cooperation in the 1990s, see Yoshihiro Otsuji, "Ajia-tsusho Senryaku no Henka" [The Deepening of Japan's Commercial Strategy toward Asia]. In *Ajia-Seiji-Keizai-ron* [Political Economy in Asia], edited by Akira Suehiro and Susumu Yamakage. Tokyo: NTT Publishing, 2001, pp. 324–28.
3   MITI, "Tsusho-hakusho" [White Paper on Trade], 2008.
4   Ibid.
5   Ibid.
6   Growth rates of GDP of ASEAN 6, JETRO HP according to <http://www.jetro.go.jp/world/asia/asean/>. Original data includes the growth rate of Vietnam.
7   Junichiro Koizumi, "Japan and ASEAN in East Asia: A Sincere and Open Partnership", 14 January 2002, Singapore.
8   Naoko Munakata, "Evolution of Japan's Policy toward Economic Integration", Working Paper, Brookings Institution, December 2001.
9   "Houkatsuteki-na-keizaijouno renkei-ni kansuru nihonkoku oyobi tounanajia-syokoku-rengo koseikoku no aida no kyotei ni tsuite" [On the Agreement of ASEAN-Japan Comprehensive Economic Partnership among Japan and ASEAN Countries] (press release, on the AJCEP METI homepage). Available at <http://www.meti.go.jp/speeches/data_ed/ed080414aaj.html>.
10   METI, Higashiajia Togo ni mukete [Toward East Asian Integration], Japan-ASEAN Comprehensive Economic Partnership (AJCEP). Available at <http://www.meti.go.jp/policy/trade_policy/east_asia/activity/nasean.html>.
11   MOFA, Nihon no FTA Seisaku [The Strategy of Japan's FTA Policy], October 2002.
12   METI, Tsusho-hakusho 2002 (White Paper on International Trade and Industry 2002), June 2002, p. 125.
13   Department of Foreign Affairs and Trade of Australia, Background to the Regional Comprehensive Economic Partnership (RCEP) Initiative, December 2012, p. 2. Available at <www.dfat.gov.au/fta> (accessed 23 January 2013).
14   Ibid.
15   METI, "Global Economic Strategy", April 2006.
16   ERIA, "Basic Concept". Available at <http://www.eria.org/about_eria/basic.html>.
17   ASEAN Leaders' Statement on ASEAN Connectivity, para. 3.
18   Master Plan of ASEAN Connectivity, December 2010.
19   Chairman's Statement at the 14th ASEAN-Japan Summit, Bali, Indonesia, 18 November 2011.
20   Declaration of the sixth East Asia Summit on ASEAN Connectivity, Bali, Indonesia, 19 November 2011.

[21]   Joint Ministerial Statement of the 11th ASEAN+3 Finance Ministers' Meeting, 4 May 2008, Madrid, Spain, para. 6.

[22]   Joint Media Statement, "Action Plan to Restore Economic and Financial Stability of the Asian Region". Phuket, Thailand, 22 February 2009.

[23]   *Nikkei Shinbun*, 11 July 2012.

[24]   Jeffery A. Bader, *Obama and China's Rise: An Insider's Account of America's Asia Strategy* (Brookings Institution, 2012), p. 4.

[25]   Hillary Rodham Clinton, Remarks at the National Convention Center, Hanoi, Vietnam, 23 July 2010.

[26]   Joint Declaration for Enhancing ASEAN-Japan Strategic Partnership for Prospering Together, Bali, Indonesia, November 2011.

5

ASEAN-JAPAN STRATEGIC PARTNERSHIP AND REGIONAL INTEGRATION: IMPACTS AND IMPLICATIONS

Moe Thuzar

INTRODUCTION

ASEAN-Japan cooperation, through Japan's milestone doctrines that set the direction for regional cooperation, has positively affected ASEAN's efforts for regionalism, including the role of ASEAN-dominated processes like the ASEAN Regional Forum (ARF), ASEAN Plus Three (A+3), and the East Asia Summit (EAS) in enhancing cooperation. These processes contribute to addressing issues and challenges faced by ASEAN and the region, and provide new opportunities for ASEAN leadership in the 21st century. Japan's role in these processes, based on the "heart-to-heart" principles of the 1977 Fukuda Doctrine, served as a bridge, initially between the non-communist ASEAN states and communist/socialist non-ASEAN mainland Southeast Asian states, and evolving gradually into constructive support for ASEAN's growth and development as the grouping's membership expanded. Japan has been most active under the A+3 framework, assisting the ASEAN countries in addressing emerging human security and development issues.

Japan has an important role in moving forward key regional processes with ASEAN. Through the ASEAN initiatives, which are complemented by sub-regional and bilateral collaboration, Japan is helping ASEAN members build national capacities to complement their regional commitments. Japan is also assisting the newer ASEAN members integrate fully into the ASEAN mainstream by sharing Japan's nation-building and development experience in areas such as economic modernization, democratization, governance, and accountability.

The recent policy statement by Prime Minister Abe on Japan's new foreign policy pillars, which focus on partnerships in the (East Asia) region for economic prosperity, provides the vision for this enhanced role in moving forward the ASEAN-Japan strategic partnership at many levels.

An important element in ASEAN-Japan relations is the integration of ASEAN's newer members, Cambodia, Myanmar, Laos, and Vietnam (collectively referred to as "CLMV"), into ASEAN. Since the 1990s, Japan has implemented focused policies and strategies to enhance the development of the CLMV to facilitate their integration into ASEAN. The Master Plan on ASEAN Connectivity provides fresh impetus to infrastructure development in the CLMV. Japan's participation in these processes takes several forms, including initiatives under the Greater Mekong Sub-region (GMS) program of the Asian Development Bank (ADB) and the Initiative for ASEAN Integration (IAI). Complementary to the IAI, the Mekong-Japan Economic and Industrial Cooperation Initiative provides another framework for Japan's partnership with the CLMV countries, to help develop the CLMV sub-region into an integrated destination for Japanese foreign direct investment (FDI).

The sub-region's potential lies in its rich natural and human resources. The question now is how ASEAN and Japan can pragmatically align the different interests of the CLMV countries in their economic development with those of the region, and with Japan, through regional and bilateral cooperation.

This chapter examines Japan's engagement of ASEAN before and after the admission of the CLMV countries into ASEAN, the methodology/approach behind the engagement, the successes/lessons of Japan's engagement with CLMV thus far, and the issues going forward, especially in light of Myanmar's recent reforms opening up to the world. To complement the other chapters, the focus is on economic engagement processes with the CLMV, and the dimension and potential of Japan's official development assistance (ODA) to these countries.

JAPAN, ASEAN, AND REGIONAL PARTNERSHIPS

The realization that Japan could not take partnership with Southeast Asia for granted dawned early. Prime Minister Fukuda, confronted with palpable anti-Japanese sentiment in Southeast Asian countries as a legacy of World War II, made the first pronouncement of a "heart-to-heart" partnership with Southeast Asia in Manila in August 1977, at the first ASEAN-Japan Summit.[1] Today, the Fukuda Doctrine stands as the collective name for three basic principles that have guided Japanese diplomacy in Southeast Asia:

1. Japan is committed to peace, and rejects the role of a military power;
2. Japan will do its best to consolidate the relationship of mutual confidence and trust based on "heart-to-heart" understanding with the nations of Southeast Asia;
3. Japan will cooperate positively with ASEAN while aiming at fostering a relationship based on mutual understanding with the countries of Indochina and will thus contribute to the building of peace and prosperity throughout Southeast Asia.[2]

The Fukuda Doctrine also set the tone for successive prime ministers of Japan to enunciate their vision for relations with ASEAN/Southeast Asia. The groundbreaking nature of the Fukuda Doctrine lay in providing the foundation for soft power diplomacy between Japan and Southeast Asia, with special emphasis on the importance of ASEAN in regional partnerships, even as Japan sought to broaden the spectrum of cooperation in other fields at different levels (including bilateral and sub-regional arrangements).

The Fukuda Doctrine had a spin-off result in Japan taking on the responsibility to act as a bridge between the then ASEAN members and countries in Indochina. It was in this context that Japan started using its ODA mechanism as an instrument to engage with the non-ASEAN states in Southeast Asia that were rapidly falling under the communist shadow. When Vietnam invaded Cambodia in December 1978, Japan adopted a "Support ASEAN" policy, essentially supporting ASEAN's approach to solving the Cambodian crisis.[3] This approach later evolved into ASEAN's modus operandi for discussions on regional peace and stability.

However, the main focus of Japan's relations with ASEAN and other Southeast Asian countries was not really in the political sphere, but in promoting economic diplomacy as a means of strengthening relations. Kesavan (2011) posits that Japan's dramatic economic growth in the 1970s, coupled with the opening up of Southeast Asian economies towards market-oriented "outward-looking" systems, led to the combination of ODA with private investments in implementing this economic diplomacy. The signing of the Plaza Accord in 1985 was thus a landmark in Japan's relations with ASEAN. The strong Japanese yen led to Japanese multinationals relocating their labor-intensive manufacturing bases to Southeast Asia, taking advantage of the low labor cost in these countries. The phenomenon became a win-win situation. The domestic economies of the ASEAN countries benefited from the Japanese investments, as they became both consumers and, later, manufacturing hubs for the export of Japanese goods to international markets. ASEAN's economic regionalization and relations with Japan thus received a boost.

During the 1997–98 financial and economic crisis that swept across Asia, Japan continued to provide assistance to ASEAN countries through bilateral and multilateral arrangements, to help them cope with the effects of the crisis. In October 1998, the New Miyazawa Initiative[4] provided the framework for the extension of US$30 billion through short-term financing arrangements to the hardest-hit economies in ASEAN (as well as the Republic of Korea). This was followed in February 1999 by a set of emergency actions designed to promote economic stabilization in Southeast Asia. In April 1999, Japan announced assistance measures for Asia as part of "Japan's Comprehensive Economic Measures". Together with other assistance detailed below, Japan has so far extended assistance totalling US$43 billion — the largest contribution of any single donor country, to address the Asian currency and financial crisis. The usefulness of the short-term currency swap arrangements under the New Miyazawa Initiative also paved the way for A+3 discussions on regional financial cooperation. A significant achievement of A+3 financial cooperation is the Chiang Mai Initiative (CMI), adopted by the A+3 Finance Ministers in May 2000 at Chiang Mai, Thailand. The CMI essentially expands on a regional swap arrangement in ASEAN and builds a network of bilateral swap agreements among the ASEAN countries, China, Japan, and the Republic of Korea. The CMI was multilateralized effective March 2010, with Japan contributing the largest share to a collective pool of US$120 billion.[5] Nemoto and Nakagawa (2013) discuss this further in their chapter on regional financial cooperation in Southeast Asia.

The 1997–98 crisis, and the advent of the A+3 mechanism, thus provided the framework for a more active role by Japan in ASEAN's regional cooperation. The statement of the 3rd ASEAN-Japan Summit held in December 1997 called for a "broader deeper partnership" and agreed to convene annual summits thereafter. Before this, the ASEAN-Japan Summit meetings took place once a decade, the first in 1977 under PM Fukuda's administration, and the second in 1987 under PM Hashimoto. At each of these summits, the Japanese leaders established or announced initiatives and proposals for deepening Japan's collaborative partnership with the ASEAN countries. The agreement to convene annual summits from 1997 onward signaled Japan's commitment to ASEAN, which complemented existing bilateral relations with individual ASEAN members.

Japan was also among the earliest supporters of ASEAN's central role in important regional processes. PM Koizumi acknowledged this in his 2002 proposal for future cooperation in East Asia, with ASEAN as the base. This notion was further propounded at the 2003 ASEAN-Japan Commemorative Summit, which celebrated 30 years of ASEAN-Japan relations. A "Declaration on ASEAN-Japan Partnership in the New Millennium" and a new concept of Mekong Region Development were also announced. However, Japan acceded to the Treaty of Amity and Cooperation (TAC) only in 2004.[6] Nevertheless, the accession by non-ASEAN states to the TAC paved the way for the TACs and ASEAN's central position in determining inter-governmental relations with ASEAN member states and participation in ASEAN-led processes such as the East Asia Summit, which ASEAN institutionalized in 2005.

Successive governments in Japan continued with development assistance as the cornerstone of its economic diplomacy with ASEAN countries. In 2006, PM Taro Aso established the Japan-ASEAN Integration Fund (JAIF) with a contribution of US$70 million from Japan. In 2007, PM Abe gave a policy speech on Japan and ASEAN at the "heart of dynamic Asia", and established the ASEAN-Japan Comprehensive Partnership Cooperation Fund and an East Asia Youth Exchange Fund. This was followed in 2008 by the signing of the Comprehensive Economic Partnership Agreement between ASEAN and Japan. When the ASEAN Charter came into effect in 2008, Japan became the first

ASEAN Dialogue Partner (DP) to appoint an Ambassador to ASEAN, resident in Jakarta.[7]

Today Japan is ASEAN's second largest trading partner, and arguably one with the most "policy clout" among ASEAN's DPs.

Japan is also a top FDI source for ASEAN. In 2011, Japan's FDI into ASEAN countries reached a record JPY15 trillion, making ASEAN the second top destination for Japanese enterprises. Figure 5.2 shows that Japan ranks second after the EU as an FDI source. However, as Figure 5.3 shows, Cambodia, Laos, and Myanmar continue to receive disproportionately low shares of the FDI inflows to ASEAN. This reinforces the imperative for these countries to develop open economies that are plugged into the global network.

In 2011 the economic overtones of the ASEAN-Japan partnership gained a more even keel. At the special ASEAN-Japan ministerial meeting following the March 2011 triple disaster in Fukushima, the ASEAN foreign ministers offered their assistance and support in helping Japanese citizens in the affected areas recover from the impact of the disaster.

Despite Japan's participation in and support of regional integration processes such as the IAI,[8] special emphasis on developing the economies

FIGURE 5.1
Percentage Share of Major Trade Partners in ASEAN's Total Trade

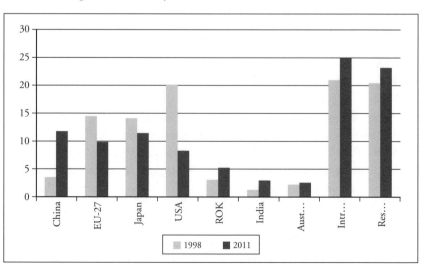

Source: "ASEAN Community in Figures 2013", ASEAN Secretariat.

FIGURE 5.2
Percentage Share of Foreign Direct Investment (FDI) by Source Country
— 2000 and 2011ᴾ

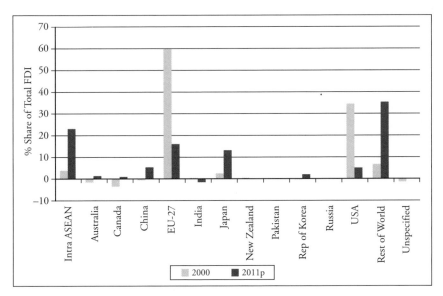

Source: "ASEAN Community in Figures 2013", ASEAN Secretariat.

FIGURE 5.3
Percentage Share of Total FDI Inflow by Host Country

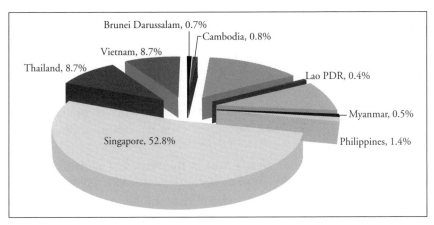

Note: Figures are as of 2010, as 2011 preliminary figures do not include data from Myanmar.
Source: "ASEAN Community in Figures 2013", ASEAN Secretariat.

of the CLMV countries became more pronounced only after 2010. The adoption of the Mekong-Japan Industrial and Economic Cooperation Initiative Action Plan indicated a growing recognition that more focused attention beyond the IAI and other ASEAN-wide mechanisms was necessary to accelerate the economic development of the CLMV. Japan-Mekong cooperation thus became a supporting feature of Japan-ASEAN partnership. A good example was the adoption of the Tokyo Strategy 2012 by the 4th Mekong-Japan Summit in April 2012 in Tokyo, where Japan pledged JPY 600 billion to support infrastructure projects in the Mekong countries.

That same year, Myanmar's reforms and the relaxation of sanctions led to Japan's forgiving a total of about US$5 billion of debt and the resumption of yen loans, which had been suspended since the late 1980s. This signals a significant moment in Japan's ASEAN relations, as well as in Japan-Myanmar bilateral relations. Myanmar's dramatic opening and fast-paced reform measures towards democratization and a market-oriented economy provided the much-needed impetus for both ASEAN (collectively and individually) and Japan to move forward with regional economic integration, particularly in the Mekong region. At the ASEAN level, PM Abe's three-pronged economic strategy reinforces the emphasis placed on assisting the CLMV countries through the Mekong-Japan and IAI processes.

Japan's partnership with ASEAN countries will thus continue to serve the interests of both parties in the decades to come. ASEAN is rich in natural resources, which Japanese industry needs; it also provides a huge market for Japanese goods and services. In particular, the CLMV now offer new/emerging market opportunities for Japan that the ASEAN-6 (the five founding members and Brunei) had provided to Japan at the start of ASEAN-Japan cooperation in the 1970s. It should also be noted that Japan has largely respected ASEAN's role in facilitating these regional partnerships. This is rooted in the Fukuda Doctrine's emphasis on "heart-to-heat" relations in pursuing growth and progress.

ASEAN has not failed Japan's trust in this respect. The demonstration effect of the ASEAN-anchored processes such as the ARF (1994), the A+3 (1998), and the EAS (2005) all indicate that Southeast Asian regionalism has matured enough to drive such forums, even as angst remains over ASEAN's central role being largely that of a convenor. Nevertheless, ASEAN's role in facilitating regional partnerships is evident in:

- the immediate reference to the formal and informal mechanisms that are employed to deal with regional issues;
- the extent of shared norms among the ASEAN member states, and expansion of these shared norms to ASEAN's partners;
- the increasing instances of ASEAN taking a lead role in tackling trans-boundary issues that affect the region (for example, Myanmar, SARS, haze); and
- ASEAN's ability and willingness to learn from its shortcomings and retool itself.

The positive impact of external (non-ASEAN) actors, such as Japan, on regional developments should not be ignored as ASEAN now moves from dialogue (and rhetoric) to more action-oriented interactions with its partners. The renewed interest in regional cooperation as the vehicle for strengthening intra- and inter-regional relations point to a new form of regionalism emerging in East Asia, centered around ASEAN. With Myanmar's opening up, the ASEAN Way has regained attention. ASEAN's regional integration moves are now balanced between providing some flexibility for compliance and promoting the "rules of the game" for regional governance through the ASEAN Charter.

Still, concerns have been raised over members' individual and collective ability to sustain and drive regional integration beyond 2015. Implementation of the Master Plan on ASEAN Connectivity requires considerable investment in the CLMV to become new nodes in the global production network. At the same time, the increasing interdependency of economic relations between ASEAN and the Plus Three countries provides both opportunities and challenges.

JAPAN AND THE CLMV

Japan's relations with the CLMV are not a new phenomenon. Even before these countries joined ASEAN, Japan provided bilateral assistance to each in helping them prepare for ASEAN membership. The IAI provided an additional regional framework for focused assistance in the areas identified as "special needs" by the recipient countries. Japan's continuation of economic diplomacy with the CLMV under the ASEAN framework could lead to a successful realization of Japan's aspirations as a bridge between the ASEAN-6 and the CLMV, helping to narrow gaps within the CLMV and stabilizing the region through these countries' economic growth. This is an ambitious aspiration. It requires building capacities for each country to meet the respective commitments for trade, services, and investment liberalization, as well as developing institutions necessary for economic development. This section assesses some of the focused economic initiatives taken by Japan to assist the CLMV and their impact on integrating these countries into ASEAN.

Uchida and Kudo (2008) report that Japan undertook "three major initiatives" to help the development of CLMV in the 1990s: the Forum for Comprehensive Development of Indochina (FCDI) in February 1995; the establishment of the AEM-METI Economic and Industrial Cooperation Committee (AMEICC) in 1998; and the New Concept of Mekong Region Development announced at the Japan-ASEAN Commemorative Summit in December 2003. Of these, Myanmar was not a participant in the FCDI, but participated in the latter two under the ASEAN framework.

Additionally, there is a plethora of projects and programs that Japan supports under the ADB's GMS programme, which has a similar aim of assisting/accelerating the economic development of the CLMV countries and thus supporting ASEAN's economic integration. The array of initiatives highlights the multi-pronged approach of Japan's economic diplomacy vis-à-vis ASEAN, with special focus on the CLMV. A prominent example would be the support provided for physical infrastructure projects to improve connectivity between the Mekong countries in mainland Southeast Asia and the maritime Southeast Asian states, under the ADB's Asian Highway Network. The ASEAN Highway Network is an integral part of the Asian Highway project. For soft infrastructure, Japan complements bilateral programs with capacity-building support under the IAI, and jointly funds training courses in the CLMV countries on topics specific to these countries' needs in order to participate more actively in the regional economic integration processes. The joint "donors" include the ASEAN-6 members (particularly Singapore) and the UN-ESCAP. The effectiveness of these multiple initiatives and multi-pronged approaches merits closer examination.

Forum for Comprehensive Development of Indochina (FCDI)

PM Miyazawa announced Japan's initiative to organize the FCDI to discuss "balanced development of Indochina" during his tour of ASEAN nations in January 1993. The FCDI was convened in February 1995 as a ministerial-level meeting. Chaired by Japan, participants included representatives from 25 nations, including Vietnam, Cambodia, Laos, the ASEAN-6, and eight international organizations, such as the European Commission.[9] Myanmar was not part of the FCDI.

At the FCDI, a study undertaken by the UN-ESCAP assessed the state of development assistance provided to the CLMV. Discussions at the FCDI led to the formation of working groups on infrastructure development (chaired by Japan) and human resources development (chaired by France). A private-sector advisory group convened in Bangkok in March 1996, to provide the business community's inputs. Working groups on the respective areas were also convened in September (for infrastructure development) and December (for human resources development). However, Uchida and Kudo (2008) observe that FCDI failed to address the subregion's needs, as no follow-up meetings were convened after 1996. The only gain seems to have been coordinating donor projects and programs in the three countries (Uchida and Kudo 2008, 209–61).

AEM-METI Economic and Industrial Cooperation Committee (AMEICC)

The ASEAN Economic Ministers-Ministry of International Trade and Industry (AEM-MITI) Economic and Industrial Cooperation Committee, or AMEICC has more potential in assisting the CLMV's participation in regional economic integration processes. In fact, it is a regional mechanism that grew out of a working group of the ASEAN-6 countries, the CLMV, and Japan's MITI to support these countries in their ASEAN membership preparations. It is a more inclusive process of CLMV integration, with Myanmar participating from the start. As far as Japan's economic diplomacy goes, the AMEICC has the right elements of building capacities for competitiveness and broadening industry-relevant assistance to the CLMV as ASEAN's new members, with attendant policy support.

Building on the CLMV Working Group established under the joint aegis of the AEM and Japan's MITI in 1994, AMEICC was established in 1998 with a mandate from the 3rd ASEAN-Japan Summit in 1997 as "a body for policy consultations to discuss enhanced industrial cooperation, improvement of ASEAN's competitiveness and development cooperation assistance to the new member countries". Annual meetings monitor work carried out under eight working groups covering: human resource development; SMEs, supporting industries, and rural industries; West-East Corridor development; the automobile industry; the chemical industry; the consumer electronic industry; the textile and garment industry; and statistics. AMEICC has been effective in bringing together the ASEAN and Japanese officials involved in the relevant sectors, and in updating the current situation and special needs of the CLMV.

As one of the key requirements is capacity-building, the AMEICC HRD working group has an important role in the AMEICC structure. This working group has created a network of "centres of excellence" across the ASEAN countries and Japan, involving a wide range of institutions involved in capacity-building. In assessing the HRD working group's impact, Uemura (2003) noted that the network included universities, government institutions, government-related training institutes, research institutions, and vocational training schools. The network facilitated consultations and sharing among the various participating institutions to develop "enhanced training curriculums" on topics such as trade, management, electrical and electronics, mechanical and information technology, to be shared among the ASEAN countries. These were the areas of interest identified by the ASEAN side. Special focus was given to developing the training centres in the CLMV, which had poorer training functions (Uemura 2003). However, the system of the national governments selecting the centers to participate in the AMEICC HRD network, and the mechanism of providing automatic assistance for training programmes proposed by individual countries (without applying some regionally applicable criteria) might have created some negative externalities, including cultures of dependency and even complacency. Additionally, the compartmentalized nature of ASEAN sectoral cooperation weakened both the internal and regional-level coordination of training projects and curricula. For example, establishing a link between the AMEICC and the ASEAN Labor Ministers may have helped support the HRD priorities towards building a competitive workforce. Nevertheless, the gains for the CLMV under the AMEICC umbrella have been reinforced with a "new" concept of developing the Mekong region and the Mekong-Japan Economic and Industrial Cooperation Initiative, especially the latter.

Mekong Region Development[10]

The concept of Mekong Region Development announced in 2003 was essentially an attempt to bring together the different strands of development assistance under Japan's ODA Charter. It covered the CLMV as well as China's Yunnan province. Taken together with ASEAN's Mekong Basin Development Cooperation (AMBDC) initiative, Japan's concept was a complementary measure to assist in narrowing the development gap for the CLMV countries and assist their economic development. Several inter-sectoral and crossborder coordination challenges soon came to the fore, including:

- emergence of disparities in development levels within countries;
- coordination issues, including donor coordination and financing arrangements, with other existing subregional bodies and initiatives such as the Mekong River Commission and the Asian Development Bank (ADB);
- the need for flexible and responsive review mechanisms;
- involvement of the private sector, especially in infrastructure investments and market access for the commercially viable areas; and
- linking and deconflicting the overlapping ODA projects under bilateral assistance programs with the regional programs.

Mekong-Japan Economic and Industrial Cooperation Initiative

Launched in 2009 at the first Mekong-Japan Economic Ministers meeting, the Mekong-Japan Economic and Industrial Cooperation Initiative is the brainchild of the former minister of METI Mr Naoshima. It is governed by a work plan monitored by the Mekong-Japan economic ministers, and has as a common vision, shared by Japan and the Mekong countries, including the CLMV and Thailand, of "peace, development and prosperity". It is noteworthy that the coverage of the Mekong region for this initiative is different from that of the 2003 concept for Mekong Region Development. Thailand's role as a key political and economic player in the Mekong region is also acknowledged.[11] The work plan also places priority on "intra-connectivity" in the Mekong region, thus linking priority construction projects with commitments made under the

Master Plan on ASEAN Connectivity. The Mekong-Japan Economic and Industrial Cooperation Initiative now forms an integral part of Japan's Comprehensive Asia Development Plan (CADP) and will serve as the link for ASEAN's connectivity with the South Asian countries, especially India. Figure 5.4 illustrates the schematic plan.

What does all this connote for Japan's trade and investment relations with the CLMV? Uchida and Kudo (2008) have observed that although Japan is the top ODA source for these countries, trade and investment relations are still weak. Carpenter, Alavi, and Zulkifli (2013) have noted that bilateral ODA is by far the most important source of external development assistance for the CLMV countries. Japan is the leading bilateral donor to each of the CLMV, with disbursement to these countries totaling US$8.7 billion from 2001–10, accounting for 26 per cent of the total aid received by CLMV. A breakdown by country indicates that Vietnam received the largest share — US$6.4 billion — while Cambodia, Laos, and Myanmar received US$1.1 billion, US$0.8 billion, and US$0.4 billion respectively. In line with the priorities listed in Japan's economic diplomacy initiatives for the CLMV, the ODA supports economic infrastructure and human resource development in a wide range

FIGURE 5.4
Comprehensive Asia Development Plan

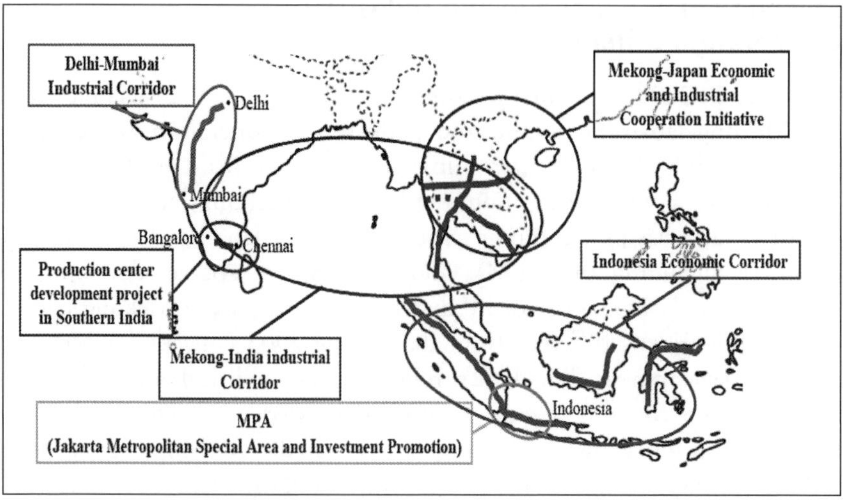

Source: "White Paper 2012", Ministry of Economy, Trade and Industry of Japan.

of sectors, as well as the sub-regional development projects for ASEAN connectivity (Carpenter, Alavi, and Zulkifi 2013, p. 147).

The picture is more or less consistent for Japan's trade relations with each of the CLMV. According to data from the ASEAN Secretariat, Japan has the largest trade relations with Vietnam. In 2011, Vietnam's total trade with Japan amounted to US$21.1 billion. Myanmar is a distant second with US$0.6 billion, followed by Cambodia at US$0.4 billion and Laos at US$0.1 billion.[12]

The state of Japan's investment relations with the CLMV is largely similar. Japan is the top investor in Vietnam. An Investment Mission organized by the ASEAN-Japan Centre and Vietnam's Ministry of Planning and Investment in August–September 2012 noted that in the period since the implementation of "Doi Moi" in 1986 till today, Vietnam has attracted a total of 14,198 investment projects with a total registered capital of US$208,115 million. Of these projects, Japan ranked as top investor, accounting for 1,758 projects and a total registered capital of US$28.064 million.[13] Key sectors of interest are infrastructure projects, sea port, and industrial zone developments. Japan and Vietnam also convene regular "Economic Dialogues" to update businesses and potential investors on investment opportunities in Vietnam. The most recent Japan-Vietnam Economic Dialogue was held in Tokyo on 18 July 2013.

As for Cambodia, the Japanese Embassy in Phnom Penh reported earlier in 2013 that Japanese investors have invested about US$300 million in Cambodia over the last three years. Cambodia's trade volume with Japan increased in 2012, reporting a 25 per cent year-on-year increase at US$641 million, according to JETRO.

With Laos, Japan ranks seventh in the list of top ten FDI sources, with US$428 million. Vietnam tops the list with US$4,913 million, followed by Thailand at US$4,082 million and China at US$3,952 million.[14] Other countries in the list include the Republic of Korea, France, Malaysia, India, the United States, and Singapore. Similar to what was done for Vietnam, the ASEAN-Japan Centre and the Lao Ministry for Planning and Investment organized a series of investment seminars in Osaka and Saitama in January 2013, to promote Japanese investments in seven "priority sectors" identified by Laos: agriculture, manufacturing, hydropower, education, healthcare, mining, and services.[15]

Myanmar seems to be the game-changer here. Although current figures indicate a low level of investment, the data has not caught up with the fast pace of reforms taking place in the country, including an ambitious economic reform agenda that is market-oriented and outward-looking. Prior to the reforms under President Thein Sein, the political situation in Myanmar had precluded the country from the benefits of participating fully in regional integration. Today's Myanmar tells a different story. Japan's economic collaboration with the CLMV also gained additional impetus with the Myanmar reforms.

Building on existing bilateral ties, Japan is now emerging as a key political and economic player that can commit large sums of aid and investment to Myanmar, to assist it in meeting its regional undertakings. This is especially important for the commitments to accomplish the ASEAN Economic Community goals by 2015. Myanmar has many areas to catch up on. The Government of Myanmar has openly recognized this — and the importance of the economic reforms to be consistent with AEC goals — in the policy priorities listed in its Framework for Economic and Social Reforms launched to donors and partners at a development cooperation forum in January 2013.

In a way, Myanmar is becoming the new poster child for how ASEAN's strategic partnerships with key DPs can be leveraged to move regional integration forward. Southeast Asia was the first foreign destination for a Cabinet member of PM Abe's administration after the Liberal Democratic Party (LDP) regained power in the November 2012 parliamentary elections in Japan. In January 2013, Deputy PM and Finance Minister Taro Aso visited Myanmar. It was PM Abe's turn in May 2013, where, accompanied by a large business delegation, he officially announced the debt forgiveness.[16] Japan was also one of the first to enter into an investment agreement under Myanmar's new Foreign Investment Law (approved in November 2012). The agreement is for the Thilawa Port project, which PM Abe also visited during his Myanmar trip. It is part of the Yangon Thilawa Development Initiative (YTDI), including a master plan for urban development in the Greater Yangon area (including Thilawa), which itself is part of a larger framework of Japan's economic cooperation to Myanmar "to spread the dividends of democratisation, national reconciliation and economic reforms" to the Myanmar people.[17] The Thilawa Port project is thus a flagship of Japan's commitment to promote industrialization, employment, and economic development in Myanmar, which will in turn boost Myanmar's role as a strategic node in the larger regional connectivity plans.

Japan's investment in Myanmar is still relatively small. Investments made between the first wave of economic reforms after 1988 and 2011 amount to US$211.9 million.[18] Japan is currently 11th in the list of investors in Myanmar. However, this will soon change. With Myanmar's aim to have more balanced relations with countries in East Asia, Japan will now have a larger role in supporting the reforms in Myanmar.[19] Japan's major political parties, various ministries, industries (including the Keidanren),[20] and NGOs are all eager to play a larger role in helping Myanmar realize her potential for economic development. PM Abe's May 2013 visit to Myanmar also underscored the economic diplomacy dimension of Japan's increasingly enthusiastic engagement with ASEAN. In addition to the Thilawa project, Japan is also assisting with Myanmar's financial sector development. Daiwa Securities and the Tokyo Stock Exchange (now the Japan Exchange Group) are aiding the establishment of Myanmar's first stock exchange. Although initially expected to be unveiled in 2014, the deadline has been pushed back to 2015 as necessary legislation and regulatory requirements are still being put into place.[21]

CONCLUDING THOUGHTS: LOOKING AHEAD

While Japan's economic diplomacy has aided the development of the CLMV, the effectiveness of the various mechanisms has been uneven. Thus far, Vietnam has benefited the most but, as indicated in the section above, this may change with Myanmar's opening. The size of their respective populations and their increasing market orientation make Vietnam and Myanmar potential "pivots" for further intensification of Japan's economic relations in the Mekong region.

The Mekong region is where ASEAN's initiatives and cooperative frameworks with Japan coincide with the latter's. Additionally, Myanmar is widely viewed as the "land bridge" linking ASEAN to South and East Asia. Currently, it is one of the region's least connected countries, although the dramatic political and economic opening-up in recent years has raised hopes for greater investments in the infrastructure necessary for better connectivity with its neighbors and the rest of the region.[22]

In the end, market forces will dictate the success or failure of economic diplomacy, as economic development ultimately has to be driven by the private sector. Governments can only provide the facilitating environment for economic activity to thrive. This is confirmed by the assessment of the Japan Bank for International Cooperation (JBIC) in Table 5.1. For

TABLE 5.1
Ranking for Promising Countries/Regions for Business Operations Over the Medium-Term

Ranking: Added this Time	→	July Survey Recounted	Country/Region	No. of Respondent Companies (Total: 288): Added this time	July Survey Recounted	Increase or Decrease	Percentage Share: Added this Time	July Survey Recounted
1	—	1	China	172	184	▲12	59.7%	63.9%
2	—	2	India	164	163	1	56.9%	56.6%
3	—	3	Indonesia	130	118	12	45.1%	41.0%
4	◀	5	Thailand	102	97	5	35.4%	33.7%
4	—	4	Vietnam	102	99	3	35.4%	34.4%
6	—	6	Brazil	63	62	1	21.9%	21.5%
7	—	7	Mexico	48	41	7	16.7%	14.2%
8	—	8	Russia	35	35	0	12.2%	12.2%
9	—	9	Myanmar	34	33	1	11.8%	11.5%
10	—	10	USA	30	26	4	10.4%	9.0%
11	—	11	Malaysia	27	23	4	9.4%	8.0%
12	◀	14	Korea	13	9	4	4.5%	3.1%
13	▶	12	Turkey	11	11	0	3.8%	3.8%
14	◀	17	Philippines	10	7	3	3.5%	2.4%
14	▶	12	Taiwan	10	11	◀1	3.5%	3.8%
16	▶	14	Cambodia	9	9	0	3.1%	3.1%
17	▶	14	Singapore	8	9	◀1	2.8%	3.1%
18	—	18	Australia	7	6	1	2.4%	2.1%
19	▶	18	Bangladesh	5	6	◀1	1.7%	2.1%
20	—	20	Germany	3	4	◀1	1.0%	1.4%

Source: JBIC FY2012 Survey Report on Overseas Business Operations by Japanese Manufacturing Companies.

the first time, Myanmar has made the grade for JBIC's assessment as a promising country for business operations in the medium-term. Other ASEAN countries in the top ten with Myanmar are Thailand, Vietnam, and Indonesia. (See Table 5.1: Ranking for promising countries/regions for business operations over the medium-term.)

Carpenter and McGillivray (2013) have suggested that, based on progress so far, it may take up to two decades for the CLMV to reach the average ASEAN-6 human development achievements. The gaps in income will take longer to converge. It may take over four decades for CLMV countries to reach the average ASEAN-6 income at current rates of growth. Significant efforts are therefore necessary on the part of ASEAN and donors like Japan to narrow these gaps.

Economic modernization and narrowing development gaps also require improving governance and institutional capacities in the CLMV. Thus, the aim of policy interventions, whether by the ASEAN-6 countries acting on their own initiative or in collaboration with key partners/donors like Japan, should be to balance out the disproportionate benefits in favor of the countries still lagging behind, notably Cambodia and Laos, which seem to be relatively ignored by investors, compared to Vietnam and, of late, Myanmar. So far, China seems to have paid the most attention to Cambodia and Laos, particularly Cambodia. Going forward, Japan and other donors should consider participating more actively in the economies of these two countries in order to provide a more inclusive and balanced approach to the economic development in these countries.

Notes

[1]   Before meeting his ASEAN counterparts in Manila, PM Fukuda had earlier toured the ASEAN countries and then Burma, where he had personally explained the main principles of what would become the Fukuda Doctrine statement.

[2]   Ministry of Foreign Affairs, Japan.

[3]   Yeo Lay Hwee 2006 (citing Sudo 2002, and Lam 2001).

[4]   Announced on 3 October 1998. Under the initiative, Japan provided financial support to ASEAN economies such as Malaysia, the Philippines, and Thailand. For the full text of the New Miyazawa Initiative, please see: <http://www.mof.go.jp/english/international_policy/financial_cooperation_in_asia/new_miyazawa_initiative/e1e042.htm>.

[5]   Japan's contribution is 32 per cent. China's contribution is also listed at 32 per cent but only if including Hong Kong.

6   India and China were the first non-ASEAN countries to accede to the TAC in 200

7   The United States had, however, "beat" the other Dialogue Partners by being the first Dialogue Partner country to appoint an ambassador to ASEAN.

8   Launched in Singapore in 2000 as an "ASEAN help ASEAN" mechanism. Still, priorities under the IAI Work Plan were opened up for support from development and dialogue partners in 2001, at an IAI Development Cooperation Forum. This practice has continued in the second IAI Work Plan timeframe.

9   Ministry of Foreign Affairs, Japan. "Japan-ASEAN Cooperation: A New Dimension in Cooperation". Available at <http://www.mofa.go.jp/region/asia-paci/asean/relation/dimens.html> (accessed April 2013).

10   This section is based on a more comprehensive examination of the Mekong Region Development by Uchida and Kudo (2008) for the ERIA Research Project Report.

11   Ministry of Foreign Affairs, Japan. "Tokyo Strategy 2012 for Mekong-Japan Cooperation". Available at <http://www.mofa.go.jp/region/asia-paci/mekong/summit04/joint_statement_en.html>.

12   ASEAN Community in Figures 2013, Table 18: ASEAN Member States' Total Trade with ASEAN+3, 2011 (based on data from the ASEAN Trade Statistics Database, November 2012).

13   ASEAN-Japan Centre, 2012. "Investment Mission to Vietnam". Available at <http://www.asean.or.jp/en/invest/about/eventreports/2012/2012-03.html/Vietnam_mission_Aug12.pdf>.

14   Ministry of Planning and Investment of Lao PDR, Investment Promotion Department, 2013. "Investment Report and Statistics", available at <http://www.investlaos.gov.la/show_encontent.php?contID=29>.

15   Ministry of Planning and Investment of Lao PDR, Investment Promotion Department, 2013. "Japan is Turning to Laos for the Next Investment Destination in ASEAN", available at <http://www.investlaos.gov.la/show_encontent.php?contID=60>.

16   The *Asahi Shimbun* edition of 26 May 2013 ("Abe ends Myanmar visit with aid, debt write-off") reported that "Japan will provide up to 20 billion yen for the Thilawa project, repayable over 40 years at 0.01 per cent interest. The money will help with electricity infrastructure in the area and an expansion of the port". See also "Japan 'Making Up for Lost Time' in Burma" by Simon Roughnee for the *Irrawaddy*, 27 May 2013, available at <http://www.irrawaddy.org/archives/35549>.

17   Ministry of Foreign Affairs, Japan. Available at <http://www.mofa.go.jp/region/asia-paci/myanmar/thein_sein_1204/pdfs/myanmar_support1204_02.pdf>.

[18] "Myanmar Boom Hits Japanese Business Sector", *The Nation*, 27 September 2012, available at <http://www.nationmultimedia.com/national/Myanmar-boom-hits-Japanese-business-sector-30191229.html>.

[19] "Japan Steps Back into Myanmar," *Nikkei Weekly*, 30 April 2012.

[20] "Japan Inc. Rushes to Myanmar," *World Street Journal*, 25 April 2012. See also "Japan Inc. at Full Force in Rebuilding of Myanmar," *International Herald Tribune*, 11 October 2012.

[21] "Myanmar's 2015 Stock Exchange Deadline at Risk", Takako Taniguchi and Kyaw Thu for Bloomberg, 4 September 2013, available at <http://washpost.bloomberg.com/Story?docId=1376-MS7YF36TTDTJ01-019N0N8COCB374QSL81C9F5BG4>.

[22] I explore this theme further in a paper on "Myanmar, India and ASEAN Connectivity" in an edited volume to be published by the Institute of South Asian Studies at the National University of Singapore.

References

Asahi Shimbun. "Abe Ends Myanmar Visit with Aid, Debt Write-off", 26 May 2013.

ASEAN Secretariat. "ASEAN Community in Figures 2013". 2013.

———. "Chairman's Statement on the Special ASEAN-Japan Ministerial Meeting," Jakarta, 9 April 2011. Available at <http://www.asean.org/news/asean-statement-communiques/item/chairman-s-statement-on-the-special-asean-japan-ministerial-meeting-jakarta-9-april-2011>.

ASEAN-Japan Centre. "Investment Mission to Vietnam", 2012. Available at <http://www.asean.or.jp/en/invest/about/eventreports/2012/2012-03.html/Vietnam_mission_Aug12.pdf>.

Asian Development Bank Institute. "Connecting South Asia and Southeast Asia: Interim Report", 2013.

Bloomberg, "Myanmar's 2015 Stock Exchange Deadline at Risk," 4 September 2013. Available at <http://washpost.bloomberg.com/Story?docId=1376-MS7YF36TTDTJ01-019N0N8COCB374QSL81C9F5BG4>.

Carpenter, David, Rokiah Alavi, and Izyani Zulkifli. "Regional Development Cooperation," in *Narrowing the Development Gap in ASEAN: Drivers and Policy Options*, edited by Mark McGillivray and David Carpenter. Routledge and ASEAN Secretariat: 2013.

Funabashi, Yoichi. "New Challenges, New Frontier: Japan and ASEAN in the 21st Century", Asia and Pacific Lecture Series No. 3. Singapore: Institute of Southeast Asian Studies, 2003.

International Herald Tribune, "Japan Inc. at Full Force in Rebuilding of Myanmar," 11 October 2012.

Irrawaddy. "Japan 'Making Up for Lost Time' in Burma", 27 May 2013. Available at <http://www.irrawaddy.org/archives/35549>.

Kesavan, K.V. *Japan and ASEAN: Their Changing Security Relations*, ORF Occasional Paper No. 22. New Delhi: Observer Research Foundation, August 2011.

Koizumi, Junichiro. "Japan and ASEAN in East Asia: A Sincere and Open Partnership," Singapore Lecture, 14 January 2002. Singapore: Institute of Southeast Asian Studies, 2002 (first reprint 2003).

Kudo, Toshihiro, Kumagai Satoru, and Umezaki So. "Five Growth Strategies for Myanmar: Re-engagement with the Global Economy," IDE-JETRO Paper No. 427, August 2013.

McGillivray, Mark and David Carpenter (eds.). *Narrowing the Development Gap in ASEAN: Drivers and Policy Options*. Routledge and ASEAN Secretariat: 2013.

Ministry of Finance, Japan. "Japan's Financial Cooperation in Asia". Available at <http://www.mof.go.jp/english/international_policy/financial_cooperation_in_asia/index.html>.

Ministry of Foreign Affairs, Japan. Available at <http://www.mofa.go.jp/region/asia-paci/asean/index.html>, <http://www.mofa.go.jp/region/asia-paci/myanmar/index.html>, <http://www.mofa.go.jp/policy/economy/asia/crisis0010.html>.

———. "Japan-ASEAN Cooperation: A New Dimension in Cooperation". Available at <http://www.mofa.go.jp/region/asia-paci/asean/relation/dimens.html> (accessed April 2013).

———. "Tokyo Strategy 2012 for Mekong-Japan Cooperation". Available at <http://www.mofa.go.jp/region/asia-paci/mekong/summit04/joint_statement_en.html>.

———. "New Miyazawa Initiative". Available at <http://www.mof.go.jp/english/international_policy/financial_cooperation_in_asia/new_miyazawa_initiative/e1e042.htm>.

Ministry of Planning and Investment of Lao PDR, Investment Promotion Department. "Investment Report and Statistics", 2013. Available at <http://www.investlaos.gov.la/show_encontent.php?contID=29>.

———. "Japan is Turning to Laos for the Next Investment Destination in ASEAN", 2013. Available at <http://www.investlaos.gov.la/show_encontent.php?contID=60>.

Nikkei Weekly. "Japan steps back into Myanmar", 30 April 2012.

Severino, Rodolfo C. *Southeast Asia in Search of an ASEAN Community*. Singapore: Institute of Southeast Asian Studies, 2006.

The Nation. "Myanmar Boom Hits Japanese Business Sector," 27 September 2012. Available at <http://www.nationmultimedia.com/national/Myanmar-boom-hits-Japanese-business-sector-30191229.html>.

Uchida, K. and T. Kudo. "Japan's Policy and Strategy of Economic Cooperation in CLMV". In *Development Strategy for CLMV in the Age of Economic Integration*, ERIA Research Project Report 2007, No. 4, edited by C. Sotharith, pp. 209–61. Chiba: IDE-JETRO, 2008.

Uemura, Toyonori. "Human Resource Activities under the AMEICC". Institute for International Studies and Training, 2003. Available at <http://www.iist.or.jp/wf/magazine/0169/0169_E.html>.

World Street Journal. "Japan Inc. Rushes to Myanmar", 25 April 2012.

Yeo, Lay Hwee. "Japan, ASEAN and the Construction of an East Asian Community." *Contemporary Southeast Asia*, vol. 28 (2), August 2006. Singapore: Institute of Southeast Asian Studies.

6

ASEAN-JAPAN COOPERATION ON MARITIME NON-TRADITIONAL SECURITY ISSUES: TOWARD A NEW PARADIGM

Jun Honna

This chapter deals with non-traditional security issues, focusing particularly on crimes at sea in Southeast Asia, and discusses how ASEAN-Japan cooperation can be effective in combating these challenges. The region, which consists of ten countries, is a hotbed of cross-border crimes, ranging from illegal unreported fishing, unlawful dumping, drug smuggling, human trafficking, timber smuggling, illegal arms trading, to armed robbery at sea. These criminal activities greatly benefit from the weak capacity of the government to control territorial boundary, especially at sea. What are the features of these maritime crimes in Southeast Asia, and in what ways do they pose a threat to the security environment in the region? How have ASEAN and Southeast Asian governments identified the problem and responded to it? How is it strategically important to involve Japan — a country that has campaigned globally for human security agendas — in the framework of regional security cooperation? We examine these questions and highlight the importance of promoting a new paradigm of maritime non-traditional security cooperation that should envisage the dynamics of security-development nexus and properly target the elimination of root causes.

We first examine the development of maritime crimes in the region. We then discuss the major limitations of the existing maritime security cooperation in Southeast Asia, which is heavily "military-oriented" due to the weak capacity of civilian law enforcement agencies at sea. Finally, we argue that a way to overcome these limitations is to shift the policy paradigm and involve Japan so as to accelerate the new paradigm.

EVOLVING MARITIME CRIMES AND HUMAN INSECURITY

The waters of Southeast Asia are subject to all sorts of cross-border crimes, and many civil society organizations question the political will of regional governments in engaging the war on crime at sea. Below, we examine four types of transnational crime that are active in both continental and maritime Southeast Asia. The scale of the crime is, however, overwhelmingly large in the latter.[1]

Piracy and Armed Robberies

Since 80 per cent of Japan's oil imports travel through the Straits of Malacca and 60 per cent of Australia's oil tankers use Indonesian waters, the problem of piracy is a vital concern for ASEAN dialogue partners. The International Maritime Bureau (IMB), whose reports are often quoted by the media, stated that in 2004, there were 329 reported cases of piracy worldwide, including thefts from vessels in harbors, armed robbery, and hostage-taking, out of which 94 took place in Indonesian waters and 38 in the Straits of Malacca (International Maritime Bureau 2012). Despite the fact that the overall number of global piracy cases has been decreasing in recent years, those in Southeast Asia account for nearly 28 per cent of the total.[2] Some of these crimes are hostage-taking seajacks of tankers, but many cases involve petty robbery targeting cargos of tugboats and small fishing boats. Thus, piracy and armed robberies have been a common threat for maritime business and the local fishery sector in Southeast Asia. However, it is always the Malacca Straits that is spotlighted by the international media and observers, due to its geo-economic significance for foreign vessels.

Trafficking in Persons (TIP)

Due to its clandestine nature, it is difficult to grasp the extent of human trafficking both globally and regionally. In the past decade, however, a growing number of reports, based on investigations by international organizations and nongovernmental agencies, point out a sharp increase in the number of trafficking victims, with Southeast Asia estimated to be the largest center of trafficking in the world. In 2000, among the estimated 600,000–800,000 victims of global human trafficking, transactions in Southeast Asia accounted for 220,000 or about one-third of the total in the years after the 1997/98 Asian economic crisis (International Organization for Migration 2000). One decade later, it has been reasonably argued that the number of victims in Southeast Asia has increased further, following the 2008 global financial crisis (U.S. Department of State 2009). Victims of this transnational crime include adults and children in forced labor, bonded labor, and forced prostitution.

Trafficking in women and children for sexual exploitation has become a source of concern for most governments in Southeast Asia since the early 1980s, and particularly in the 1990s, due to a variety of factors including the boom in sex tourism in the 1980s, the global campaign for gender equality, the spread of HIV/AIDS, the feminization of migrant workers, and the economic crisis in the 1990s. Encouraged by the development of information and communication technology, the business of trafficking, which involves the recruitment of women, preparation for travel, contracts with brothels, and supervision of labors, has become increasingly sophisticated, with an operational network that has expanded beyond national borders. The regionalization of the trafficking business has divided Southeast Asia into sending, transit, and receiving countries, although these categories are not fixed as the market forces of supply and demand change over time.

Illegal Logging and Smuggling of Woods

Illegal logging, destructive cutting, and wood smuggling are also major transnational maritime crimes that require an urgent response. Because the pace of forest destruction in Southeast Asia is so rapid, there is growing concern that the region's tropical forests may vanish within ten years. Such a loss would be devastating, and even if this apocalyptic scenario is averted, the region faces serious problems due to environmental degradation. Loss of wildlife habitat will endanger many species; barren mountainsides are also prone to the landslides and floods that plague Southeast Asia every year, swallowing villages and inhabitants. Floods also destroy local fishing communities near the river and result in the flow of migrant workers into urban slums. Illegal logging has also contributed significantly to the decrease of the water-holding capacity of mountains, causing less water to flow to dams and thus shortages of water. As such, illegal logging is a serious threat to human security. Both importing and supplying countries need to establish an improved monitoring system and effective enforcement mechanisms to curb the illicit-wood trade and smugglers' transnational networks.

Illegal logs are usually distributed to domestic and foreign markets with the collaboration of criminal groups and timber companies. In many cases, corrupt local officials are involved in the process, for example, through the issuing of certificates that obscure the illicit origins of the timber being exported. One of the regional centers of the illegal log trade is in Papua, Indonesia. A credible investigation reveals the process by which the forests are destroyed by the timber mafia, domestic legal safeguards are evaded by criminals, and the illegal timber is transported and "laundered" to pass inspections by importing nations (EIA/Telapak 2005). It is widely believed that Singapore functions as the business hub of log traffickers.

Illicit Drugs Smuggling

Myanmar is the second largest cultivator of opium poppy in the world after Afghanistan. Afghanistan's production dropped temporarily after the Taliban banned poppy production in 2000, but the ousting of the Taliban by U.S. forces has led to an increase in poppy cultivation since 2002. Before the comeback of Afghanistan, Southeast Asia's Golden Triangle, which straddles the border area of Myanmar, Laos, and Thailand, constituted the world's largest territory (96,000 hectares) of opium cultivation, accounting for nearly half of opium-producing land (180,000 hectares) in the world (United Nations Office on Drugs and Crime (UNODC) 2003, p. 16). As the major supplier of opium in the world, Southeast Asian governments were pressured by the international community to crack down on the narcotic threat. The golden age of the Golden Triangle was during the Cold War, as the drug production helped fund anticommunist military intelligence operations by the CIA.

In the post-Cold War era, the scale of opium production in the region has decreased. A boom in chemical drug production has contributed to the declining production of opium. For organized crime syndicates, the mass production of chemical drugs, namely, the amphetamine-type stimulant, or ATS, can be done anywhere in a short time at low cost. Evading law enforcement is much easier. Popular drugs such as MDMA (or ecstasy) and "ice" (speed) are "market leaders" and distribution of these drugs has expanded rapidly in the region.

DEVELOPMENT OF REGIONAL COOPERATION

The problems of maritime piracy, TIP, illegal woods trading, and illicit drugs are all transnational, requiring a regional cooperative response based on securitizing these criminal activities. ASEAN's collective concern about the need for promoting anticrime regional cooperative measures was first officially expressed in December 1997, when it held the first ASEAN Conference on Transnational Crime in Manila and produced the ASEAN Declaration on Transnational Crime. Following the Declaration, an Action Plan was adopted the following year, leading to the establishment of an annual Senior Officials' Meeting on Transnational Crime (SOMTC) and a biennial ASEAN Ministerial Meeting on Transnational Crime (AMMTC).[3] This Action Plan identified eight areas of transnational crime that required action by member countries: terrorism, sea piracy, illegal logging, trafficking in persons, illicit drugs, arms smuggling, cybercrime, and money-laundering. Among these, only cybercrime and money-laundering can be excluded from the category of maritime crime. The other six issues are related to the vulnerability of maritime governance in Southeast Asia.

Following these developments, in October 2003, leaders of ASEAN countries met in Bali, Indonesia to open the 9th ASEAN Summit Meeting. The agenda of this Summit was historically significant because it declared a vision for regional integration in Southeast Asia. The Summit proposed establishing an ASEAN Community by 2020 and unanimously adopted the Declaration of ASEAN Concord II, which espoused the idea of "ASEAN Vision 2020".[4] The Vision calls for the realization of ASEAN integration and establishes three community pillars — ASEAN Economic Community, ASEAN Social-Cultural Community, and ASEAN Security Community (ASC) — to enhance functional cooperation in each field.[5] The ASEAN Concord II describes the role of the ASC as " ... bringing ASEAN's political and security cooperation to a higher plane to ensure that countries in the region live at peace ... in a just, democratic and harmonious environment".[6] Regarding security cooperation, ASC clearly prioritized transnational crime, calling on member states to "strengthen national and regional capacities to counter terrorism, drug and human trafficking, and others".[7] This statement suggests that ASEAN has been reshaping its paradigm in tackling transnational crime (both on land and at sea). Viewing the threat as a shared security problem, ASEAN has expressed its determination to securitize cross-border maritime crime in the region.

In 2004, following ASEAN Concord II, an important initiative was made by Malaysia, Singapore, Indonesia, the three littoral states that share the Malacca Straits. They agreed to conduct trilateral Malacca Straits Coordinated Patrols (Operation Malsindo) and to launch naval patrols to reduce piracy and smuggling activities in the troubled waters. Seventeen naval vessels from the three countries were allocated to Malsindo's year-round patrols. This was the first significantly operationalized multilateral maritime cooperation in Southeast Asia to develop without an extra-regional partner (Bradford 2005, p. 68). Malsindo was upgraded the following year when another initiative, Eyes in the Sky (EiS), was introduced, involving the three littoral countries and Thailand. Air patrols were provided by the EiS to support the surveillance of Malacca Straits. In 2006, both Malsindo and EiS were integrated under the umbrella of the Malacca Straits Patrol (MSP) network.

Another multilateral effort was made in November 2004 when 16 countries (ASEAN plus Japan, China, South Korea, Bangladesh, India, and Sri Lanka) got together to create the Regional Cooperation Agreement on Combating Piracy and Armed Robbery against Ships in Asia (ReCAAP). This agreement was first proposed by Japanese Prime Minister Junichiro Koizumi at ASEAN Plus 3 Summit in 2001, and it gained wide support in ASEAN countries. However, when it came to decide the location of the ReCAAP Information Sharing Center (ISC), which would develop databases and analyze incidents, both Malaysia and Indonesia insisted on locating the center in their own countries, claiming sensitivity of data-gathering. After months of deadlock, ReCAAP finally decided to locate ISC in Singapore, but Malaysia and Indonesia declined to sign the agreement. Until today, Malaysia and Indonesia have not ratified the agreement, but ISC, officially set up in 2007, is important as it brings critical analysis to bear on the issue of piracy, with data gathered from the governmental agencies themselves, and can supplement the data received from the IMB — a nongovernmental international organization under the International Chamber of Commerce (Ho 2007, p. 31).

Alongside these measures that aim mainly to boost antipiracy cooperation, ASEAN has also initiated broader maritime security cooperation via the ASEAN Maritime Forum (AMF). Following up on ASEAN Concord II, the 2004 ASEAN Summit in Vientiane adopted the ASEAN

Security Community Plan of Action (ASC PoA). Then, at the ASC PoA Coordinating Conference in 2006, Indonesia proposed to convene the Workshop on the Establishment of AMF. The Workshop was supported by the Japan-ASEAN Integration Fund (JAIF), and it formulated a Concept Paper proposing that the agenda of the AMF include "addressing transnational maritime issues related to crimes" and "promoting cooperation among maritime law enforcement agencies".[8] In 2010, the AMF was officially launched during its first meeting in Surabaya (Termsak and Ibanez 2012, pp. 139–64).

In this way, ASEAN has developed various regional mechanisms since ASEAN Concord II in 2003 to demonstrate its seriousness in combating transnational crimes at sea. These constitute a significant progress, as dialogue and information-sharing have contributed to building confidence among member countries in security matters. It is also through these mechanisms that hotlines of communication have been strengthened between security agencies of different countries. However, this progress does not mean that ASEAN, as a regional organization, has operationalized effective counter-crime policies; the illegal smuggling of goods and people has not declined either. As we have seen above, Southeast Asian waters are still vulnerable to serious cross-border crimes, and it is in this context that the existing maritime cooperation is regarded as insufficient and ineffective. There are three reasons to support this claim.

TOWARD A NEW PARADIGM

From Navy to Coast Guard

First, it is increasingly obvious that regional military cooperation at sea, as symbolized by Malsindo-MSP, faces inherent limitations. Navies are, above all, designed and trained to defend national sovereignty from foreign military attacks. Thus it is logical that they should wish to maintain secrecy concerning fighting abilities, including the performance of vessels. This professional orientation has effectively blocked the promotion of joint naval operations, for example, in the Malacca Straits where piracy and other maritime crime rings conduct cross-border operations. Importantly, the MSP is a "coordinated" operation in which warships of the three countries merely conduct patrols at the same time and place without an integrated command structure. Such a structure is essential to counter cross-border criminal activities but hard to realize due to strong mutual suspicion among the navies and concerns of possible leakage of defense intelligence. Naval officers themselves concede the ineffectiveness of coordinated patrols, yet doing nothing may invite foreign powers' intervention in the management of the Malacca Straits — avoiding such a scenario seems to be the foremost concern for both Malaysia and Indonesia (Mak 2006, p. 86).

Another reason for the ineffectiveness of MSP is attributed to the dubious performance of the military, for example, in Indonesia. Piracy specialists believe that the Indonesian Navy is involved in the piracy business. It is reported that Malaysian authorities arrested a number of pirates in their waters who were identified as members of the Indonesian military. In order to avoid an "international incident", the perpetrators were not charged for their offences; instead they were repatriated quickly (Liss 2011, p. 282).

Moreover, as Simon (2010, p. 10) points out, the EiS component of MSP has been expected to report suspicious activities of ships in the Malacca Straits, but its patrols are conducted only in daylight hours, whereas most piracy and armed robbery occur at night. EiS has also been criticized as being merely "for show" because of the insufficient number of sea patrol vessels available to carry out investigation and interdiction upon sightings of suspect vessels by the aerial patrols (Raymond 2007, p. 74).

A lack of provision for "hot pursuit" into the territorial waters of respective countries further compromises effectiveness. Responding to the criticism, Malaysia, Singapore and Indonesia agreed in 2006 to allow patrol vessels to cross over into territorial waters when in pursuit of a vessel engaged in maritime crime, provided that the patrol vessel does not open fire or carry out any other military actions. This agreement is no doubt a significant step toward deepening regional cooperation, but whether it is actually implemented remains to be seen.

Finally, regarding ReCAAP, it is the first intra-governmental agreement to promote data-sharing on maritime violence in the Malacca Straits, and the initiative is a significant step. However, the agreement does not oblige members to any specific action other than sharing information that they deem pertinent to imminent piracy attacks (Bradford 2005, p. 69). Clearly, ReCAAP alone cannot combat maritime crime, including piracy in Southeast Asian waters.

There are expectations for the ASEAN Maritime Forum (AMF) to evaluate these problems, formulate alternative policies, and provide a guideline for the practical implementation of measures aimed at strengthening regional efforts against crimes at sea. However, the role of the AMF is largely limited to that of a forum, which is designed to discuss regional concerns and address common issues among AMF members, rather than to formulate particular policies for specific problems. Indeed, at the 3rd AMF in 2012, issues such as maritime security and cooperation, marine environment and ecotourism were raised, and the importance of promoting maritime security cooperation, maintaining freedom and safety of navigation, and respecting the rules concerning the South China Sea were underlined.[9] Although addressing these issues is important to demonstrate and institutionalize ASEAN centrality in regional maritime affairs, discussions in this forum are too broad to produce any specific policy outcome.

It is thus evident that while the current regional architecture, represented by MSP, ReCAAP, and AMF, is designed to promote maritime cooperation to combat piracy and crimes at sea, these initiatives are not effective enough to operationalize practical countermeasures. Clearly, the main reason lies in the use of the military (the navy) for non-military matters such as counter-crime operations.

In recent years, it has become common practice for the regional security community to set up civilian coast guard agencies in order to deal professionally with maritime crime in sovereign territory and to promote regional cooperation. Combating crime at sea mostly requires speedy patrol boats with policing capacity, that are not professionally associated with the navy. "The navy is trained to 'kill the enemy', rather than collecting evidence and apprehending perpetrators, and emphasizes expanding its fleet of large-scale naval vessels with high-tech war abilities".[10] The navy's warships are not equipped to deal with transnational crime; patrol boats are better equipped and cost less to operate.

Assessing the need to build maritime security capacity, the Philippines established its coast guard (PCG) in 1998 and so did Malaysia in 2004 with the Malaysia Maritime Enforcement Agency (MMEA). Both PCG and MMEA were established in cooperation with the Japan Coast Guard (JCG), which provided technical assistance. Malaysia and the Philippines expected Indonesia — the biggest maritime state in Southeast Asia — to follow in their footsteps and play a more active role in promoting regional cooperation among regional law enforcement agencies.[11] Clearly, the navy was out of the loop in the region's newly emerging maritime strategic environment.

Faced with the changing strategic environment of Indonesian waters in the age of transnational crime — and the navy's limits to deal with it — the Indonesian government under Yudhoyono issued a presidential decree in 2005 to create a new government body, the Maritime Security Coordinating Board (Badan Kordinasi Keamanan Laut, or Bakorkamla).[12] Bakorkamla was established to lead the formulation of national maritime policy and to coordinate the activities of 12 maritime-related institutions, including the navy, water police, and customs. Bakorkamla does not have any operational arms so that actual law enforcement activities are conducted by other agencies, but it is the first attempt at reorganizing the roles and responsibilities of stakeholders in maritime governance in Indonesia.

The international community has welcomed Bakorkamla despite considerable domestic skepticism that the new body will enhance maritime security management. Overseas, there is concern about the ambiguous structure of authority in Indonesia's maritime sector, which includes various agencies without efficient coordination. Drawing on international support to fight on the domestic turf, Bakorkamla is establishing its presence.[13] According to a high-ranking navy general, "It is difficult for the [Indonesian] navy to respond fully to the changing demands of maritime security, therefore we encourage Bakorkamla to take further steps to build our Coast Guard and streamline the inefficient structure of maritime authority today".[14] The navy suggests that the new Coast Guard take on the following primary roles: maritime law enforcement, customs, aid to navigation (ATON) and shipping safety, fishery protection, search and rescue (SAR) at sea, and assistance to the navy in times of war by taking on port security and coastal patrols. The new shipping law was enacted in 2008 and Indonesia started to transform Bakorkamla into the Indonesian Sea and Coast Guard (ISCG), as in the case of the Philippines and Malaysia. With this new organization, Indonesia is expected to promote regional maritime cooperation with foreign counterparts, and to establish a new framework of civilian policing cooperation at sea that cannot be achieved by the navies. As it takes time to develop such a regional framework, it is too early to be optimistic, and Japan is expected to maintain its technical cooperation for Bakorkamla/ISCG.

Beyond Malacca

The military legacy cannot be dealt with on a sustainable basis as long as the issue of piracy dominates the maritime security concerns of policy-makers both regional and international. Media coverage on piracy tends to "dramatize" the acts of armed pirates; similarly policy-makers tend to play up the security aspects of piracy. The call for safer navigation arises largely from the strong demand of the foreign shipping industry. Under such circumstances, a discourse claiming that powerful navies can be mobilized to fight against armed pirate ships is legitimized.

However, as we have discussed above, many cases of armed robberies at sea in the region are in fact petty crimes and are closely related to other types of illegal activities such as the smuggling of goods and people. Thus the prevailing conceptualization of piracy is too narrow to embrace the broader context of everyday maritime crimes, leading to an almost exclusive focus on the Malacca Straits and Indonesian waters, rather than the regional field of operation. It is in this sense that the "de-Malacca-ization" of maritime security concerns is needed in order to leave navies to more professional military functions and to pave the way for civilian law enforcement agencies to establish more effective regional maritime policing cooperation.

From Sea to Land

The border surveillance in non-Malacca areas, for example, between Indonesia and the Philippines, Malaysia and the Philippines, Vietnam and Thailand is also critical to curbing cross-border transgressions. In these places, villagers are mobilized in various ways by piracy groups and other criminal agencies for logistical missions. This criminalization of coastal villages is essentially a problem of human insecurity caused by poverty and unemployment. In particular, the almost uncontrolled large-scale poaching by domestic and foreign fishing companies in the aftermath of the Asian financial crisis of 1997/98 led to the rapid diminution of fish stocks available for local small-scale fishermen.

Poverty is clearly a primary root cause of various maritime crimes, hence the relevance of "on-land" counter-crime approaches. Promoting the rural development of coastal communities may significantly reduce the number of people involved in transnational crimes at sea. In essence, the problem of maritime crime is not the problem at sea — it is the problem on land. Without confronting the issue of coastal poverty, real and sustainable success of counter-crime measures at sea is not possible. In this sense, bringing the human element back to the core of maritime security seems to be imperative.

THE ROLE OF JAPAN IN THE NEW PARADIGM

In promoting such a paradigm shift in maritime security cooperation aimed at eradicating crimes at sea, Japan — as a stakeholder in building a public good in Southeast Asian waters — can play a significant role. As we have discussed above, the current ASEAN architecture dealing with maritime non-traditional security issues has serious limitations, due mainly to its heavy reliance on naval cooperation. The "demilitarization" of counter-crime schemes is thus expected and can be enhanced by mobilizing three alternative approaches: strengthening regional cooperation among civilian law enforcement agencies at sea, extending the attention beyond the Malacca Straits, and formulating strategic policies to tackle root causes of maritime crimes, including poverty reduction, vocational training, and job creation in coastal villages. It is through these initiatives that the prospect of establishing a new paradigm can be reinforced. Importantly, Japan is in the position to accelerate these moves toward the new paradigm. At least four areas in which Japan may extend further cooperation can be identified.

The first is to sustain capacity-building cooperation for regional coast guard agencies. As seen above, Japan provided technical assistance to build coast guards in the Philippines, Malaysia, and Indonesia. Next the Japan Coast Guard Academy (JCGA) launched an international program called the Asian Coast Guard Junior Office Course of Japan (AJOC) in 2011. Young officers from maritime law enforcement agencies in Malaysia, Vietnam, the Philippines, and Indonesia were invited to spend one year in JCGA to learn about maritime issues in Asia and gain specialized knowledge in coast guard operations. This training program emphasizes the importance of regional coast guard cooperation in dealing with common maritime challenges in Asia such as crimes, environmental conservation, and safety navigation. Through AJOC, JCGA not only expects participants to develop operational skills but also encourages value-sharing and norm-sharing among junior officers from different countries who may lead regional cooperation in future. In the words of one participant, "A strong friendship is cultivated here and our class network will be a great asset when we become senior officers and are expected to conduct joint operations with the neighboring countries".[15] From 2014, JCGA plans to launch a similar program for senior officers aimed at "training the trainers".

Since there is no such multilateral education project for maritime law enforcers in ASEAN, Japan's initiative is valuable. However, whether it is sustainable or not remains to be seen. In order to maximize the benefits of JCG's capacity-building program, the Japanese government is expected to underline the strategic importance of building a maritime regime of the new generation and to prioritize budget allocation for the long-term implementation of the program. Also important from the perspective of sustainability, is a vision to transfer JCG's program to ASEAN in the future and to institutionalize the joint training and education of cadets at the regional level. For this, the establishment of an ASEAN coast guard academy is desirable. Japan may initiate the proposal, send trainers, and allow JCG's junior officers to join the academy in order to develop their international experience, a cornerstone of JCG's future cooperation with ASEAN countries.

The second area is development assistance to eradicate root causes of maritime crime on land. As Manicon (2010, p. 38) suggests, Japan is expected to direct ODA funding toward reducing poverty, improving governance, and addressing human security challenges in known pirate havens among the coastal communities in Sumatra, the Riau Islands, and Southern Philippines. It is noteworthy that development assistance is more "friendly" to the sovereignty issue; Japan also has a long history of rural development cooperation in Southeast Asia. It is time to utilize the ODA framework to promote the root-cause eradication approach in the context of maritime security cooperation. Perhaps the best scheme is the Grant Assistance for Grassroots Human Security Projects (GGP), which was established to assist local NGOs and public authorities in responding to various development needs. Since the promotion of human security characterizes Japan's foreign policy, it is a chance to demonstrate to the international community that the human security agenda is not only compatible with the non-traditional security agenda, it is also a core element in building a regional consensus about Japan's active engagement in security issues in Southeast Asia.

Thirdly, it is also important, in the context of local governance of coastal communities, to promote partnership between local police and citizens, which is indispensable for improving anticrime operations on land. In many places, trust between the police and the community is lacking and residents hesitate to report crime to the police — a situation exploited by criminal organizations. This calls for an initiative to change the situation and promote the concept of "community policing". Community policing aims to build trust between the police and the local community by reforming the police to engage actively in public activities related to the safety of residents. "The police as part of the community" and "the police as the protector of the community" — this is the philosophy of community policing. The Japanese National Police Agency has dispatched many police experts to the community police assistance program in Indonesia since 2000, and the program site in the Bekasi district in West Java Province is now regarded as a model district police implementing effective community policing, as evident in a series of public surveys conducted by international survey company AC Nielsen (2009).

There is no reason to confine the fruit of this Japanese cooperation to the Bekasi district. Bekasi's experience can be shared with other police stations in Indonesia, especially in areas facing serious maritime crimes.

Bekasi could also invite other countries, for example, Malaysia, the Philippines, and Vietnam, to study the practice of community policing and apply the model to their own coastal communities. A scheme called South-South Cooperation (SSC) exists in Japan's ODA, which can be used to facilitate such an international sharing of "best practice".

Finally, Japan can deepen its cooperation with the ASEAN Secretariat in promoting the new paradigm of regional maritime non-traditional security cooperation. The empowerment of the ASEAN Secretariat (ASEC) is an important agenda for the successful management of the ASEAN Political and Security Community, but current conditions suggest that the lack of resources has minimized the role of ASEC in formulating regional cooperation policies. An empowered ASEC is expected to play a leading role in, for example, mapping out the capacity level of civilian maritime law enforcement agencies (that is, coast guards and marine polices) in ASEAN countries; identifying the gap in capacity among them; illustrating best practices to fill the gap; standardizing anticrime operations; harmonizing various regional cooperation agendas; and synchronizing sea and land approaches to best balance the symptom-cause countermeasures. For ASEC to be the center of these regional initiatives, external backup is crucial and this is where Japanese cooperation should be directed.

All these four areas of Japan's further contribution to ASEAN's maritime non-traditional security cooperation are strongly expected to have a synergistic effect, but doing so requires a "new paradigm" for the Japanese government to effectively package these different initiatives involving several Japanese agencies into one scheme, under the flag of deepening maritime non-traditional security cooperation with ASEAN. Cross-sectoral policy formulation/implementation is traditionally weak in Japan; overcoming this weakness will thus be the homework for policymakers in Tokyo.

CONCLUDING REMARKS

We have discussed the significance of changing the current paradigm of maritime non-traditional security cooperation in ASEAN, which has been heavily military-oriented, highly Malacca-centric, and dealing essentially with the symptoms instead of causes. Initiatives such as AMMTC, MSP, ReCAAP, and AMF are all important to demonstrate a political will of the states to combat expanding maritime crime and to address common security concerns in the region. The institutions created by these initiatives no doubt contribute to promoting dialogue, narrowing perception gaps, strengthening mutual confidence, and consolidating regional partnership. These developments surely provide a positive pathway to the building of the ASEAN Political and Security Community.

However, from a practical viewpoint, these initiatives have shown their limitations in the effective operationalization of regional countermeasures. As a result, while the number of piracy incidents in the Malacca Straits has declined, pirates are still active in other areas, including the South China Sea, Sulu Sea, and Indonesia's huge territorial waters. Human trafficking has been on the rise in the past decade, and this criminal activity has benefited tremendously from the lingering weak maritime governance in Southeast Asian waters. The same can be said of the smuggling of woods and illegal drugs, which has expanded operations in Southeast Asia in recent years. Clearly, criminal networks have been strengthened at the regional level and are less affected by the ASEAN initiatives above.

It is against this backdrop that we have discussed the need for reviewing the current paradigm after ten years of ASEAN Concord II and shaping a new paradigm aimed at enhancing countermeasures. We have highlighted the importance of establishing civilian law enforcement agencies at sea and securing their cooperation. This is a smoother, less costly, and less problematic method than the current approach of using naval vessels for crime patrols. We have also underlined the importance of focusing more on root-cause treatment by improving the living conditions of coastal communities where villagers are vulnerable to recruitment from criminal groups, including piracy syndicates. Thus, "non-military" and "on land" are two key components of the new paradigm that is expected to overcome the limitations of the current one.

In promoting this paradigm shift, we have seen how Japan can play an important role. The ongoing regional coast guard training at JCGA is a good start, and it should be sustained to produce young cadets who share the goal of fighting against a common enemy at sea, even if the results of the program may not be immediately perceptible. Coast guard cooperation is not limited to the training program of junior officers — the program targeting senior officers should be well designed so as to be effective rapidly.

The root-cause approach is also what is expected with Japan taking the initiative. As the promoter of a global campaign for mainstreaming human security, Japan has a long and rich global experience allowing it to understand the dynamics of development-security nexus. This perspective is useful in dealing with the poverty-crime nexus widely seen in coastal communities in Southeast Asia. Thus, the community development approach should be highlighted by the government of Japan, which has shown eagerness to promote cooperation with ASEAN in the field of maritime security. Mainstreaming human security entails the improvement of local governance, and it is in this context that the philosophy and practice of community policing should be introduced in areas where distrust between law enforcers and community residents has benefited criminal groups in their illegal businesses at sea. Again, Japan's experience and long-time cooperation in Indonesia can be shared widely with other ASEAN countries.

In this way, there is still much room for deepening ASEAN-Japan cooperation in the field of maritime non-traditional security, and involving Japan will help ASEAN to advance the paradigm shift above. For Japan, non-traditional security is the only area where it can demonstrate its active commitment in the building of the region's security community. The mutual interests of ASEAN and Japan should be constantly reaffirmed at the top level, and it is important — especially for the Japanese side — to avoid creating a situation that may undermine mutual interest. Such a risk can be found in the debate on the rearming of Japan, the revisionist historical view that attempts to justify Japan's wartime activities in Asia, and other ultra-nationalistic statements on developments in East Asia, which are all led by conservative politicians from the ruling party. These "noises" should be firmly contained in order to eliminate the risk of undermining ASEAN-Japan mutual interests in promoting further cooperation on maritime security in Southeast Asia.

Notes

[1] For a detailed discussion on this, see Honna, 2007, pp. 97–114.

[2] The region accounted for 42 per cent in 2003, 51 per cent in 2004, 42 per cent in 2005, 36 per cent in 2006, 26 per cent in 2007, 18 per cent in 2008, 11 per cent in 2009, 15 per cent in 2010, and 18 per cent in 2011. The average from 2003–11 is thus 28 per cent. International Maritime Bureau, January 2012.

[3] The ASEAN Plan of Action to Combat Transnational Crime is available at <http://www.aseansec.org/16133.htm>.

[4] The target year was consequently brought forward to 2015.

[5] The ASC is not a regional security organization per se but is aimed at promoting regional cooperation in tackling "common" security issues. Nevertheless, the ASC is considered a major step because during the Cold War, asymmetrical threat perceptions preoccupied Southeast Asian countries and discouraged them from enhancing security cooperation. For the history of ASEAN's security

environment, see the comprehensive study by Caballero-Anthony, 2005. ASEAN Concord II is a follow-up to the Concord adopted in 1976 during the Cold War.

[6] "Declaration of ASEAN Concord II (Bali Concord II)", 7 October 2003, Section A, Paragraph 1.

[7] Ibid, Paragraph 10.

[8] See "Concept Paper for the Establishment of an ASEAN Maritime Forum", 7(f) and 8(c).

[9] See "Chairman's Statement, 3rd ASEAN Maritime Forum", ASEAN Secretariat, October 9, 2012.

[10] Interview with Captain Joel S. Garcia, Communications and Information System Command, Philippine Coast Guard, 15 August 2007.

[11] Interviews with Vice Admiral Danilo A. Abinoja, Deputy Commandant for Operations, PCG (13 August 2007) and Rear Admiral Dato' Noor Aziz Yunan, Deputy Director General of MMEA (17 August 2007).

[12] For this development, see Honna, 2008, pp. 63–80. For Bakorkamla, see also Goldrick and McCaffrie, 2013, pp. 85–86.

[13] Interview with Vice Admiral Djoko Sumaryono, Chief Executive of Bakorkamla, 22 August 2007.

[14] Interview with Vice Admiral Tedjo Edhy Purdijatno, Director-General of Defense Planning at the Defense Ministry, 24 August 2007. Purdijanto later became Navy Chief-of-Staff.

[15] Author's communication with an AJOC participant at JCGA, 14 December 2012.

References

A.C. Nielsen. "INP and Measuring Response to Police Reform in Bekasi: 2009 Reading". 2009.

ASEAN Secretariat. "Chairman's Statement, 3rd ASEAN Maritime Forum", 9 October 2012.

Bradford, John F. "The Growing Prospects for Maritime Security Cooperation in Southeast Asia". *Naval War College Review* 58, no. 3 (2005).

Caballero-Anthony, Mely. *Regional Security in Southeast Asia: Beyond the ASEAN Way*. Singapore: Institute of Southeast Asian Studies, 2005.

EIA/Telapak. "The Last Frontier: Illegal Logging in Papua and China's Massive Theft". London: Environmental Investigation Agency, 2005.

Goldrick, James and Jack McCaffrie. *Navies of South-East Asia: A Comparative Study*. London: Routledge, 2013.

Ho, Joshua. "The Importance and Security of Regional Sea Lanes". In *Maritime Security in Southeast Asia*, edited by Kwa Chong Guan and John K. Skogan. London: Routledge, 2007.

Honna, Jun. "Instrumentalizing Pressures, Reinventing Missions: Indonesian Navy Battles for Turf in the Age of *Reformasi*". *Indonesia* 86 (October 2008): 63–80.

———. "Transnational Crime and Human Insecurity in Southeast Asia". In *Protecting Human Security in a Post 9/11 World: Critical and Global Insights*, edited by Giorgio Shani *et al*. London: Palgrave Macmillan, 2007.

International Maritime Bureau. "Piracy and Armed Robbery Against Ships: Annual Report 1 January–31 December 2011". Essex: ICC-IMB, January 2012.

International Organization for Migration. "Combating Trafficking in South-East Asia: A Review of Policy and Program Responses". Geneva: IMO, February 2000.

Liss, Carolin. *Oceans of Crime: Maritime Piracy and Transnational Security in Southeast Asia and Bangladesh*. Singapore: Institute of Southeast Asian Studies, 2011.

Mak, J.N. "Securitizing Piracy in Southeast Asia: Malaysia, the International Maritime Bureau and Singapore". In *Non-Traditional Security in Asia: Dilemmas in Securitization*, edited by Mely Caballero-Anthony, Ralf Emmers, and Amitav Acharya. Hampshire: Ashgate, 2006.

Manicom, James. "Japan's Role in Strengthening Maritime Security in Southeast Asia". In *Maritime Security in Southeast Asia: U.S., Japanese, Regional, and Industry Strategies*, edited by John Bradford, James Manicom, Sheldon W. Simon, and Neil A. Quartaro. NBR Special Report No. 24. Washington, D.C.: The National Bureau of Asian Research, November 2010.

Raymond, Catherine Zara. "Piracy in the Waters of Southeast Asia". In *Maritime Security in Southeast Asia*, edited by Kwa Chong Guan and John K. Skogan. London: Routledge, 2007.

Simon, Sheldon W. "Safety and Security in the Malacca Strait: The Limit of Collaboration". In *Maritime Security in Southeast Asia: U.S., Japanese, Regional, and Industry Strategies*, edited by John Bradford, James Manicom, Sheldon W. Simon, and Neil A. Quartaro. NBR Special Report No. 24. Washington, D.C.: The National Bureau of Asian Research, November 2010.

Termsak, Chalermpalaupap and Mayla Ibanez. "ASEAN Measures in Combating Piracy and Other Maritime Crimes". In *Piracy and International Maritime Crimes in ASEAN: Prospects for Cooperation*, edited by Robert C. Beckman and J. Ashley Roach. Massachusetts: Edward Elgar Publishing, 2012.

United Nations Office on Drugs and Crime (UNODC). *Global Illicit Drug Trends 2003*. New York: UNODC, 2003.

U.S. Department of State. "Trafficking in Persons Report 2009". Washington, D.C.: U.S. Department of State, 2009.

7

JAPAN'S EVOLVING SECURITY CONCERNS IN MARITIME SOUTHEAST ASIA: FROM SAFETY OF NAVIGATION TO "LAKE BEIJING"

Ian Storey

In a speech that was due to be delivered in Jakarta on 18 January 2013 — but postponed due to the hostage crisis in Algeria — Japanese Prime Minister Shinzo Abe stressed the vital importance of Asia's maritime domain to Japan:

> Japan's national interest lies eternally in keeping Asia's seas unequivocally open, free, and peaceful —in maintaining them as the commons for all the people in the world, where the rule of law is fully realized ... In light of our geographic circumstances, the two objectives are natural and fundamental imperatives for Japan, a nation surrounded by ocean and deriving sustenance from those oceans — *a nation that views the safety of the seas as its own safety.*[1]

That Abe chose to focus on maritime security during his first overseas trip since assuming office on 26 December 2012 was unsurprising for two reasons. First, as an island nation largely bereft of natural resources, Japan depends for its economic prosperity on the free flow of maritime trade. Japan relies on Asia's sea lines of communication (SLOCs) for the transportation of its manufactured goods to world markets and for the importation of natural resources, including more than 90 per cent of its imported energy supplies. SLOC security has been, and remains, a critical national security concern for Japan's leaders, strategic thinkers, and security planners. The SLOCs that thread through the maritime chokepoints of Southeast Asia (including the Malacca-Singapore Straits, Sunda Straits, and Lombok-Makassar Straits) and the South China Sea link the Indian and Pacific Oceans and are therefore of singular importance to Japan's economic well-being and national security. In 2010 Japan's two-way trade with the ten members of the Association of Southeast Asian Nations (ASEAN) amounted to US$214 billion, with South Asia (India, Pakistan, and Bangladesh) to US$17.8 billion, and with the European Union (EU) to US$147 billion — the bulk of this trade being borne along Southeast Asia's sea lanes.[2] Regional sea lanes are routinely utilized also by the Japan Maritime Self Defense Force (JMSDF), including by warships operating in the Indian Ocean as part of international efforts to counter pirates off the coast of Somalia and in the Gulf of Aden. It would not, therefore, be an exaggeration to state that the sea lanes constitute Japan's lifelines, and that Southeast Asia plays a key role in the country's survival as a maritime trading nation. The critical importance of maritime trade routes is reflected in the fact that since the 1960s Japan has invested considerable financial and political capital to improve the safety and security of Southeast Asia's sea lanes by funding safety of navigation mechanisms and, in the 1990s and first decade of the 21st century, promoting regional cooperation to tackle transnational threats such as sea piracy and maritime terrorism.

The second reason that Abe focused on maritime security was that although North Korea's nuclear weapons program is perceived as a major national security concern, Japan seems more concerned with the territorial and maritime boundary disputes in the East China Sea — where Tokyo and Beijing contest ownership of the Senkaku/Diaoyu Islands — and the South China Sea. Although Southeast Asians may regard these disputes as separate, Japan views the two issues as inextricably linked. While Japan is not a claimant in the South China Sea, it sees striking parallels with the situation in the East China Sea: renewed Chinese assertiveness fueled by growing nationalism, and Beijing's willingness to apply coercive pressure on the other claimants made possible by the rapid modernization of the People's Liberation Army Navy (PLA-N) and the expansion of China's civilian maritime law enforcement agencies. Japan is greatly concerned that Beijing's position on the South China Sea has the potential to undermine international legal norms, including the principle of freedom of navigation.

It also worries that growing instability in the South China Sea could ultimately disrupt shipping flows to Japan. Indeed, in an opinion piece published the day after he took office, Abe warned that there was a risk of the South China Sea being transformed into "Lake Beijing".[3] As a result of this angst, Japan's new government has stepped up existing policies to encourage ASEAN unity over the South China Sea; strengthen the maritime capabilities of certain Southeast Asian claimants; and foster closer coordination and cooperation with other stakeholders, especially the United States.

This chapter traces the evolution of Japan's maritime security interests in Southeast Asia, from navigational issues in the Cold War period and nontraditional security threats in the first two decades of the post-Cold War era, to the current anxieties associated with China's emergence as Asia's preeminent military power and how Tokyo hopes to mitigate its security concerns in Southeast Asia's maritime domain.

JAPAN AND MARITIME SECURITY IN THE COLD WAR

As Japan experienced its "economic miracle" from the 1960s onward, the country's dependence on Southeast Asia's sea lanes deepened. Of particular importance to Japan were access to, and the safety of navigation in, the region's principal maritime chokepoints: the Malacca-Singapore, Sunda, and Lombok-Makassar Straits. But given Japan's constitutional restrictions and aggressive role in Southeast Asia during World War II, Tokyo was unable to employ traditional instruments of power — such as a strong navy — to protect its maritime interests. Instead, Japan relied on quiet, regional diplomacy while simultaneously piggybacking on the strategic imperatives of the superpowers.

The Malacca Straits, the 500-mile-long channel between Sumatra and the Malay Peninsula, provides the shortest passage for ships traveling from the Indian Ocean to Japan via the South China Sea. As such, the waterway is heavily congested (more than 60,000 international vessels pass through it each year), which raises the risk of collision at sea, especially in poor weather. At 25 meters it is also relatively shallow and therefore unsuitable for ships with deep drafts, such as supertankers. The Malacca Straits can be bypassed through the Sunda and Lombok Straits, which, at depths of approximately 37 and 180 meters respectively, are deeper — but these routes add time and hence cost to a ship's journey.[4]

As with all great maritime trading powers throughout modern history, sea-lane security became a matter of great importance to Japan from the

1960s onward. Unlike the seafaring nations of Holland, Portugal, Britain, and the United States, however, Japan could not use naval power to secure its maritime interests, for two main reasons. First, Japan's constitution placed restrictions on the operational parameters of the JMSDF; indeed, it was not until the 1980s that the nation was allowed to defend the country's sea lanes out to 1,000 nautical miles.[5] Second, Japan's wartime legacy in Southeast Asia dictated that an overt Japanese security role would be rejected by regional states. As a consequence, Japan was forced to rely heavily on its treaty ally the United States to ensure freedom of navigation. But Japan was no free-rider: it also instituted a proactive but low-key policy of providing aid to littoral states such as Indonesia and Malaysia to secure its navigational interests. As Euan Graham explains, Japan adopted a "composite" approach "blending official and private diplomacy (via non-government and commercial organizations) as well as relying on other maritime states to pursue the more confrontational aspects of freedom of navigation in the region".[6]

The principal mechanism through which Japan provided aid to the littoral states was the Malacca Strait Council (MSC), established in 1968 and funded by the Japanese government and private shipping organizations in Japan. The MSC funded hydrographic surveys of the Malacca Straits and financed the purchase, installation, and maintenance of navigational aids such as buoys, light beacons, and lighthouses.[7] Following the grounding of a Japanese tanker in the straits in 1975, the MSC implemented a Traffic Separation Scheme and an under-keel clearance scheme that required vessels over 230,000 tons to use alternative and deeper channels such as the Sunda and Lombok Straits. According to Graham, between 1968 and 2001 the MSC provided 13 billion yen in financial and technical support to the littoral states.[8] Japan's support for the MSC was designed to enhance the country's economic security and was thus far from altruistic. Nevertheless, Japanese aid ensured safety of navigation for all shipping, a public good of critical importance to the expansion of world trade and the spread of globalization.

Fortunately for Japan, its economic security interests in maritime Southeast Asia during the Cold War largely coincided with the strategic interests of the superpowers. Both the United States and the Soviet Union argued that the Straits of Malacca should be regarded as an international strait, a position Japan supported. Indonesia and Malaysia, however, maintained that as coastal states they should have the right to regulate shipping through the strait, both commercial and naval.[9] The littoral states were backed by China, which saw itself as the target of Soviet containment from the 1970s until the late 1980s and was therefore keen to limit Moscow's military presence in Southeast Asia. China's stance also reflected the country's belief that coastal states should exercise sovereignty and control over their maritime domains, a position it maintains until today.[10] Moreover, unlike the United States and the Soviet Union, China at that time did not possess an oceangoing navy, and the PLA-N was an infrequent user of the Straits of Malacca. During the third United Nations Conference on the Law of the Sea (1974–82), the littoral states were persuaded to accept the principle of transit passage rights through international straits in return for archipelagic rights.

In short, through a combination of low-key financial aid to the littoral states for the purchase of navigational safety equipment — which avoided arousing painful historical memories — reliance on U.S. naval power, and a congruence of strategic interests with the superpowers, Japan was able to protect and advance its economic and security interests in Southeast Asia's maritime domain throughout the Cold War period.

JAPAN AND THE PROBLEM OF PIRACY/SEA ROBBERY IN SOUTHEAST ASIA

Post-Cold War, the safe passage of shipping through Southeast Asia's sea lanes remained a key priority for Japan's national security establishment. Japanese governments and the private sector continued to fund the upkeep of navigational aids in the region's vital chokepoints. Military threats to shipping were judged to be at an all-time low during the 1990s and for much of the next decade as the Soviet Navy no longer presented a potential threat to Japanese maritime interests; and while China's military modernization program was closely monitored by Japanese analysts, it was not judged to pose a threat to national security. Similarly, while the disputes in the South China Sea over the sovereignty of atolls and maritime boundaries began to generate serious friction between China and each of the Southeast Asian claimants — principally Vietnam and the Philippines and, to a lesser extent, Malaysia and Brunei — they did not arouse undue concern in Tokyo. Indeed, as will be discussed later, Japanese governments remained largely silent on the South China Sea dispute until the end of the first decade of the 21st century.

Japan's primary concern vis-à-vis sea-lane security in Southeast Asia for the first two decades of the post-Cold War period was piracy and sea robbery.[11] During the 1990s the number of reported attacks against ships in Southeast Asia rose steadily (see Table 7.1). A number of interlinked

TABLE 7.1

Reported Piracy and Sea Robbery Attacks in Southeast Asia, 1994–2011

Location	1994	1995	1996	1997	1998	1999	2000	2001	2002	2003	2004	2005	2006	2007	2008	2009	2010	2011
Indonesia	22	33	57	47	60	115	119	91	103	121	94	79	50	43	28	15	40	46
Malacca Straits	3	2	3	0	1	2	75	17	16	28	38	12	11	7	2	2	2	1
Malaysia	4	5	5	4	10	18	21	19	14	5	9	3	10	9	10	16	18	16
Singapore Straits	3	2	2	5	1	14	5	7	5	2	8	7	5	3	6	9	3	11
Philippines	5	24	39	16	15	6	9	8	10	12	4	0	6	6	7	1	5	5
Thailand	0	4	16	17	2	5	8	8	5	2	4	1	1	2	0	1	2	0
Myanmar	0	0	1	2	0	1	5	3	0	0	1	0	0	0	1	1	0	1
South China Sea	6	3	2	6	5	3	9	4	0	2	8	6	1	3	0	13	31	
Cambodia	1	1	1	1	0	0	0	0	0	0	0	0	N/A	N/A	N/A	N/A	N/A	13
Vietnam	2	4	0	4	0	2	6	8	12	15	4	10	3	5	11	9	12	8
Total	**46**	**78**	**126**	**102**	**94**	**166**	**271**	**165**	**170**	**187**	**170**	**118**	**87**	**78**	**65**	**67**	**113**	**101**

Source: International Maritime Bureau, "Piracy and Armed Robbery against Ships Annual Report", various issues 2001–11. Figures include actual and attempted attacks.

factors contributed to the rising tide of maritime crime.[12] Weak political control, poor governance (including corruption in the armed forces and marine police), and lack of state capacity to address the threat as a consequence of severe defense cuts provided a conducive environment for maritime criminals. This was especially true in Indonesia following the fall of President Suharto in 1998, when political control at the center was severely weakened. By the middle of the first decade of the 21st century, nearly two-thirds of all piracy and sea robbery attacks in Southeast Asia were occurring in Indonesian waters.[13] Poor socioeconomic conditions in coastal communities encouraged unemployed mariners to turn to piracy and sea robbery to supplement meager incomes. Access to high technology such as fast boats, satellite navigation, and automatic weapons often gave maritime criminals an edge over poorly funded law enforcement agencies, though it should be noted that the vast majority of attacks in Southeast Asia were opportunistic and usually perpetrated by criminals wielding nothing more than knives. The problem of violent attacks against shipping was compounded by the lack of security and military cooperation among Southeast Asian states, primarily due to extreme sensitivity over sovereignty and jurisdictional issues, heightened by problems of interoperability.

While ships of all flags came under attack in Southeast Asia, Tokyo felt that Japanese shipping was bearing the brunt (though statistics produced by the International Maritime Bureau's Piracy Reporting Centre did not support this view).[14] The hijacking of the Japanese-owned vessel *Alondra Rainbow* in Indonesian waters in 1999 — during which the crew were set adrift in a raft — triggered a more proactive approach to the problem by Tokyo.[15] However, Prime Minister Keizo Obuchi's suggestion that Japan lead the formation of a regional coast guard found little support within Southeast Asia and China, in part because of Japan's wartime record.[16] Recognizing this opposition, Japan changed tack and instead emphasized bilateral cooperation with regional coast guards as well as encouraging regional cooperation through information sharing.

Beginning in 2000, the Japan Coast Guard (JCG) stepped up cooperation with its regional counterparts. The JCG conducted anti-piracy training programs and exercises with civilian maritime law enforcement agencies from Brunei, Indonesia, Malaysia, the Philippines, Singapore, Thailand, and Vietnam.[17] In addition to training, Japan also sought to improve the capacity of regional coast guards through the transfer of equipment and the provision of funding using overseas development aid. For example, in 2006–07 Japan transferred three patrol boats to the Indonesian marine police and provided funding to the country's Maritime Security Coordination

Agency (Bakorkamla).[18] In 2008 Japan transferred a training vessel and gave US$4.7 million to the newly established coast guard of Malaysia, the Malaysian Maritime Enforcement Agency (MMEA), for the upgrade of radars.[19] Tokyo also furnished financial support and training for the Philippine Coast Guard (PCG).[20]

To promote greater cooperation among regional coast guards and navies, in 2001 Japanese Prime Minister Junichiro Koizumi proposed a government-to-government agreement to fight piracy. His proposal was followed by a series of Japanese-funded conferences in Tokyo, Bangkok, Kuala Lumpur, and Manila, leading to agreement in 2004 among 16 countries (the ten ASEAN members plus Japan, South Korea, China, India, Bangladesh, and Sri Lanka) to the Regional Agreement on Combating Piracy and Armed Robbery against Ships in Asia (ReCAAP).[21] ReCAAP establishes a framework for cooperation among member states based on three main activities: information sharing, capacity building, and operational cooperation. In 2006 ReCAAP established the Information Sharing Centre in Singapore, the purpose of which is to facilitate communications, information exchange, and operational cooperation among ReCAAP members to improve incident response by member countries. Since the center's establishment in 2006, Singapore has made the largest financial contribution to it (US$4 million between 2006 and 2009) followed by Japan (US$1.4 million during the same period).[22] The center's inaugural executive director and his successor have both been Japanese nationals. To date, 17 countries have become contracting parties to ReCAAP, though two key Southeast Asian states — Malaysia and Indonesia — have refused to ratify the agreement, citing sovereignty concerns.[23]

Reported incidents of piracy and sea robbery attacks in Southeast Asia fell dramatically between 2004 and 2009 (see Table 7.1). This was due to a combination of factors. First, coordinated naval patrols in the Straits of Malacca by Singapore, Malaysia, and Indonesia, launched in 2004 and joined by Thailand in 2008, seem to have had a deterrent effect. Second, the littoral states put in place national initiatives to crack down on pirates and sea robbers: Singapore tightened security at its ports and in its territorial waters, Malaysia established the MMEA as its national coast guard, and, most important, Indonesia increased naval patrols in its territorial waters. Third, capacity-building support from the United States and Japan helped improve the maritime interdiction and surveillance capabilities of regional navies and coast guards.[24] ReCAAP, through its training programs, information exchange, and sharing of best practices, has also contributed to the improved maritime security situation in Southeast

Asia. Although in 2010 the number of reported attacks in Southeast Asia experienced an upsurge, especially in Indonesian waters, incidents in the Straits of Malacca remained negligible (see Table 7.1). Thus, by the end of the first decade of the 21st century, Japan, together with the rest of the international community, had turned its attention to the dramatic increase in maritime attacks off the coast of Somalia and in the Gulf of Aden, resulting in JMSDF participation in international counter-piracy patrols. At the same time, negative developments closer to home in the South China Sea quickly supplanted piracy as Japan's primary security concern in Southeast Asia.

JAPAN AND THE SOUTH CHINA SEA DISPUTE

The South China Sea dispute centers on competing sovereignty claims to hundreds of small geographical features (such as atolls, rocks, reefs, and islands) and their adjacent maritime space. In the northern waters of the South China Sea lie the Paracel Islands, which China occupied in 1974 but which Vietnam still claims sovereignty over. Farther south, sovereignty of the Spratly Islands is contested in whole by China, Taiwan, and Vietnam, and in part by the Philippines, Malaysia, and Brunei.[25] The parties base their sovereignty claims on the grounds of discovery, occupation, and administration, though from a legal perspective all of their claims have significant weaknesses. Each of the claimants except Brunei has occupied and garrisoned features in the Spratlys.

While tensions have been cyclical since the late 1980s, they have risen steadily since 2007–08 due to a combination of factors. First, popular nationalism concerning sovereignty of the disputed atolls has been growing in intensity, especially in Vietnam and China. Rising nationalism has been fueled by claimant governments so as to bolster their legitimacy; however, volatile nationalism also constrains governments' policy options as any attempt to compromise their sovereignty claims would be perceived as weakness by nationalists. Second, and related, over the past several years nearly all the claimants have moved to strengthen their jurisdictional claims through national legislation and submissions to the United Nations Commission on the Limits on the Continental Shelf. Third, competition over access to maritime resources such as crude oil, natural gas, and fisheries has been rising, resulting in a number of tense standoffs and incidents at sea. Fourth, the dispute has become increasingly militarized. The rapid modernization of the PLA-N and the expansion of China's civilian maritime law enforcement agencies have enabled China to increase its presence in the South China Sea and bring coercive pressure to bear on the Southeast Asian claimants, particularly Vietnam and the Philippines. Fifth, the United States' more active interest in the dispute since 2008 has added an extra layer of complexity to the dispute. The United States does not take a position on the territorial claims but regards freedom of navigation in the South China Sea as a national interest and has voiced concern at growing tensions. While the United States' more proactive stance toward the South China Sea has generally been welcomed by Southeast Asian countries, China has criticized Washington for "meddling" in the dispute and using it as a pretext to "pivot" or "rebalance" its military forces toward Asia. Conflict management mechanisms, such as the 2002 ASEAN-China Declaration on the Conduct of Parties in the South China Sea (DoC), have failed to reduce tensions; and the dispute, together with other maritime territorial problems, has quickly worked its way to the top of Asia's security agenda, where it is likely to stay for the foreseeable future.

Japan's Concerns

Japan has played an important role in China's reemergence as a Great Power. When China opened up its economy in the late 1970s, Japan was an early and enthusiastic investor; bilateral trade boomed and in 2011 hit US$345 billion.[26] Today, however, high levels of economic interdependence coexist alongside low-level rivalry and mutual suspicions: the legacy of Japan's aggressive behavior during the 1930s and World War II continues to negatively shape Chinese perceptions of Japan, while Tokyo is palpably concerned at Beijing's more assertive behavior in the maritime domain, perceived lack of respect for international norms, and growing military might.

Japan recognizes that China's phenomenal economic growth and generally stable domestic politics have given Beijing a newfound confidence on the world stage. This confidence has been bolstered by China's rapid emergence as Asia's preeminent military power. As the PRC's economy has expanded, greater financial resources have been devoted to the armed forces even as defense spending has remained more or less constant as a percentage of GDP — around 2 per cent according to most analysts.[27] Between 1988 and 1997 China raised defense spending by an annual average of 14.5 per cent, and between 1998 and 2007 it raised defense spending to 15.9 per cent.[28] In 2012 China's official defense spending rose to US$106 billion, the second highest in the world — admittedly a long way behind the United States, whose spending was US$614 billion, but nevertheless the highest in Asia.[29] These trends stand in marked contrast to

Japan's political, economic, and military milieu. Since the early 1990s the Japanese economy has been mired in recession, a problem compounded by weak political leadership. As a direct consequence of economic stagnation, defense spending has remained flat: in 1999 Japan spent US$54.39 billion on its armed forces, and in 2011 it spent US$54.53 billion (in constant 2010 U.S. dollars).[30] In January 2013 the Abe government promised to raise defense spending by 0.8 per cent, the first increase in 11 years.[31]

Japan has repeatedly criticized China for its lack of transparency concerning defense spending (many analysts estimate that the true level of Chinese defense expenditure is two or three times higher than the official budget), PLA modernization, and strategic intentions. Japan's 2010 defense white paper assesses that "China has not yet achieved the levels of transparency expected of a responsible major power" and that this lack of transparency "could lead to a sense of distrust and misunderstandings" by other countries.[32] A year earlier, Japan's Ministry of Defense had noted there was "concern how the military power of China will influence the regional state of affairs and the security of Japan" and that the modernization of the PLA was something "Japan should keep a careful watch over".[33]

Japan's security analysts believe that China's growing military power has already altered the strategic context in both the East China Sea and the South China Sea. Since the beginning of the current century, Tokyo has been concerned over the growing presence of Chinese military and paramilitary vessels in waters close to Japan, including in its 200-nautical-mile exclusive economic zone (EEZ). Such presence includes a Chinese submarine entering Japan's territorial waters in 2004, the increasing frequency of transits by PLA-N vessels through Japan's international straits such as Okinawa and Miyako (these are perfectly legal, but Tokyo has accused Chinese military helicopters of aggressively "buzzing" shadowing JMSDF vessels), and intrusions by Chinese vessels into Japan's territorial waters and EEZ around the Senkaku/Diaoyu Islands in September 2010, August 2011, and February-March 2012.[34] The activities of Chinese vessels near the Senkaku/Diaoyu Islands is a particularly emotive issue, and a collision between a Chinese trawler and two JCG ships in September 2010, as well as the presence of Chinese patrol boats near the islands in September 2012 following the Japanese government's "nationalization" of three of the Senkaku/Diaoyu, have provoked serious crises in Sino-Japanese relations and raised tensions between the two countries to their highest level since the end of World War II.

Japanese security analysts have also expressed concern over the worsening situation in the South China Sea. The National Institute for Defense

Studies, for example, noted in its 2011 review of regional security that after pursuing a more "cooperative stance" in the previous decade, China had "once again begun adopting a hardline stance on the South China Sea".[35] A year later, the institute went on to observe that China's more assertive posture had provoked sporadic clashes with the other claimants, facilitated greater security cooperation between the United States and Southeast Asian countries, and "significantly influenced" the arms acquisitions programs of some ASEAN states.[36] Japan's anxiety was reflected in the 2012 defense white paper, which, for the first time, devoted a separate section to the South China Sea dispute. The white paper noted "growing concern among the international community in recent years over issues such as the freedom of navigation in the sea" and that the dispute "is considered to have a potential impact on the peace and stability of the regional and international community, and attention will continue to be paid to trends in the countries concerned as well as the direction of dialogues aimed at resolution of the issue".[37]

These comments reflect Japan's two main concerns regarding the situation in the South China Sea: the potential impact on sea lane security and international legal norms.

Instability fueled by rising tensions has the potential to disrupt Southeast Asia's sea lanes on which Japan's economic security depends. While few observers expect a major conflict over ownership of the Spratlys, the increasing frequency of incidents at sea involving warships, patrol boats, fishing trawlers, and survey vessels raises the risk that an accidental clash could quickly escalate into a major diplomatic and military crisis. The hardening of positions by the claimant states, rising nationalism, and the almost complete absence of conflict prevention and management mechanisms compound the risk. Similar scenarios involving the armed forces of China and Japan could also occur in the East China Sea for precisely the same reasons.

Japan's second main concern is related to legal norms. Most of the disputants base their claims to sovereignty of the Spratly Islands on discovery, historical usage, and administration. Because China did not begin to occupy features in the Spratlys until the 1980s, it places a strong emphasis on historical "evidence" going back to the Han Dynasty in the second century BC. China points to a number of maps to support its claims, including one drawn up by the Nationalist Chinese government in 1947. The map shows nine discontinuous lines encompassing 80 per cent of the South China Sea. China has studiously avoided providing a detailed explanation of what these dashes indicate. In fact, there seem to be differing interpretations within

China on what the map means: from a claim only to the geographical features and their adjacent waters, to the notion that China is entitled to "historic rights" within the nine dashes, including ownership of all living and nonliving resources therein.[38] While the first interpretation would broadly be in line with the United Nations Convention on the Law of the Sea (UNCLOS), the latter is clearly incompatible. The ambiguity of the map, and the presumption that China is claiming sovereignty over all of the insular features plus exclusive rights to maritime resources within the nine-dash line, has generated unease across the region and beyond. Japan's disquiet was heightened in 2009, when China officially submitted the map attached to a *note verbale* protesting Vietnam and Malaysia's joint submission to the United Nations Commission on the Limits on the Continental Shelf. Japan does not believe that the nine-dash line can be legally justified, and it believes that should other Asian nations be persuaded or coerced into accepting China's claims, UNCLOS would be undermined. A settlement that recognizes Beijing's claims would also strengthen China's position in the East China Sea, thus undermining Japan's claims. Japanese concerns regarding the need to preserve the legal norms enshrined in UNCLOS are shared by other countries around the world, including the United States and members of the European Union.

A related issue is the principle of freedom of navigation. Thus far, the dispute has not interrupted the transit of maritime traffic through the South China Sea. Nevertheless, concerns that one day freedom of navigation may be put at risk by a preponderant China have been voiced. Attempts by Beijing to put these fears to rest have had a mixed reception. In September 2012, for instance, then Chinese Foreign Minister Yang Jiechi stated, "Freedom and safety of navigation in the South China Sea is assured."[39] The Philippine government articulated the unease of other governments when it issued a statement arguing that it was not for China to bestow freedom of navigation in the area — a "privilege" that could, presumably, be taken away if China so wished.[40] Japan has not voiced this concern in public but does so in private.

China's interpretation of freedom of navigation is, moreover, at odds with other countries'. While most governments view foreign military surveillance activities in the EEZ of a coastal state as legitimate and permissible under UNCLOS, China regards such actions as illegal.[41] This interpretation (which is supported by a dozen or so countries around the world, including in Asia) puts the United States and China at odds and is what led to the 2001 EP-3 surveillance plane and 2009 *Impeccable* incidents. The issue of foreign military surveillance activities in the EEZ of a coastal state poses a dilemma for Japan. In general Tokyo supports the position of the United States, but it does not do so publicly because this would prevent it from criticizing China for conducting the same kinds of activities in Japan's EEZ, which it views with great concern.

Japan's Response

Japan seeks to ameliorate its concerns in the South China Sea in four ways: raising maritime disputes at international forums; encouraging ASEAN unity; addressing the issue bilaterally with Southeast Asian countries; and strengthening relations and policy coordination with the United States and other countries.

China is opposed to the "internationalization" of the South China Sea on the grounds that the dispute is bilateral in nature and can only be resolved by Beijing and each of the claimant countries on a one-on-one basis. Accordingly Beijing has tried to limit discussion of the issue at regional security forums such as the ASEAN Regional Forum (ARF) and the East Asia Summit (EAS), and also rejects submission of the dispute to international legal arbitration such as at the International Court of Justice (ICJ) or, as the Philippines did in 2013, to the International Tribunal on the Law of the Sea.[42] The latter position means it is highly unlikely that Beijing would advocate submitting the Senkaku/Diaoyu dispute to the ICJ as it would set a precedent for other disputes, including the Paracels and Spratlys. With regard to the former, however, Japan has, at least over the past few years, ignored Chinese opposition. Thus, at the ARF meeting in Hanoi in July 2010, Japan was one of 12 countries that expressed concern at developments in the South China Sea, a move it repeated in 2011 and 2012. At the 2012 ARF, for instance, Japan described the South China Sea dispute as "directly related to the peace and stability of the Asia-Pacific region", called on all parties to clarify their claims in accordance with UNCLOS, and expressed "serious concern" over the Sino-Philippine Scarborough Shoal Incident in May-June.[43] Prime Minister Yoshihiko Noda reiterated these concerns at the EAS in November 2012.[44] By raising the issue at such forums, Japan aims to highlight the importance of preserving freedom of navigation, effective conflict management, and a peaceful resolution of the dispute.

As tensions in the South China Sea have escalated, the divisions within ASEAN have become more pronounced. The ten members of ASEAN have differing interests in — and positions on — the South China Sea: Vietnam and the Philippines view the problem as a major national security concern; fellow claimants Malaysia and Brunei tend to downplay tensions; Indonesia and Singapore have both called on China to clarify its claims; the four non-claimants in mainland Southeast Asia — Thailand, Myanmar, Cambodia, and Laos — do not perceive a direct stake in the dispute and in any case wish to avoid jeopardizing close economic and political links with China by taking positions inimical to Beijing's interests.[45] ASEAN does have a lowest common denominator consensus on the dispute: that all parties and stakeholders have a vested interest in peace and stability in the South China Sea; that the dispute should be resolved peacefully in accordance with international law and without the use of force; and that China and ASEAN should pursue confidence-building measures to reduce tensions. But beyond this there is no consensus on how to move forward with conflict management and conflict resolution. The problem of ASEAN solidarity over the South China Sea was brought into sharp relief in July 2012, when, for the first time in the organization's 45-year history, ASEAN foreign ministers failed to issue a joint communiqué because of differences over whether the dispute should be mentioned.[46] Japan was extremely disappointed with Cambodia's chairmanship of ASEAN and particularly the lack of progress on developing a formal Code of Conduct (CoC) for the South China Sea.[47]

ASEAN disunity over the South China Sea worries Tokyo for two reasons: first, because it impedes efforts to better manage the dispute, allowing tensions to fester and increase; and second, because it raises the unwelcome prospect that China could exploit the divisions and cut separate deals with individual claimants that would benefit its national interests. Japan has therefore tried to foster ASEAN unity, and called for the implementation of the 2002 DoC and the negotiation of a CoC.[48] In 2011, Japan suggested that the ASEAN Maritime Forum be expanded to include the organization's dialogue partners.[49] Japan's aim was to push discussions on implementing concrete conflict-management mechanisms such as the DoC and CoC. ASEAN accepted Japan's proposal; and in October 2012 the Expanded ASEAN Maritime Forum (EAMF) met in Manila, with the participation of EAS members. Although no major progress was achieved, Japan would like to see the EAMF convene on an annual basis, a sentiment supported by the United States.[50]

Japan has supplemented its multilateral approach with bilateralism. Japanese ministers now regularly discuss the South China Sea dispute with their Southeast Asian counterparts. In October 2011, for instance, then Foreign Minister Koichiro Gemba raised the issue during visits to Singapore,

Malaysia, and Indonesia.[51] The dispute was also addressed during summit meetings between Japan and the Philippines and Vietnam in September and October 2011 respectively.[52] Within weeks of the Abe administration taking office in December 2012, senior Japanese leaders fanned out across Southeast Asia: Taro Aso, former prime minister and now deputy prime minister and finance minister, visited Myanmar in early January 2013; Foreign Minister Fumio Kishida visited the Philippines, Singapore, and Brunei in mid-January; and Abe himself took in Vietnam, Thailand, and Indonesia from 16–18 January. The purpose of these trips was twofold: first, to reenergize economic relations between Japan and Southeast Asia; and second, to discuss maritime security issues, that is, the ongoing disputes in both the South and East China Seas. In his Jakarta speech, the prime minister outlined the "Abe Doctrine." Of the five principles he enunciated, the second was that Japan would work to ensure that the maritime domain remained "governed by laws and rules, not might".[53] The "not might" clause was clearly a reference to the possibility that China might seek to resolve its claims through coercion.

Japan is paying particular attention to the Philippines. Tokyo was perturbed by the Scarborough Shoal standoff in April-May 2012, in which the Philippines was forced to back down and China essentially seized control of the reef. Japan is concerned that China is pursuing a similar strategy in the East China Sea — using its maritime law enforcement agency vessels to undermine Japanese administrative control over the Senkaku/Diaoyu Islands with the ultimate objective of exercising de facto control. Japan has found a willing partner in the Philippines. After meeting with Japanese Foreign Minister Kishida in January 2013, his Philippine counterpart, Albert del Rosario, told a news conference that the two sides shared "mutual concern" over China's position on maritime disputes, and that the nine-dash line posed a threat to regional stability and freedom of navigation.[54] In an effort to strengthen the Philippines' maritime capabilities, Tokyo has moved to expand contact with the Philippine Navy and has offered capacity-building support to the PCG. During Philippine President Benigno Aquino's visit to Japan in September 2011, agreement was reached on an exchange of visits by the heads of navy, increased port calls by JMSDF vessels to the Philippines, and enhanced cooperation between the Japanese and Philippine coast guards.[55] In 2012, Japan offered to transfer up to ten patrol boats worth US$12 million each to enhance the PCG's maritime surveillance capabilities in disputed waters.[56] The patrol boats will be funded from Japan's Overseas Development Aid budget and will be delivered over a two-year period. Similar capacity-building support may also be extended to Vietnam.

Japan's fourth strategy to cope with perceived threats in the South China Sea is to pursue closer ties with democratic countries that share its concerns over recent developments in Asia's maritime domain. The Abe government's priority is to strengthen Japan's alliance with the United States, but the prime minister has also identified India and Australia as important partners. Japan has welcomed the United States' "pivot" or rebalancing of military forces toward Asia. In December 2012 Abe proposed a "Democratic Security Diamond" comprising Japan, the United States, India, and Australia, in which those four countries would work together to "safeguard the maritime commons stretching from the Indian Ocean region to the Western Pacific".[57] Even before Abe came to power, Tokyo and Washington had agreed to coordinate their positions at multilateral security forums such as the ARF so as to encourage China to adhere to international norms of behavior.[58] And in terms of providing capacity-building support to the Philippines, a division of labor is apparent: the United States is helping to modernize the armed forces of the Philippines through the transfer of refurbished military assets such as ex-U.S. Coast Guard cutters, while Japan seeks to improve the capabilities of the PCG by providing patrol boats and training.

Japan's strategies do, of course, have their limitations. While Japan is keen to promote ASEAN solidarity on the South China Sea dispute, the member states are acutely conscious of the need to avoid giving the impression that they are "ganging up" on China at Tokyo's behest. Japan's capacity-building support for certain Southeast Asian countries is constrained by constitutional restrictions and budgetary pressures. And while U.S. and Japanese views on the situation in the South China Sea overlap to a considerable degree, the overlap is less when it comes to Indian and Australian perceptions. Both New Delhi and Canberra have significant reservations about a "Democratic Security Diamond", which would almost certainly be seen in Beijing as part of a wider U.S.-led strategy to contain or encircle China.

CONCLUSION

Japan's principal security interests in Southeast Asia are tied to sea-lane security, on which the country's economic security depends. Since Japan's economic liftoff in the 1960s, and continuing into the current period of recession, successive governments have invested considerable resources to enhance the safety and security of regional SLOCs. For much of the Cold War period the Japanese government and private industry financed the installation and upkeep of navigational safety equipment in Southeast Asia's strategic chokepoints, especially the Straits of Malacca. Post-Cold War, attention shifted to the threat posed by pirates and sea robbers. In order to address the threat, Japan stepped up capacity-building support for regional coast guards and provided leadership to encourage greater regional cooperation through information exchange. Japan's support was a major factor in the downward trend in maritime violence in Southeast Asia from 2005 to 2010.

While safety of navigation and piracy remain important issues for Tokyo, since 2008–09 Japanese security analysts have expressed quiet but growing concern at rising tensions in the South China Sea over contested territorial and maritime boundary claims. While Japan is not a claimant, and does not take a position on the territorial claims, it has been perturbed by China's more assertive behavior and the potential for disruption to vital SLOCs. More important, Japan is concerned that should China prevail in its dispute with Southeast Asian countries, international legal norms will be undermined, and the country's national interests in both the South China Sea and East China Sea would be harmed. In order to preserve the status quo, Japan is pursuing multiple strategies simultaneously: internationalizing the dispute at multilateral forums; encouraging ASEAN unity; providing capacity-building support to claimant countries, especially the Philippines; and coordinating its positions with the United States. China rejects Japanese "meddling" in the dispute, but for Japan the stakes are too high for it to be a mere bystander. Even as the two countries face off in the East China Sea, the South China Sea is likely to become an increasing point of contention in Sino-Japanese relations.

Notes

[1]   Prime Minister Abe did not deliver the speech in person, as his trip to Southeast Asia was cut short due to a hostage crisis in Algeria in which 14 Japanese nationals were killed. See "The Bounty of the Open Sea: Five New Principles for Japanese Diplomacy", 18 January 2013, available at <http://www.kantei.go.jp/foreign/96_abe/statement/201301/18speech_e.html> (Emphasis added).

[2]   Statistics compiled from *Direction of Trade Statistics: Yearbook 2011* (Washington, D.C.: International Monetary Fund, 2011).

3   Shinzo Abe, "Asia's Democratic Security Diamond", *Project Syndicate* (27 December 2012), available at<http://www.project-syndicate.org/ commentary/a-strategic-alliance-for-japan-and-india-by-shinzo-abe>.

4   R.G. Boyd, *The Strategic Significance of the Malacca Strait* (Ottawa: Department of National Defence, 1977), p. 3.

5   James Manicom, "Japan's Role in Strengthening Maritime Security in Southeast Asia". In *Maritime Security in Southeast Asia: U.S., Japanese, and Industry Strategies*, edited by John Bradford, James Manicom, Sheldon W. Simon, and Neil A. Quartaro. Seattle: National Bureau of Asian Research, 2010, p. 33.

6   Euan Graham, *Japan's Sea Lane Security, 1940–2004: A Matter of Life and Death?* London and New York: Routledge, 2006, p. 152.

7   Yaacov Y.I. Vertzberger, *Coastal States, Regional Powers, Superpowers and the Malacca-Singapore Straits.* Berkeley: University of California, 1984, p. 9.

8   Graham, *Japan's Sea Lane Security*, p. 163.

9   Vertzberger, *Coastal States*, p. 3.

10   Ibid., p. 62.

11   Under international law, an act of piracy is defined as an illegal act of violence or detention involving two or more ships on the high seas, that is, outside a coastal state's 12-nautical-mile territorial waters; acts of maritime depredation that occur within a state's territorial waters are known as sea robbery and are subject to the national jurisdiction of the state.

12   See Ian Storey, "Securing Southeast Asia's Sea Lanes: A Work in Progress". *Asia Policy* 2 (July 2008): 106–09.

13   Ibid., p. 107.

14   Manicom, "Japan's Role", p. 35.

15   Michael Richardson, "Challenging Marauders' Spread, Navy Recovers Hijacked Ship", *International Herald Tribune*, 23 November 1999.

16   Mark Valencia, "Piracy and Terrorism in Southeast Asia". In *Piracy in Southeast Asia: Status, Issues and Responses*, edited by Derek Johnson and Mark Valencia. Singapore: Institute of Southeast Asian Studies, 2005, p. 110.

17   Ibid., pp. 93, 107.

18   "Japan to Provide Assistance for RI's Maritime Security Agency", Antara News, 19 September 2007.

19   "Japan Gives Malaysia Grant for Malacca Strait Security", Kyodo News, 25 January 2008.

20   Manicom, "Japan's Role", p. 37.

21   ReCAAP was finalized on 11 November 2004 and came into effect on 4 September 2006.

22   *The Asian Initiative: Enhancing Regional Cooperation 2006–2008* (Singapore: ReCAAP, 2009), p. 55, available at <http://www.recaap.org/DesktopModules/ Bring2mind/DMX/Download.aspx?Command=Core_Download&EntryId=35 &PortalId=0&TabId=78>.

23   Storey, "Securing Southeast Asia's Sea Lanes," p. 115.

24   Ian Storey, "Maritime Security in Southeast Asia: Two Cheers for Regional Cooperation". In *Southeast Asian Affairs 2009*, edited by Daljit Singh (Singapore: Institute of Southeast Asian Studies, May 2009), pp. 36–60.

25   For an overview of the South China Sea dispute, see Clive Schofield and Ian Storey, *The South China Sea Dispute: Increasing Stakes and Rising Tensions*, Jamestown Foundation Occasional Paper (November 2009).

26   "JETRO Survey: Analysis of Japan-China Trade in 2011 and Outlook for 2012," Japan External Trade Organization, press release, 23 February 2012, <http://www.jetro.go.jp/en/news/releases/20120223142-news>.

27   Andrew S. Erickson and Adam P. Liff, "Understanding China's Defense Budget: What It Means and Why It Matters". PacNet 16, 10 March 2011.

28   Ibid.

29   "China's Defense Budget to Grow 11.2 pct in 2012: Spokesman", Xinhua, 4 March 2012.

30   See SIPRI Military Expenditure Database, available at <http://milexdata. sipri.org>.

31   "Japan Defense Budget to Increase for First Time in 11 Years", Bloomberg, 30 January 2013.

32   *Defense of Japan 2010* (Tokyo: Ministry of Defense, 2010), pp. 55, 5.

33   *Defense of Japan 2009* (Tokyo: Ministry of Defense, 2009), p. 4.

34   *Defense of Japan 2008* (Tokyo: Ministry of Defense, 2009), pp. 55–56; *Defense of Japan 2012* (Tokyo: Ministry of Defense, 2012) [no page numbers available].

35   National Institute of Defense Studies, *East Asian Strategic Review 2011*. Tokyo: The Japan Times, 2011, p. 121.

36   National Institute of Defense Studies, *East Asian Strategic Review 2012*. Tokyo: The Japan Times, 2012, p. 155.

37   *Defense of Japan 2012*.

38   Duong Danh Huy, "China's 'U-shaped' Line in the South China Sea". *Asia Sentinel*, 19 September 2012.

39   "China Vows Freedom, Safety in S. China Sea". *The Straits Times*, 6 September 2012.

40   Department of Foreign Affairs, "Statement on Freedom of Navigation in the West Philippine Sea", 6 September 2012.

41   Jonathan Odom, "A China in the Bull Shop? Comparing the Rhetoric of a Rising China with the Reality of the International Law of the Sea". *Ocean and Coastal Law Journal* 17, no. 2 (2012): 201–49.

42   "Manila Ups the Ante in the South China Sea". *China Brief* 13, no. 3 (1 February 2013).

43   "Statement of Japan at the 19th ARF Ministerial Meeting 2012", copy provided by the Ministry of Foreign Affairs, Japan, September 2012.

44 "Japan to Challenge China on Security". *Wall Street Journal*, 19 November 2011.
45 Ian Storey, "Asean Is a House Divided". *Wall Street Journal*, 14 June 2012.
46 Ian Storey, "China Pushes on the South China Sea, ASEAN Unity Collapses". *China Brief* 12, no. 15 (4 August 2012).
47 Author interviews with Japanese officials at the Ministry of Foreign Affairs, Tokyo, in September and December 2012.
48 "Statement of Japan at the 19th ARF Ministerial Meeting 2012", copy provided by the Ministry of Foreign Affairs, Japan, September 2012.
49 "ASEAN Leaders Agree to Study 'Expanded' ASEAN Maritime Forum", Kyodo News, 24 August 2011.
50 "U.S. Wants Expanded ASEAN Maritime Forum Institutionalized". *The Philippine Star*, 7 October 2012.
51 "Govt Must Boost Security, Economic Ties with ASEAN". *The Yomiuri Shimbun*, 15 October 2011.
52 "Japan-Philippines Joint Statement on the Comprehensive Promotion of the 'Strategic Partnership' between Neighboring Countries Connected by Special Bonds of Friendship", 27 September 2011, available at <http://www.mofa.go.jp/announce/pm/noda/joint_statement110927.html>; "Japan-Viet Nam Joint Statement on the Actions Taken under Strategic Partnership for Peace and Prosperity in Asia", 31 October 2011, available at <http://www.mofa.go.jp/mofaj/kaidan/s_noda/vietnam1110/pdfs/1.pdf>.
53 Abe, "The Bounty of the Open Sea".
54 "Philippines Seeks Patrol Ships, Communications Equipment from Japan amid Disputes with China", Associated Press, 10 January 2013.
55 National Institute for Defense Studies, *East Asian Strategic Review 2012*. Tokyo: The Japan Times and NIDS, 2012, p. 144.
56 "Japan to Give Patrol Boats to Manila amid China Tensions". Agence France-Presse, 11 February 2013.
57 Abe, "Asia's Democratic Security Diamond".
58 Author interviews with senior officials, Ministry of Foreign Affairs, Tokyo, September 2012.

8

EVOLUTION OF INSTITUTIONS AND POLICIES FOR ECONOMIC INTEGRATION IN EAST ASIA: THE RISE OF CHINA AND CHANGES IN THE REGIONAL ORDER

Yoshihiro Otsuji and Kunihiko Shinoda

The signing of the Plaza Accord on currency alignment in the mid-1980s marked the beginning of substantial progress toward genuine economic integration in East Asia in the decade that followed. Multinational companies became established in the region and new business clusters were formed. Progress was also made in terms of systems and policy: efforts were made to liberalize trade and put in place a set of rules that would encourage regional economic integration. A number of Free Trade Agreements (FTA) and Economic Partnership Agreements (EPA) have been signed, and we can be optimistic that economic integration on the systems front will continue in the years to come.

This chapter discusses the game-changing effects of China's increased involvement in the East Asian economic integration process since it joined the World Trade Organization (WTO). We look at how the Association of Southeast Asian Nations (ASEAN) and Japan have responded to date, and consider how they ought to respond in the future.

WTO MEMBERSHIP PROMPTS GREATER CHINESE INVOLVEMENT

How and when did China become fully integrated into the East Asian regional economy, involved diplomatically not just in bilateral but also multilateral efforts? For many years, Japan and ASEAN were the main drivers of de facto economic integration in East Asia. This began to change after China joined the WTO in 2001. China opened FTA negotiations with ASEAN soon after, and became much more directly involved in the regional economic integration process, calling for preliminary studies on an FTA involving ASEAN+3 (Japan, China, and South Korea).

Until the Asian currency crisis of the late 1990s, the main hubs for regionalization in East Asia were Japan and ASEAN. After World War II, the countries that would later form ASEAN passed tough laws regulating foreign investment and attempted to achieve import substitution through steep tariffs. When this approach reached a dead end, the ASEAN countries shifted to an export-driven model of industrialization. It was around this time, with the value of the yen soaring following the Plaza Accord in 1985, that Japanese companies, particularly in the electronics sector, began to make serious investments in ASEAN in order to maintain their international competitiveness.

This brought about the so-called "flying geese" model of economic development with Japan at the head of the flock, and led to greater regional integration in East Asia.[1] Throughout the 1990s there was concentrated investment in the automotive, electrics, and electronics industries, as well as in components and other supporting industries, as ASEAN developed as a base for exports. ASEAN became a major part of the global factory. Singapore and Malaysia became important centers for the electronics industry, and Thailand for the automotive industry. ASEAN, originally created as a mechanism for political cooperation, increasingly evolved into an economic cooperation organization. In the post-Cold War years of the 1990s, ASEAN was expanded, with the participation of Vietnam, Laos, Cambodia, and Myanmar, into a framework for massive regional economic integration comprising a population of more than 500 million people. One of the chief goals of the organization was the formation of an ASEAN Free Trade Area (AFTA).

The situation in China was quite different. Indeed, for much of the immediate postwar period, it would be no exaggeration to say that China was outside the East Asian regional framework as it worked to build a communist system. The first wave of changes came with Deng Xiaoping's shift to a policy of "reform and opening-up" in 1989. Deng's reforms aimed to develop a state-controlled market system based on state-owned enterprises under a "socialist market economy". But China's relationship with the wider East Asian regional system was still limited. Although China encouraged foreign direct investment, the reforms did not go far enough to build bilateral trade relationships in any true sense.

The second wave of change came quite suddenly in the second half of the 1990s. This began when Japanese companies, under pressure from the high value of the yen, began to invest heavily in Guangdong Province and the Yangtze River region. Taiwanese and Korean firms did likewise, so that China was pulled quickly into the triangular trade system centered on the United States, Japan, and ASEAN. The second aspect of this change was China's move to join the WTO, which suddenly gained momentum around this time. Defining the amount of triangle trade as the total amount of intermediate goods exported from Japan and NIEs to ASEAN and China, plus the amount of final goods exported from ASEAN and China to the United States, we can calculate the changes in share of the amount of trade in the East Asia production network for the whole economy. In 2003 the amount traded in the triangle trade structure increased five times from that in 1990. In addition, share of triangle trade in total trade more than doubled from 11.7 per cent in 1990 to 23.1 per cent in 2003.

Initially, many thought that China would be less than wholehearted in its commitment to the WTO, but that turned out to be false. One recalls remarks made in China during the late 1990s to the effect that China's comeback on the international stage would be marked by three major turning points: a return to the United Nations, membership of WTO, and hosting of the Olympics. Politically at least, the idea that China would become involved in the international community as a great power or rule-maker was starting to be accepted. Economically speaking, it seemed that the intention was to use external pressure to spur reforms of the domestic economy. This was similar to Japan's aims in participating in multilateral trade negotiations. Political and economic reforms were the two main reasons why China joined the WTO; the same is true of FTAs.

Despite the Asian currency crisis in 1997, foreign investment poured into China after the country joined the WTO in 2001. This coincided with huge expectations of a rapid expansion of business within China itself. The influx of foreign capital led to an expansion of the domestic production base and increased production in manufacturing industry, notably steel and consumer electronics. China began to develop as a major exporter. Driven by investment and strong exports, China underwent dramatic economic growth, and fluctuations in the Chinese economy soon had a major global impact. In order to increase its political influence in Asia, China began to actively leverage its economic strength in its foreign policy. As we will see, China was the first to propose an FTA with ASEAN in 2001. China has been a hugely important presence since the turn of the century, displaying considerable autonomy and launching private sector feasibility studies on an FTA encompassing ASEAN, Japan, China, and South Korea.

However, this dramatic economic development has brought a number of serious problems to the surface. Perhaps the most serious of these is the issue of severe income disparities. The production capacity of the Chinese economy has soared through increased investment, but the rapid growth carries the risk of economic overheating and a hard landing for the economy as a whole. In the shadow of this development is a widening of the economic disparities between urban and rural areas, and between the coastal regions and the interior.

Initially, China was not particularly enthusiastic about regional integration efforts such as the ASEAN+3 summit meetings. This position changed as WTO membership approached. For China, joining the WTO fulfilled a long-held ambition. But it was certain that Western countries would demand that China open its markets as soon as it joined the WTO. China needed to cultivate partners who would stand by it in responding to these demands. It was also clear that restructuring China's domestic markets following entry into the WTO would involve considerable costs. Building overseas markets was therefore a matter of urgency for China, particularly in areas where China had a comparative advantage, such as the textiles and electronics industries.

At the same time, a joint study on an FTA with Japan and Singapore was underway in March 2000. This prompted the Chinese government to take a political decision to commit to East Asian regionalism. In November 2000, Chinese Premier Zhu Rongji proposed negotiations for an FTA between China and ASEAN, and in November 2001, not long after China joined the WTO, an agreement was reached to sign an FTA within the next ten years.

In its FTA negotiations with ASEAN, China's strategy made speed a priority. As well as pushing liberalization of trade in agricultural products such as fruit and vegetables and some mineral and industrial products, China plunged into regional cooperation on agriculture, information technology, human resources development, investment, and development of the Mekong River region.[2] Negotiations on liberalization of trade in services and investment followed on the heels of liberalization of goods trading.

With many ASEAN countries fearful of China's rapid rise to political and economic prominence, China hurried to produce concrete results in the fields of commodities trade and economic cooperation that would bring tangible benefits to ASEAN. Trade between the two regions was central to the real economy, and there was relatively little exchange in trade in services and investment, making it more difficult to move forward with negotiations on liberalization right away in areas where China still needed to carry out further domestic structural reforms.

Then, in 2004, China started to take the initiative in promoting a regional FTA for East Asia. It was China that proposed launching a study by private sector specialists on the feasibility of an East Asian Free Trade Agreement (EAFTA) composed of ASEAN+3.[3] There were probably two main reasons for this change: first, China had already made substantial progress toward an FTA with ASEAN; and second, it was aiming to increase its influence on ASEAN, comprising primarily developing countries, in an ASEAN+3 context.

EAST ASIA REGIONAL ECONOMIC INTEGRATION: A CHANGING GAME

China's increasing involvement in the regional integration process has changed the game in terms of economic relations among East Asian countries. This change is an ongoing process. First, it has come to have a huge impact on the FTA strategies of other East Asian countries. Second, it has accelerated the move to further de facto economic integration.

China's November 2001 agreement to conclude an FTA with ASEAN within ten years acted as a spur to other partners engaged in a dialogue on a possible FTA with ASEAN, and led to a number of negotiations on new FTAs with ASEAN as their hub. Under the influence of the agreement between China and ASEAN, Japan began expert meetings on beefing up economic partnership with ASEAN. In November 2002 a joint statement was adopted on the ASEAN-Japan Comprehensive Economic Partnership (AJCEP) and an agreement reached to make an economic partnership agreement a reality within ten years.[4] In rapid succession, a number of other dialogue partners subsequently reached agreements to begin FTA negotiations with ASEAN, including India (2002), South Korea (2004), Australia and New Zealand (2004). As a result, stimulated by China's FTA negotiations, similar negotiations for FTAs spread around East Asia with ASEAN as the hub, accelerating the economic integration process.

China's 2004 calls for a study on an FTA encompassing ASEAN+3 (Japan, China, and South Korea) led to new ideas on the FTA concept both within the East Asia region and beyond. These included ASEAN+6 (Japan, China, South Korea, India, Australia, New Zealand) and the Asia-Pacific Economic Cooperation (APEC).

In 2004 China called for discussion of an East Asia FTA, and following consideration at a study meeting, a report was published on an FTA for East Asia in 2006. In the same year, Japan responded by calling for a study group to consider an ASEAN+6 FTA (Comprehensive Economic Partnership in East Asia, CEPEA). This was approved at the East Asian Summit that year.[5]

Underlying these developments were the following three facts: (1) Trade and investment were expanding in the actual economic activities between ASEAN and India, Australia, and New Zealand; (2) With relations frosty between Japan and China, ASEAN was looking to India, Australia, and New Zealand to play the role of balancing powers; and (3) India, Australia, and New Zealand were also hoping for wider FTAs with ASEAN within the East Asia region.

Japan's proposal to pursue economic cooperation within the framework of ASEAN+6 prompted the United States, one of the leading members of APEC, to demand that Japan make a greater contribution to the APEC forum, and that the United States be involved in the economic integration process in East Asia. As a result, following a proposal from the United States, an agreement was reached at the APEC meeting in 2006 to move forward with studies aimed at regional economic integration. These would include a Free Trade Area of the Asia-Pacific (FTAAP) as a medium- to long-term prospect, with the results reported to heads of government.[6] Since the Obama administration was established in 2009, the United States has become more engaged in maintaining a power balance, enhancing political partnerships, and creating trade rules in the Asia-Pacific region.

In its FTA negotiations with ASEAN, China's approach has realistically reflected the actual conditions of its trade and investment exchanges with ASEAN, moving to liberalize trade in certain agricultural, mineral, and industrial products first, followed by the goods trade as a whole, and trade in services and investment last of all.

In the early stages of the negotiations, the emphasis was on cooperation in priority areas such as agriculture, information technology, human resources training, investment, and development of the Mekong River region. More recently, this has expanded to include cooperation efforts such as the China-ASEAN Cooperation Investment Fund, which is worth approximately

US$10 billion for developing infrastructure and energy development within the ASEAN region.[7]

Since the ASEAN-Japan Comprehensive Economic Partnership (AJCEP) came into effect in 2008, Japan too has been devoting considerable energy to improving both hard and soft infrastructure in the region — aspects not fully covered by the liberalization and facilitation of trade and investment under the AJCEP. In addition to committing some US$20 billion in official development assistance to countries in Asia, Japan is also pushing ahead with wide-area infrastructure improvements in East Asia, as part of its initiative to double the size of the East Asian economy.[8] In this way, Japan and China have been competing to develop hard and soft infrastructure within the East Asia region, quite apart from their ASEAN+3 and ASEAN+6 FTA strategies.

De facto economic integration in East Asia has made progress at the same time as China has increased its involvement in the economic integration process. It has been driven by the networks of multinational companies and the emergence of a middle class, which have brought about supply chains of manufacturing industries, a domestic demand-driven growth, and a common lifestyle within the region.

The first point to note is the emergence of a middle class throughout the region. There is now a well-established class of consumers whom we can consider to represent the middle class, not just in Japan and South Korea, but also in China, where an estimated 640 million people are actively purchasing consumer goods in 2010. China's middle class is freely spending the wealth that has accrued as a result of greater economic freedom, and is using the Internet in order to enjoy the consumer lifestyle. In ASEAN countries, as a result of high growth since the mid-1980s, a middle class emerged in the 1990s. Politically, this class has supported gradual democratization in Thailand and other Southeast Asian countries. The middle class was hit hard by the Asian currency crisis owing to heavy dependence on loans, but prosperity has now returned. There are some estimated 240 million middle-class consumers in Southeast Asia. In total, there are around 1,460 million consumers in Asia in 2010 affluent enough to be considered middle-class.[9] Members of this emergent middle class demonstrate certain things in common regardless of nationality, a tendency encouraged by globalization and the increasing use of information technology. Although this middle class is more diverse and lacks the shared religious foundation that marked the emergence of the middle class in Europe, in practical terms, we can expect that this emergent middle class across has a largely similar lifestyle.

The second point, which is closely related to the first, is the search for mechanisms of endogenous development within the region. Even after the currency crisis, economic growth in China and Southeast Asia remained reliant on exports and direct investment from overseas. Once a middle class has formed, however, the next step needs to be a political focus on reducing inequalities between urban and rural regions, and the rich and the poor. This is becoming an increasingly urgent issue in a number of East Asian countries, as it was in Japan during the 1970s. When Prime Minister Thaksin Shinawatra was in power in Thailand, for instance, his administration announced promises to eradicate rural poverty and foster small businesses, and adopted policies to stimulate local entrepreneurship using the "One Tambon One Product" program. These initiatives had the common goal of achieving endogenous, autonomous development.[10]

In China, similarly, the Seventh National Congress of the Communist Party of China advanced the "Harmonious Society" concept in October 2005.[11] In the Chinese case, glaring inequalities in wealth meant that the authorities had no choice but to address the situation officially. This coincided with a shift from external demand to domestic demand as the main engine of growth, suggesting that China's development was moving beyond the stage of "factory of the world". China began efforts to develop its domestic market and reduce its dependence on the U.S. and European markets. This eventually led to cross-border projects that treated the whole East Asian region as one market. This coincided with a shift from external demand to domestic demand as the main engine of growth.

The third change that has taken place is the rise of corporate networks spanning the entire Asian region. Direct investment by foreign companies became the driving force of the growth in Asia, resulting in a concentration of multinational corporations in the region, particularly in manufacturing. These multinationals, most of them based in Japan, the United States, Europe, South Korea, and Taiwan, built supply chains for electronics, automobiles, and other products in the 1970s and 1980s. No other region has yet matched the supply chain infrastructure developed in East Asia in this period. Japanese corporations in particular built expansive networks for international production, sales, and procurement in East Asia, and the region made up a larger share of Japan's total trade and overseas investment every year. Against the backdrop of this development of supply chains by multinationals, trade in intermediate goods, such as parts for the general machinery and electrical equipment industries, expanded. For instance, the share of the intermediate goods trade within the total trade in East Asia increased from 18.3 per cent in 1990 to 32.5 per cent in 2010.[12]

On the investment front, if Japanese corporations focused on Southeast Asia before the Asian currency crisis, since the turn of the 21st century, China has been the main investment destination. At present, most Japanese companies adopt a "China+1" strategy, with plants and facilities in China and at least one other Asian country. Companies are building a sophisticated labor division system across the entire East Asian region, Japan included. In autos, household appliances, and other processing and assembly industries, Japan's firms tend to leave the production of engine parts, liquid crystal display components, and other high-value-added inputs at home even as they step up investments to manufacture other less-competitive inputs and finished products elsewhere in East Asia. In order to be a winner in a highly competitive world, multinationals must maintain and improve networks not just for production but also for procurement and sales. No longer can countries choose which companies they wish to invite in, not even fast-growing China. We have entered an age in which companies choose countries and regions.

ASEAN LOOKS TO BECOME AN INTEGRATION HUB

The Asian currency crisis exposed several weaknesses in the economic structure of Southeast Asian countries. In the years that followed, ASEAN continued to pursue internal economic integration in order to enhance its attractiveness as a production base and expand its presence in overseas markets. Since its decision to conclude an FTA with China, it has actively pursued free trade agreements with Japan and other dialogue partners.

Prior to the Asian currency crisis, ASEAN countries promoted the inflow of vast amounts of foreign capital while keeping their currencies essentially pegged to the dollar. This brought in a period of prosperity in which speculative bubbles formed. The crisis taught these countries that they had become excessively dependent on foreign investment and exports for their growth. The structure of their economies was clearly weak when it came to achieving autonomous development. In macroeconomic terms, domestic demand was inadequate to sustain autonomous development. From a microeconomic perspective, inadequate development of financial and economic systems acted as constraints on sustained growth.[13] At the same time, despite ASEAN's image as a well-structured organization, it became clear that the region as a whole needed to be more economically integrated. Immediately after the crisis struck, for example, ASEAN found itself unable to make an effective economic policy response that had the backing of all its members. Similarly, plans to accelerate economic integration by reducing tariffs within the region ran into resistance from some members, worried about the impact this might have on their own domestic industries.[14]

Even in the midst of the currency crisis, ASEAN continued to work on regional integration in the political and economic spheres. It expanded its membership, incorporating Vietnam in 1995, Laos and Myanmar in 1997, and Cambodia in 1999. While giving special consideration to the slower economic development of its new members, the organization drafted the ASEAN Vision 2020 blueprint for the future,[15] and progressed toward regional economic integration, using such tools as the dismantling of tariff barriers under the ASEAN Free Trade Area (AFTA) and the ASEAN Industrial Cooperation scheme (AICO).[16] All these initiatives are long-term arrangements for achieving economic integration gradually. An understanding grew that increasing the size of the region's internal markets would not be sufficient on its own to achieve a complete economic recovery.

In its early years, ASEAN aimed to achieve economic growth through investment from the advanced industrialized countries, particularly Japan and the United States, and by boosting exports to markets outside the region. The reasoning was that closer collaboration with external dialogue partners could be an effective means of overcoming the currency crisis. In 1997 ASEAN invited China, Japan, and South Korea to join what became known as ASEAN+3, marking the beginning of efforts to improve East Asian cooperation in a wide range of fields.[17] After the turn of the century, ASEAN initiated negotiations on FTAs for liberalizing and facilitating trade and investment. Positioning itself in the driver's seat, ASEAN pressed China, Japan, and other dialogue partners to compete for the opportunity to get on board.

ASEAN members signed the Declaration of ASEAN Concord II (Bali Concord II) at their October 2003 Summit.[18] The Concord set the goal of establishing an ASEAN Community by 2020, supported by the three pillars of political and security cooperation, economic cooperation, and sociocultural cooperation. In 2007 the target date for this community was moved forward from 2020 to 2015.[19] In the economic arena, an ASEAN Economic Community (AEC) is to be established. The aim of the AEC is to transform ASEAN into a region with free movement of goods, services, investment, and skilled labor, along with freer flows of capital. ASEAN is eager to complete its economic integration as quickly as possible because of its greater need to grow its markets, compared with rapidly rising China and India. At the same time, it hopes to make itself more attractive as a production base and, by integrating its markets, acquire a larger voice in diplomatic negotiations with countries outside the region.

Even as it took steps toward economic integration, ASEAN also made progress toward economic collaboration by means of FTAs with dialogue partners. Both China and South Korea wanted to expand exports to Southeast Asia's markets for industrial products and gain greater investment opportunities in the region. They were therefore open to finalizing free trade arrangements with ASEAN, making their target the deadline for ASEAN's elimination of its own internal tariffs under AFTA, and offering to open their own markets for agricultural products in exchange. In 2005 China began to lower its tariff rates for ASEAN countries, and in 2007 South Korea's FTA with ASEAN went into effect. Australia, New Zealand, and India also began working on FTAs with ASEAN, albeit more slowly than China and South Korea. Their aim in the long run is to gain entry to the community-building process in East Asia.

In the midst of these activities, Japan began working on regional and bilateral economic partnership agreements with ASEAN and its individual members. The ASEAN-Japan Comprehensive Economic Partnership Agreement (AJCEP) came into force at the end of 2008.[20] Japan hopes that the bilateral EPAs will stimulate Japanese investment in Southeast Asian countries and result in an improved division of labor once tariffs on parts and materials are eliminated. With the regional AJCEP also in place, finished products manufactured within ASEAN will gain an advantage in cost competitiveness when ASEAN's own tariffs on parts and materials reach zero, at least in the case of trade deals that satisfy Japan and ASEAN's rules of origin. From Japan's perspective, regional and bilateral EPAs offer the promise of reducing tariff costs, optimizing production bases, expanding markets, and increasing investment targets — all of which should help Japanese companies to be more competitive internationally.

JAPAN'S ROLE IN PROMOTING EAST ASIAN ECONOMIC INTEGRATION

The Asian currency crisis prompted a major change in Japan's regional strategy. Hitherto Tokyo had only endorsed arrangements consistent with WTO rules, but after the crisis, it shifted course and began approving schemes for regional integration in Asia. The opening of negotiations on a Japan-Singapore EPA proved to be a powerful stimulant. It sparked off a sequence of events that prompted the start of FTA negotiations between ASEAN and China, paved the way for talks on the AJCEP, and encouraged other moves to establish FTAs and EPAs in the East Asian region.

The currency crisis of the late 1990s prompted a serious discussion in Japan on how the country should respond to moves toward regional integration around the world. Initially most Japanese took a negative view of regionalism, and Tokyo's policy concentrated on promoting multilateral negotiations, such as the talks in the WTO. In fact, regionalization had already made considerable progress, as witnessed by the development of regional supply chains in East Asia after the 1985 Plaza Accord on currency realignment, following the rapid appreciation of the value of the yen and the resulting direct investment by Japanese companies. Nonetheless, Tokyo remained skeptical of regionalism, and few such schemes were realized. But with moves to promote regional economic integration spreading around the world, it became clear that the risks of region-building efforts were more than offset by the advantages of expanded trade and investment.

In this context, Japan for the first time gave consideration to a regional arrangement, collaborating with Singapore on a joint study on a free trade agreement.[21] Prompting the shift in direction was the background setting in 1998 and 1999, when APEC's plans for sectoral liberalization were making little progress and the WTO's bid to launch a new round ended in failure, with Singapore seeking to set up bilateral FTAs in East Asia. The discussions on signing a bilateral FTA with Singapore marked a major turning point in Japan's trade policy, which ceased to require that all arrangements be in line with the multilateral WTO format. Regional integration became the new catchphrase.

On the occasion of the currency crisis, Tokyo approved vast infusions of financial assistance to reduce the distress in Southeast Asian nations, where many Japanese companies were operating. In the years that followed, however, delay in the recovery of the Japanese economy diminished to some extent its presence in East Asia. But Japan appeared to be winning its battle to halt a long period of deflation, and Japanese companies made an earnest attempt to get involved in overseas businesses once again. Accordingly, Japan's corporations and overseas subsidiaries were ready to rebuild their Asian strategies when FTA activity moved into full swing.

In October 2001, not long after this shift in trade policy, Japan and Singapore made major progress in their negotiations for an EPA. It was officially signed in January 2002 and entered into force in November the same year.[22] As an economic partnership agreement, it goes beyond the scope of an FTA, which basically just liberalizes trade. Among other provisions, it provides for mutual cooperation in the fields of information technology, human resources development, and trade and investment facilitation. These include measures for investment rules, mutual recognition of standards, and digitalizing trade procedures. Because the agreement emphasizes harmonization of systems as well as trade liberalization, it was named the "Japan-Singapore New Age Economic Partnership Agreement".

This agreement marked the start of serious work on bilateral FTAs in East Asia. It also triggered political decisions in China and ASEAN to open negotiations on a regional FTA. The opening of talks between China and ASEAN in turn prompted a Japanese response, and one year later, in November 2002, Japan and ASEAN adopted a joint declaration on realizing a comprehensive economic partnership within the next ten years.[23] In other words, the Japan-Singapore EPA touched off a chain reaction that prompted Beijing to swing into action and encouraged Tokyo to step up its economic collaboration with ASEAN.

When Japan began to consider additional EPAs with ASEAN, it had to choose between prioritizing bilateral EPAs with individual Southeast Asian nations or concentrating on a single EPA covering all of ASEAN's members. In contrast to the Chinese approach, Japan opted to work first on bilateral EPAs with the original ASEAN members including Malaysia, the Philippines, and Thailand. This seemed a reasonable approach because it built on the high-level bilateral agreement Japan had already arranged with Singapore. Another consideration was that if Japan tried to secure agreement from all the ASEAN members, countries that were not keen on liberalization might drag their feet, resulting in a low-level agreement that merely paid lip service to the highest common factors.

As a result of its decision to prioritize bilateral EPAs, however, Tokyo came in for criticism, mostly from ASEAN members that were not yet ready for EPA talks. Their concern was that the Japanese policy approach might drive a wedge into ASEAN's economic integration. A further concern concerned the supply from Japan of high-value-added parts that ASEAN members were unable to manufacture (plasma panels, for example). There were worries that shipments of the assembled finished products (plasma TVs) to markets within the ASEAN region might not be eligible for the reduced tariff rates under bilateral FPAs and the AFTA agreement.

It was in this context that Japan and ASEAN issued their joint declaration to establish a regional AJCEP.[24] Negotiations between Japan and ASEAN got underway two-and-a-half years later, in April 2005. The accord was signed and went into force in 2008, as previously noted.[25] That was after both China and South Korea had finalized their own FTAs with ASEAN but before the FTAs between ASEAN and Australia/New Zealand and between ASEAN and India went into effect.

TRENDS TOWARD INTRA- AND INTER-REGIONAL ECONOMIC INTEGRATION IN EAST ASIA

ASEAN+3 cooperation may have begun with a ministerial meeting held at Japan's initiative, but it was a proposal from China — which had taken the lead by negotiating its own FTA with ASEAN — that set in motion the first formal study for an East Asia Free Trade Agreement (EAFTA).[26] Later Japan countered with its own proposal for an ASEAN+6 economic framework (dubbed the Comprehensive Economic Partnership in East Asia). This decision reflected the evolving economic reality inside and outside the region, as well as changing relations among the key parties. Meanwhile, the United States began promoting a Free Trade Area of the Asia-Pacific (FTAAP) that would cover all APEC countries.

Moves toward economic integration of the ASEAN+3 countries can be traced all the way back to 1990, when Malaysian Prime Minister Mahathir Mohamad floated his vision for an East Asia Economic Group, a concept later modified and renamed the East Asia Economic Caucus.[27] This ultimately led to the idea of an East Asian Community. At the time, some in Japan urged Tokyo to support Mahathir's initiative in the interests of Asian economic integration. But Washington opposed the idea, warning that it would "draw a line down the Pacific" and lead to a schism between Japan and the United States, and the plan never materialized. Efforts toward East Asian economic integration resumed in 1996, when Japan convened a ministerial meeting of the ASEAN countries, plus Japan, China, and South Korea, on the occasion of the first Asia-Europe Meeting (ASEM).

ASEAN+3 dialogue and cooperation officially began in 1997, when the leaders of Japan, China, and South Korea were invited to attend the ASEAN Informal Summit held to mark the 30th anniversary of ASEAN. This was the first ASEAN+3 Summit. It was the year the East Asian financial crisis broke out, and this time Washington raised no objections to a multilateral East Asian framework for addressing the region's financial and currency problems. Indeed, the currency crisis and the immediate and long-term challenges it posed for the region were the main items on the agenda at the first ASEAN+3 Summit.[28] On this occasion, the ASEAN leaders expressed high hopes for Japan's role in regional cooperation. At the 2002 summit, the East Asia Study Group (EASG) released its final report, recommending a number of high-priority and relatively feasible short-term and medium-to-long-term measures to advance East Asian economic integration.[29] Among the medium- and long-term measures were recommendations to inaugurate an East Asia Summit and to begin exploring an EAFTA.

The period following the 2002 ASEAN+3 Summit and the release of the EASG report saw a variety of international cooperation projects implemented according to the recommendations of the report. But it also witnessed structural changes in the region's economic environment. These included the ongoing de facto economic integration in East Asia, the maturation of the ASEAN Free Trade Area (AFTA), progress in negotiations for bilateral and multilateral FTAs and EPAs, and the emergence of region-wide problems requiring concerted action (rising resource prices, environmental problems, sustainable growth, etc.). At the 2007 ASEAN+3 Summit, commemorating the tenth anniversary of ASEAN+3 cooperation, the leaders issued their Second Joint Statement on East Asia Cooperation, outlining the basic direction for regional cooperation in the future.[30] Under the heading of Economic and Financial Cooperation, the ASEAN+3 agreed to work toward economic integration and free trade, pursue structural reforms, encourage investment, promote transfer of technology, protect intellectual property rights, build research and policy-making capacity, multilateralize the Chiang Mai Initiative, and strengthen the Asian Bond Markets Initiative.

The negotiation of an EAFTA was one of the medium- to long-term recommendations of the 2002 EASG report. In 2004, China took an important step in that direction by calling for an EAFTA feasibility study by a panel of experts from the private sector. Agreeing to launch a two-year study, the ASEAN+3 set up a Joint Expert Group for Feasibility Study on EAFTA in line with China's proposal. In its final report, submitted in August 2006, the group recommended: (1) that ASEAN+3 leaders begin work on forming an EAFTA with the goal of completing the agreement by 2016 and admitting Cambodia, Laos, Myanmar, and Vietnam by 2020; (2) that the EAFTA begin within the framework of the ASEAN+3 but should remain open to the possibility of participation by countries in neighboring regions, including Australia, New Zealand, and India; (3) that the EAFTA should be a high-quality, comprehensive agreement going beyond existing bilateral and ASEAN+1 FTAs and achieving substantial liberalization in all sectors; and (4) that liberalization be accompanied by economic cooperation, including aid to the region's developing nations, to help lower trade barriers, build capacity, and so forth.[31]

In accordance with the EASG's recommendations and other proposals, the first East Asia Summit was held in Kuala Lumpur in December 2005, attended by Australia, New Zealand, and India, as well as the ASEAN+3 countries. Among the items on the agenda was the concept of an East Asian Community that would aim to bring about regional integration in the political, economic, and security spheres. At this time, the debate turned on whether the East Asia Summit (EAS) or the ASEAN+3 Summit should take the lead in regional community building in East Asia.[32] Japan, India, Australia, and New Zealand took the position that the EAS was part of the community-building process and should hold substantive discussions on the building of an East Asian Community. China and Malaysia led the opposition to this approach, insisting that the EAS was not intended for discussions on forming an East Asian Community, which should take place within the ASEAN+3 framework. The standoff reflects a basic difference of perception between Beijing, which sees the ASEAN+3 framework as an opportunity to increase China's influence over ASEAN unchecked by the United States, and Japan, which seeks to liberalize trade with less China's influence by including India, Australia, and New Zealand in the community-building process.

In August 2006, immediately after the Joint Expert Group submitted its recommendations for an EAFTA, Japan called for a panel of scholars and other experts to study the feasibility and merits of a 16-member ASEAN+6 economic partnership including Australia, New Zealand, and India — the Comprehensive Economic Partnership in East Asia (CEPEA). The aim was to make economic cooperation in East Asia more comprehensive and open to the outside world. Although China and South Korea opposed the idea, insisting that the community-building process remain within the ASEAN+3 framework, the ASEAN countries argued that the best way to further East Asian economic integration was to pursue the economic integration of ASEAN and conclude separate ASEAN+1 FTAs and EPAs with various partners. In the end, it was agreed that the ASEAN+3 would set up a high-level working group to look further into the EAFTA concept proposed by the Joint Expert Group.[33] Meanwhile, thanks to strong support from the ASEAN countries, the ASEAN+6 agreed in principle to Japan's proposal for a joint study by academics and other experts on a CEPEA.[34]

The CEPEA initiative seeks to bundle the various EPAs and FTAs concluded separately between ASEAN and its partners — Japan, China,

South Korea, India, Australia, and New Zealand — into a comprehensive, high-quality 16-nation EPA embracing tariff reductions, investment liberalization, and protection for intellectual property rights. Given the role of direct investment in powering the region's economic growth, such an agreement cannot be limited to trade in goods. The CEPEA would also cover investment, as well as trade in services, intellectual property rights, and economic cooperation.[35] The main aims of the CEPEA initiative are to promote further development of the region's vertically specialized production networks in the manufacturing sector, to build a regional market economy based on freedom and fairness, in which all players observe the rules, and to support ASEAN's role as the driver of wider economic integration while encouraging the dynamism to extend this integration to include other partners involved in the region.

At the same time, meaningful and effective economic integration will require not only an agreement on rules and systems for free trade and investment but also a mechanism to oversee and guide the process of integration. Accordingly, when Japan proposed the CEPEA in 2006, it also called for the creation of a regional organ to provide intellectual support for East Asian economic integration: the Economic Research Institute for ASEAN and East Asia (ERIA).[36]

In order to harmonize its diverse systems and coordinate its response to common challenges, East Asia needs an international mechanism that can move quickly and flexibly to facilitate the adoption and implementation of compatible policies. At present, however, the only mechanisms for economic integration are the very loose, cooperative framework of the EAS, on the one hand, and the tightly binding rules of FTAs and EPAs, on the other. We need an intermediary approach based on policy coordination to deal flexibly with issues as they arise. Japan proposed the establishment of the ERIA as a region-wide organization comparable to the OECD. This would collect and publish statistics, make policy recommendations, and help coordinate and harmonize policies in such matters as trade, investment, industrial policy, energy, the environment, industrial standards and certification, and protection of intellectual property rights. ERIA's research activities are expected to encompass trade and investment, intellectual property and industrial standards and certification, environment and energy, logistics and infrastructure, as well as SMEs and human resources. After its official establishment, ERIA set to work holding symposiums and sponsoring contract research on a wide range of topics. The initial aim is to identify the most urgent issues and those requiring more in-depth study. The focus will then shift to working groups and finally to submitting policy recommendations.[37]

As we have seen, trends in East Asian economic integration have proceeded in a concentric fashion, beginning with ASEAN and gradually expanding through separate ASEAN+1 agreements, the ASEAN+3 framework, and finally the ASEAN+6 concept. Meanwhile, incipient efforts toward an economic integration in the broader Asia-Pacific region are also under way.

As early as 2004 the APEC Business Advisory Council suggested that the forum consider the idea of an APEC-wide FTA.[38] But concerns over feasibility, as well as the potential impact on negotiations for the WTO Doha Development Agenda, delayed any serious consideration at the government level. All of this changed after Japan's 2006 proposal for a CEPEA (embracing all the ASEAN+6 countries) and an ERIA. Shortly after this, at Washington's initiative, APEC agreed to begin exploring prospects for a Free Trade Area of the Asia-Pacific (FTAAP).[39] WTO negotiations had stalled, and Washington seemed to have grown alarmed by moves toward East Asian economic integration that the United States might not participate in.

Serious economic and political obstacles stand in the way of economic integration of the entire Asia-Pacific region, given that the region includes countries at widely disparate levels of economic and social development and political system. But momentum is building behind efforts to use existing economic agreements among smaller groups of Pacific Rim countries as the building blocks for a larger FTA that could ultimately encompass the entire region. One promising initiative would use the Trans-Pacific Strategic Economic Partnership concluded by Singapore, New Zealand, Brunei, and Chile in 2005 (also known as the P4) as the basis for a larger Trans-Pacific Partnership (TPP) encompassing the United States, Australia, Peru, and others.[40]

Japan faced a tough political decision regarding its role in the FTAAP process during the months when it hosted the 2010 APEC ministerial meeting and economic leaders' meeting to assess progress toward the Bogor goals and adopt new targets. Tokyo needs to consider how the process of participating in the TPP and FTAAP in the long term will mesh with ASEAN+3 and ASEAN+6 integration efforts, and how it will liberalize and facilitate trade and investment with major countries of the Asia-Pacific region, such as China and the United States, in the interim. Given the ever-growing role of the "triangular trade" model, in which East Asia's vertically specialized production networks manufacture goods for export to the United States and Europe, the idea of extending economic integration to countries outside the East Asian region is sure to draw increasing attention in the years ahead.

POSSIBLE THRUSTS FOR DEEPER REGIONAL INTEGRATION

In this section, we discuss five effective measures for promoting deeper regional integration in East Asia, namely: (1) comprehensive support for developing infrastructures; (2) fostering middle-class communities and deepening international exchanges among them; (3) creating a new mechanism for regional economic development; (4) resolving energy and environmental issues; and (5) developing high-level comprehensive FTAs. We will examine each of these measures with special reference to Japan's role. Further economic integration in East Asia requires development of infrastructure, in both physical and "soft" forms. Here we look at each of these in some detail.

The expansion of multinational corporations' networks of production, procurement, and sales in East Asia has led to the progress of de facto economic integration in East Asia. Against this background, it is necessary to develop cross-border physical infrastructure, which will contribute substaintially to industrial development and the improvement of logistics in East Asia. Specifically, master plans should be formulated to develop the India-Mekong Industrial Corridor, which will enhance connectivity between India and the Mekong subregion (mainland Southeast Asia), and to develop the BIMP-EAGA, which consists of island Southeast Asia.[41] In addition, it is important to develop nodal cities and relevant industrial and logistic infrastructure in Hanoi and Ho Chi Minh City, the Jakarta Metropolitan Area of Indonesia, and the Chennai-Bangalore Industrial Corridor, which form the nodes of regional industrial and infrastructure development in East Asia.

ASEAN faces various issues, including a delay in liberalization as well as in facilitation and system harmonization. Harmonization of economic institutions, such as those for intellectual property rights, standards and conformance, and customs procedures, is indispensable for realizing seamless economic activities in the region. Problems such as the lack of system harmonization and delays in the liberalization of service industries have more serious repercussions in ASEAN than in China, Japan, and South Korea. Trade facilitation, harmonization of economic systems, and liberalization of the service market would oblige ASEAN to commit itself to the acceleration of economic integration.

In the case of China, it is widely recognized that China has succeeded in establishing a free economic system by entering into the WTO, but has not yet secured a level playing field for foreign investors. According to a JETRO survey on the problems experienced by Japanese companies in operating in the trade and investment environment in China, among the priority issues that need to be tackled are the insufficiency and unpredictability of the legislation and tax systems, unfair enforcement and non-uniformity in the legislation system, infringement of intellectual property rights, and restrictions on currency exchange and remittances.[42] Taking these points into consideration, it is imperative to develop a soft infrastructure, including an antimonopoly law, intellectual property rights, a judicial system, corporate governance, and information disclosure, so as to guarantee free business activities.

In addition, Japan has comparative advantages in business practices and know-how, including the fostering of skilled labor, trade practices, and the development of supporting industries, as well as in economic systems and policy measures including IT skill standards, SME policies, energy conservation, recycling methods, and logistics standards. It is to be hoped that Japan will conceptualize these practices and systems and share them with East Asian countries as possible regional standards.[43]

With a view to fostering a new middle class, it is important to create transparent and participatory systems in terms of politics, the economy, and society. For instance, the development of a sustainable economy and society is expected to be achieved through the strengthening of the economic/legal infrastructure, including financial sector reforms (above all, the disposal of non-performing loans), as well as improvements in bankruptcy and antimonopoly legislation for a fair and competitive environment. These have become important issues ever since the Asian currency crisis of 1997. It will also be crucial to develop human and management resources through the promotion of small- and medium-sized enterprises; human resources development in the field of information technology; and educational reforms. In addition, development of transparent and fair tax systems and social security systems are likely to lead to the improvement of economic and social stability.

In order to realize regional integration in East Asia, it is more important than ever to deepen international exchanges not only between young people who carry the future of Asia in their hands, but also between educated middle-class people who share a similar lifestyle and values. It is imperative for Japan to: (1) promote the globalization of universities, research institutes, and personnel; (2) enhance international competitiveness in tourism and services to attract foreign visitors; and (3) convey Japanese culture and branding to the rest of East Asia.[44]

It is important to establish a policy coordination mechanism for economic integration in East Asia. Examples include financial cooperation schemes, for example the Chiang Mai Initiative, that were developed to address emergent financial problems caused by large external shocks such as the Asian currency crisis. One of the most important challenges facing East Asia is the establishment of a policy coordination mechanism that harmonizes economic policies and systems from a mid- to long-term perspective. An example is discussions on how to mobilize savings for investment in this region through the Asian Bond Market Initiative and the Asian Infrastructure Fund, so as to realize sustainable growth. While East Asian countries established and utilized the Economic Research Institute for ASEAN and East Asia (ERIA) for regional economic policy formulation, the ASEAN+3 and +6 frameworks, under which various ministerial meetings have been established, should be reorganized to function in practical terms as a policy coordination mechanism. A permanent policy coordination mechanism can be expected to play a useful role in harmonizing economic policies and systems in East Asia in the future.

Lately, the international energy market has been tight because Chinese demand for energy has risen swiftly as a result of rapid economic growth and energy-consuming manufacturing plants and equipment in China. Japan has proactively implemented energy cooperation with Asian countries in such areas as energy conservation, new energy, clean coal technology, oil stockpiling, and nuclear energy.[45] It has also promoted environmental cooperation aimed at limiting emissions of CO_2 and SO_2, and at accelerating the creation of a recycling-oriented society. China and Japan should continuously carry out joint cooperative projects in the areas of energy and the environment under the framework of ASEAN+3 and the East Asia Summit. Cooperation in these areas could make an important contribution toward the building of mutual economic and political trust in the region.

Modalities of bilateral FTAs in East Asia may well need to be reviewed. For instance, China has been trying to be proactive and expeditious as regards the negotiations of the ASEAN-China FTA. However, so far, it has focused mainly on trade liberalization, and has taken a longer time to proceed with negotiations in such important areas as trade in services and investment. It was also apparent that important items related to the automobile and electronics industries were excluded from normal track negotiations.

Efforts should now be made to apply the brakes on the proliferation of low-level FTAs in the region in order to realize comprehensive and high-level economic integration in terms of trade and investment liberalization and facilitation. In the medium and long term, East Asian countries might explore the possibilities of realizing FTAs under the framework of EAS and APEC, in cooperation with the United States and Australia, both of which are promoters of high-level liberalization and rule-making in trade and investment.

Notes

1   <http://www.meti.go.jp/english/report/downloadfiles/2008WhitePaper/3-5.pdf>.
2   <http://www.asean.org/communities/asean-economic-community/item/framework-agreement-on-comprehensive-economic-co-operation-between-asean-and-the-people-s-republic-of-china-phnom-penh-4-november-2002-3>.
3   <http://www.asean.org/news/item/chairman-s-statement-of-the-8th-asean-3-summit-vientiane-29-november-2004>.
4   <http://www.asean.org/news/item/asean-japan-summit-phnom-penh-5-november-2002-joint-declaration-of-the-leaders-of-asean-and-japan-on-the-comprehensive-economic-partnership-2>.
5   <http://www.asean.org/news/item/chairman-s-statement-of-the-second-east-asia-summit-cebu-philippines-15-january-2007>.
6   <http://www.apec.org/Meeting-Papers/Leaders-Declarations/2006/2006_aelm.aspx>.
7   <http://www.china-asean-fund.com/>.
8   <http://www.kantei.go.jp/foreign/asospeech/2009/04/09speech_e.html>.
9   <http://www.meti.go.jp/english/report/downloadfiles/2011WhitePaper/3-1.pdf>.
10 <http://www.meti.go.jp/english/report/downloadfiles/gWP2004ke.pdf>.
11 <http://en.wikipedia.org/wiki/Socialist_Harmonious_Society>.
12 <http://www.meti.go.jp/english/report/downloadfiles/2012WhitePaper/2-2.pdf>.
13 It has been pointed out that, at the time of the Asian currency crisis, Asian countries were faced with a variety of issues concerning the need for corporate and financial sector reform. These included enhancing the functions of financial institutions, promoting small business finance, developing domestic bond markets, strengthening the enforcement of bankruptcy law, and improving corporate governance.
14 Malaysia delayed the introduction of tariff reductions on completed cars and the Philippines delayed tariff reductions on petrochemicals under the Common Effective Preferential Tariff (CEPT) Scheme for the AFTA.

15   <http://www.asean.org/news/item/asean-vision-2020>.

16   <http://www.asean.org/news/item/statement-on-bold-measures-6th-asean-summit-hanoi-16-december-1998>.

17   <http://www.asean.org/asean/external-relations/asean-3/item/asean-plus-three-cooperation>.

18   <http://www.asean.org/news/item/declaration-of-asean-concord-ii-bali-concord-ii>.

19   <http://www.asean.org/news/item/chairman-s-statement-of-the-13th-asean-summit-one-asean-at-the-heart-of-dynamic-asia-singapore-20-november-2007>.

20   <http://www.asean.org/images/archive/agreements/AJCEP/Agreement.pdf>.

21   <http://www.meti.go.jp/english/information/data/cJSEPA1e.html>.

22   <http://www.meti.go.jp/english/policy/external_economy/trade/FTA_EPA/epa_sing1_e.pdf>.

23   <http://www.asean.org/images/2013/economic/afta/AJFTA/2-%202002%20-%20Joint%20Declaration%20on%20CEP.pdf>.

24   <http://www.asean.org/news/item/asean-japan-summit-phnom-penh-5-november-2002-joint-declaration-of-the-leaders-of-asean-and-japan-on-the-comprehensive-economic-partnership-2>.

25   <http://www.asean.org/images/archive/agreements/AJCEP/Agreement.pdf>.

26   <http://www.asean.org/news/item/chairman-s-statement-of-the-8th-asean-3-summit-vientiane-29-november-2004>.

27   <http://en.wikipedia.org/wiki/East_Asia_Economic_Caucus>.

28   <http://www.asean.org/news/item/asean-plus-three-cooperation>.

29   <http://www.asean.org/images/archive/pdf/easg.pdf>.

30   <http://www.asean.org/news/item/second-joint-statement-on-east-asia-cooperation-building-on-the-foundations-of-asean-plus-three-cooperation>.

31   <http://www.thaifta.com/thaifta/Portals/0/eafta_report.pdf>.

32   <http://www.asean.org/news/item/external-relations-asean-3-chairman-s-statement-of-the-ninth-asean-plus-three-summit-kuala-lumpur-12-december-2005 http://www.asean.org/news/item/chairman-s-statement-of-the-first-east-asia-summit-kuala-lumpur-14-december-2005-2>.

33   <http://www.mofa.go.jp/region/asia-paci/asean/conference/asean3/state0701.html>.

34   <http://www.asean.org/news/item/chairman-s-statement-of-the-second-east-asia-summit-cebu-philippines-15-january-2007>.

35   <http://www.thaifta.com/thaifta/Portals/0/cepea_report.pdf>.

36   <http://www.eria.org/>.

37   <http://www.eria.org/about_eria/basic.html>.

38   <http://publications.apec.org/publication-detail.php?pub_id=459>.

39   <http://www.apec.org/Meeting-Papers/Leaders-Declarations/2006/2006_aelm.aspx>.

40   <http://www.sice.oas.org/TPD/TPP/TPP_e.asp>.

41   <http://www.eria.org/RPR-2009-7-1.pdf>.

[42] <http://www.jetro.go.jp/en/reports/survey/pdf/2012_03_01_biz.pdf>.
[43] <http://www.meti.go.jp/english/topic/downloadfiles/GlobalEconomicStrategy (Summary).pdf>.
[44] <http://www.meti.go.jp/english/topic/downloadfiles/GlobalEconomicStrategy (Summary).pdf>.
[45] <http://www.meti.go.jp/press/2012/04/20120423002/20120423002-3.pdf>.
<http://www.meti.go.jp/press/2012/09/20120913002/20120913002-4.pdf>.

References

APEC Secretariat. "Bridging the Pacific: Coping with the Challenges of Globalization, APEC Business Advisory Council Report to APEC Economic Leaders 2004". December 2004.

———. "Leaders' Declaration, Ha Noi Declaration — Towards a Dynamic Community for Sustainable Development and Prosperity". November 2006.

ASEAN Secretariat. "ASEAN VISION 2020". December 1997.

———. "Statement on Bold Measures". 6th ASEAN Summit, Hanoi. 16 December 1998.

———. "Framework Agreement on Comprehensive Economic Co-Operation between ASEAN and the People's Republic of China". Phnom Penh, 4 November 2002.

———. "Final Report of the East Asia Study Group". November 2002.

———. "ASEAN-Japan Summit Joint Declaration of the Leaders of ASEAN and Japan on the Comprehensive Economic Partnership". Phnom Penh. 5 November 2002.

———. "Declaration of ASEAN Concord II (Bali Concord II)". October 2003.

———. "Chairman's Statement of the 8th ASEAN + 3 Summit". Vientiane. 29 November 2004.

———. "Chairman's Statement of the Ninth ASEAN Plus Three Summit". Kuala Lumpur. 12 December 2005.

———. "Chairman's Statement of the First East Asia Summit". Kuala Lumpur. 14 December 2005.

———. "Towards an East Asia FTA: Modality and Road Map — A Report by Joint Expert Group for Feasibility Study on EAFTA". July 2006.

———. "Chairman's Statement of the Tenth ASEAN Plus Three Summit". Cebu, Philippines. 14 January 2007.

———. "Chairman's Statement of the Second East Asia Summit". Cebu, Philippines. 15 January 2007.

———. "Chairman's Statement of the 13th ASEAN Summit: One ASEAN at the Heart of Dynamic Asia". Singapore, 20 November 2007.

———. "Second Joint Statement on East Asia Cooperation Building on the Foundations of ASEAN Plus Three Cooperation". November 2007.

————. "Agreement on Comprehensive Economic Partnership among Japan and Member States of the Association of South Asian Nations". April 2008.

————. "Report of the Track Two Study Group on Comprehensive Economic Partnership in East Asia (CEPEA)". June 2008.

————. "Overview — ASEAN Plus Three Cooperation". October 2012.

Aso, Taro. "Japan's Future Development Strategy and Growth Initiative Towards Doubling the Size of Asia's Economy". April 2009.

Economic Research Institute for ASEAN and East Asia (ERIA). "The Comprehensive Asia Development Plan". October 2010.

Japan, Ministry of Economy, Trade and Industry. "Agreement between Japan and the Republic of Singapore for a New-age Economic Partnership". January 2002.

————. "White Paper on International Trade". June 2004.

————. "White Paper on International Trade". July 2005.

————. "Global Economic Strategy". April 2006.

————. "New Economic Growth Strategy". June 2006.

————. "White Paper on International Trade". August 2008.

————. "White Paper on International Trade". July 2011.

————. "Joint Ministerial Statement of the Fifth East Asian Summit Energy Ministers Meeting". September 2011.

————. "Joint Ministerial Statement of the Sixth East Asian Summit Energy Ministers Meeting". September 2012.

————. "White Paper on International Trade". September 2012.

Japan, JETRO (Japan External Trade Organization). "The Current Situation of ASEAN Economic Community (AEC) and Changes in the Business Environment". February 2006.

————. "FY2011 Survey on the International Operations of Japanese Firms — JETRO Overseas Business Survey". March 2012.

Mori, Kazuko. "Higashi Asia Community Ni Do Approach Suru Ka" [How Should We Approach East Asian Community?]. *Asia Kenkyu* 51, no. 2 (2005).

Otsuji, Yoshihiro and Takashi Shiraishi. "Nihon-ASEAN No Kakudai FTA O Teisho Suru" [Building Closer Ties with ASEAN]. *Chuo Koron* 117, no. 2 (2002): 68–76.

9

MANAGING INTEGRATION IN EAST ASIA: BEHIND BORDER ISSUES IN JAPAN-ASEAN TRADE AGREEMENTS

Yose Rizal Damuri

INTRODUCTION

Economic integration in East Asia has been undergoing a massive trans-formation for more than a decade. The search for markets, combined with a quest for low-cost production sites, has resulted in a set of formal trade agreements — at the regional, plurilateral, and bilateral levels — among countries in the region. Not only the number of trade agreements but also their content has evolved to cover various aspects aside from trade liberalization. This transformation reflects the complexity of problems surrounding economic integration in East Asia, as well as the need for better governance and discipline.

When talking about regional economic integration and the rise of regionalism in East Asia, one cannot neglect the importance of economic relations between Japan and Southeast Asian countries. Market-driven integration in the region was initiated, to a large extent, by the economic relations of Japanese business groups with their ASEAN counterparts. The relations created networks of trade, production, investment, and services spanning across developing countries of ASEAN and later included other countries in East Asia. Formal economic cooperation and trade agreements between Japan and ASEAN countries, at the regional and bilateral levels, also set the practice of including new features of free trade agreements (FTAs) known as behind-border issues (BBIs). BBIs include provisions on investments, competition policy, intellectual property rights, and other non-trade issues. The inclusion of BBIs into ASEAN-Japan FTAs created a 21st century regionalism that is different from the relationships created by traditional trade agreements.

This paper is an attempt to examine regional economic integration in East Asia, particularly between Japan and ASEAN countries, and how it has evolved into 21st century regionalism. The premise is that economic relations, while initiated by market forces, require some kind of management to address emerging issues and problems. This can be delivered by providing various elements within the framework of FTAs.

We begin the analysis by looking at the nature of economic relations between Japan and ASEAN countries and how formal trade agreements emerged. This is done through both historical and analytical assessment. We then explore more technical details of trade agreements by looking at various new behind-border issues in FTAs between Japan and ASEAN countries and place them in the context of implementing economic integration in the region. Some questions regarding the effectiveness of such implementation are also discussed in the paper before we close it with a conclusion and recommendation.

REGIONALISM IN EAST ASIA

Unlike regional integration in other areas of the world, where integration is driven mostly by government initiatives, the process in East Asia has taken place mainly in the form of trade and business relations, principally among Japanese multinationals and businesses in Southeast Asian countries. This has made formal regionalism in the region have the specific purpose to answer the increasing needs of market-driven economic integration. Here we look back on how regionalism has emerged in East Asia, and how trade agreements with deeper commitments were intended to answer the need for better governance of economic integration.

Market-Driven Integration: Internationalization of Production

East Asia has been known as one of the most integrated economic regions in the world. Countries in the region have been trading with each other for a long time. As can be observed from the trade statistics presented in Table 9.1, intra-regional trade dominated trade patterns in East Asian countries even in the early 1980s, accounting for up to more than 32 per cent of the countries' global trade. It is gaining even more importance over time, with the 2010 statistics showing that more than 40 per cent of the region's trade was conducted within the region. Stronger patterns of integration can be observed also in manufacturing, whose share of intra-regional trade has doubled within the last 30 years.

Trade relations between South East Asian countries and Japan have increased significantly within the last several decades. The relations go back to the early period of regional economic development in the 1970s. By the early 1980s, as shown in Table 9.1, trade between ASEAN and Japan dominated the trade pattern of countries in the southern part of the region. With around 15 per cent of Japan's total trade and 9 per cent of its manufacturing trade consisting of imports from and exports to ASEAN countries, the two economies have engaged in a dynamic reciprocal trade relationship. In later years the share declined slightly, particularly due to the emergence of China. But ASEAN countries' position in Japan's trade remains very important, as seen by its positive growth.

Statistics of trade between ASEAN countries and Japan tell only part of the story. Beyond trade statistics, the relationship between those economies takes complex forms, which involve (1) internationalization of production, (2) cross-border investments and subcontracting, (3) transfer of technology and know-how, and (4) trade in services. Many scholars have pointed out the development and importance of such networks of production in East Asia.[1] Richard Baldwin (2006) goes even further to refer to the network as "Factory Asia," where "conveyor belts" of production connect thousands of firms operating in various countries, many specializing in certain tasks of the production process.

Several indicators of internationalization of production also show that countries in East Asia are highly integrated. Using network analysis, Yose Rizal Damuri (2012a) shows that networks of production in the region have been developing rapidly since the 1980s, with Japan serving as the most important hub, particularly during the early period of the former's development. The vertical specialization index presented in Figure 9.1 shows that the region's index is relatively higher than other regions'. This index measures the share of production, in terms of intermediate inputs and value added, originating from overseas. The figure also shows that an important turning point in this trend occurred in the 1980s.

TABLE 9.1
East Asia's Trade Pattern 1981–2010

	1981			1991			2001			2010		
	ASEAN 6	Northeast Asia	Japan	ASEAN 6	Northeast Asia	Japan	ASEAN 6	Northeast Asia	Japan	ASEAN 6	Northeast Asia	Japan
Manufacturing												
ASEAN 6	10.2	35.5	28.6	16.2	30.6	21.7	21.3	29.4	16.2	22.3	35.7	12.2
ASEAN Countries	10.2	35.5	28.6	16.3	30.5	21.7	21.4	29.4	16.1	22.3	35.9	12.1
East Asia 15	8.1	20.0	10.2	10.4	30.0	11.4	13.8	32.6	11.4	13.6	35.9	9.6
Japan	8.9	10.8	0.0	11.0	15.1	0.0	14.0	23.1	0.0	13.9	36.7	0.0
Northeast Asia	7.7	16.3	5.9	8.6	29.8	8.2	10.8	33.9	9.5	10.9	35.9	8.9
Non-oil												
ASEAN 6	13.1	30.3	23.1	16.2	29.9	20.7	20.9	28.6	15.5	21.9	33.3	11.5
ASEAN Countries	13.1	30.3	23.1	16.3	29.8	20.7	21.1	28.6	15.5	21.9	33.5	11.5
East Asia 15	9.8	18.8	9.5	10.8	28.3	10.9	13.8	31.3	10.9	13.8	33.3	9.1
Japan	9.8	10.0	0.0	11.3	14.1	0.0	13.9	22.1	0.0	14.4	34.2	0.0
Northeast Asia	8.8	15.3	5.3	9.0	27.8	7.6	11.0	32.4	9.1	11.1	33.3	8.3
Total												
ASEAN 6	16.5	29.6	23.0	16.1	31.5	20.4	18.6	28.8	15.2	23.5	28.3	10.8
ASEAN Countries	16.5	29.6	23.0	16.3	32.0	20.9	19.0	29.1	15.3	23.7	28.5	10.7
East Asia 15	13.7	18.7	9.7	12.3	30.7	11.4	12.3	32.4	10.6	14.5	26.5	8.4
Japan	14.2	9.8	0.0	14.5	16.7	0.0	13.2	24.0	0.0	14.3	28.1	0.0
Northeast Asia	12.5	14.2	4.2	10.8	30.2	7.9	9.9	33.6	9.0	11.1	25.7	7.5

Source: Comtrade Database.

FIGURE 9.1
Vertical Specialization Index of Various Regions

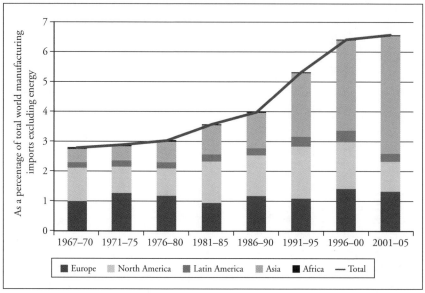

Source: Amador and Cabral (2008).

Internationalization of production can take two main forms: foreign direct investment (FDI) and cross-border subcontracting and outsourcing. In the first form, firms set up subsidiaries abroad to conduct certain production tasks, for instance, producing parts and components or performing assembly tasks. The tasks are organized directly by the principal firms or headquarters. Under a subcontracting arrangement, tasks are assigned to independent contractors outside the multinational companies and often take place in other countries. Whether multinationals choose FDI or subcontracting, there is an intensive transfer of technology. Subsidiaries and suppliers use designs and blueprints provided by the principal companies. The multinationals also make technical know-how and detailed production methods available to ensure high product quality.

The availability of an excellent services industry and appropriate organizational management are necessary to ensure that all production tasks are performed properly and that international linkages of the production units can take place in an efficient and timely manner. High-quality telecommunication services and information technology enable the communication and exchange of ideas between different production units and headquarters. Excellent transport and logistics services allow companies to ship parts and components as well as final products across borders to support further production processes or to meet consumer demands.

This kind of new arrangement — the so-called trade-investment-services nexus (Baldwin, 2011) — is easily observed among countries in East Asia. Again, internationalization of production in the region has been dominated by Japan and ASEAN member countries. Japanese multinationals are known to have set up their subsidiaries in Southeast Asian countries back in the 1970s (Figure 9.2), initially as a way to avoid trade barriers to serve the domestic market but later evolving to become suppliers of parts and components and important elements of regional production networks. Ando and Kimura (2009) documented the latter development of Japanese MNCs' activities in the region, not only holding and operating their own production units but also initiating subcontracting and outsourcing to domestic firms as well as companies in neighboring countries.

FIGURE 9.2
Japanese FDI Destinations (% of Outward FDI)

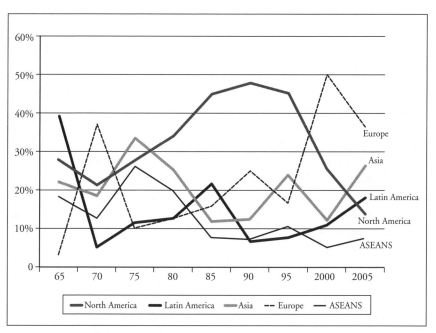

Source: Ministry of Finance Statistics.

From Market-Driven Integration to Governance

Market-based economic integration in East Asia has been so successful that it raises concerns regarding the sustainability of the region's gigantic network of economic and business relations. Initiatives to support economic relations were initially unilateral efforts by countries pursuing trade-related policies and reform they thought would best serve their interests. The most favoured nation (MFN) tariff rates of Indonesia and Thailand, for example, fell from around 25 per cent and 35 per cent (simple average) in the mid-1980s to 15 per cent and 23 per cent in 1995. Reforms in other areas of development also occurred in many countries in the region.

While these unilateral efforts have boosted economic development in the region, the lack of international commitment makes such an arrangement prone to disruption from countries backtracking on their reform process. For instance, Indonesia's average WTO bound rates remained at around 40 per cent in 1995. With countries having no binding commitment to the WTO's multilateral trade arrangement, unilateral tariff reduction in many countries of East Asia can be reversed easily. This happened during the Asian Financial Crisis of 1998, when Indonesia raised the import tariffs of several products to their WTO bound rates. In addition, further reforms of economic policy may need a certain amount of international cooperation to promote regional development even more. To address cross-border problems related to regional integration, some level of regulatory harmonization and coherence needs to be present at the regional level. We will take a more detailed look at this when talking about behind-border measures in trade agreements.

In the 1990s, virtually only ASEAN countries made an effort to create a free trade area in East Asia and to harmonize limited aspects of economic policies, such as investment and services. The lack of a formal regional arrangement was due to a combination of factors, ranging from a lack of vision to then sufficient unilateral actions, a lack of importance given to intra-regional economic relations by regional governments, and external pressure — mainly from the United States.[2] It is interesting to note that before the new millennium, Japan did not have a single treaty for investment protection — such treaties normally take the form of a bilateral investment treaty — with an East Asian country, while it had established intensive trade and investment relations for decades. Again, the lack of formal regionalism resulted in some difficulties during the Asian crisis and limited economic integration in the region.

Regionalism in East Asia entered a new phase when China announced its intention to have an FTA with ASEAN, which was implemented in 2003. Partly because of the domino effect and fear of trade diversions, other countries in the region — including Japan — started to embrace regionalism. This opened up an opportunity for Japan to address some problems related to market-driven integration with its counterparts. Economic and trade relations between Japan and other countries in the region have grown so extensive that they require a more harmonized international regulatory framework. Japan came up with a strategy of building comprehensive economic partnerships with ASEAN countries that went beyond traditional trade liberalization.

This was done by including various provisions and commitments on behind-border issues in an agreement between ASEAN member countries and Japan — the ASEAN Japan Economic Partnership Agreement. Those BBIs' provisions set international rules for various economic matters normally determined domestically. The agreement provides cross-border governance for trade, investment, and production relations between Japan and ASEAN countries. This move was followed by other countries in East Asia, including South Korea and Australia.

Before taking a look at such provisions in various trade agreements in East Asia, we describe briefly what actually defines BBIs. We also discuss how provisions in trade agreements can help in defining governance in regional integration.

BEHIND-BORDER ISSUES: AN OVERVIEW

Disciplining Integration: Importance of Behind-Border Issues in East Asia

A firm's objective in opening production bases and sourcing intermediate inputs overseas is to take advantage of geographical differences in price of production. While this strategy offers many advantages, it also brings up problems that do not exist with more conventional production activities. For example, a Japanese multinational willing to open up a subsidiary in a Southeast Asian country might find that its investments are exposed to many unfavorable business and legal practices.

One of the most significant problems is related to the protection of business activities. Multinational investors from capital-exporting countries feel the need to protect their assets against financial damage due to political risks in the host countries. Another crucial protection is related to intellectual property rights (IPR). Firms subcontracting work to suppliers in other countries may be required to share their proprietary knowledge, such as trademarks, industrial designs, and patents. The risk of losing valuable IPR assets increases as international production becomes a more substantial component of the production process.

There are also problems related with market failure, such as information asymmetry and anticompetitive behavior. Multinational firms are exposed to many difficulties, since contracts with input suppliers are normally "incomplete" and cannot specify all aspects of the business relation. This can lead to hold-up problems and may result in inefficient or low production. Parts and components produced by subcontracting suppliers need to conform to standards set by the contracting firm in the importing countries, where consumption takes place. Offshoring also has the potential to create new forms of anticompetitive behavior, since contracts between companies are normally long-term, non-competing, and exclusive. This may lead to an abuse of power by the final producers, who gain vertical market power.

Another type of market failure is international externalities. Knowledge spillover, leakage from lower regulatory standards, and the need for reliable infrastructure and information exchange are among the types of externalities that can occur at the international level; their significance becomes larger in international production networks.

With production networks in East Asia becoming larger and more complex, the above problems are becoming more prevalent. Multinationals operating such networks, usually from Japan and South Korea, find the risks increasing as they expand their production bases in countries such as the ASEAN nations and China. While the problem can be handled at the national level to some extent, international cooperation increases the effectiveness of actions. A country's attempt to adopt international best practice for investment protection and IPR, for example, is more compelling when it is made as part of an international commitment. A more harmonized framework for competition is needed in order to address international anticompetitive behaviors. Many trade liberalization and facilitation measures, such as agreements on customs procedures and standards, also need to be taken at the international level. An effective arrangement for production and trade, in short, requires new and deeper internationally accepted disciplines and governance.

This is where behind-border provisions in FTAs play an active role. These provisions offer the deeper disciplines required in international trade and production-sharing practices. While the best option is to go for multilateral agreements, the delay in the WTO's Doha Development Agenda has made countries pursue cross-border economic governance using regional agreements instead. The blueprint for the ASEAN Economic Community (AEC) signed in 2007, for example, provides for a deeper commitment that envisages a more coherent regulatory environment among the member countries. Comprehensive trade agreements between Japan and ASEAN countries also offer such systems of rules that were previously almost nonexistent between them.

What Constitute Behind-Border Issues?

BBIs' provisions in FTAs can cover a broad range of issues, from economic and commercial to political and social. Henrik Horn *et al.* (2010) have tried to define a complete list of provisions observed in FTAs involving the European Union and the United States. The list includes 52 provisions ranging from the conventional provision of tariff elimination to less common provisions such as corruption and social cooperation. Damuri (2012*b*) finds that among the 52 provisions, there are only 18 that are commonly found in trade agreements and have substantial commercial meaning. Of these, six can be categorized as behind-border commitments (Table 9.2). We will briefly discuss some of these important new features of FTAs.

Provisions on investment protection and policy seek to apply national treatment principles to the investment interests of foreign firms. These provisions may include various types of prohibition, a subrogation clause, and a state-investor dispute-settlement mechanism. Investment provision is among the most extensive areas of commercial regulation found in FTAs.

Provisions on IPR seek to ensure returns on intellectual property by promoting international standards and preventing/dissuading from counterfeiting and piracy. Such provisions include protection on copyright and related rights, trademarks, patents, and geographical indications. The focus on improved enforcement in partner countries is particularly strong and typically requires legal and institutional changes in the partner countries.

Provisions on competition policy force trade partners to conform to the general principles of open and competitive domestic markets. This often involves the introduction of new domestic legislation on competition law, or a whole new competition policy program. The same spirit can be found in provisions on state-owned enterprises (SOEs), which attach importance to more competitive behaviors and treatments toward SOEs.

TABLE 9.2
"Core" Provisions of Regional Trade Agreements

Provisions	Description	Category
FTA industrial goods (FTA ind.)	Tariff liberalization; elimination of non-tariff measures on industrial goods	Border-Tariff
FTA agricultural goods (FTA agr.)	Tariff liberalization; elimination of non-tariff measures on agricultural goods	Border-Tariff
Customs administration	Provision of information; publication on the Internet of new laws and regulations; training	Border-Non-Tariff
Export taxes	Elimination of export taxes	Border-Non-Tariff
Sanitary and phytosanitary (SPS measures)	Affirmation of rights and obligations under the WTO Agreement on SPS; harmonization of SPS measures	Border-Non-Tariff
Technical barriers to trade (TBT)	Affirmation of rights and obligations under WTO Agreement on TBT; provision of information; harmonization of regulations; mutual recognition agreements	Border-Non-Tariff
State trading enterprises (STE)	Establishment or maintenance of an independent competition authority; nondiscrimination regarding production and marketing conditions; provision of information; affirmation of Art XVII GATT provisions	Behind-Border protection
Antidumping (AD)	Retention of AD rights and obligations under the WTO Agreement (Art. VI GATT)	Border-Tariff
Countervailing measures (CVM)	Retention of CVM rights and obligations under the WTO Agreement (Art VI GATT)	Border-Tariff
State aid	Assessment of anticompetitive behavior; annual reporting on the value and distribution of state aid given; provision of information.	Behind-Border protection

Provisions	Description	Category
Public procurement	Progressive liberalization; national treatment and/or nondiscrimination principle; publication of laws and regulations on the Internet; specification of public procurement regime	Behind-Border Market Access
Trade-related investment measures (TRIMs)	Provisions concerning requirements for local content and export performance on foreign direct investment	Border-Tariff
Trade-related intellectual property rights (TRIPs)	Harmonization of standards; enforcement; national treatment, most favored nation treatment	Border-Tariff
GATS	Liberalization of trade in services	Behind-Border Market Access
Competition policy	Maintenance of measures to proscribe anticompetitive business conduct; harmonization of competition laws; establishment or maintenance of an independent competition authority	Behind-Border protection
Investment	Information exchange; development of legal frameworks; harmonization and simplification of procedures; national treatment; mechanisms for settlement of disputes	Behind-Border protection
Movement of capital	Liberalization of capital movement; prohibition of new restrictions	Border-Non-Tariff
Intellectual Property Rights (IPR)	Accession to international treaties not referenced in the TRIPs Agreement	Behind-Border protection

Source: Damuri (2012*b*).

BEHIND-BORDER ISSUES IN JAPAN AND
ASEAN TRADE AGREEMENTS

In this section we examine the pattern of commitments in some FTAs in
East Asia. The focus of the discussion is trade agreements between Japan
and ASEAN members, although for the sake of comparison other ASEAN
FTAs are discussed. We examine the depth of commitments based on
provisional areas discussed in the text of agreements and evaluate whether
they are deep enough to provide a set of internationally accepted disciplines
considered in the previous section.

How Deep Are the Commitments?

Table 9.3 presents commitments in FTAs between Japan and ASEAN
members. Traditional border provisions, such as tariff elimination and
rules of origin, appear on all agreements between those trading partners,
including in an agreement where ASEAN acts as a single trading partner.
More recent and complex issues on border barriers are also discussed in
many agreements. Commitments to eliminate barriers on trade in services
and to regulate non-tariff measures can also be found in those series of
agreements, although the contents vary among them.

Some behind-border issues can virtually be observed in the agreements.
Although the ASEAN-wide agreement seems to pay little attention to those
provisions, agreements between Japan and individual members cover the
issues to some extent. Commercially heavy provisions, such as investment
and IPR provisions, are found in most of the agreements. Commitments
on sector-specific rules and regulations are also common features of those
FTAs, especially on financial industries.

Unlike many other trade agreements involving major developed
economies such as the European Union and United States, Japan's FTAs
have a visible lack of attention to various aspects that contain less commercial value. Issues such as the environment and labor standards are
rarely mentioned in those agreements. However, Japan also emphasizes
the economic cooperation aspect of trade agreements. This provision, both
general and sector-specific commitments, can be seen as a leverage for the
inclusion of behind-border commitments in Japan's agreements with its
trading partners.

While BBIs are common in Japan's agreements, the extent of such
provisions varies significantly between one trading partner and another. One
way to see the depth of the commitments is by comparing the contents of

TABLE 9.3
Provisions of RTAs between Japan and ASEAN Members

	Singapore	Malaysia	Philippines	Brunei	Indonesia	Thailand	Vietnam	ASEAN
Border Issues								
Tariff elimination	✓	✓	✓	✓	✓	✓	✓	✓
Rules of origin	✓	✓	✓	✓	✓	✓	✓	✓
Services trade	✓	✓	✓	✓	✓	✓	✓	✓
Customs cooperation and trade facilitation	✓	✓	✓	✓	✓	✓	✓	✓
Sanitary and phytosanitary measures	✓	✓					✓	✓
TBTs and standard conformity	✓	✓					✓	✓
Behind-Border Issues								
Intellectual property	✓	✓	✓	✓	✓	✓	✓	
Investment	✓	✓	✓	✓	✓	✓		
Government procurement	✓		✓	✓	✓	✓		
Competition policy	✓	✓	✓		✓	✓	✓	
Environment standards								
Sustainable development								
Labor standards								
Financial services	✓	✓	✓	✓	✓		✓	
Telecommunications	✓							
E-commerce	✓	✓	✓	✓	✓	✓	✓	
Economic cooperation	✓	✓	✓	✓	✓	✓	✓	✓

Source: Original text of the agreements.

behind-border issues with the related subjects discussed at the multinational level. The provision of investment rights in an FTA can be evaluated with respect to the agreement in trade-related investment measures of GATT. The agreement, which was reached in the Uruguay Round, requires GATT member countries to phase out various investment measures that affect trade performance and decisions. Such measures include requiring investors to utilize a certain amount of local input in production or export a proportion of their production.

Table 9.4 compares selected agreements between Japan and several ASEAN members. Singapore has been selected to see how far Japan's trade agreement can go to include behind-border provisions, since the more developed country is relatively ready to embrace such disciplines. Thailand is unique since this country is quite aggressive in pursuing trade agreements with its trading partners: as of 2012, Thailand had signed 25 bilateral and regional free trade agreements. Indonesia has been selected since the country has the lowest number of trade agreements among ASEAN members.

Investment provisions in the agreements between Japan and selected members of ASEAN seem to be quite deep, encompassing agreements set in the WTO's trade-related investment issues. Deep commitments are negotiated in individual agreements between ASEAN countries and Japan, while ASEAN-wide agreement does not cover such provisions. A similar pattern is found in other agreements between ASEAN and other East Asian countries.

Commitments on property rights can be compared to trade-related intellectual property rights, which define national laws on various aspects of property rights that affect trade policy. Table 9.5 shows that the agreements between Japan and ASEAN members do not specify many areas beyond multilateral agreement. In terms of provisions on competition policy, there is not much effort from Japan and ASEAN countries to define a more harmonized and coherent competition policy in the region. ASEAN countries so far do not have specific agreement on such policy, although the AEC blueprint envisages deeper cooperation between member countries in that policy area.

Are the Commitments Sufficient?

An interesting question regarding the commitments in Japan's FTAs is whether they can sufficiently deliver the discipline and rules required to manage the complex arrangement of international trade and production in East Asia. One way to evaluate the efficacy of the provisions is to see what they do not mean and the limitations of those commitments.

TABLE 9.4
Investment Provisions in Selected RTAs

	Japan – Singapore	Japan – Indonesia	Japan – Thailand	ACIA	ACFTA	KAFTA
No provisions					?	?
Commitment to future negotiation				✓		
Stated compliance to existing WTO (TRIMs) agreements on Investment		✓	✓	✓		
Information exchange and transparency commitments	✓	✓	✓	✓		
TRIMs Provisions						
National treatment principle (Article III of GATT)	✓	✓	✓	✓		
Prohibition of performance requirements	✓	✓				
Prohibition of controls on investor international financial transfers	✓	✓	✓	✓		
TRIMs Plus						
Most Favored Nation (MFN) treatment (in relation to that already afforded to non-Parties)		✓	✓	✓		
Prohibition of nationalization or expropriation of assets	✓	✓	✓	✓		
Prohibition of appointing key personnel (e.g. senior managers) of particular nationality				✓		

TABLE 9.4 *(Cont'd)*

	Japan – Singapore	Japan – Indonesia	Japan – Thailand	ACIA	ACFTA	KAFTA
TRIMs Plus						
Subrogation clause	✓			✓		
Minimum standard of treatment clause						
Environmental clause		✓	✓			
Protective Clauses and Exceptions						
Exceptions on investor performance requirements	✓	✓	✓	✓		
Safeguard measures on financial transfers during periods of financial instability	✓	✓	✓	✓		
Industrial policy assistance awarded exclusively to domestic investors or investments	✓					
Exceptions on government procurement		✓	✓	✓		
Sectoral exemptions and limitations	✓	✓	✓	✓		
Taxation exemption	✓	✓	✓	✓		
Investor-state dispute settlement mechanism	✓	✓	✓	✓		
Compensation rights clause	✓	✓	✓	✓		

Source: Original text of the agreements and Dent (2010).

TABLE 9.5
Intellectual Property Rights in Selected RTAs

	Japan – Singapore	Japan – Indonesia	Japan – Thailand	ASEAN FTA	ACFTA	KAFTA
Recourse or reference to WTO (TRIPS) rules only					✓	✓
Conformance to general principles of IPR	✓	✓	✓			
Stated compliance to existing WTO (TRIPS)/WIPO agreements on IPR		✓	✓	✓		
Information exchange and transparency commitments	✓	✓	✓	✓		
TRIPs Provision Areas						
Copyright and related rights		✓	✓			
Trademarks		✓	✓			
Geographical indications		✓	✓			
Industrial designs		✓	✓			
Patents		✓	✓			
Protection of undisclosed information		✓	✓			
Control of anticompetitive practices in contractual licenses		✓	✓			
TRIPs-Plus						
New varieties of plants		✓	✓			
Recourse for judicial review and compensation from IPR infringement		✓	✓			

Source: Original text of the agreements and Dent (2010).

TABLE 9.6
Competition Policy in Selected RTAs

	Japan – Singapore	Japan – Indonesia	Japan – Thailand	ASEAN	ACFTA	KAFTA
No provisions						✓
Conformance to general principles of open and competitive markets	✓	✓	✓	✓	✓	
Information exchange and transparency concerning subsequent developments in competition policy	✓	✓	✓	✓		
Recourse to consultations and review on competition policy actions and policy changes	✓	✓	✓			
Explicitly and equally applies to government/ public sector						
Stated obligation to enact new competition policy legislation						
Stated obligation to reduce size of the public enterprise sector generally						
Exempted sectors or organizations specifically listed						

Source: Original text of the agreements and Dent (2010).

There are three main issues normally covered in provisions on investments: (1) liberalization, (2) protection, and (3) promotion. The liberalization aspect of investment, including Japan's FTAs with ASEAN countries, can be found in two chapters of the ASEAN-Japan agreement dealing with two separate but related issues. Market access issues for investment in the services sector are normally discussed in the agreement on trade in services, particularly for mode 3 (commercial presences of service providers). Another aspect, namely the principle of national treatment, which maintains nondiscriminatory treatment toward foreign investors, is specified in the investment chapter.

While the principle of national treatment is specified clearly in Japan's FTAs, it is also followed by long lists of exceptions and reservations regarding foreign investment. Such measures include horizontal ones — such as the acquisition of lands and properties, and limitations on asset transfers — and sector-specific measures such as equity limitations in the banking sector. Those exceptions reduce the significance of investment provisions in FTAs between Japan and ASEAN.

Moreover, commitments specified in other related chapters are normally below the actual rules and regulations.[3] In terms of investment liberalization, FTAs in East Asia, including among ASEAN members, do not really provide substantial improvement. A better arrangement can be observed when it comes to protection of investment rights. Protection provisions in FTAs between Japan and ASEAN members stipulate the limits of government actions to restrict activities of investors and to expropriate their investment. The provisions increase the certainty of investor activities of both parties. This is a significant improvement in the attempt to regulate integration in the region, considering that Japan has virtually no bilateral investment treaty with any ASEAN member, which normally provides such protection.

In agreements on competition policy, FTAs in the region do not seek to set up an aligning mechanism on competition policy or to harmonize domestic policy between trading partners. Rather, the agreements aim to construct more effective enforcement mechanisms through the promotion of transparency and cooperation in implementation. This is understandable, since many ASEAN countries, such as the Philippines and Malaysia, do not even have a comprehensive competition law. It is still a long way to suggest that FTAs in East Asia, especially between Japan and ASEAN members, would provide better attempts at harmonizing such policy at the regional level. Even among ASEAN countries, which envisage greater integration of the AEC in 2015, there is no apparent direction for such harmonization.[4]

One aspect related to competition policy that is missing from Japan's FTAs is the provision of state aid and the conduct of SOEs. In many economies SOEs receive special privileges from the government, including monopoly rights that may harm a pro-competition environment. The implementation of a national competition policy, as well as provisions in trade agreements, often exclude special rights for SOEs.

The lack of commitment on the part of SOEs in FTAs between Japan and ASEAN members indicates that state-owned companies remain a sensitive issue in the region. The reason for this is that in virtually all economies in the region, SOEs maintain a significant role and receive massive state aid and special rights in conducting business. SOEs' monopoly in various economic sectors has hampered the delivery of goods and services needed for the development of production networks in the region. For example, since logistics and transportation are one of the main aspects of the network, monopoly in these sectors holds back the delivery of economical and high-quality logistics services.

For the protection of IPR, FTAs between Japan and ASEAN countries provide substantial provisions. The chapter on IPR in those agreements even includes several enforcement measures that require both parties to act in order to support IPR protection. This provision seems to be a comprehensive arrangement for managing integration in the region. Unfortunately, besides Japan-ASEAN FTAs there is no similar arrangement among countries in the region. ASEAN itself, while it has been discussing IPR for more than a decade, still focuses on how to improve IP creation rather that enforcing laws and protection. Finding a balanced regional arrangement for IPR creation and protection among ASEAN members would increase support for regional integration.

From the discussion above, it is quite obvious that behind-border provisions of FTAs in the region can be improved to provide better governance and discipline for economic integration in the region. One point worth mentioning on BBIs in trade agreements between Japan and ASEAN countries is the absence of behind-border provisions in such FTAs. Commitments in such region-wide agreements seem to be weaker than the agreements between Japan and individual countries. This is apparent not only on new issues such as BBIs, but also on traditional subjects, including rules of origin and tariff elimination. This may arise from Japan's strategy in pursuing regional economic cooperation: seeking a general framework of economic cooperation in region-wide agreements while discussing the details in individual agreements.

However, this approach might undermine the initiatives toward a more coherent and harmonized regulatory framework in the region. The "noodle bowl" effects of different BBI arrangements in East Asia may not be as severe as the problems created by border-barriers commitments — e.g., different preferential tariffs or rules of origin — but they indicate that initiatives toward harmonized and deeper formal arrangements in the region are still far from being realized.

CONCLUSION

Regional economic integration in East Asia has evolved to become a complex arrangement of cross-border trade, production, services, and investment. Decades of intensive market-driven economic relations have induced an increasing need for well-defined disciplines and governance for such integration. The answer lies in the emerging trade agreements in the region, especially the new behind-border issues of FTAs. Trade agreements between Japan and ASEAN countries, the major components of Factory Asia, are among the critical instruments in developing the needed governance.

Many such disciplines are embodied in the behind-border provisions of those agreements, for instance, investment protection, competition policy, and IPR protection. However, commitments on BBIs in those agreements seem to be weak and insufficient to promote the development of economic integration in East Asia. There are two important issues that need to be addressed in order to increase the effectiveness of BBIs in East Asia's trade agreements. The first is the depth of BBIs' commitments in East Asian FTAs. While many trade agreements already include such commitments, especially commerce-related provisions, there are many yet to be discussed; some are quite important, such as provisions on the conduct of state-owned enterprises. Commitments and provisions that are already specified in FTAs seldom include measures that deal directly with the issues at hand. The long list of exceptions and reservations attached to various commitments raises questions on the seriousness of the countries in providing the necessary international governance for regional integration.

Another issue is related to the uniformity of commitments on BBIs in East Asia's FTAs. Many agreements at the bilateral level incorporate such commitments, but at various levels of depth. The agreements between Japan and individual ASEAN members are different from one another. There is little discussion about BBIs in the Japan-ASEAN Partnership Agreement, which indicates Japan's strategy is to confine itself to the bilateral level. While the "noodle-bowl" effects of BBIs' commitments seem to be relatively low compared to those of trade in goods and services, more harmonized provisions in BBIs are important in order to create effective governance.

Notes

[1]   See, for example, Ando and Kimura (2005), which provides an extensive survey on the East Asian production network. Many case studies at the industrial and firm level also provide insights into the development of production in East Asia, most notably of Japanese companies' networks. See, for example, Hiratsuka (2011) for the hard disk industry in Thailand and Pasha and Setiati (2011) for Indonesia's automotive industry.

[2]   In 1990 Malaysian Prime Minister Mahathir Mohamad came up with the idea of an East Asia Economic Caucus to cover six members of ASEAN along with Japan, China, and South Korea. This idea was abandoned, mostly due to strong objections from Japan and the United States. ASEAN countries therefore embarked on an ASEAN Free Trade Area, while in the greater region of Asia-Pacific, APEC took over the initiative.

[3]   For example, in a more sector-specific of trade in services agreement, Indonesia does not specify any commitment to liberalization in the retail sector in the services chapter of its economic partnership agreement with Japan, while the sector has already been fully liberalized for around a decade — for instance, foreign equity participation can reach 100 per cent.

[4]   The AEC blueprint stipulates that greater cooperation in competition policy will be attained, mainly through capacity building and sharing of knowledge. There have also been attempts to create a comprehensive national competition policy in all member countries, such as by adopting a national law on competition or creating a national agency. But there is no visible approach toward harmonizing policies at the regional level.

References

Amador, João, and Sónia Cabral. "Vertical Specialization across the World: A Relative Measure". *North American Journal of Economics and Finance*, Elsevier, (December 2009): 267–80.

Ando, Mitsuyo, and Fukunari Kimura. "The Formation of International Production and Distribution Networks in East Asia". NBER Chapters, in *International Trade in East Asia, NBER-East Asia Seminar on Economics*, vol. 14 (2005): 177–216. National Bureau of Economic Research.

Ando, Mitsuyo, and Kimura Fukunari. "Fragmentation in East Asia: Further Evidence". ERIA Working Papers DP-2009-20. Economic Research Institute for ASEAN and East Asia, 2009.

Baldwin, Richard E. "Managing the Noodle Bowl: The Fragility of East Asian Regionalism". *CEPR Discussion Paper* no. 5561. Centre for Economic Policy Research, 2006.

————. "21st Century Regionalism: Filling the Gap between 21st Century Trade and 20th Century Trade Rules". WTO Working Paper ERSD-2011-08. World Trade Organization, 2011.

Damuri, Yose Rizal. "International Production Sharing: Insights from Exploratory Network Analysis". Centre for Trade and Economic Integration Working Paper no. 03/2012. Graduate Institute Geneva, 2012*a*.

————. "21st Century Regionalism and Production Sharing Practice". Centre for Trade and Economic Integration Working Paper no. 04/2012. Graduate Institute Geneva, 2012*b*.

Dent, Christopher. "Freer Trade, More Regulation? Commercial Regulatory Provisions in Asia-Pacific Free Trade Agreements". *Competition and Change* 14, no. 1 (March 2010): 48–79.

Hiratsuka, Daisuke. "Production Networks in Asia: A Case Study from the Hard Disk Drive Industry". ADBI Working Papers no. 301. Asian Development Bank Institute, 2011.

Horn, Henrik, Petros C. Mavroidis, and André Sapir. "Beyond the WTO? An Anatomy of EU and U.S. Preferential Trade Agreements". *The World Economy* 33, no. 11, Wiley Blackwell (November 2010): 1565–88.

Pasha, Mochamad, and Ira Setiati. "Trade Liberalization and International Production Networks: Indonesia's Automotive Industry". In *Fighting Irrelevance: The Role of Regional Trade Agreements in International Production Networks in Asia. A Study by the Asia-Pacific Research and Training Network on Trade*. United Nations ESCAP, 2011.

10

REGIONAL FINANCIAL COOPERATION IN EAST ASIA: DEVELOPMENT AND CHALLENGES[1]

Yoichi Nemoto and Satoshi Nakagawa[2]

DEVELOPMENT OF REGIONAL FINANCIAL COOPERATION IN EAST ASIA

East Asian Miracle and Asian Financial Crisis of 1997–98

In the late 20th century East Asian economies achieved rapid economic growth, a phenomenon that is often called the "East Asian Miracle". According to the World Bank (1993), from 1965 to 1990 East Asian economies grew faster than economies in any other region of the world. Eight high-performing Asian economies — Japan, the Four Tigers (Hong Kong, South Korea, Taiwan, and Singapore), Indonesia, Malaysia, and Thailand — grew roughly three times as fast as Latin American and South Asian economies, and five times faster than Sub-Saharan African economies. An export-oriented policy and a strategy to attract foreign direct investment, accompanied by high savings and investment in physical and human capital, contributed to the development of export-oriented manufacturing industries that drove growth in these economies.

Under the sustained high growth, the financial sector liberalization of the 1990s, and a de facto U.S. dollar-pegged foreign exchange rate regime, the East Asian economies attracted large cross-border capital inflow. As nominal domestic interest rates were significantly higher than interest rates on the U.S. dollar, local banks (including non-banking financial institutions) and local corporates sought to take advantage of lower interest rates by taking U.S. dollar loans from foreign lenders. The foreign lenders viewed such lending as lucrative investment opportunities as they placed high confidence in these economies owing to their sustained growth.

But these economies were also subject to the accumulated risks emanating from the capital inflow, that is, heightened vulnerability to external shocks. First, such capital inflow took the form of short-term, unhedged U.S.-dollar-denominated bank loans to local banks, non-banking financial institutions, and corporates. Second, the borrowers were not only in export industries — which could generate foreign exchange income — but also in non-tradable sectors, even channeling those funds into asset markets such as equity and real estate. Third, the capital inflow took place against a background of a market infrastructure that had weak banking supervision and legal systems (e.g., bankruptcy laws), and there were concerns about the robustness of their statistics and transparency. As a result of these conditions, there was a greater exposure to balance-sheet losses in the event of currency depreciation ("currency risks") and greater exposure to the risk of a "run" ("liquidity risk"), which could easily develop into a full-fledged financial and economic crisis. Indeed, at the end of June 1997 the ratio of short-term external debt to foreign exchange reserves exceeded 100 per cent in Indonesia, South Korea, and Thailand.[3]

Against such backdrop, these economies experienced a sudden reversal of capital flow and fell into profound, full-fledged, and self-fulfilling financial and economic crises in 1997–98, an event that became known as the Asian Financial Crisis. Thailand, Indonesia, and South Korea were among the countries that faced significant pressure of currency depreciation and a sharp fall in their foreign exchange reserves. They had to request a rescue package from the International Monetary Fund (IMF) to regain market confidence and overcome the crisis. The IMF, to address the liquidity crisis, applied a conventional program that had been used to improve macro-imbalances (solvency) and imposed rigorous structural conditionalities to implement long-outstanding reforms that may not have been critical to the resolution of the liquidity crisis.

With the perception in the market that the program was underfinanced or not fully owned by the authorities, the prescriptions by the IMF were not effective in restoring market confidence; rather, the organization's policy advice exacerbated the situation. For example, the immediate suspension or closure of a large number of financial institutions without a blanket deposit guarantee caused a self-fulfilling panic among depositors in Indonesia. In South Korea, the advice to sharply raise interest rates and to defend currencies in an environment where corporates were highly leveraged turned the liquidity difficulty into a solvency problem. The austerity measures, based on a misjudgment of the economic situation, resulted in an additional contraction when the economy was already depressed in these countries.[4] As a result, these countries underwent a "full-fledged financial panic and massive withdrawal of foreign capital"[5] and thereby fell into a vicious cycle of a currency crisis ("depreciation of currency"), a financial crisis ("surge in non-performing loans"), and an economic crisis ("economic depression"). In 1998, real GDP contracted by 10.5 per cent in Thailand, 13.1 per cent in Indonesia, and 6.9 per cent in South Korea.[6]

Burgeoning of Regional Financial Cooperation

In response to the painful experiences of the Asian Financial Crisis and in order to better prepare for the future, authorities in the region realized the importance of regional financial cooperation. The initial attempt to develop regional financial cooperation began as early as September 1997, when Japan proposed the establishment of the Asian Monetary Fund (AMF) right after the support meeting for Thailand in August 1997. According to Eisuke Sakakibara (2000), Japan's Finance Minister Hiroshi Mitsuzuka proposed the establishment of the AMF for 10 economies in the region — Australia, China, Hong Kong SAR of China, Japan, South Korea, Indonesia, Malaysia, Singapore, Thailand, and the Philippines — on 12 September 1997. The proposal was discussed at the Regional Finance Deputies' Meeting held in Hong Kong on 21 September 1997, in which the ten Asian economies participated and the United States and the IMF attended as observers. While ASEAN and South Korea expressed support for the AMF proposal, the United States and Australia opposed it. China voiced no opinion.[7] As such, consensus was not reached. A few reasons have been put forth for why the United States opposed the AMF proposal. According to C. Randall Henning (2002), the United States rejected the AMF proposal because it could displace the IMF and undercut its ability to secure policy adjustments from borrowing countries. Phillip Lipscy (2003) noted that the United States had weak ties with East Asia, unlike the case of Mexico during its 1994 crisis, and tilted toward emphasizing moral hazard concerns rather than rapid liquidity provision. This was in contrast to Japan, which had a high level of banking exposure and close economic ties with East Asia. Sakakibara (2000) even suspected that the United States might have believed that the proposal, which was developed without its input, was a challenge by Japan to U.S. hegemony.

Although the AMF proposal itself did not materialize, the deputies of the finance ministers and central bank governors of Australia, Brunei Darussalam, Canada, the People's Republic of China, Hong Kong SAR of China, Indonesia, Japan, South Korea, Malaysia, New Zealand, the Philippines, Singapore, Thailand, and the United States met in Manila in November 1997 to develop a concerted approach to restoring financial stability in the region.[8] The deputies at the meeting recognized the challenges that accompanied globalization of financial markets and the increased volatility of capital flows, and therefore agreed to establish a framework for regional cooperation to enhance the prospects for financial stability. This became known as the "Manila Framework".

The Manila Framework, endorsing the central role of the IMF in the international monetary system, had four initiatives: (1) a mechanism for regional surveillance to complement global surveillance by the IMF; (2) enhanced economic and technical cooperation, particularly in strengthening domestic financial systems and regulatory capacities; (3) measures to strengthen the IMF's capacity to respond to financial crises; and (4) a cooperative financing arrangement that would supplement IMF resources. Although the Manila Framework itself ended its activities in 2004, it laid an important first step for regional financial cooperation in East Asia.

In the meantime, the government of Japan in October 1998 announced a new facility to provide short-term funds in the form of swap arrangements between U.S. dollars and local currencies with the aim of addressing potential short-term financing needs of the countries in East Asia. This was known as the New Miyazawa Initiative (see box).[9] Under the initiative, Japan reached bilateral swap arrangements with South Korea (up to US$5 billion) and Malaysia (up to US$2.5 billion).[10] This demonstrated the usefulness of short-term currency swaps using foreign exchange reserves as a financing arrangement to cope with liquidity crises.

China also gradually realigned its foreign policy for regional cooperation.[11] In November 1997, on the occasion of the fifth APEC Informal Leadership Meeting, then President Jiang Zemin stated, "It is beneficial to all countries to enhance regional and international financial cooperation, maintain normal international financial order, jointly ward off the impact of excessive speculation of hot money in the world and create a favourable financial environment. We adopt a positive attitude towards strengthening financial cooperation in Asia and is ready to participate in discussions on relevant mechanism for cooperation."[12] During this period China also refrained from devaluing its currency, which was perceived as a relief by the crisis-hit countries as it allowed those countries to retain their export competitiveness against China.[13]

Japan's New Miyazawa Initiative (MOF of Japan, 1998)

- In order to assist Asian countries in overcoming their economic difficulties and to contribute to the stability of international financial markets, the government of Japan announced the New Miyazawa Initiative on 3 October 1998. According to the initiative, Japan stood ready to provide a package of support measures totaling US$30 billion, of which US$15 billion would be made available for medium- to long-term financial needs for economic recovery in Asian countries, and another US$15 billion would be set aside for possible short-term capital needs during the process of implementing economic reform.
- With "Medium- to Long-Term Financial Support to Asian Countries", Japan stood ready to provide official financial assistance through the Export-Import Bank of Japan (by extending loans to Asian countries, purchasing bonds issued by Asian countries, issuing guarantees to bank loans to and bonds issued by Asian countries), to provide insurance to bank loans to Asian countries, and to extend ODA yen loans to Asian countries. Japan also requested the World Bank and the Asian Development Bank to provide co-financing and technical assistance to Asian countries.
- With "Short-Term Financial Support to Asian Countries", Japan set aside US$15 billion in short-term funds that would take the form of swap arrangements to cope with short-term capital needs such as facilitation of trade finance.
- At the Asian Finance Ministers' and Central Bank Governors' meeting on 3 October 1998, the following statement was issued: "The Ministers and Governors welcomed the initiative announced today by Japan, to support Asian countries overcome the current economic difficulties by providing a package of support measures totaling US$30 billion."

Beginning of ASEAN+3 Regional Financial Cooperation

Building upon the success of the Asia-Europe Meeting (ASEM) in Bangkok in 1996, which was attended by the leaders of seven ASEAN member states plus China, Japan, and South Korea, the ASEAN leaders invited their counterparts from China, Japan, and South Korea to their ASEAN Summit in Kuala Lumpur, Malaysia, in 1997 — the first ASEAN+3 Summit. Since then, the ASEAN+3 Summit has been held yearly. In 1999, the ASEAN+3 leaders issued a joint statement on East Asia Cooperation.[14] In this statement, it was announced that the ASEAN+3 leaders agreed, in the area of monetary and financial cooperation, to strengthen policy dialogue, coordination, and collaboration on financial, monetary, and fiscal issues of common interest. The initial focus would be on issues related to macroeconomic risk management, enhancing corporate governance, monitoring regional capital flows, strengthening banking and financial systems, reforming the international financial architecture, and enhancing self-help and support mechanisms in East Asia through the ASEAN+3 Framework, including the ongoing dialogue and cooperation mechanism of the ASEAN+3 finance and central bank leaders and officials.

Cooperation among the ASEAN+3 finance ministries and central banks started in 1999, following the agreement at the second ASEAN+3 Summit in December 1998 in Hanoi, Vietnam, to establish a forum at the level of finance deputies to discuss issues of international finance. In March 1999 the first ASEAN+3 Finance and Central Bank Deputies Meeting (previously known as "AFDM+3", now renamed "AFCDM+3") was held in Hanoi, Vietnam, where the delegates regarded the ASEAN+3 forum as "very important, timely and very useful".[15] Subsequently, in Chiang Mai, Thailand, in May 2000, the ASEAN+3 finance ministers made a number of significant agreements.[16]

First, they established "a network of contact persons of the ASEAN+3 finance and central bank officials to facilitate regional surveillance in East Asia" and agreed to conduct the mutual economic surveillance called "economic reviews and policy dialogues (ERPD)" on an informal basis. Second, they agreed on the "Chiang Mai Initiative (CMI)" to establish a regional financing arrangement to supplement the existing international facilities, in order to strengthen their self-help and support mechanisms in East Asia through the ASEAN+3 framework. The CMI was composed of an expanded ASEAN Swap Arrangement that would include five original ASEAN countries, and a network of bilateral swap and repurchase agreement facilities among ASEAN countries, China, Japan, and South Korea. Its core objectives were defined as follows: (1) to address short-term liquidity difficulties in the region, and (2) to supplement the existing international financial arrangements.

Development of CMI: Network of Bilateral Swap Agreements

Since the agreement in Chiang Mai in May 2000, 16 bilateral swap agreements (BSA) under the CMI have been concluded among eight countries (China, Indonesia, Japan, South Korea, Malaysia, the Philippines, Singapore, and Thailand). The total size reached US$36.5 billion by May 2004. The ASEAN Swap Arrangement, the other main component of the CMI, was increased to US$1 billion on 17 November 2000 and expanded to cover all ASEAN member countries.[17]

After the establishment of the network of bilateral swap agreements, in May 2004 the ASEAN+3 finance ministers agreed to undertake a further review of the CMI to explore ways of enhancing its effectiveness.[18] As a result, in May 2005 the finance ministers decided on the following four measures:

1. Integration and enhancement of ASEAN+3 economic surveillance into the CMI framework to enable early detection of irregularities and swift remedial policy actions, with a view to developing effective regional surveillance capabilities that complement the current undertaking by international financial institutions (IFIs);

2. Clear defining of the swap activation process and the adoption of a collective decision-making mechanism of the current network of bilateral swap arrangements (BSAs) as a first step of multilateralization so that the relevant BSAs would be activated collectively and promptly in case of an emergency;

3. Significant increase in the size of swaps: The size of the BSAs should be increased by (i) increasing the amount of existing bilateral commitment, (ii) concluding new BSAs, for example, among ASEAN countries, and (iii) transforming one-way BSAs to two-way BSAs. Member countries favored an enhancement of up to 100 per cent increase in the existing individual arrangements while noting that the size could be flexibly decided by bilateral negotiations. In this context, the ASEAN Swap Arrangement was doubled from US$1 billion to US$2 billion; and

4. Improving the drawdown mechanism: The size of swaps that could be withdrawn without the IMF-supported program would be increased from the current 10 per cent to 20 per cent in order to better cope with sudden market irregularities while the current framework to complement the international financial arrangements and other disciplined conditions would be firmly maintained.[19]

Subsequently, in May 2006 the ASEAN+3 finance ministers further agreed on the following measures:

1. A collective decision-making procedure for swap activation was adopted. All swap-providing countries could simultaneously and promptly provide liquidity support to any parties involved in bilateral swap arrangements (BSAs) at times of emergency;
2. To explore the ways for further strengthening surveillance capacity in East Asia, the Group of Experts (GOE) and the Technical Working Group on Economic and Financial Monitoring (ETWG) would be launched. The GOE, composed of several regional professional experts, would serve as an independent economic assessment vehicle for the region. The ETWG would play an important role in developing and spreading the Early Warning System to facilitate early detection of irregularities; and
3. The total swap size had reached US$75 billion, almost double from the previous year. It was noted that nine BSAs had been revised since the previous year to enhance the effectiveness of CMI reflecting the Istanbul Agreement.[20]

Global Financial Crisis and Enhancement of ASEAN+3 Regional Financial Cooperation

Against the steady development of the CMI, the ASEAN+3 region experienced the harsh spillover of the Global Financial Crisis in 2008–9. Being deeply integrated with the global economy and having strong financial ties with the advanced economies, the ASEAN+3 economies — including Japan — were hit hard by the crisis in both trade and financial channels. In 2008/Q4–2009/Q3, exports by the major economies plummeted by up to 40 per cent year on year. In the midst of global deleveraging, foreign exchange reserves in Indonesia and South Korea dropped by 9 per cent and 23 per cent year on year respectively at the end of 2008.

To cope with the mounting pressure, South Korea and Singapore established bilateral swap arrangements up to US$30 billion with the

TABLE 10.1
Impact of Global Financial Crisis

	2008				2009				2010			
	Q1	Q2	Q3	Q4	Q1	Q2	Q3	Q4	Q1	Q2	Q3	Q4
Exports					(%, yoy)							
China	21.2	22.2	23.3	4.4	(19.7)	(23.4)	(20.5)	0.1	28.7	40.8	32.2	24.8
Japan	20.5	17.6	12.9	(10.0)	(40.6)	(34.0)	(24.5)	(1.0)	48.3	40.8	28.3	19.4
Korea	17.4	23.1	37.0	(9.9)	(25.2)	(21.1)	(17.6)	11.7	35.8	33.1	22.7	23.8
Indonesia	31.9	29.6	27.9	(5.6)	(31.9)	(26.2)	(19.3)	23.9	54.7	36.9	27.7	28.9
Singapore	22.2	26.1	20.7	(14.2)	(32.7)	(30.9)	(22.3)	12.2	38.3	36.4	27.8	22.0
Thailand	24.6	25.0	24.5	(12.1)	(33.4)	(23.6)	(16.7)	13.3	34.2	39.2	23.2	21.0
Foreign Reserve					(US$, billion)							
China	1,688.4	1,815.1	1,911.8	1,953.3	1,960.9	2,145.0	2,298.3	2,425.9	2,473.4	2,481.0	2,676.7	2,875.9
Japan	1,015.6	1,001.6	955.9	1,030.6	1,018.6	1,019.2	1,052.6	1,049.4	1,042.7	1,050.2	1,109.6	1,096.2
Korea	264.2	258.1	239.7	201.2	206.3	231.7	254.3	270.0	272.3	274.2	289.8	291.6
Indonesia	59.0	59.5	57.1	51.6	54.8	57.6	62.3	66.1	71.8	76.3	86.6	96.2
Singapore	177.3	176.4	168.6	174.0	166.0	173.0	181.8	187.6	196.9	199.7	214.5	225.5
Thailand	110.0	105.7	102.4	111.0	116.2	120.8	131.8	138.4	144.1	146.8	163.2	172.1
Real GDP					(%, yoy)							
China	11.3	10.1	9.0	6.8	6.6	8.1	9.1	10.7	12.1	10.3	9.6	9.8
Japan	1.3	(0.0)	(0.7)	(4.8)	(9.2)	(6.5)	(5.5)	(0.6)	5.1	4.4	5.8	3.5
Korea	5.3	4.2	3.1	(3.2)	(4.0)	(2.0)	1.2	6.3	8.6	7.4	4.5	5.0
Indonesia	6.2	6.3	6.3	5.3	4.5	4.1	4.3	5.6	5.9	6.3	5.8	6.8
Singapore	8.4	2.8	(0.3)	(3.2)	(9.0)	(2.1)	2.3	5.7	16.5	19.7	10.8	12.6
Thailand	6.3	5.2	3.1	(4.1)	(7.0)	(5.2)	(2.8)	5.9	12.0	9.2	6.6	3.8

Source: EIU.

Federal Reserve of the United States respectively.[21] However, no ASEAN+3 members resorted to the CMI. This could be attributable to the following reasons: (1) a certain buffer provided by self-defense, that is, the level of foreign reserves was much higher than that during the Asian Financial Crisis; (2) a complicated and intertwined mechanism of the CMI as a network of bilateral swap arrangements; (3) the stigma of the IMF program during the Asian Financial Crisis — more than 20 per cent of the CMI was conditional upon the existence of the IMF supported-program.

Recognizing such issues, the ASEAN+3 finance ministers adopted two measures to enhance the CMI: (1) multilateralization of the CMI, and (2) the establishment of an independent surveillance unit. Multilateralization of the CMI was a way to streamline the CMI's complicated and intertwined network of bilateral swap arrangements. After thorough discussions at the working levels, the ASEAN+3 finance ministers in May 2009 agreed on all the main components of the CMIM, including the individual countries' contribution, borrowing accessibility, and surveillance mechanism.[22] As a result, the Chiang Mai Initiative Multilateralization Agreement (CMIM Agreement) came into effect on 24 March 2010.[23] The CMIM Agreement is aimed at further enhancing regional capacity to safeguard against downside risks and challenges in the global economy, with the following core objectives: (1) addressing balance of payment short-term liquidity difficulties in the region, and (2) supplementing the existing international financial arrangements.

Key Points of the CMIM Agreement[24]

1. Total size: US$120 billion.
2. Each member's contribution: China (32 per cent, including Hong Kong), Japan (32 per cent), South Korea (16 per cent), Indonesia/Thailand/Malaysia/Singapore/Philippines (3.793 per cent each), Vietnam (0.833 per cent), Cambodia (0.1 per cent), Myanmar (0.05 per cent), Brunei/Lao PDR (0.025 per cent)
3. Drawing: Central banks of the members are to swap their local currencies with the U.S. dollar for an amount up to their contribution multiplied by their respective purchasing multiples.
4. Maturity: Each drawing of liquidity support in the form of bilateral currency swaps shall mature basically 90 days after the

date of drawing, and can be rolled over a maximum of seven times (over approximately two years).

5. Decision making: Fundamental issues (total size of CMIM, contribution of each CMIM party, etc.) for the CMIM will be determined by consensus approval at the Ministerial Level Decision Making Body, which consists of ASEAN+3 finance ministers. Executive-level issues (initial execution of drawing, renewal of drawing, events of default) will be determined by a two-third majority at the Executive Level Decision Making Body (ELDMB), which comprises the deputy-level representatives of members.

6. Conditions precedents and covenants: A CMIM party that requests for a drawing has to meet conditions before the voting for a swap request, such as completion of review of the economic and financial situation and no events of default. As well, each CMIM party is requested to comply with covenants such as submission of the periodic surveillance report and participation in the ASEAN+3 Economic Review and Policy Dialogue.

7. Escape: In principle, each of the CMIM parties may only escape from contributing to a swap request by obtaining the approval of the ELDMB. In exceptional cases such as an extraordinary event or instance of *force majeure* and domestic legal limitations, escape is possible without obtaining ELDMB approval.

In February 2009, in order to further strengthen the regional surveillance mechanism into a robust and credible system that would facilitate prompt activation of the CMIM, the ASEAN+3 finance ministers agreed to establish an independent regional surveillance unit called the "ASEAN+3 Macroeconomic Research Office (AMRO)".[25] In May 2010, the ASEAN+3 finance ministers agreed on key elements of AMRO, announcing that "AMRO will be located in Singapore to monitor and analyze regional economies, which contributes to the early detection of risks, swift implementation of remedial actions, and effective decision-making of the CMIM."[26]

Following the appointment of Wei Benhua[27] as the first AMRO Director and Yoichi Nemoto as the second AMRO Director, AMRO was established in Singapore in May 2011 by 27 finance ministries and central banks of the ASEAN+3 countries.[28] Its work is defined as follows:[29]

1. Peacetime
   - To prepare quarterly consolidated reports on the overall macroeconomic assessment of the ASEAN+3 Region as well as on individual ASEAN+3 countries
2. Crisis time
   - To provide an analysis of the economic and financial situation of the CMIM Swap Requesting Country
   - To monitor the use and impact of the funds disbursed under the CMIM Agreement
   - To monitor the compliance by the CMIM Swap Requesting Country with any lending covenants to the CMIM Agreement

As of May 2013, AMRO had 25 staff under AMRO Director Yoichi Nemoto, of whom 15 were economists.

Eurozone Crisis and Further Strengthening of the CMIM

Even after overcoming the spillover from the Global Financial Crisis, the ASEAN+3 region has not been immune from external shocks. Among other shocks, the deepening of the eurozone crisis posed the risks of deleveraging and withdrawal of credit supply by European banks to the region. In such a volatile global economic and financial environment, the ASEAN+3 financial authorities took various measures to further strengthen the CMIM. In May 2011, the ASEAN+3 finance ministers set forth the "Operational Guidelines for Enhancing Effectiveness of CMIM", which is an operational manual for currency swaps pursuant to the CMIM Agreement. It includes the CMIM's activation process in relation to the existence of IMF programs, which will contribute to the swift and smooth activation of a CMIM Agreement.[30] Also, the ASEAN+3 finance ministers decided to invite ASEAN+3 central bank governors to their annual meetings from 2012, in order to strengthen regional economic monitoring and to enhance regional financial cooperation.

Moreover, in order to adapt to the new volatile environment, the ASEAN+3 finance ministers and central bank governors in May 2012 decided to strengthen the CMIM in the following ways:

1. Double the total size of the CMIM from US$120 billion to US$240 billion;
2. Increase the IMF de-linked portion to 30 per cent in 2012 with a view to increasing it to 40 per cent in 2014 subject to review should conditions warrant;

3. Lengthen the maturity and supporting periods for the IMF-linked portion from 90 days to one year and from two years to three years, respectively; and for the IMF de-linked portion from 90 days to six months and from one year to two years, respectively;
4. Introduce a crisis prevention facility called the "CMIM Precautionary Line (CMIM-PL)".[31]

The introduction of the crisis prevention facility, particularly, is regarded as a major step forward for the CMIM. With this amendment, the CMIM will have the functions to not only cope with the actual balance of payment short-term liquidity difficulties (i.e., "crisis resolution function") but also to prevent potential balance of payment short-term liquidity difficulties (i.e., "crisis prevention function"). This will be important to protect innocent bystanders from external shocks, especially when the global uncertainty lingers, particularly in the euro area.

CHALLENGES OF REGIONAL FINANCIAL COOPERATION IN EAST ASIA

Volatile and Uncertain Global Environment and Increasing Interlinkage in East Asia

Regional financial cooperation in East Asia started only in the aftermath of the Asian Financial Crisis in 1997–98. Nevertheless, it has so far made good progress and, despite a series of major blows from advanced economies such as the Lehman shock and the European sovereign debt crisis, the East Asian economies have weathered such storms fairly well. This is summarized in the ASEAN+3 finance ministers and central bank governors' joint statement in May 2012: "The ASEAN+3 region has been posting steady growth, which was underpinned by robust domestic demand and effective intermediation function provided by financial institutions in the region."[32]

That said, the global economic and financial environment surrounding the ASEAN+3 region remains uncertain, and this uncertainty may last for some time. The advanced economies may need time until they come back to a steady growth trajectory. In the meantime, extremely accommodative monetary policies in the form of quantitative easing in these advanced economies may also continue to keep interest rates low and supply enormous levels of financial liquidity to the market. This may directly or indirectly disturb East Asian economies through the suppressed interest rates and heightened capital inflows and outflows in, for example, the stock, bond, foreign exchange, commodity, and property markets. As the East Asian economies have more favorable economic performance compared to other global regions, they may attract the world's abundant liquidity. However, given the relatively small size of most of the East Asian economies, the impact of such volatile capital inflows and outflows could be significant (even if they are small amounts from the perspective of the advanced economies). It is also important to prepare for a possible capital reversal upon the recovery of the advanced economies and withdrawal of their accommodative monetary policies.

At the same time, the interconnectedness of East Asian economies continues to increase. The ADB (2012) pointed out that economic integration was most strongly evident in the form of trade, tourism, and capital markets. In 2008–11, Asia's intra-regional trade reached 55 per cent and intra-regional equity holding stood at 25 per cent.[33] This may have two implications. On the one hand, the East Asian economies can gain benefits from their neighboring economies' buoyant growth underpinned by solid domestic demand. On the other hand, the East Asian economies are becoming more and more susceptible to each other's economic situation. If any of the East Asian economies — especially the large ones — falls into difficulties, it will significantly affect other economies in the region through trade and financial channels.

Under such circumstances, there is no doubt about the importance of regional financial cooperation. The issue for the ASEAN+3 finance and central bank authorities is whether the current framework of regional cooperation can effectively prevent balance of payment short-term liquidity difficulties in the region and if there is a crisis effectively resolve them. The key concern here could be how to gain and retain market confidence.

In this context, the following perspectives may be identified as challenges to regional financial cooperation:

1. Measures to gain and retain market confidence during peacetime: (a) Good economic policies and regional policy coordination underpinned by regional mutual surveillance, (b) addressing the limitation of data and statistics, (c) good communication with the market;
2. Measures to gain and retain market confidence during crisis time: (1) Size and promptness of the liquidity provision mechanism, (2) collaboration with global and bilateral framework.

"Peace Time" Measures for Market Confidence

Good economic policies are the foundation to gain any market confidence. Without sound macroeconomic policies and without adequate macro-prudential policies, stability of the domestic economy may not be maintained and market credibility may be undermined. The loss of market confidence in any economy may easily transmit to other economies, due to the increasing interlinkage among East Asian economies.

It is therefore very important and necessary to conduct effective regional mutual surveillance so that the authorities are able to continually monitor the economic situation and place peer pressure on other economies to adopt good economic policies and make rectifications if needed. The increase in cross-border banking activities in the region means, for example, that there needs to be coordination in banking supervision among East Asian economies. Moreover, amid the heightened cross-border capital flows, discussions and possible coordination of monetary and macro-prudential policy measures could be useful. The ASEAN+3 ERPD as part of the CMIM, supported by AMRO, is a central plank of the policy to conduct regional surveillance in East Asia. An important challenge is therefore how to continuously improve the quality of the ERPD discussions and their effectiveness.

In conducting economic and financial surveillance, the biggest practical challenge is the limitation of data and statistics. This data limitation can be classified into the following: (1) the lack of data, (2) limited disclosure, and (3) lack of credibility. For example, the scope and frequency of the availability of economic data in some of the East Asian economies are quite limited. Even quarterly GDP figures are not published in some economies. And even if data and statistics are compiled, there are cases where only some limited data are published. Not all the published official data are trusted by market participants, as they sometimes differ substantially from the partici-pants' perceptions of the situation. Addressing these data issues is likely to take a long time, but steps need to be taken to improve data credibility because, as observed in the case of Greece, they can precipitate a crisis.

The importance of transparency and good communication with market participants cannot be overemphasized. Market participants' views are fluid and may change overnight based on the participants' business strategy. Over the last decade some East Asian economies have substantially improved their communications with market players, including foreign market participants. One central bank in the region has established an investor relations unit and started providing news and statistics in English in a timely manner. A loss of market confidence can occur due to the lack of dissemination of proper information. Therefore, these efforts need to be strengthened across the region.

"Crisis Time" Measures for Market Confidence

To gain and retain market confidence, it is equally important to show that there is an effective mechanism in place in the region to resolve balance of payment short-term liquidity difficulties if they occur. To this end, the ASEAN+3 authorities have increased, in a number of stages, the size of the regional financial arrangement. For the CMI, the total size of the network of bilateral swap agreements reached US$36.5 billion in May 2004 and US$75 billion in May 2006.[34] This figure was further increased to US$120 billion when the CMI was multilateralized.[35] In May 2012, it was agreed that the total size of the CMIM would double to US$240 billion.[36] It is also important to ensure that the liquidity support mechanism can be activated in a timely manner when needed, and the ASEAN+3 authorities have been making efforts to ensure this is in place. In May 2011, an operational manual was produced ("Operational Guidelines for Enhancing Effectiveness of CMIM") with the aim of contributing to a swift and smooth activation of the CMIM Agreement.

An adequate size for the regional liquidity facility is difficult to gauge. This is because the mechanism is designed to retain and restore market confidence, as this will be a key to resolving any crisis. An important task remaining is to design an effective linkage between the global financial arrangement (i.e., the IMF program), the regional financial arrangement (i.e., the CMIM Agreement), and bilateral financial arrangements (e.g., bilateral swap arrangements). For example, Indonesia can draw US$22.8 billion from the CMIM on top of US$6.3 billion from the IMF and US$12 billion from Japan through a bilateral swap arrangement. If combined, the amount would be US$41.1 billion. The eurozone crisis has shown that if a crisis originates within the region, then regional mechanisms alone may not be sufficient to restore market confidence. As the troika of the EU, the ECB, and the IMF demonstrates, for a liquidity crisis, especially if such a crisis is triggered by the loss of market confidence due to an event in a neighboring economy in the region, consolidated support including the global facility could be critical to the restoration of market confidence. So far, the CMIM Agreement has never been activated, so there has been no precedent for the coordination framework. Now, the CMIM Agreement includes a crisis prevention facility. As both the global and regional financial arrangements also have a crisis prevention facility, effective collaboration between the different financial arrangements is likely to be an important agenda for further discussions.

Future Agendas

There are two additional agendas that the ASEAN+3 authorities have embarked on, as announced in the ASEAN+3 Finance Ministers and

Table 10.2
Selected Economic Indicators: China, Indonesia, Korea, Malaysia and Thailand

	1991	1992	1993	1994	1995	1996	1997	1998	1999	2000	2001	2002	2003	2004	2005	2006	2007	2008	2009	2010	2011	2012
Real GDP Growth (%)																						
China	9.2	14.2	13.9	13.1	10.9	10.0	9.3	7.8	7.6	8.4	8.3	9.1	10.0	10.1	11.3	12.7	14.2	9.6	9.2	10.4	9.3	7.8
Indonesia	8.9	6.5	8.0	7.5	8.2	7.8	4.7	13.1	0.8	5.4	3.6	4.5	4.8	5.0	5.7	5.5	6.3	6.0	4.6	6.2	6.5	6.2
South Korea	9.4	5.9	6.1	8.5	9.2	7.0	4.7	6.9	9.5	8.5	4.0	7.2	2.8	4.6	4.0	5.2	5.1	2.3	0.3	6.3	3.7	2.0
Malaysia	9.5	8.9	9.9	9.2	9.8	10.0	7.3	7.4	6.1	8.9	0.5	5.4	5.8	6.8	5.3	5.6	6.3	4.8	-1.5	7.2	5.1	5.6
Thailand	8.6	8.1	8.3	9.0	9.2	5.9	-1.4	-10.5	4.4	4.8	2.2	5.3	7.1	6.3	4.6	5.1	5.0	2.5	-2.3	7.8	0.1	6.4
Current Account (% of GDP)																						
China	3.1	1.3	-1.8	1.2	0.2	0.8	3.8	3.0	1.9	1.7	1.3	2.4	2.6	3.5	5.8	8.3	10.1	9.2	5.1	4.0	2.8	2.7
Indonesia	-3.0	-1.8	-1.2	-1.4	-2.9	-3.0	-2.0	3.9	3.7	4.8	4.3	4.0	3.50	0.6	0.1	3.0	2.4	0.0	2.0	0.7	0.2	-2.7
South Korea	-2.4	-0.7	0.8	-0.8	-1.5	-4.0	-1.5	11.9	5.3	2.8	1.7	1.3	2.4	4.5	2.2	1.5	2.1	0.3	3.9	2.9	2.4	4.6
Malaysia	-8.5	-3.7	-4.5	-6.1	-9.7	-4.4	-5.9	13.2	15.9	9.1	7.9	7.1	12.1	12.1	13.9	16.1	15.4	16.8	15.7	11.1	11.0	8.2
Thailand	-7.7	-5.7	-5.1	-5.6	-8.1	-8.1	-2.0	12.7	10.1	7.6	4.4	3.7	3.3	1.7	-4.3	1.1	6.3	0.8	8.3	3.1	1.7	0.7
Foreign Reserves (US$ billion)																						
China	44.3	21.2	23.0	53.6	76.0	107.7	143.4	149.8	158.3	168.9	218.7	295.2	412.2	618.6	825.6	1,072.6	1,534.4	1,953.3	2,425.9	2,875.9	3,212.6	3,340.9
Indonesia	10.3	11.4	12.4	13.2	14.8	19.3	17.4	23.5	37.3	29.3	28.0	32.0	36.3	36.3	34.7	42.6	56.9	51.6	66.1	96.2	110.1	112.8
South Korea	13.7	17.2	20.3	25.7	32.7	34.1	20.4	52.0	74.1	96.2	102.8	121.4	155.4	199.1	210.4	239.0	262.2	201.2	270.0	291.6	306.4	327.0
Malaysia	11.0	17.3	27.4	25.5	23.9	27.1	20.9	25.7	30.6	28.6	29.8	33.7	44.1	66.2	70.2	82.4	101.3	91.5	96.7	106.5	133.6	139.7
Thailand	18.4	21.2	25.4	30.3	36.9	38.6	26.9	29.5	34.8	32.7	33.0	38.9	42.1	49.8	52.1	67.0	87.5	111.0	138.4	172.1	175.1	181.6
Exchange Rate (LCU/US$, period average)																						
China	5.32	5.51	5.76	8.62	8.35	8.31	8.29	8.28	8.28	8.28	8.28	8.28	8.28	8.28	8.19	7.97	7.61	7.95	7.83	6.77	6.64	6.31
Indonesia	1,950	2,030	2,087	2,161	2,249	2,342	2,909	10,014	7,855	8,422	10,261	9,311	8,577	8,939	9,705	9,159	9,141	9,699	10,390	9,090	8,770	9,387
South Korea	733	781	803	803	771	804	951	1,401	1,189	1,131	1,291	1,251	1,192	1,145	1,024	955	929	1,102	1,277	1,156	1,108	1,126
Malaysia	2.75	2.55	2.57	2.62	2.50	2.52	2.81	3.92	3.80	3.80	3.80	3.80	3.80	3.80	3.79	3.67	3.44	3.33	3.52	3.22	3.06	3.09
Thailand	25.52	25.40	25.32	25.15	24.92	25.34	31.36	41.36	37.81	40.11	44.43	42.96	41.48	40.22	40.22	37.88	34.52	33.31	34.29	31.69	30.49	31.08

Public Debt (% of GDP)

China	5.9	5.6	5.0	5.8	6.1	6.7	7.4	12.2	27.2	27.6	27.3	27.1	26.8	25.0	23.2	20.7	17.1	15.1	16.4	16.2	15.4	15.8
Indonesia	32.9	32.0	30.2	30.4	27.2	22.3	35.9	50.9	67.1	82.8	71.5	59.7	54.4	51.0	42.8	33.0	31.2	29.5	26.4	25.6	24.1	24.4
South Korea	n.a.	n.a.	n.a.	n.a.	n.a.	n.a.	n.a.	n.a.	n.a.	n.a.	n.a.	19.2	19.7	23.3	25.6	28.6	28.8	30.4	33.5	34.3	356.2	36.7
Malaysia	73.3	64.4	55.7	47.6	41.1	35.3	31.9	36.4	37.3	35.2	41.3	43.0	45.1	45.7	42.1	40.6	40.1	39.8	50.8	51.2	51.8	53.5
Thailand	n.a.	n.a.	21.8	20.0	18.1	16.7	31.8	40.2	56.6	57.8	57.5	55.1	50.7	49.5	47.6	41.1	37.6	38.0	44.8	43.1	40.3	44.5

External Debt (% of GDP)

China	14.2	14.5	13.4	17.2	15.6	14.4	14.9	13.8	13.5	12.2	14.0	12.7	12.5	12.6	12.4	11.6	10.7	8.4	8.7	9.4	9.5	8.9
Indonesia	56.0	56.9	50.8	54.9	55.4	51.1	56.9	142.9	97.6	87.1	82.5	65.5	57.0	53.5	49.6	37.3	34.2	30.9	33.2	27.5	25.2	23.6
South Korea	17.0	17.0	16.5	18.2	17.7	21.8	27.6	42.2	30.1	25.8	22.8	20.4	19.3	21.4	21.4	27.5	37.0	43.5	50.1	42.4	40.3	38.1
Malaysia	4.8	33.8	39.1	40.7	38.7	39.3	47.1	58.7	53.0	44.7	48.7	47.9	44.1	41.9	36.3	34.3	32.6	29.3	34.5	34.5	32.8	32.9
Thailand	38.4	37.5	42.1	45.4	59.5	62.0	72.7	93.8	79.0	65.0	58.2	46.9	35.8	30.7	26.4	22.2	18.4	18.4	23.2	25.3	23.2	24.1

Public Debt (% of Exports)

China	86.1	85.2	93.5	79.9	77.0	71.4	67.6	66.5	63.7	49.0	58.3	48.1	40.0	35.2	32.0	28.7	25.9	22.1	30.3	29.1	30.2	29.8
Indonesia	237.4	230.1	212.6	231.8	226.7	219.4	207.1	262.4	258.0	193.4	200.8	187.3	185.9	158.6	131.7	110.2	105.5	95.6	126.8	106.3	92.3	93.6
South Korea	62.6	62.2	60.9	68.1	61.4	79.0	86.5	92.2	78.9	63.5	61.1	58.3	51.4	49.2	51.6	64.3	80.6	74.0	93.5	76.1	67.5	63.0
Malaysia	43.1	43.0	47.7	44.2	39.9	41.8	49.2	49.8	42.7	36.6	43.2	43.6	39.7	35.0	31.0	28.9	28.9	27.8	35.1	34.8	33.5	35.5
Thailand	97.2	96.4	103.8	109.2	132.0	146.2	141.0	148.5	127.5	91.0	82.8	69.0	51.8	41.7	35.0	29.3	24.1	23.2	32.4	34.3	29.2	30.5

Source: EIU

Central Bank Governors Meeting in May 2013. One is on the usefulness of using local currencies for settlements in trade, investment, and capital transactions in the region. China has been promoting the cross-border use of the Chinese yuan in recent years. As of May 2013, China had bilateral local currency swap arrangements with Japan, South Korea, Malaysia, Singapore, and Thailand among the ASEAN+3 members.[37] The other agenda is on the possible joint response to capital flows, which could be an important pillar of ASEAN+3 ERPD discussions.

CONCLUSION

This paper reviews the history of regional financial cooperation in East Asia. The ASEAN+3 (China, Japan, and South Korea) authorities have established a liquidity support mechanism called the Chiang Mai Initiative (CMI) and multilateralized it (CMIM), and created a regional surveillance mechanism called the Economic Review and Policy Dialogue (ERPD), for which the ASEAN+3 Macroeconomic Research Office (AMRO) was also established.

Amid the volatile and uncertain global environment and increasing interlinkages in East Asia, there is no denying the importance of regional financial cooperation. Under such circumstances, this paper presents challenges in deepening ASEAN+3 regional financial cooperation. The first category of challenges is how to gain and retain market confidence during peacetime. Such challenges include (1) good economic policies and regional policy coordination underpinned by regional mutual surveillance, (2) addressing the limitation of data and statistics, and (3) good communication with the market. The second category of challenges consists of measures to gain and retain market confidence during periods of crisis (crisis time), such as (1) the size and promptness of the liquidity provision mechanism, and (2) collaboration among a global, a regional and bilateral frameworks.

Notes

[1]   This paper was prepared for the GRIPS-ISEAS Workshops on the ASEAN Japan Relationship held in Tokyo on 5 October 2012 and in Singapore on 4 April 2013. The views expressed in this paper are those of the authors and do not necessarily reflect those of the ASEAN+3 Macroeconomic Research Office (AMRO).

[2]   Yoichi Nemoto is the AMRO Director and Satoshi Nakagawa the senior coordination officer of AMRO.

3   See Rocha (2007) and Thorbecke, Lambarte, and Komoto (2010). Rochar
    pointed out that the ratios of short-term debt to reserve in Indonesia, South
    Korea, and Thailand were 170 per cent, 206 per cent, and 145 per cent,
    respectively.

4   See Rocha (2007) and Independent Evaluation Office of the IMF (2003) for
    details.

5   As described by Radelet and Sachs (1998).

6   See Blustein (2001) for an analysis of how the crisis deepened.

7   The 15th National Congress of the Communist Party of China was held between
    12 and 18 September 1997.

8   <http://www.mof.go.jp/english/international_policy/convention/manila_
    framework/if000a.htm>.

9   <http://www.mof.go.jp/english/international_policy/financial_cooperation_in_
    asia/new_miyazawa_initiative/e1e042.htm>.

10 <http://www.mof.go.jp/english/international_policy/convention/bilateral_
    meetings_between_finance_ministers/e1e063.htm>; <http://www.mof.go.jp/
    english/international_policy/financial_cooperation_in_asia/new_miyazawa_
    initiative/if005.htm>.

11 See Tsai *et al.* (2011).

12 <http://www.fmprc.gov.cn/eng/wjdt/zyjh/t24914.htm>.

13 See Lum *et al.* (2008) and Tsai *et al.* (2011).

14 <http://www.mofa.go.jp/region/asia-paci/asean/pmv9911/joint.html>.

15 <http://www.amro-asia.org/wp-content/uploads/2011/11/AFDM+3-Hanoi-Mar-
    19991.pdf>.

16 <http://www.mof.go.jp/english/international_policy/convention/asean_plus_3/
    if014.htm>.

17 <http://www.mof.go.jp/english/international_policy/convention/asean_plus_3/
    ekaigi008.htm>.

18 <http://www.mof.go.jp/english/international_policy/convention/asean_plus_3/
    as3_040515e.htm>.

19 <http://www.mof.go.jp/english/international_policy/convention/asean_plus_3/
    as3_050504.htm>.

20 <http://www.mof.go.jp/english/international_policy/convention/asean_plus_3/
    as3_060504.htm>.

21 <http://www.federalreserve.gov/newsevents/press/monetary/20081029b.htm>.

22 <http://www.mof.go.jp/english/international_policy/convention/asean_plus_3/
    as3_090503.pdf>.

23 <http://www.mof.go.jp/english/international_policy/convention/asean_plus_3/
    as3_100502.pdf>.

24 <http://www.amro-asia.org/wp-content/uploads/2011/12/Key-Points-of-CMIM.
    pdf>.

25 <http://www.mof.go.jp/english/international_policy/convention/asean_plus_3/
    as3_090222.pdf>.

[26] <http://www.mof.go.jp/english/international_policy/convention/asean_plus_3/as3_100502.pdf>.

[27] Former deputy chief of China's State Administration of Foreign Exchange (SAFE).

[28] <http://www.amro-asia.org/wp-content/uploads/2011/11/AFDM+3-PR-2011-000-20110406-Appointmeent-of-the-AMRO-Director-PR20110503.pdf, http://www.amro-asia.org/about-amro/overview/membership/>.

[29] <http://www.amro-asia.org/about-amro/overview/how-we-do/>.

[30] <http://www.mof.go.jp/english/international_policy/convention/asean_plus_3/as3_110504.pdf>.

[31] <http://www.mof.go.jp/english/international_policy/convention/asean_plus_3/as3_120503.pdf>.

[32] <http://www.amro-asia.org/wp-content/uploads/2012/05/120503AFMGM+3-JS.pdf>.

[33] <http://www.adb.org/publications/asian-economic-integration-monitor-july-2012>.

[34] <http://www.mof.go.jp/english/international_policy/convention/asean_plus_3/as3_040515e.htm>; <http://www.mof.go.jp/english/international_policy/convention/asean_plus_3/as3_060504.htm>.

[35] <http://www.mof.go.jp/english/international_policy/convention/asean_plus_3/as3_090222.pdf>.

[36] <http://www.amro-asia.org/wp-content/uploads/2012/05/120503AFMGM+3-JS.pdf>.

[37] China has been actively establishing bilateral local currency swap arrangements with non-ASEAN+3 members as well, such as Australia, Kazakhstan, Mongolia, Pakistan, Turkey, UAE, and Ukraine.

References

ASEAN+3 Macroeconomic Research Office. "Joint Ministerial Statement of the ASEAN+3 Finance Ministers Meeting (Tashkent, Uzbekistan, 2 May 2010)". Available at <http://www.amro-asia.org/wp-content/uploads/2011/11/JMS-Tashkent-May-20101.pdf> (accessed May 2013).

————. "Joint Statement of the ASEAN+3 Finance Ministers and Central Bank Governors' Meeting (3 May 2012, Manila, the Philippines)". Available at <http://www.amro-asia.org/wp-content/uploads/2012/05/120503AFMGM+3-JS.pdf> (accessed May 2013).

————. "Joint Statement of the ASEAN+3 Finance Ministers and Central Bank Governors' Meeting (Delhi, India, 3 May 2013)". Available at <http://www.amro-asia.org/wp-content/uploads/2013/05/16th-AFMGM+3-Joint-Statement_2013-India.pdf> (accessed May 2013).

Asian Development Bank. "Asian Economic Integration Monitor — July 2012". Available at <http://www.adb.org/sites/default/files/pub/2012/aem-201207.pdf> (accessed May 2013).

Blustein, Paul. *The Chastening: Inside the Crisis that Rocked the Global Financial System and Humbled the IMF*. New York: Public Affairs, 2001.

Henning, C. Randall. *East Asian Financial Cooperation*. Washington, D.C.: Peterson Institute for International Economics, 2002.

Independent Evaluation Office of the International Monetary Fund. "IMF and Recent Capital Account Crises: Indonesia, Korea, Brazil". Available at <http://www.imf.org/external/np/ieo/2003/cac/pdf/all.pdf> (accessed May 2013).

Lipscy, Phillip Y. "Japan's Asian Monetary Fund Proposal". *Stanford Journal of East Asian Affairs* 3 (Summer 2003): 93–104.

Lum, Thomas, Wayne Morrison, and Bruce Vaughn. "China's 'Soft Power' in Southeast Asia". Washington, DC: U.S. Senate Committee of Foreign Relations, Congressional Research Service, 2008.

Ministry of Finance, Japan. "A New Framework for Enhanced Asian Regional Cooperation to Promote Financial Stability: Meeting of Asian Finance and Central Bank Deputies — Agreed Summary of Discussions, Manila, Philippines, 18–19 November 1997". Available at <http://www.mof.go.jp/english/international_policy/financial_cooperation_in_asia/manila_framework/if000a.htm> (accessed May 2013).

———. "Joint Ministerial Statement of the ASEAN+3 Finance Ministers Meeting (Chiang Mai, Thailand, 6 May 2000)". Available at <http://www.mof.go.jp/english/international_policy/convention/asean_plus_3/20000506.htm> (accessed May 2013).

———. "Joint Ministerial Statement of the ASEAN+3 Finance Ministers Meeting (Honolulu, USA, 9 May 2001)". Available at <http://www.mof.go.jp/english/international_policy/convention/asean_plus_3/20010509.htm> (accessed May 2013).

———. "Joint Ministerial Statement of the ASEAN+3 Finance Ministers Meeting (Jeju, Korea, 15 May 2004)". Available at <http://www.mof.go.jp/english/international_policy/convention/asean_plus_3/20040515.htm> (accessed May 2013).

———. "Joint Ministerial Statement of the ASEAN+3 Finance Ministers Meeting (Istanbul, Turkey, 4 May 2005)". Available at <http://www.mof.go.jp/english/international_policy/convention/asean_plus_3/20050504.htm> (accessed May 2013).

———. "Joint Ministerial Statement of the ASEAN+3 Finance Ministers Meeting (Hyderabad, India, 4 May 2006)". Available at <https://www.mof.go.jp/english/international_policy/convention/asean_plus_3/20060504.htm> (accessed May 2013).

————. "Joint Ministerial Statement of the ASEAN+3 Finance Ministers Meeting (Phuket, Thailand, 22 February 2009)". Available at <https://www.mof.go.jp/english/international_policy/convention/asean_plus_3/20090222.pdf> (accessed May 2013).

————. "Joint Ministerial Statement of the ASEAN+3 Finance Ministers Meeting (Bali, Indonesia, 3 May 2009)". Available at <https://www.mof.go.jp/english/international_policy/convention/asean_plus_3/20090503.pdf> (accessed May 2013).

————. "Joint Ministerial Statement of the ASEAN+3 Finance Ministers Meeting (Hanoi, Vietnam, 4 May 2010)". Available at <http://www.mof.go.jp/english/international_policy/convention/asean_plus_3/20110504.pdf> (accessed May 2013).

————. "A New Initiative to Overcome the Asian Currency Crisis: New Miyazawa Initiative". Available at <http://www.mof.go.jp/english/international_policy/financial_cooperation_in_asia/new_miyazawa_initiative/e1e042.htm> (accessed May 2013).

Ministry of Foreign Affairs, Japan. "Joint Statement on East Asia Cooperation, ASEAN+3 Summit in Manila, November 1999". Available at <http://www.mofa.go.jp/region/asia-paci/asean/pmv9911/joint.html> (accessed May 2013).

Radelet, S., and J. Sachs. "The Onset of the East Asian Financial Crisis". NBER Working Paper no. 6680 (1998).

Rocha, Bruno. "At Different Speeds: Policy Complementarities and the Recovery from the Asian Crisis". ADB Institute Discussion Paper no. 60 (2007).

Sakakibara, Eisuke. *Nihon to Sekai ga Furueta Hi: Saiba Shihonshugi Hokai no Kiki* 日本と世界が震えた日 [The Day That Shook Japan and the World: Cyber Capitalism in Danger of Collapse]. Tokyo: Chuo Koron Shinsha, 2000.

Thorbecke, W., M. Lamberte, and G. Komoto. "Promoting Learning and Industrial Upgrading in ASEAN Countries". ADB Working Paper Series no. 250 (2010).

Tsai, Tung-Chieh, Hung Ming-Te, and Tony Tai-Ting Liu. "China's Foreign Policy in Southeast Asia: Harmonious Worldview and Its Impact on Good Neighbor Diplomacy". *Journal of Contemporary Eastern Asia* 10, no. 1 (2011): 25–42.

World Bank. 1993. *The East Asian Miracle: Economic Growth and Public Policy.* Washington, D.C.: World Bank. Available at <http://documents.worldbank.org/curated/en/1993/09/698870/east-asian-miracle-economic-growth-public-policy-vol-1-2-main-report> (accessed May 2013).

11

JAPANESE DEVELOPMENT ASSISTANCE TO ASEAN COUNTRIES

Naohiro Kitano[1]

INTRODUCTION

Japan has been promoting bilateral economic cooperation with the Association of Southeast Asian Nations (ASEAN) member countries (ASEAN countries) since the 1960s, using development assistance[2] as a major tool. In recent years, Japan has also enhanced regional cooperation with ASEAN. Shimomura (2013) noted that Japan's economic cooperation with East Asia, including ASEAN countries, produces "synergy effects of trade, investment and aid" and considered that this approach is common in the economic cooperation of other Asian countries such as China. This paper provides an overview of Japan's development assistance to ASEAN countries, its relationship with Japan's foreign direct investment (FDI), and other characteristics of Japan's development assistance, such as supporting a balanced urban and rural development. Lastly, recent developments in Japan's regional cooperation with ASEAN are outlined. As a reference, China's external economic cooperation is also described briefly in the footnotes.[3]

IMPACTS OF DEVELOPMENT ASSISTANCE TO ASEAN COUNTRIES

This paper begins with an introduction to some of the previous studies on the impact of Japan's development assistance to ASEAN countries. Kawai

(2005), in his report on a coherent policy for development, states that "the economic development of developing countries in East Asia since the 1980s was made possible by the inflow of FDI from developed countries and the subsequent activation of regional specialization and trade." He points out that "there are links between the development of infrastructure in Asian developing countries supported by Japan's development assistance, the increase in Japanese FDI as a result of Japanese manufacturing companies entering those countries, the increase in exports of industrial products by those countries due to the increase in the intra-company division of labor and transactions, and the increase in household income in those countries." He concluded that "Japan's development assistance policy, which focused on infrastructure development, was coherent with the strategies of the developing countries in the region, which had promoted export-oriented and industrialization policies."

Meanwhile, Kimura and Todo (2010) scrutinized the role played by development assistance in inducing FDI. They classified the FDI-inducing effects of the cumulative amount of development assistance of the five main OECD countries[4] from 1990 to 2002 into three types — "positive infrastructure effect", "negative rent-seeking effect", and "positive vanguard effect" — and performed an empirical analysis using the Gravity Model. Here, "vanguard effect" means a specific effect whereby Japan's development assistance serves only to attract Japanese FDI as a "vanguard". The results of the analysis showed that development assistance in general did not have a significant effect on FDI in terms of those three effects, but that Japan's development assistance for infrastructure development had a significant "vanguard effect".

Kimura and Todo argue that if only the six major countries in East Asia[5] are considered, 6 per cent of the increase in Japanese FDI during the period of 1997–2002 is attributable to the increase in Japan's development assistance to those countries. Furthermore, Sung Jin Kang et al. (2010) contend that, using the same model as that of Kimura and Todo, Korea's development assistance also had a significant "vanguard effect".

Mitsubishi Research Institute (2011) analyzed the impact of Japan's development assistance on the formation of economic infrastructure stock in the three ASEAN countries of Thailand, Indonesia, and Vietnam,[6] and concluded that for Thailand and Indonesia, Japan's development assistance, through its outstanding contribution to the formation of economic infrastructure in the 1980s, may have acted as a catalyst for the activation of FDI from all over the world, including from Japan, and that a similar pattern has been observed in Vietnam since the 1990s.[7] Mitsubishi Research Institute estimates that the formation of economic infrastructure may have boosted productivity in the private industrial sector by 3 per cent to 30 per cent.

JAPAN'S FOREIGN DIRECT INVESTMENT AND DEVELOPMENT ASSISTANCE TO ASEAN COUNTRIES

The studies presented in the previous section suggest that Japan's development assistance for some ASEAN countries has encouraged FDI, especially from Japan, and contributed to the economic growth of these countries. Let us examine whether the same tendency can be observed in other ASEAN countries. In this section, we compare the trends in FDI and development assistance from Japan to the ASEAN-4 of Indonesia, Malaysia, Thailand, and the Philippines, now becoming middle-income countries, with that to the CLMV (Cambodia, Laos, Myanmar and Vietnam) or the latecomer ASEAN countries (Cambodia, Laos, and Myanmar). Cambodia, Laos, and Myanmar are classified as least developed countries (LDCs), while Vietnam is the only country among the CLMV that is becoming a middle-income country. For this purpose, both the ODA gross disbursements in OECD International Development Statistics and the Japanese FDI flow in the "Outward and Inward Foreign Direct Investment" as well as "Balance of Payments Statistics" of Japan[8] (JETRO website) have been used.

ASEAN-4

(i) Trend of Japan's development assistance and FDI to ASEAN-4

Figure 11.1 shows the trend in development assistance and FDI from Japan to the ASEAN-4. The overall trend is that FDI increased as the volume of development assistance increased until the Asian financial crisis in the late 1990s, and increased sharply in the 2000s despite the Lehman shock in 2008.

A close-up graph in Figure 11.1, which covers the period 1960–75, shows that the original grant aid was gradually replaced by Japanese ODA loans (Yen Loans) from 1966.[9] During this period, Indonesia's Brantas River Basin Development Plan in East Java,[10] which was the

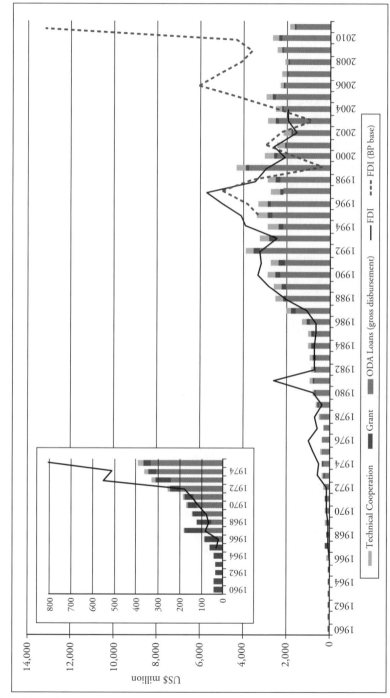

FIGURE 11.1

Japan's Development Assistance and FDI to ASEAN-4 Countries

Source: OECD International Development Statistics and JETRO.

first comprehensive regional development plan and served as a model for Japan's subsequent development assistance, was implemented (Fujimoto 2013). Japanese FDI increased sharply as a result of the Nixon Shock of 1971,[11] and the amount of investment in the ASEAN-4 also sharply increased, exceeding US$500 million in 1973. There was remarkable progress in the small-scale textile industry in particular, while investment in the development and import of oil progressed in Indonesia.[12] Although infrastructure development in these countries was far from adequate, the provision of Yen Loans every year may have produced a "vanguard effect" and reduced the sovereign risk of the ASEAN-4, as well as Vietnam, as described later.[13]

(ii) Social issues encountered by Japan in the early stage of ASEAN-Japan relations

The surge in Japanese FDI led to a backlash from the recipient countries. In particular, Japan was criticized for its rapid entry into and over-presence in East Asia, where 26 per cent of its total FDI was directed (Japan Overseas Enterprises Association 1999). In response to this criticism, the Federation of Economic Organizations (Keidanren),[14] together with four other economic organizations,[15] published "Guidelines for Investment Activities in Developing Countries"[16] in 1973;[17] the Japan Overseas Enterprises Association was also established in 1974.[18] Since then, the Japanese private sector has accumulated the knowledge and experience to handle social and environmental issues.

(iii) Eastern Seaboard Development Program in Thailand: A case of "synergy effects of trade, investment, and aid"

Since the late 1970s, the reduction of Japan's large trade surplus has become a serious diplomatic issue. One of Japan's most effective measures to achieve this was to launch four consecutive medium-term policies that aimed to significantly increase the amount of ODA (Japan Bank for International Cooperation 2003). The subsequent sharp increase in development assistance to the ASEAN-4 was used to enhance infrastructure development through the construction of power plants and the improvement of transport facilities.[19] In addition to the improved investment environment and the liberalization of investment policies of these countries, the surge in the yen resulting from the Plaza Accord of 1985 was the decisive factor that led Japanese companies to increase FDI in the ASEAN-4 from the late 1980s.[20]

At around this time the government of Thailand formulated the "Eastern Seaboard Development Program" in order to develop the strategically located eastern seaboard region. This program proposed the construction of a deepwater port with easy access to Bangkok to foster export-oriented industries. Between 1982 and 1993, Japan provided Yen Loans totaling ¥178.8 billion for the construction of Laem Chabang and Map Ta Phut ports, trunk roads connecting to Bangkok, water pipes, industrial parks, and so forth. Mieno (2013) and Muto *et al.* (2007) argue that the development of the eastern seaboard helped to attract FDI, especially in the auto industry, and led to the subsequent development of industrial agglomerations in Thailand.[21] The amount of Japanese FDI in the ASEAN-4 fell after the Asian financial crisis in the late 1990s and the Lehman Shock in 2008, and then recovered to US$13 billion in 2011.

(iv) Japan's inclusive approach to support a balanced urban and rural development

As mentioned above, "synergy effects of trade, investment, and aid" is observed in the case of the Eastern Seaboard development in Thailand. During this period, Japan simultaneously supported the Thai government to redress regional disparities between the metropolitan areas and the northeastern as well as northern regions, which has been an important policy issue. Nagashima (2012) compared the migration of workers from rural to urban areas in the 1980s against migration in the 2000s. In the 1980s, as rural migrants without sufficient education flowed into urban areas as unskilled workers without access to formal labor markets, income inequality increased significantly. By contrast, in the 2000s, with the formalization of labor markets as a result of the formation of FDI-led industrial agglomerations, including the eastern seaboard, and improvement in education in rural areas, it became possible for rural workers to gain access to formal labor markets. The study concludes that migrant workers have been able to secure a certain level of income, thereby reducing the income disparities of the previous decades. Japan has not only cooperated in infrastructure development, which has enabled the establishment of industrial agglomerations, but has also supported inclusive rural development, including small-scale irrigation programs, new village development programs, rural finance (BAAC[22] loans), and vocational education in rural areas, such as an industrial college in Chiang Mai. Japan's balanced support in these areas has helped to alleviate disparities.

(v) *Human resource development: technical cooperation for ASEAN-4 plus Singapore*

Human resource development is another area that Japan has been emphasizing. Japan has actively provided technical cooperation by sending experts to ASEAN-4 as well as Singapore and by receiving trainees in Japan. The number of trainees from the ASEAN-4 increased from fewer than 500 in 1968 to over 2,000 in 1989. A typical example is the comprehensive technical cooperation with Singapore during 1983–90, called the Productivity Development Project (PDP), which aimed to transfer Japan's know-how in productivity improvement. Singapore successfully internalized the know-how and began its technical cooperation by setting up the Singapore Cooperation Program (SCP) in 1992 as south-south cooperation.[23]

Meanwhile, Japanese technical cooperation at King Mongkut's University of Technology, Thonburi, Thailand, and at the Malaysian Institute of Industrial Weighing enhanced technical capabilities of its counterparts and indirectly contributed to improving productivity in the respective countries through human resource development (Japan International Cooperation Agency, the Center for International Development/International Development Journal 2010).

Another example is the Southeast Asia Engineering Education Development Network Project, started in 2001 as an autonomous sub-network of the ASEAN University Network (AUN/SEED-Net), aimed at promoting human resources development in engineering in ASEAN. The Network consists of 26 leading member institutions from 10 ASEAN countries, supported by 14 leading Japanese universities, all of which engage in a number of activities focused on joint research.[24] The third phase, from 2013, is aimed at (a) fostering human resources for advanced industry and supporting regional industry by providing technical assistance; (b) responding to global challenges that are common to the region; and (c) forming a platform for the development of science and technology in Asia.

(vi) *Recent efforts to improve the investment environment in metropolitan areas of ASEAN countries*

As the ASEAN-4 become middle-income countries, they face the new challenge of avoiding the middle-income trap and advancing to a high-income level through sustainable and inclusive growth. Japan has started to provide development assistance to meet this challenge in innovative ways.

In recent years, Japan has been supporting urban development for the metropolitan areas of ASEAN countries in order to further improve their investment environment to attract FDI. In the Jakarta metropolitan area, which is the driving force of the Indonesian economy, urban infrastructure has not met the vast need for economic activities. Thus, a master plan (M/P) study for establishing a Metropolitan Priority Area for Investment and Industry (MPA) was conducted by the Japan International Cooperation Agency (JICA) to formulate an overall plan on infrastructure development, by adopting a public-private partnership (PPP) and specifying 45 priority infrastructure projects such as the development of a new international port, smart communities, and the Jakarta Mass Rapid Transit (MRT).[25] A joint venture consisting of 11 Japanese companies participated in the M/P study team in order to share their professional knowledge and experiences on investments in and operation of infrastructure projects, as well as provide policy recommendations to the Indonesian government.

(vii) Science and technology cooperation

Another innovative approach is in the field of science and technology, which forms the basis of innovation and sustainable growth. In 2008, Japan introduced a new program for promoting international joint research targeting global issues, including global warming, infectious diseases, and natural disasters. This program, called Science and Technology Research Partnership for Sustainable Development (SATREPS),[26] works through three- to five-year projects involving partnerships between researchers in Japan and researchers in developing countries, in collaboration with two Japanese government agencies — Japan Science and Technology Agency (JST) and JICA.

So far, 78 projects have been approved, of which the share in ASEAN countries is the largest (30 projects), followed by Africa (20 projects). One example is the Integrated Study Project on Hydro-Meteorological Prediction and Adaptation to Climate Change in Thailand (IMPAC-T), led by the Institute of Industrial Science, the University of Tokyo, and Kasetsart University (KU), whose objective is to propose effective techniques for managing water resources and models for water-related disaster mitigation, especially in the Chao Phraya river basin, which suffered from flooding in 2011, as well as to create support systems for policy implementation.

Vietnam

The principle of Japan's development assistance to the ASEAN-4 was extended to Vietnam in the 1990s. Figure 11.2 shows the trend of Japan's development assistance to and FDI in Vietnam. Japan paid war reparations to South Vietnam in the 1960s. This was followed by grant aid as well as commodity loans after the unification of the South and the North in the 1970s.[27] Immediately after the signing of the Paris Peace Agreement for Cambodia in 1991, Japan resumed full-scale development assistance, starting with a ¥44.5 billion commodity loan intended to clear past arrears.

Figure 11.2 shows that Japanese FDI increased immediately after the resumption of development assistance. Tomoda and Takeda (2005) argue that the resumption of Yen Loans reduced sovereign risk and encouraged the private sector to invest and advance into Vietnam, which suggests that Japan's development assistance in this period had a significant "vanguard effect". The amount of Japanese development assistance rapidly increased, covering a wide range of sectors such as national road and railway, electric power, urban and rural infrastructure development, public health, and education. In order to provide economic policy advice to the leaders of the country, a survey on supporting the transition to a market economy in Vietnam (1995–2001) known as the Ishikawa Project, was also conducted. This was followed by a number of capacity development, and policy and institutional reform projects. Subsequently, Japanese FDI increased again in the 2000s, reaching US$1.8 billion in 2011.

An example of Japan's approach as "synergy effects of trade, investment, and aid" is transport infrastructure projects in Northern Vietnam. Tran Van Tho *et al.* (2003) conclude that the widening and improvement works of National Highway No. 5, connecting Hai Phong to Hanoi, and the rehabilitation of Hai Phong Port, contributed to the development of an industrial park located at the suburban area of Hanoi, Thang Long Industrial Park, which was initiated by a Japanese trading company. A major Japanese manufacturing company, Canon, made a decision to make FDI to establish a printer factory for export in this industrial park. Canon's decision became the catalyst for the formation of industrial agglomerations in northern Vietnam by inducing FDI by parts suppliers. Canon performed the role of "anchor company". Consequently, trade volumes have increased and new employment has been created.

Similar to the case of Thailand, in order to support a balanced urban and rural development in Vietnam, Japan also extended Yen Loans for

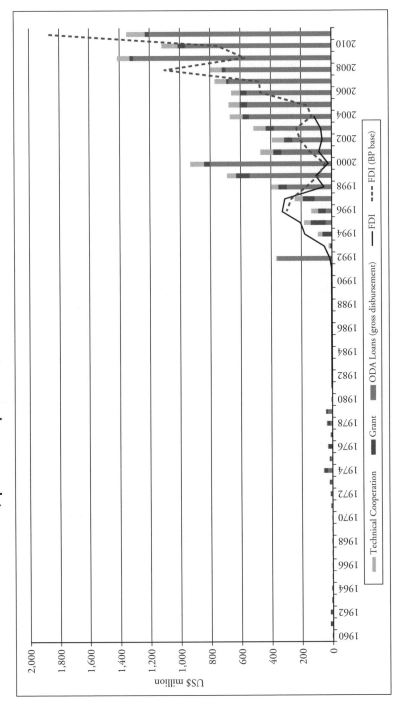

FIGURE 11.2
Japan's Development Assistance and FDI to Vietnam

Source: OECD International Development Statistics and JETRO.

a series of small-scale pro-poor infrastructure development projects in rural areas.

Cambodia, Laos, and Myanmar

This section summarizes the situation in Cambodia, Laos, and Myanmar. Just as the political conditions in these countries are different from those in the ASEAN-4 and Vietnam examined so far, so is the trend in Japan's development assistance and FDI. However, in recent years, Japanese manufacturing companies have been seeking opportunities to invest in production bases in the CLMV partly because of the increasing cost of labor in China.

(i) Cambodia

Figure 11.3 shows the trend of Japan's development assistance to and FDI in Cambodia. Economic cooperation with Cambodia commenced with the 1959 signing of the economic cooperation agreement between Japan and Cambodia, after which grant aid as "quasi-reparations", as well as Yen Loans were provided to Cambodia. However, bilateral economic cooperation with the country was suspended following the coup d'état by General Lon Nol in 1970 and the establishment of the Pol Pot regime in 1975.

Japan actively helped to establish peace in Cambodia at the end of the 1980s. After the general election in 1993, it resumed full-scale assistance by supporting the rehabilitation and reconstruction of the country. Assistance centered on grant aid and various types of cooperation is on the rise. The development of infrastructure, including trunk roads, bridges,[28] Sihanoukville Port, and transmission lines, as well as irrigation, were carried out through grant aid and Yen Loans, while capacity enhancement of water corporations, dissemination of maternal and child health care, TB control, development of the judicial system, private sector development, and mine clearance were facilitated through technical cooperation.

Although FDI from Japan is still limited, it reached US$80 million in 2011. Cambodia has just built a Special Economic Zone adjacent to Sihanoukville Port by utilizing a Yen Loan to attract Japanese investment.[29]

(ii) Laos

Figure 11.4 shows the trend of Japanese FDI in Laos. Economic cooperation with Laos began in the late 1950s with feasibility studies for water

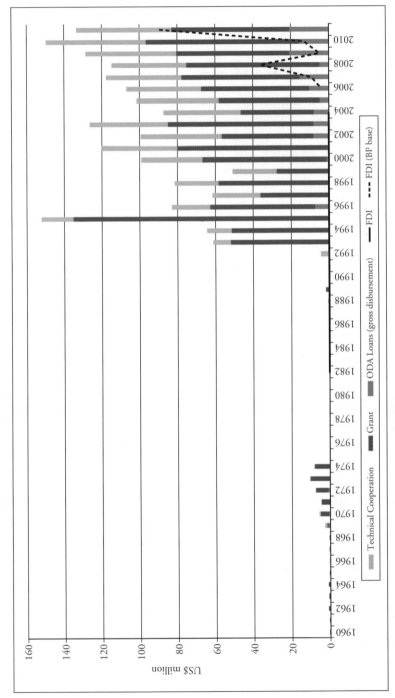

FIGURE 11.3
Japan's Development Assistance and FDI to Cambodia

Source: OECD International Development Statistics and JETRO.

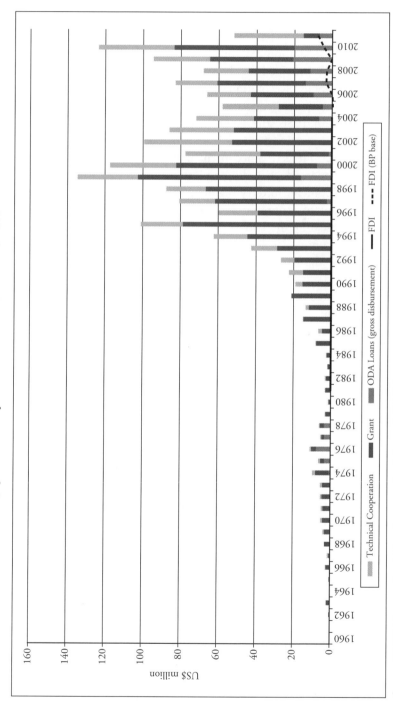

FIGURE 11.4
Japan's Development Assistance and FDI to Laos

Source: OECD International Development Statistics and JETRO.

supply and bridge construction projects, and the acceptance of trainees as well as the dispatch of experts. In 1965, part of the first group of Overseas Cooperation Volunteers was sent to Laos. In the mid-1970s, a Yen Loan was provided for the Nam Ngum Hydropower Project. However, after the People's Revolutionary Party formed a government in 1975, the amount of aid was reduced. After the economic liberalization policy was introduced in 1986, the Japanese government increased its grant aid and technical cooperation, and in 1996 provided a Yen Loan for the Nam Leuk Hydropower Project. Since then, a variety of cooperative ventures have been implemented, including education and medical care, agriculture and rural development, forestry maintenance, development of the private sector, development of economic and social infrastructure, and governance.

Japanese FDI in Laos is still very limited, although Japanese manufacturing companies located in Thailand have been building factories there since the mid-2000s as a direct result of the sharp rise in salaries in Thailand. In 2007, the Lao Japan Public and Private Sector Dialogue was launched with the aim of improving the trade and investment environment. The following year, the Japan-Laos Investment Agreement was inaugurated, paving the way for the expansion of investment from Japan, which reached US$7 million in 2011.[30]

(iii) Myanmar

Finally, we turn our attention to Myanmar. Figure 11.5 shows the trend of Japan's development assistance to and FDI in Myanmar. Starting with war reparations in the 1950s, Myanmar received a greater amount of development assistance, especially Yen Loans, from Japan, than did Laos and Cambodia, in a wide range of fields including electric power, manufacturing, transportation, health, improving the living standard of minority populations in border areas, counter-narcotics efforts, and structural economic reform.[31] Shrouded by the cloak of the "Burmese way to socialism" since 1962, however, the country remained closed to the outside world. Western countries imposed sanctions on the country after a military government took power in 1988, even though the government abandoned socialism and introduced a market economy with the consequent opening up of the country to the outside world. As such, Japan did not invest as much in Myanmar as it did in the ASEAN-4 and Vietnam.

The bilateral economic relationship with Myanmar was suspended in principle after 1988. In 1995, however, the Japanese government reviewed its aid policy toward Myanmar and decided to consider or implement

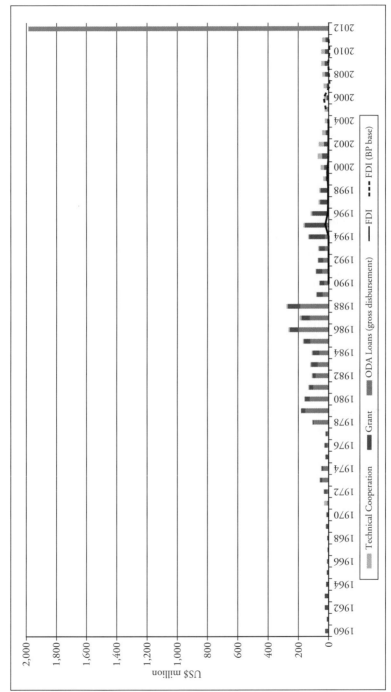

FIGURE 11.5
Japan's Development Assistance and FDI to Myanmar

Source: OECD International Development Statistics and JETRO.

suspended projects and projects that would directly benefit the people of Myanmar by addressing their basic human needs, on a case-by-case basis, while monitoring the progress toward democracy and the improvement of human rights.[32] Since 2003 Japan has continued to provide cooperation, mainly to developing ASEAN countries, as well as ASEAN as a whole, focusing on those facets of humanitarian assistance that contribute to democratization and economic reform.

At the summit meeting between Japan and Myanmar in April 2012, (a) a debt-relief measure in order to resume new Yen Loans was agreed on; (b) Japan announced that it would provide support to improve people's livelihood, including assistance to ethnic minorities, capacity building and institutional development to sustain the economy and society, and development of the infrastructure required for sustainable economic growth; and (c) a memorandum was exchanged for the development of the Tirawa Special Economic Zone.[33]

As in the case of Vietnam, JICA extended approximately the equivalent of US$2 billion (¥198.9 billion) in Yen Loans to Myanmar in January 2013, as part of Japan's debt relief measures. A loan, provided by three Japanese banks for clearing a part of the debt, is bridged to this Yen Loan.[34] During Prime Minister Abe's visit to Myanmar in May 2013, he announced Japan's intent to implement assistance totaling ¥91 billion — comprising ¥51 billion as Yen Loans and ¥40 billion as grant aid and technical assistance — to Myanmar by the end of FY 2013. Japan's projected development assistance to Myanmar is thus starting to catch up with the level of its assistance to Vietnam. Although Japanese FDI in Myanmar in 2011 was only US$0.5 million, it is expected to increase significantly.[35]

As social inclusion of ethnic minorities, who predominantly live in rural and border areas, is one of the most crucial issues for Myanmar, an inclusive approach to support a balanced urban and rural development is essential for Japan's future development assistance.

COOPERATION WITH ASEAN

This section deals with Japan's cooperation with ASEAN, which has come to play an important role in recent years, alongside bilateral cooperation.[36]

(1) Commitment at the Summit Level

For the past few decades, Japan has been committed to supporting ASEAN and the Mekong region. In 1977, Prime Minister Takeo Fukuda met with leaders of ASEAN countries and promised financial assistance of US$1 billion for ASEAN industrialization projects.[37] In 1997, Prime Minister Hashimoto announced at the first Japan-ASEAN Summit Meeting that Japan would accept up to 20,000 trainees and students from ASEAN countries over the subsequent five years as part of the Japan-ASEAN Comprehensive Human Resources Cultivation Program. In 1998, Prime Minister Obuchi made a commitment at the second Japan-ASEAN Plus Three Summit Meeting to implement a series of support measures including the realization of the New Miyazawa Initiative aimed at resolving the Asian financial crisis, the implementation of special Yen Loans of ¥600 billion in three years, the training of 10,000 people, and cooperation to strengthen higher education.

At the Japan-ASEAN Special Summit Meeting (Japan-ASEAN Commemorative Summit), which was held for the first time in Japan in 2003, the Tokyo Declaration for a Dynamic and Enduring Japan-ASEAN Partnership in the New Millennium was agreed upon. As an attachment to the Tokyo Declaration, the Japan-ASEAN Action Plan was formulated. The latter covered about 120 items for cooperation and included an announcement by Prime Minister Koizumi for cooperation consisting of over US$1.5 billion in three years for the development of human resources, as well as cooperation consisting of US$1.5 billion for the development of the Mekong region. At the 9th Japan-ASEAN Summit Meeting in 2005, a contribution of ¥7.5 billion for ASEAN integration was announced. This was followed by an announcement at the 10th Meeting, held in January 2007, of a contribution of US$52 million for the Japan-ASEAN Comprehensive Economic Alliance Cooperation Fund, intended to encourage economic alliances, as well as a contribution of US$67 million for measures to combat avian influenza. At the 11th Meeting held in November of the same year, cooperation consisting of US$300 million over five years for securing security and safety, and the training of 300 personnel was announced. In the meantime, at the first Japan-Mekong Region Summit Meeting in 2010, ODA totaling more than ¥500 billion over three years was announced for the Mekong region as a whole. In 2011, at the 14th Japan-ASEAN Summit Meeting, 1,000 people from East Asia were invited to participate in programs on the development of human resources in the field of infrastructure development. At the 4th Mekong-Japan Summit Meeting, a list of 57 major infrastructure projects worth a total of ¥2,300 billion, which would contribute to the development of the countries in the Mekong region, was presented. Approximately ¥600 billion in the form of ODA was also pledged in the three years starting the following year.[38]

As described above, Japan's commitment is characterized by the following: (a) Since the Fukuda Doctrine, emphasis has been placed not only on support for the development of infrastructure, but also on the development of human resources and personnel exchanges; (b) focus has been placed not only on bilateral cooperation but also on cooperation with ASEAN through the Japan-ASEAN Comprehensive Economic Partnership Cooperation Fund and the Economic Research Institute for ASEAN and East Asia (ERIA), referred to below; and (c) commitment to the Mekong region is on the rise (US$1.5 billion over three years from 2003, ¥500 billion over three years from 2010, and ¥600 billion over three years from 2012).

(2) Cooperation for the Master Plan on ASEAN Connectivity

In preparation for the regional economic integration scheduled for 2015, ASEAN adopted the Master Plan on ASEAN Connectivity (MPAC), which aims to develop regional infrastructure. As part of its own growth strategy, and in tandem with the Free Trade Agreement in Asia within the framework of the East Asia Summit (ASEAN Plus Six), Japan is poised to support the plan in view of the importance of its geographical connectivity with East Asia.

ERIA, which plays a core role in the plan, was the brainchild of the Japanese government, and in accordance with the agreement at the 3rd East Asia Summit in 2007, its inaugural meeting was held at the Secretariat of ASEAN in Jakarta in 2008. ERIA is a regional think tank with a research network composed of research institutions of the 16 East Asia Summit member countries. In order to promote further economic integration among East Asian and ASEAN countries, the think tank makes recommendations on specific policies and programs based on an analysis of a range of issues in the region, working toward its main goals of "deepening economic integration", "narrowing development gaps", and "sustainable development".[39]

At the 6th East Asia Summit in 2010, the Comprehensive Asia Development Plan (CADP), compiled by ERIA making use of the Geographical Simulation Model, which was developed by applying Spatial Economics Theory, was approved. The Plan focuses on the integral development of both software and hardware infrastructure in order to improve ASEAN connectivity. This involves building a range of infrastructure including roads, ports, airports, industrial parks, power plants, transmission lines, etc., while simultaneously improving a range of systems and programs. The latter include the framework for trade and business over a wide area including the Industrial Artery, comprising the Mekong, India, Brunei, Indonesia, Malaysia, and the Philippines (BIMP); the East Asia Growth Area (EAGA); and the so-called growth triangle of Indonesia, Malaysia, and Thailand (IMT). A total of 695 projects have been identified, listed, and classified by priority.

Using the results of data compiled by CADP, ERIA also played an active role in planning strategies for implementing the MPAC adopted at the 17th ASEAN Summit in 2010, in cooperation with the ADB, the World Bank, and UNESCAP. MPAC is designed to develop infrastructure for strengthening connectivity among ASEAN countries with the objective of full integration by 2015.

In 2012, in partnership with the private sector, the government of Japan decided to implement through the ADB, a technical cooperation plan called the Master Plan on ASEAN Connectivity Implementation, by leveraging the Japan-ASEAN Integration Fund. In addition, JICA, which signed a cooperation agreement with ERIA in 2010, will assist in the creation and implementation of individual projects based on CADP and MPAC, in cooperation with the Japanese private sector, including the Federation of Economic Organizations.

(3) Cooperation for the Maritime ASEAN Economic Corridor Initiative

In addition to the MPAC, there is yet another initiative supported by Japan: the Maritime ASEAN Economic Corridor. This initiative was devised to develop the islands in conjunction with the continental economic corridor initiative that ASEAN has promoted so far. In response to the proposal made by ASEAN, JICA conducted a survey on creating a development guideline for the ASEAN network of 47 ports and harbors, and the selection of the 10 highest priority ports, including Lach Huyen Port in Vietnam.[40]

In addition, the "Study on the Establishment of an ASEAN Ro-Ro Shipping Network", which is a top priority item and will serve to strengthen connectivity between the islands in the ASEAN countries, is currently under way, in cooperation with ASEAN. Ro-Ro (Roll on-Roll off) ships, which utilize a loading ramp to enable wheeled vehicles to be rolled on and off, and which are capable of loading and unloading at any port without a crane, are expected to be widely used in the ASEAN islands. The Asia Cargo Highway initiative is also under consideration.[41]

(4) Disaster Management

In the field of disaster management, a preparatory office for the establishment of the ASEAN Coordinating Center for Humanitarian Assistance on Disaster Management (AHA Center) was established in Jakarta in 2011 to promote cooperation with ASEAN countries and related international organizations, and to identify, evaluate, and monitor risks. In addition to providing communication equipment and stockpiling supplies through the Japan-ASEAN Integration Fund, Japan sent an adviser via JICA to enhance the capacity of the center.[42]

(5) Efforts to Alleviate Intra-regional Disparities

Against the backdrop of impressive economic growth, ASEAN countries continue to suffer intra-regional disparities, which need to be alleviated for the stability of the whole region. To this end, the forerunning ASEAN countries (Indonesia, Malaysia, the Philippines, Singapore, Thailand, and Brunei) and the latecomer ASEAN countries (Cambodia, Laos, Myanmar, and Vietnam: CLMV) launched a framework called the Initiative for ASEAN Integration (IAI) in 2002.[43] A total of 134 training sessions and seminars were held during the IAI Work Plan I (2002–08) on human resource development, information and communication technology, infrastructure development, regional economic integration, and tourism and poverty. In the meantime, for the IAI Work Plan II (2009–2015), it was decided that each country would choose subjects according to its needs (IAI Priority List). JICA supports the creation of a more specific CLMV Priority Action List in conjunction with the ASEAN Secretariat. In Laos, the Laos Pilot Program, based on a tripartite collaboration consisting of the government of Laos, the ASEAN Secretariat, and JICA, is under way. Currently, technical cooperation is provided by ASEAN and Japan in the three priority areas of the environment, agriculture, and environmental protection.[44]

CONCLUSION

This paper has provided an overview of Japan's development assistance to ASEAN countries, focusing on its relationship with Japanese FDI, as well as its other characteristics such as an inclusive approach that considers urban and rural balance, as well as human resource development. Japan's bilateral development assistance and FDI to the ASEAN-4 and Vietnam has yielded "synergy effects of trade, investment and aid". Japan's recent innovative development assistance with private sectors and research institutions to ASEAN-4 is expected to contribute to avoiding the middle-income trap and advancing to a high-income level.

Japanese companies' advance into the late entrants of Cambodia, Laos, and Myanmar in recent years is a positive signal; however, whether the same modus operandi will apply to these countries remains to be seen. An inclusive approach and emphasizing the importance of human resource development are also crucial to the sustainable development of the three countries, especially Myanmar, which faces ethnic minority issues.

Regarding ASEAN-Japan development cooperation, aside from commitments at summit level, new initiatives have emerged, such as the establishment of ERIA and the AHA Center, measures to improve ASEAN connectivity, as well as collaboration in IAI, aimed at alleviating intra-regional disparities. Deepening development cooperation with ASEAN is necessary for Japan, as an important partner, in view of ASEAN integration in 2015 and beyond.

Lastly, China, as described briefly in the footnotes, has been rapidly strengthening economic ties with ASEAN countries through economic cooperation. However, until recently, China had not coordinated with other providers of development assistance — not only in the region but also in other parts of the world. It seems that China has recently changed its stance and has started to coordinate with other countries, such as UK and Australia, in the region. The disclosure level of statistical information on China's aid is in general still low, for example, in its first white paper on foreign aid issued in 2011, except where Cambodia is concerned, because the host country has maintained the transparent aid statistical system. However, it is expected to improve in the second white paper scheduled for the end of 2013.

Being providers of development assistance in the same region, it is important for Japan and China to have positive interactions with each other — both on the field and at the central level — so that both countries can better understand each other's approaches and practices in the region, and compete and coordinate with each other to improve the quality of their development assistance and truly aid ASEAN countries. In this regard, fully utilizing the existing frameworks is a pragmatic approach, such as the Japan-China Policy Dialogue on the Mekong Region[45] initiated by the foreign ministries of both countries in 2008 and the Asian Development Forum (ADF)[46] started in 2010.

Notes

[1] The opinions expressed and arguments employed in this paper are the sole responsibility of the author and do not necessarily reflect those of JICA Research Institute, Japan International Cooperation Agency.

[2] In this paper, "development assistance" is used instead of Official Development Assistance (ODA).

[3] Due to its economic development, China is rapidly increasing its economic cooperation globally, including with ASEAN countries. According to its first white paper on foreign aid issued in 2011, China places "[u]nremittingly helping recipient countries build up their self-development capacity" at the core of its foreign aid policy, and systematizes its own 60 years of experience in development to share with other developing countries. The third point in its policy is: "Adhering to equality, mutual benefit and common development." This implies that Chinese foreign aid is not only beneficial to host countries but also to China's economic development. Currently, China is addressing a number of issues such as correcting its trade imbalance and considering the environment and local community, alongside promoting economic activities. The statistical information in the first white paper is limited; for example, only the total amount of aid from 1950–2009 is disclosed. The second white paper, which is supposed to be issued by the end of 2013, is expected to disclose more statistical information. Regarding the recent ASEAN-China relationship, refer to ASEAN-CHINA Dialogue Relations, <http://www.asean.org/asean/external-relations/china/item/asean-china-dialogue-relations>.

[4] The five countries are Japan, France, Germany, Great Britain, and the United States.

[5] The six countries are China, Korea, Indonesia, Malaysia, the Philippines, and Thailand.

[6] The total amount of Japanese development assistance for economic infrastructure in these countries from 1970–2009 amounted to ¥4.39 trillion, of which ¥1.53 trillion was for Thailand, ¥1.82 trillion for Indonesia, and ¥1.04 trillion for Vietnam.

[7] Grant aid and Yen Loan projects for individual sectors of ASEAN countries total, for example, 76 per cent in Thailand, 85 per cent in Vietnam, and 45 per cent in Myanmar for airports in terms of passenger traffic; 35 per cent in Laos, 53 per cent in Malaysia, and 62 per cent in Indonesia for hydropower plants in terms of GWh; 37 per cent in Vietnam for thermal power plants in terms of GWh; and 51 per cent in the Philippines, 36 per cent in Indonesia, and 22 per cent in Thailand for railways in terms of kilometers.

[8] "Outward and Inward Foreign Direct Investment" represents the total amount of investment at the time of agreement; it does not include return on investment. The data in "Balance of Payments Statistics" is the total amount involved, including return on investment. The former was discontinued in

2004. Because of the difference in definition, two sets of data are shown in the graphs. The latter displays data from 1996 (Ministry of Finance, Policy Research Institute 2006).

[9]   Japan signed reparations treaties with Myanmar, the Philippines, Indonesia, and the Republic of Vietnam (South Vietnam) in the 1950s. Grant aid known as "quasi-reparations" was provided to Cambodia, Laos, Thailand, Malaysia, and Singapore. Japan established Yen Loans as a means to provide financial assistance first to India in 1958. This was followed by extending tied Yen Loans mainly to ASEAN countries until the early 1970s.

[10]   This integrated water resource and regional development plan was intended to increase the country's grain production as well as economic development in the Basin. Development projects such as dams and irrigation facilities were carried out steadily in accordance with master plans that committed to the "One River, One Plan, and One Integrated Management" principle, on a ten-year review basis. In order to strengthen the institutional framework, an independent Project Management Unit, the Brantas Office, was established in 1965. The long-term commitment by the Indonesian and Japanese governments, JICA, and Japanese consultants and contractors, as well as synergies between hard aid and soft aid, encouraged local institutions to develop along with the infrastructure, resulting in good capacity development. Through cooperation in this river basin over the last half century, 7,000 engineers and technicians were trained and have gone on to work in other projects across Indonesia, which met one-third of the country's total demand for manpower in water resource development. Their skills were honed through a series of joint works with foreign experts or OJT, which is why the project is known as "The Brantas School".

[11]   According to the Japan Overseas Enterprises Association (1999), Japan invested heavily in overseas enterprises during this period. Its FDI totaled US$858 million and covered 902 projects in fiscal year (FY) 1971, US$2.33 billion covering 1,770 projects in FY 1972, and US$3.49 billion covering 3,093 projects in FY 1973, which was nearly equivalent to the cumulative total investment of US$3.57 billion over the 20 years from 1951 up to FY 1970.

[12]   Figure 11.1 shows a sharp increase in FDI in 1975 in petroleum-related investments in Indonesia. The hike in 1981 is also attributed to large LNG base-related investments in Indonesia.

[13]   Economic cooperation with the ASEAN-4 in this period centered on export promotion through tied Yen Loans, the securing of civil works orders overseas, as well as the securing of natural resources, etc., which resembles China's current economic cooperation overseas.

[14]   The current Japan Business Federation.

[15]   Japan Chamber of Commerce and Industry; Japan Federation of Employers' Associations, which was merged with the Federation of Economic Organizations

in 2002; Japanese Association of Corporate Executives; and Japan Foreign Trade Council.

[16]   The guidelines clearly stipulate as their basic policy that "any foreign investment is welcomed by the recipient country and will contribute both to the development of Japanese companies and the progress and the development of the recipient country, and will also serve for the harmonization of the economy and society of the recipient country". The guidelines focus on (a) the establishment of a long-term vision, (b) localization of management, (c) education of personnel, and (d) relationships within the community. In 1987 the Japan Federation of Economic Organizations, Japan Chamber of Commerce and Industry, Japanese Association of Corporate Executives, Japan Federation of Employers' Associations, Japan Foreign Trade Council, Kansai Economic Federation, and Japan Overseas Enterprises Association published "Guidelines for Japanese Overseas Direct Investment", which was not limited to developing countries.

[17]   In 2012, the "Guide on Social Responsibility for Chinese International Contractors" was released by the China International Contractors' Association, under the direction of the Ministry of Commerce. This is the first standard for voluntary social responsibility of the international project contracting industry (China International Contractors' Association 2012).

[18]   Direct contact between Japan and ASEAN also started during this period with the establishment of the ASEAN-Japan Forum on Synthetic Rubber in 1973 to resolve the dispute over Japan's rapid increase in the production and export of synthetic rubber, which competed with natural rubber made in ASEAN countries, especially Malaysia (Chng and Hirono 1984).

[19]   In order to reduce the surplus, Japan provided the ASEAN-4 countries not only with development assistance but also untied loans from the Export-Import Bank of Japan, which were classified as Other Official Flows (OOF) of cofinancing with the World Bank and the Asian Development Bank (ADB).

[20]   Of the four countries, the relatively low economic performance of the Philippines was attributed to poor infrastructure development, especially in the metropolitan area, which was a prerequisite to attract FDI and the subsequent creation of industrial agglomerations.

[21]   Based on the experience of its Economic and Technological Development Zones, China developed Special Economic Zones (SEZs) in Africa and built the Khorgos International Center of Border Cooperation across the border with Kazakhstan. The 12th National Five-Year Plan, the 12th Yunnan Province Five-Year Plan, and the 12th Guangxi Zhuang Autonomous Region Five-Year Plan stipulate the establishment of economic cooperation districts at the borders with Myanmar, Laos, and Vietnam in the Mekong region. Some of those border districts are at the preparatory stage, with assistance from the ADB as part of the Greater Mekong Sub-region (GMS) Program. Currently, SEZs are either under construction or have been completed in five locations in Thailand,

Indonesia, Cambodia, Laos, and Vietnam. As Sato Yuri (2011) rightly points out, the imbalance of trade between Indonesia and China is a serious issue and China is encouraged to invest more in manufacturing. The SEZs are expected to play an important role in attracting Chinese investment in manufacturing, and could evolve as industrial agglomerations.

22   Bank for Agriculture and Agricultural Cooperatives (BAAC) is the only governmental agricultural bank in Thailand.

23   Based on Ohno and Kitaw 2011. Since 1994, Japan has supported Singapore in its efforts to cooperate with ASEAN countries through the Japan-Singapore Partnership Program (JSPP), aimed at sharing the accumulated technology and knowledge that Singapore received from Japan, including productivity improvement. In 1997, the Japan Singapore Partnership Program for the 21st Century (JSPP21) was initiated to promote triangular cooperation as part of SCP, based on 50 per cent cost sharing. The cooperation program between the two countries is represented by a joint training program on productivity management in the Southern African Development Community (SADC) countries, implemented from 1997–2004.

24   In 1998, Prime Minister Obuchi made a commitment at the second Japan-ASEAN Plus Three Summit Meeting to implement a series of support measures, including cooperation for the enhancement of higher education. In response, AUN/SEED-Net was formulated.

25   See <http://www.jica.go.jp/english/news/press/2012/121009.html>.

26   For more information, see the website of SATREPS, <http://www.jst.go.jp/global/english/about.html>.

27   For China's aid to North Vietnam during this period, see Zhu (2001).

28   Recently, China has been the predominant provider of economic assistance to Cambodia's road sector, followed by Japan and Korea. Having implemented economic cooperation in the same countries and the same sectors, information sharing is essential to enhance the effectiveness of development assistance and to avoid the duplication of activities. In Cambodia, the Council for the Development of Cambodia (CDC) is actively working on aid information sharing. Every year, detailed information on aid volume from OECD countries and non-OECD countries, including China, is published by CDC. This suggests the importance of improving transparency in recipient countries.

29   In addition to extending concessional loans and preferential export buyer's credit for the development of infrastructure such as trunk roads in Cambodia in recent years, China has also started to invest in a wide range of fields. For economic cooperation with emerging countries such as China, and between South Korea and Cambodia, see Sato Jin *et al.* (2011). For China's economic cooperation in the Mekong region, see N. Kitano (forthcoming).

30   In the framework of the GMS program, China has completed the Laos section of the North-South Economic Corridor connecting Bangkok to Kunming, funded by tripartite financing between the ADB, Thailand, and China. The

fourth Thailand-Laos Mekong Bridge is scheduled for completion in 2013 within the framework of the GMS program. Meanwhile, Chinese companies are engaged in a number of investment programs for real estate development and mining.

31   A survey aimed at supporting policies for the development of economic structural adjustment was carried out from 2000–03.

32   See <http://www.mofa.go.jp/region/asia-paci/myanmar/myanmar.html>.

33   Joint Press Statement on Japan–Myanmar Summit Meeting on 21 April 2012, <http://www.mofa.go.jp/region/asia-paci/myanmar/thein_sein_1204/joint_press_statement_en.html>.

34   For details on the package of debt clearance operations, refer to <paci/myanmar/thein_sein_1204/myanmar_debt_issues_en.html>.

35   China's economic cooperation with Myanmar has undergone changes since the announcement by Myanmar President Thein Sein of the discontinuation of the joint construction by China and Myanmar of the Myitsone hydroelectric power plant on the Irrawaddy River.

36   The Japanese government appointed the first ambassador to ASEAN in October 2008, following the signing of the ASEAN Charter at the 13th Summit Meeting in 2007, and officially opened the Japan Diplomatic Representation Office as the second non-ASEAN member. JICA, meanwhile, signed an MOU with the secretariat of ASEAN and appointed a principal representative for ASEAN coordination in order to form an alliance with the secretariat of ASEAN, ASEAN sectorial ministerial bodies, and the Committee of Permanent Representatives to ASEAN. This section is based on the data of the Southeast Asia and Pacific Department, Japan International Cooperation Agency (2011) as well as data on the websites of JICA and the Ministry of Foreign Affairs.

37   In Manila, at the end of a tour of Southeast Asia in 1977, Prime Minister Fukuda made a historic speech later known as the "Manila Declaration (Fukuda Doctrine)," referring to the doubling of ODA in five years as promised by Japan, the main portion of which would be reserved for industrialization and the development of infrastructure in ASEAN countries and Burma, including welfare, agriculture, health care, and education projects. According to M. Kitano (2001), the speech focused on the following three points: (a) Japan, with its firm determination not to be a major military country, was poised to contribute to the peace and prosperity not only of Southeast Asia but of the world as a whole; (b) Japan aimed to build a relationship of mutual trust with countries in Southeast Asia that would encompass not only the political and economic fields, but also social and cultural aspects; (c) Japan would cooperate with other countries to strengthen the self-development of ASEAN as an equal partner. Surin Pitsuwan, the then secretary-general of ASEAN who attended the Future of Asia Symposium held in May 2012, stated that the Fukuda Doctrine played a major role in the construction of the relationship with ASEAN and the foundation of

regional cooperation (*Nikkei Shinbun*, 25 May 2012). The full text of the Manila Declaration is available at <http://www.ioc.u-tokyo.ac.jp/~worldjpn/documents/texts/docs/19770818.S1J.html>.

[38] At the 12th summit in 2009, China expressed its intention to establish a China-ASEAN Investment Cooperation Fund, but also committed to a loan to ASEAN countries amounting to US$15 billion, including US$6.7 billion with preferential conditions. In addition, it announced special aid of RMB 270 million for Cambodia, Myanmar, and Laos. At the 14th China-ASEAN meeting held in 2011 to celebrate the 20th anniversary of the establishment of dialogue between the two parties, China committed a further US$10 billion in loans to ASEAN countries, of which around US$4 billion were loans with preferential conditions. For more information, see N. Kitano (forthcoming).

[39] See ERIA's website <http://www.eria.org/research/activities.html>.

[40] At the 13th meeting of the Ministers of Transport of ASEAN in 2007, the Roadmap Towards an Integrated and Competitive Maritime Transport in ASEAN, consisting of 20 items for achieving a more open, efficient, and competitive maritime transport system, was adopted and implemented by the ASEAN Working Group on Maritime Matters. JICA provided cooperation in two areas (6 and 8 below) targeted at infrastructure, and measures 5 and 7 were implemented with the cooperation of the Korean team. Following a request from the working group, Japan and South Korea, in principle, jointly conducted the survey (30 ports were jointly surveyed).

Measure 5: "Creation of database on maritime trade within ASEAN"
Measure 6: "Formulation of a guideline for the evaluation of priorities for development of ASEAN network ports (47 ports in total)"
Measure 7: "Selection of challenging issues within ASEAN"
Measure 8: "Selection of prioritized development projects within ASEAN"

[41] With the cooperation of the Customs and Tariff Bureau of the Ministry of Finance, JICA, the ADB, and the World Customs Organization (WCO), it is intended (a) to build a system based on authorized dealers and to conclude the agreement, (b) to build a National Single Window for international systems cooperation, and (c) to reform the system of customs clearance to allow smooth trade transactions.

[42] Japan provided emergency relief supplies and dispatched flood experts to Thailand as part of bilateral cooperation following the 2011 flood that hit the Mekong region. Japan is also implementing the Project on a Comprehensive Flood Management Plan for the Chao Phraya River Basin, which involves upgrading the existing flood management master plan to a medium-term flood protection measure.

[43] At the 4th ASEAN Informal Summit in 2000, the Initiative for ASEAN Integration (IAI) was instituted. It aimed to alleviate economic disparities within ASEAN and strengthen the competitiveness of ASEAN.

[44] Singapore established IAI training centers in Cambodia, Laos, Myanmar, and Vietnam, and has devised and implemented training in accordance with the needs of each country in the established IAI training centers. Within ASEAN countries, Singapore contributes the most to IAI.

[45] For the 4th Japan-China Policy Dialogue on the Mekong Region, see <http://www.mofa.go.jp/mofaj/press/release/23/9/0901_06.html> (in Japanese).

[46] For the Fourth Asian Development Forum, see <http://www.jica.go.jp/english/news/field/2013/130409_01.html>.

References

China International Contractors Association. "Guide on Social Responsibility for Chinese International Contractors". Available at <http://www.chinca.org/cms/sites/shzr/resource/Guide%20on%20Social%20Responsibility%20for%20Chinese%20International%20Contractors.pdf>, 2012.

Chng, Meng King and Ryokichi Hirono, eds. *ASEAN-Japan Industrial Co-Operation: An Overview*. Singapore: Institute of Southeast Asian Studies, 1984.

Fujimoto, Koji. "Brantas River Basin Development Plan of Indonesia". In *Aid as Handmaiden for the Development of Institutions: A New Comparative Perspective*, edited by Machiko Nissanke and Yasutami Shimomura. Palgrave Macmillan, 2013.

Japan Bank for International Cooperation (JBIC). *Kaigai kyoryoku kikin shi* [Overseas economic cooperation fund history] (in Japanese). 2003.

Japan International Cooperation Agency (JICA), International Development Center of Japan/International Development Journal. *Ajia chiiki tonan ajia hitozukuri senryaku sakutei nimuketa johoshushu/kakunin chosa saishu hokokusho* [Data collection survey on strategy formulation on human resources development in Southeast Asia: final report] (in Japanese). Available at <http://libopac.jica.go.jp/images/report/P0000253231.html>, 2010.

Japan International Cooperation Agency (JICA), Southeast Asia and Pacific Department. 2011. *ASEAN togo ni mukete: Renketsusei jitugen e no kadai to JICA no torikumi* [For integration of ASEAN: Issues of realizing connectedness and JICA's activities] (in Japanese). Available at <http://www.jica.go.jp/topics/2011/pdf/20111115_01_09.pdf>, 2011.

Japan Overseas Enterprises Association (JOEA). "Nichigaikyo nijugonen no ayumi" [JOEA's footsteps for 25 years] (in Japanese). *Nichigaikyo Monthly* (June 1999). Available at <http://www.joea.or.jp/wp-content/uploads/pdf/joea_history1999.pdf>.

Kang, Sung Jin, Hongshik Lee, and Bokyeong Park. "Does Korea Follow Japan in Foreign Aid? Relationships between Aid and Foreign Investment". Available at <http://www.rieti.go.jp/jp/events/10101201/pdf/2-1_Lee_paper_en.pdf>, 2010.

Kawai, Masahiro. "Hokokusho naiyo" and "Dai juyonsho nihon ni okeru kaihatsu no tame no seisaku no ikkansei", *Chiiki keizai apurochi wo fumaeta seisaku no ikkansei bunseki: higashi ajia no keiken to ta donaa no seisaku* ["Content of this report" and "Chapter 14 Policy coherence for development in Japan." In Analysis of policy coherence based on local economy approaches: Experience in East Asia and policies by other donors] (in Japanese). Japan Bank for International Cooperation. Available at <http://jica-ri.jica.go.jp/IFIC_and_JBICI-Studies/jica-ri/research/archives/jbic/pdf/pcd/all.pdf>, 2005.

Kimura, Hidemi and Yasuyuki Todo. "Is Foreign Aid a Vanguard of FDI? A Gravity-Equation Approach". *World Development* 38, no. 4 (2010): 482–97. Available at <http://www.rieti.go.jp/jp/events/10101201/pdf/2-3_Todo_paper_en.pdf>.

Kitano, Mitsuru. *Gaiko saizensen dai san kai Burunei kara no shogeki: Tonan ajia seisaku wo megutte* [Diplomatic forefront No. 3, Impact from Brunei: Over Southeast Asian policies] (in Japanese). Research Institute of Economy, Trade and Industry (RIETI). Available at <http://www.rieti.go.jp/users/foreign-policy/01003_1.html>, 2001.

Kitano, Naohiro. "The Impact of Economic Cooperation on Asian Countries: Focus on the Mekong Region and Central Asia". In *A Study of China's Foreign Aid*, edited by Shimomura and Ohashi. Palgrave Macmillan, forthcoming.

Kokado, Takeshi. *ASEAN yonjunana nettowaaku koo no chosa katsudo ni tsuite* [Research activities of ASEAN 47 network ports] (in Japanese). *OCDI Quarterly* 81 (2010), available at <http://www.ocdi.or.jp/pdf/81_butsuryu03.pdf>.

Mieno, Fumiharu. "The Eastern Seaboard Development Plan and Industrial Cluster in Thailand: A Quantitative Overview". In *Aid as Handmaiden for the Development of Institutions: A New Comparative Perspective*, edited by Machiko Nissanke and Shimomura Yasutami. Palgrave Macmillan, 2013.

Ministry of Finance, Policy Research Institute. Tainaigai chokusetsu toshi no gaiyo [Outline of direct inward and outward investment]. *Finance Statistics Monthly Report* No. 645 (in Japanese). Available at <http://www.mof.go.jp/pri/publication/zaikin_geppo/hyou/g645/645_a.pdf>, 2006.

Mitsubishi Research Institute. "Yusho shikin kyoryoku/musho shikin kyoryoku no keizaiteki inpakuto hyoka" hokokusho ["Economic Impact Assessment of ODA Loans and Grant Aid" report] (in Japanese). Japan International Cooperation Agency. Available at <http://www.jica.go.jp/activities/evaluation/tech_ga/after/pdf/2011/201112_01.pdf>, <http://www.jica.go.jp/english/our_work/evaluation/reports/2011/pdf/part2-2.pdf> (the English summary of the report in Annual Evaluation Report 2011, JICA), 2011.

Muto, Megumi, Takuro Takeuchi, and Norifumi Koike. *Policy Coherence in Development: Case Study of East Asia*. JBICI Working Paper No. 24. Available at <http://www.jbic.go.jp/en/research/report/working-paper/pdf/wp24_e.pdf>, 2007.

Nagashima, Masaharu. *Tai ni okeru chiikikan kakusa zesei ni shisuru chosa/kenkyu* [Research/study on rectifying disparities among regions in Thailand] (in Japanese). Southeast Asia and Pacific Department, Japan International Cooperation Agency, 2012.

Ohno, Izumi and Daniel Kitaw. "Productivity Movement in Singapore." In *Kaizen National Movement: A Study of Quality and Productivity Improvement in Asia and Africa*, edited by Japan International Cooperation Agency (JICA) and GRIPS Development Forum. Available at <http://www.grips.ac.jp/forum-e/pdf_e12/JICA&GDFReport_Ethiopia_phase1/Kaizen_National_Movement/Kaizen_ch3.pdf>, 2011.

Sato, Jin, Hiroaki Shiga, Takaaki Kobayashi, and Hisahiro Kondoh. "Emerging Donors from a Recipient Perspective: Institutional Analysis of Foreign Aid in Cambodia". *World Development* 39, no. 12 (2011): 2091–104.

Sato, Yuri. "Indoneshia kara mita chugoku keizai kankei" nisenjuichinendo seisaku teigen kenkyuu "Chugoku/indo no taito to higashi ajia no henyo", dai jusankai kenkyukai ["Economic relations with China from the viewpoint of Indonesia"-FY2011 Policy Issue Research "The Rise of China/India and the implications for East Asia", 13th workshop] (in Japanese). Available at <http://www.ide.go.jp/Japanese/Publish/Download/Seisaku/pdf/1203_satoyuri.pdf>, 2011.

Shimomura, Yasutami. "Ajia gata enjo moderu" no kanosei. "Chugoku no taigaienjo" ["Asian model for aid" in "China's foreign aid"] (in Japanese). Nihon Keizai Hyouronsha, 2013.

Tomoda, Takahisa and Souichi Takeda. "Dai yon sho mitsui bussan no kyujunendai shoto betonamu shijo eno sannyu ni tsuite", *Chiiki keizai apurochi wo fumaeta seisaku no ikkansei bunseki* ["Chapter 4: Mitsui & Co. Ltd.'s entry into the market in Vietnam in the early 1990s", in Analysis of policy coherence based on local economy approaches: Experience in East Asia and policies by other donors] (in Japanese). Japan Bank for International Cooperation, Institute for Development and Finance. Available at <http://jica-ri.jica.go.jp/IFIC_and_JBICI-Studies/jica-ri/research/archives/jbic/pdf/pcd/all.pdf>, 2005.

Tran, Van Tho, Akifumi Kuchiki, Fumi Idei, and Shozo Sakata. *Impact Assessment of Transport Infrastructure Projects in Northern Vietnam*. Japan Bank for International Cooperation. Available at <http://www.jica.go.jp/english/our_work/evaluation/oda_loan/post/2003/pdf/1-03_smry.pdf>, 2003.

Zhu, Jianrong. *Motakuto no betonamu senso* [Mao Zedong's Vietnam War] (in Japanese). University of Tokyo Press, 2001.

12

JAPANESE FOREIGN DIRECT INVESTMENT IN THE ASEAN-4 COUNTRIES

G. Sivalingam

INTRODUCTION

Indonesia, Malaysia, the Philippines, and Thailand or the IMPT countries are usually referred to as the ASEAN-4 countries. Japanese foreign direct investment (FDI) in the ASEAN-4 countries has evolved through various stages after the post-World War II period. The Cold War saw the Japanese not being involved in the ASEAN-4 countries in an active manner, as they were not interested in war or in containing communism in Southeast Asia as were the Americans. In the 1950s and 1960s, the focus of the Japanese government's policy was to encourage direct investments to secure reliable flows of raw materials (Guisinger 1991, p. 30). From the late 1950s, the ASEAN economies were also becoming increasingly involved in import substitution industrialization (ISI) and there was little scope for Japanese direct investments in ASEAN. Japanese electrical products and cars were, however, sold in ASEAN countries.

The oil shocks in the early and late 1970s also saw increased Japanese investments in oil drilling in Indonesia to secure reliable supplies of oil for home consumption. There were Japanese investments also in textiles, chemicals, and metals in the ASEAN-4 countries in the 1970s. It was the next phase of export-oriented industrialization in the ASEAN-4 countries, which coincided with the Plaza Accord of 1985, that saw the active involvement of Japanese multinational corporations (MNCs) as direct and greenfield investors in several of the ASEAN-4 countries. In the 1980s Japanese corporations began to focus their investments in food processing, machinery, electrical and electronics goods, and more technologically advanced products (Guisinger 1991, p. 30).

This active phase of Japanese FDI in the ASEAN-4 countries lasted for about a decade, when, as a result of the opening up of China, Japanese investors took their capital to China to take advantage of cheaper unskilled labor and to exploit the advantages of a relatively huge domestic market. There were also divestments by Japanese multinational corporations in some of the ASEAN-4 countries after the Asian Financial Crisis (AFC) of 1997–98. In divesting, the Japanese multinational corporations exhibited tendencies of being "footloose" and revealed their preference for commercialism over benevolence. The slowing down of Japanese investments in the ASEAN-4 countries also coincided with the AFC of 1997–98, the bursting of the Japanese bubble, the deflationary cycle in Japan, and the admission of China into the World Trade Organization (WTO) in 2001.

The reversal of Japanese FDI from the ASEAN-4 countries also brought into question the notion that there was a sustainable "East Asian Miracle" as claimed by the Japanese-government-financed 1993 World Bank study titled *The East Asian Miracle* (World Bank 1993). Similarly, the assertion by W. Easterly (2002) in refuting the Japanese-inspired World Bank study that growth in some of the ASEAN-4 countries, for example, Malaysia was "home grown" is an understatement of the effect of FDI on the growth process in Malaysia and other ASEAN-4 countries.

Since 2004, however, there has been a change in direction of Japanese FDI from China to the ASEAN-4 countries because of changes in production network strategies, the rising cost of labor in China, the implementation of the China+1 strategy, and the territorial dispute between China and Japan.

Several writers have overstated Japan's contribution to the development process by asserting that Japan provided development aid for the building of infrastructure to facilitate the relocation of Japanese industries in the ASEAN-4 countries. While there was some technical and other assistance as well as soft yen loans from Japan, the ASEAN-4 countries went back into Japan's "warm" embrace after more than four decades of the Japanese occupation of several ASEAN countries probably because of the need to create low-value-added, unskilled, and labor-intensive jobs for unemployed youth in urban and rural areas.

However, all of the ASEAN-4 countries that were the recipients of Japanese aid and FDI for more than four decades since the 1970s have not graduated to the ranks of high-technology-intensive economies and still have a lot of catching up to do to reach the status of developed economies. In this sense, then, the "Flying Geese" model may not apply to the ASEAN-4 countries; it may apply more appropriately to the Newly Industrializing Economies (NIEs) of South Korea, Hong Kong, Taiwan, and Singapore. Although the ASEAN-4 countries are known as the "follower geese" and Japan is known as the "lead goose", the followers have yet to catch up with the leader. This is probably because there has been very little transfer of technology, use of local resources, or linkages with the domestic private sector.

JAPANESE FDI IN ASEAN-4 FROM WORLD WAR II TO THE PLAZA ACCORD, 1985

The relationship between several of the ASEAN-4 countries and Japan was strained after World War II as a result of the occupation of several of these ASEAN-4 countries by the Japanese during the war. The Japanese were not active participants in the ASEAN-4 countries immediately after the war, and in the 1950s and 1960s the Japanese government was averse to foreign investments except where it was necessary to secure reliable flows of raw materials (Guisinger 1991, p. 30). Protectionism in the ASEAN-4 countries was also high, as these countries were pursuing a policy of import substitution. There was limited scope for FDI in the import substituting industries, as the domestic markets were small. During this period the Japanese were more interested in gaining access to natural resources, and "the oil shock in the 1970s prompted Japanese investors to secure oil supplies especially in Indonesia" (Guisinger 1991, p. 30).

There was a tripartite relationship between Japan, the United States, and the ASEAN-4 countries, but the Japanese still found it difficult to develop a positive relationship with the ASEAN-4 countries. As part of the effort to win the hearts and minds of the ASEAN-4 countries, the Japanese government initiated reparation agreements with these nations in the 1950s and 1960s. The Japanese were able to reduce the resistance and harmonize relations with ASEAN-4 governments by offering not only reparations but also financial and technical aid that was focused on gaining access for Japanese direct investments in these ASEAN-4 countries. According to Akrasanee and Prasert (2003, p. 67), "financial and technical aid to the ASEAN countries had long been used as a tool to alleviate trade friction and facilitate Japanese investment in the region."

Consistent with its philosophy and strategy to use aid to facilitate trade and investment, the Japanese began the period after World War II by signing peace and reparation agreements with several Southeast Asian countries. Japan signed reparation agreements with the Philippines, Indonesia, and the Republic of Vietnam and quasi-reparation agreements with Cambodia, Laos, Thailand, Malaysia, and Singapore. The Japanese also signed technical cooperation agreements with the ASEAN-4 countries. The Japanese initiative in joining the Colombo Plan for Economic and Social Development in Asia and the Pacific in 1954 also endeared the Japanese to the developing Southeast Asian countries that participated in and benefited from the Colombo Plan.

In an effort to build a meaningful relationship with the ASEAN-4 countries, then Japanese Prime Minister Kishi Nobusuke proposed the establishment of the Asian Development Fund in 1957. It appears that "the Japanese government" not only initiated and concluded "reparation agreements with Southeast Asian countries from the late 1950s … but also devised several ideas for establishing an anti-communist regional economic zone, such as the Asian version of the Marshall Plan or the Southeast Asian Development Fund plan … The Japanese government also developed its own regional strategy to support Japanese firms' move on to the region and to a lesser extent maintain its political presence" (Yun 2004, pp. 4–5).

It was obvious that Japan was not disinterested in the ASEAN-4 countries after World War II, as "the Kishi government hammered at a concrete formula for Japanese economic re-entry, based on a trinity of reparation payments, economic development and economic cooperation" (Suehiro 1999, p. 85). The Japanese government also built institutions to facilitate the reentry of Japan in the region, as "Kishi's ideas was crystalized in the founding of two important government funded organizations engaged in economic cooperation (i.e., OECF and AOTS) and a government sponsored research institute specializing in Asian Studies."

The government of Japan was active also at the political level, as "Kishi's policy was ultimately put into effect by the Sato government when it hosted the first Ministerial Meeting on Southeast Asian Development in Tokyo in 1966, which marked the beginning of both Japan's full-fledged commitment to support the USA in the Vietnam War and Japan's re-entry into Asian markets" (Suehiro 1999, p. 85).

The impetus for these peace and goodwill efforts were U.S. pressure and the need in a resource-poor Japan for a mechanism to gain access to the resources of a resource-rich Southeast Asia. The focus of aid policy in the 1960s was also in promoting Japanese exports to aid-recipient countries (Orr 1990, p. 79). M. Sorderberg (1996) concurs with Orr (1990, p. 79) when he asserts that during the initial period and until the beginning of the 1970s, Japanese aid was closely linked to Japanese business interests and to the promotion of export markets of Japanese firms.

In the early period of Japan's re-entry into ASEAN, the Japanese government preferred to use the term "economic cooperation" (*keizai kyoroku*) rather than "aid" as it was involved not only in providing official aid but also in providing export credits to Japanese firms and encouraging private capital flows for the extraction of natural resources, especially energy resources in Indonesia (Blaise 2009, p. 4). According to Orr (1990, p. 79), the focus of aid policy changed in the 1970s to the development of natural resources, especially to large capital projects in the energy sector.

With the formation of ASEAN in 1967, the Japanese found an opportunity to further their economic interests beyond the provision of aid and the exploitation of natural resources of the ASEAN-4 countries. When ASEAN-4 came into being on 8 August 1967, Tokyo officials turned to the Ministerial Conference for the Economic Development of Southeast Asia as a forum to further bilateral relations with the ASEAN-4 countries (Akrasanee and Prasert 2003, p. 65). However, Japan encountered problems in penetrating ASEAN countries as it continued to be distrusted and resented by the latter. In 1972, Thailand organized a boycott of Japanese goods. Malaya was perturbed by the Japanese production and export of synthetic rubber in competition with natural rubber, which was then the mainstay of the Malaysian economy. Indonesia's frustrations with Japan were manifested in "violent demonstrations during the mid-January (1974) visit by Japanese Prime Minister Tanaka" (Hansen 1975, p. 148).

The ASEAN-4 economies appeared to have recovered from the devastating effects of World War II, as in the 1960s they achieved high rates of economic growth. These high growth rates were due in part to the period of rehabilitation and reconstruction in the 1950s. Of the ASEAN-4 countries, Thailand experienced the highest economic growth: its economy grew by about 8.3 per cent from 1960 to 1970. Comparative growth rates over the same period for the Philippines and

Indonesia were respectively 5.2 per cent and 3.9 per cent (Akrasanee and Prasert 2003, p. 64). The Malaysian economy grew by 6 per cent over the same period (Young *et al.* 1980, p. 13). The Japanese economy, however, grew much faster at 10.6 per cent over the same decade and it appeared that there was scope for ASEAN-4 to benefit from the recycling of the Japanese trade surpluses as investments in the ASEAN-4 countries. The ASEAN-4 economies were predominantly agrarian in the 1970s and were dependent on the export of primary commodities and the terms of trade of these primary commodities. The industrial sector was small in the ASEAN-4 countries and was dominated by import substituting industries, although some of the ASEAN-4 economies, such as Malaysia, had established export processing zones in the early 1970s to lure export-oriented MNCs.

The OPEC oil embargo in 1973 raised questions about the appropriate strategies to generate economic growth in the emerging economies, including the ASEAN-4 economies. The recommended strategy by multilateral institutions was an FDI-led export-oriented strategy. The view that FDI would serve as an engine of growth and development gained currency. To gain access to ASEAN-4 countries and to prepare them to provide the capacity for the establishment of Japanese plant and equipment, the Japanese government provided aid and technical assistance (Rix 1990).

The visit of Japanese Prime Minister Takeo Fukuda to several ASEAN-4 countries in 1977 provided the impetus for further FDI inflows into export-oriented industries in the ASEAN-4 countries. According to Atarashi (1985), Fukuda's visit in August 1977 marked a new era in bilateral relations between Japan and each of the ASEAN-4 countries. The *Asahi Shimbun* (2013) reported that "in a speech delivered in Manila, Fukuda announced the 'Fukuda Doctrine' about Japan's diplomacy. He declared that Japan will never become a military power and would do its best to build a relationship of friendship and mutual trust based on 'heart-to-heart' understanding with Southeast Asian nations. These principles have set the tone for Japan's foreign policy towards Asia."

As a follow-up to the Fukuda Doctrine, the Japanese government stepped up its efforts to provide aid and development assistance to the government of the ASEAN-4 countries to build new infrastructure and upgrade existing infrastructure, including roads, ports, and export processing zones. The aid had a vanguard effect in the sense that it was provided in strategic areas to build infrastructure that was conducive to the establishment of Japanese plants and factories and that contributed to the reduction of the transaction costs of Japanese MNCs, which were focused mainly on exploiting the rich natural resources and cheap labor of the ASEAN-4 countries.

It can be seen that after the Fukuda Doctrine was enunciated, the relationship between Japan and Southeast Asia was to change as Japan became a major or important source of FDI that created a vibrant manufacturing and resource extraction based trade sector that augmented the already existing primary commodity based trade sector of the ASEAN-4 countries. The inflow of FDI over the years not only created an FDI-trade nexus in the ASEAN countries, but as aid policy after the Fukuda Doctrine became more focused on facilitating the entry of Japanese FDI in a conducive environment, there also developed an aid-FDI-trade nexus between the ASEAN-4 countries and Japan.

After 1977, Japan became the world's largest donor and Southeast Asia became the major recipient of its aid that was focused on facilitating Japanese FDI in Malaysia. It has been estimated that during 1975–87, 65 per cent of Japanese foreign aid went to Asia (Rix 1990). "Indonesia had been the major destination for Japan's ODA until 1982, when it was replaced by China" (Akrasanee and Praser 2003, p. 67). The aid flows were essentially "allocated in the form of loans for infrastructure in the transport and energy production sector" (Blaise 2009, p. 4), including electricity production, telecommunications, railways, and motorways (Blaise 2009, p. 11).

Before 1980 the Japanese were interested in energy resources, especially because of the two oil crises in 1973 and 1979. As a consequence, most of the Japanese FDI in ASEAN-4 before 1980 was concentrated in Indonesia's oil resources and in energy, minerals, and agricultural and natural resources that were exported to Japan via Japanese trading companies (Patrick 2008, p. 19). In Malaysia, Japanese FDI was focused on iron ore mining, and in the Philippines it was focused on copper mining (Urata 1993, p. 275). During the initial postwar period, Japan imported natural resources and materials that it paid for with exports of machinery and equipment. Southeast Asian countries found the Japanese reparations useful, as they could be used to pay for Japanese imports. They also exported manufactured consumer goods to Japan.

As noted earlier, Japanese FDI in the 1970s in Indonesia was largely in petroleum followed by manufacturing. In the other three ASEAN-4 countries, Japanese FDI was mainly concentrated in manufacturing, that is, export-oriented manufacturing (Doner 1993, p. 169). Exports from

Japanese FDI factories in the 1970s were mainly textiles and apparel (Doner 1993, p. 171).

The Japanese became active in investing in the ASEAN-4 countries after the Fukuda Declaration of 1977 and as they recovered after the first oil crisis in 1973. The impetus for increasing FDI was the appreciation of the yen, as it made it cheaper for Japanese firms to produce in Asia, where labor costs were much lower. However, the focus of FDI was in the developed world, and FDI in the ASEAN-4 countries did not increase until the early 1980s, when there was an outflow of Japanese FDI from the NIEs to the ASEAN-4 countries as labor costs in the NIEs had increased. Although Japanese FDI outflows had increased in the early 1980s, the increases were not sustained and they remained at the same level until 1986 (Urata 1993, p. 276). Among the reasons Japanese FDI did not increase was that the yen had depreciated against the U.S. dollar and there was little reason for Japanese firms to migrate to ASEAN countries to reduce labor costs. Furthermore, the ASEAN-4 countries were faced with a problem of increasing external debt and an unsustainable fiscal deficit, making them undesirable as investment locations for affiliates of Japanese firms.

RECESSION AND LIBERALIZATION IN THE ASEAN-4 COUNTRIES, 1985–86

The mid-1980s were eventful years for the ASEAN-4 countries as commodity prices collapsed in 1985 and 1986, causing a recession in several countries and calling for a reassessment of development strategies from an overdependence on primary commodity exports and an inefficient import substitution strategy. In addition, these countries had incurred an increasing amount of unsustainable external debt: they had incurred excessive public expenditure, creating a fiscal crisis; and as exports were declining, these ASEAN-4 countries were also facing a current account deficit.

Malaysia was one of several ASEAN-4 countries that experienced a contraction in the economy by 1 per cent in 1985 because of the collapse of commodity prices. The economy of Singapore also contracted by 1 per cent in 1985, while Indonesia's economy grew by 1.9 per cent and Thailand's by 3.5 per cent (Phongpaichit 1990, p. 84). Chintayarangsan *et al.* (1992, p. 356) pointed out, "The year 1985 was a nightmare for all ASEAN countries: growth rates were low in Indonesia and Thailand and negative in Malaysia, Singapore and the Philippines."

According to Urata (2001, p. 418):

> ... after their favorable economic performance in the 1970s, a number of developing economies in East Asia experienced an economic slowdown in the early 1980s. The second oil crisis in the late 1970s and its aftermath were major factors behind the slowdown, as were inward-looking import substitution policies and active public investment ... The slowdown in the world economy exerted a negative influence on the economic performance of developing East Asian economies, mainly by reducing the demand for their products.

The economies were also rethinking their development strategies, as it was realized that import substitution had reached a limit due to the smallness of the market. The import substitution strategy also limited competition and encouraged rent seeking and the misallocation of resources, as it was not based on the comparative advantage of the economies. There was a discernible shift to an export-oriented industrial strategy in reaction to the collapse of commodity prices. Export-oriented manufacturing was preferred as a strategy for generating scarce foreign exchange that was needed to import capital-intensive and technology-intensive goods. This was consistent with the philosophy of diversifying sources of foreign exchange and stabilizing the economy against external shocks.

In response to the twin deficits, that is, the deficit in the current account of fare balance of payments and the fiscal deficit, the East Asian economies on the prodding or prompting of the World Bank, initiated the Structural Adjustment Program (SAP). The SAP consisted

> mainly of liberalization in foreign trade and FDI and deregulation in domestic economic activities. The change in policy from inward-looking protection to outward-looking liberalization was attributable to the recommendations of donors, such as the World Bank and the International Monetary Fund. Such policy changes were also due to the realization that liberalization would promote export oriented economic growth. The liberalization of trade and FDI led to the expansion of exports and inward FDI because it shifted the incentives from import substituting production to export production and increased the attractiveness of these ASEAN-4 economies to foreign investors (Urata 2001, p. 419).

Many developing East Asian countries liberalized restrictions on FDI, with measures such as (1) liberalization of restrictions on market access, (2) most-favored-nation treatment, and (3) National treatment (Urata 2001, p. 419). Malaysia made a strategic commitment to expand its manufacturing base by reformulating its Investment Incentive Act 1972 into the Promotion of Investment Act 1986.

THE PLAZA ACCORD AND THE BOOM IN JAPANESE INVESTMENTS

According to Henning and Destler (1988, p. 317):

> ... when United States Secretary of the Treasury James A. Baker announced a new international monetary accord among the Group of Five (G-5) centers at the Plaza Hotel in New York City in September 1985, he signaled a dramatic change in U.S. exchange rate policy ... U.S. exchange rate policy shifted from unilateralist non-intervention to actively promoting dollar depreciation and multilateral cooperation.

The Plaza Accord was historic because it was agreed by nations that the U.S. dollar would depreciate against the yen to correct the trade balance of the United States. It was historic also because it drove Japanese corporations to look for cheaper production bases and export platforms as goods produced in Japan would not be internationally competitive. The realignment of the major currencies by non-market forces together with liberalization of trade and investment regimes in the East Asian economies led to the inflow of Japanese FDI into ASEAN-4 countries.

According to Urata (2001, p. 423):

> ... in addition to trade and FDI liberalization policies, several external developments in the mid-1980s precipitated the expansion of exports from and of FDI inflows to the developing East Asian economies. One is the substantial realignment of the exchange rates of major currencies, notably the appreciation of the Japanese yen vis-à-vis the U.S. dollar and other currencies. In September 1985, to correct the imbalances in the current accounts among major industrial countries — a huge current account surplus in Japan and Germany and a huge current account deficit in the United States were major causes of instability of the world economy — the G-5 countries agreed to realign the exchange rates of their currencies. As a result, the Japanese yen and the Deutsche Mark appreciated in value vis-à-vis the U.S. dollar and other currencies.

Urata (2001, p. 424) added:

The drastic yen appreciation stimulated Japanese FDI to developing East Asian economies in two ways (see Kawai and Urata 1998 for a detailed discussion). To cope with the loss in international price competitiveness, many Japanese firms moved their base of production from Japan to foreign economies where production costs were lower. The yen appreciation also had a positive impact on outflows of Japanese FDI through the liquidity or wealth effect. To the extent that yen appreciation made Japanese firms relatively more wealthy by increasing their collateral and liquidity, it enabled them to finance outward FDI relatively more cheaply than their foreign competitors. In addition, liquidity was injected into the economy in the second half of the 1980s, with the objective of reactivating the Japanese economy from a recession caused by a decline in exports, pushing up the prices of shares and land and creating the so-called bubble economy. Such an increase in liquidity and the subsequent asset-price inflation further promoted Japan's FDI by making it easier for Japanese firms to obtain loans. The bubble economy contributed to the expansion of exports from developing East Asian economies by Japan by increasing Japan's demand for imports.

At the same time that the ASEAN-4 countries were liberalizing their foreign investment regime, Japanese firms were relocating their plant and machinery to these countries to take advantage of relatively cheaper labor to produce output for export. This was to get over the high cost of production in Japan as a consequence of the appreciation of the yen in the aftermath of the Plaza Accord of 1985.

According to Goldberg and Klein (1998), Japanese investments in ASEAN have been very sensitive to exchange rate changes of not only the Japanese yen but especially exchange rate changes between the yen and the U.S. dollar. According to them, a depreciation of the dollar in terms of the yen leads to a surge in investments from Japan into ASEAN, probably because the ASEAN currencies are tied to the U.S. dollar. The appreciation of the yen then makes labor in ASEAN much cheaper and hence makes ASEAN countries attractive as a production base and possibly an export platform for the Japanese. The appreciation of the yen also makes Japanese products cheaper in the United States and hence increases Japanese exports from ASEAN to the United States. The appreciation of the yen after the Plaza Accord led to a deepening of the trilateral relationship between ASEAN, Japan, and the United States via Japanese direct investments in ASEAN.

According to Goldberg and Klein (1998), exchange rates may affect FDI through various channels. The most significant path lies in their effects on labor and other costs that change the comparative advantage of certain goods between two centers and thus encourage the transfer of production bases from one country to another.

According to Nakamura and Oyama (1998), the outflow of FDI from Japan into Southeast Asia is strongly affected by changes in the real bilateral exchange rates between Japan and the ASEAN countries. The authors note that Taiwan and Korea are closely linked with Japanese capacity utilization, which indicates that their industries are integrated with the Japanese economy. In the case of Indonesia and the Philippines, Japanese FDI increased due to the appreciation of the yen against the U.S. dollar, which also lowered labor costs in these countries. In the case of China, Malaysia, Singapore, and Thailand, Nakamura and Oyama (1998) make the argument that Japanese FDI flew in to take advantage of the market. While this may be true in the case of the large market in China, it has limited validity in the case of the relatively small markets of Malaysia and Thailand, where the main attraction for Japanese MNCs was cheap labor cost. The writers are also sharp in noting that Japanese FDI in ASEAN was export-augmenting, or supportive of trade expansion to Japan, and also stimulated imports from Japan. However, they stop short of arguing whether ASEAN-4 exported more to Japan or whether it in fact imported more from Japan.

Although affiliates of the ASEAN-4 countries exported to Japan as Japan liberalized its import regime, Japanese affiliates in the ASEAN-4 countries also sold in the domestic market. For example, Matsushita sold Panasonic radios and TV sets as well as National refrigerators, washing machines, and dryers in Malaysia. Japanese affiliates obtained most of their imports from Japan and exported the assembled products to Japan and other ASEAN-4 economies. This promoted interdependence and provided the stimulus for regionalism in ASEAN. Exports from Japanese affiliates to Japan — or "reverse imports", as they were called — increased as the appreciation of the yen made imports from the ASEAN-4 economies cheaper. The Japanese economy was booming and hence had an appetite for imports; and the Japanese government was promoting imports, especially if they originated from Japanese affiliates overseas, including the ASEAN-4 economies. It appears that one of the main motivations for

Japanese FDI overseas, including to the ASEAN-4 economies, is to increase "reverse imports" and to use economies such as the ASEAN-4 economies as an export platform. It appears that the ASEAN-4 economies import more from Japan than they export to Japan. This is in sharp contrast to the NIEs, which have a much better net export position than the ASEAN-4 economies with Japan. This is probably because the Japanese affiliates source and procure their inputs in the home country. Despite the fact that ASEAN-4 economies have policies to encourage local procurement and the use of local content, the net export position is adversely affected by imports from Japan. According to Urata (2001, p. 297), this situation will change over time as Japan's trading and investment relationship with the NIEs has been in place for a much longer period than its relationship with the ASEAN-4 countries. Over time it may be possible that Japan will import more from the ASEAN-4 countries than it exports to the ASEAN-4 countries.

THE FLYING GEESE MODEL OF JAPANESE FDI

It has been argued that the pattern of Japanese FDI inflows into the ASEAN-4 economies can be captured by the simplistic and general "Flying Geese" or FG model of capital, plant, and equipment flows. According to this model, which has many variations and interpretations, there is a "lead goose" and a "follower geese". Japan was the "lead goose" and the ASEAN-4 countries were the "follower geese", as capital, plant, and equipment flowed from Japan to the ASEAN-4 countries. However, the trend of industrialization in the ASEAN-4 countries did not follow the pattern depicted by the FG model.

The reason for choosing geese for this analogy is because the original conceptualizer, Kaname Akamatsu, found a pattern of development in industries when plotted on a piece of paper that was similar to geese flying. Flocks of geese fly in an inverted U pattern, which is similar to the pattern of development of industries in a country like Japan. Originally, Japan will have to import (M) the goods that it requires; and after some time as costs go up and the imitative capacity of the nation increases, Japan will start producing (P) goods for domestic consumption; and as sales and demand increase, output and investment will increase, and to achieve further economies of scale Japanese corporations will start to export (E) their goods and services.

According to Akamatsu, the originator of the Flying Geese model, the M-P-E process of development follows the pattern of flying geese. This is because initially imports of goods desired increase until they reach a peak and the government starts an ISI strategy. As a result, as M declines, P will go up; but once the country starts to produce the same goods for external markets, P will go down as E goes up and reaches a peak. E will go down as long as Japanese affiliates move their FDI and create export bases or platforms overseas, including in ASEAN-4 economies. The growth, peaking, and fall of M, P, and E follow an inverted U pattern, similar to how geese fly. If one puts the charts one has drawn for the development stages of M, P, and E, one will see three sets of geese flying in three inverted U patterns.

Cumings offers a good explanation of the Flying Geese phenomenon, although he has been dismissed as a dependency theorist by Kojima, a disciple of Akamatsu. According to Cumings (1984, pp. 150–51):

> For Japan the product cycle has not been mere theory; it has melded with conscious practice to make Japan the preeminent example of upward mobility in the world system through successive waves of industrial competition. In the 1930s, Kaname Akamatsu elaborated his famous FG model of industrial development in follower countries, predating Vernon's work by several decades. Time-series curves for imports, import-substitution form the domestic market, and subsequent exports of given products tend to form a pattern like wild geese flying in ranks. The cycle in given industries — textiles, steel, automobiles, light electronics — of origin, rise, apogee, and decline has not simply been marked, but often mastered, in Japan; in each industrial life cycle there is also an appropriate jumping off place, that is, a point at which it pays to let others make the product or at least provide the labor. Taiwan and Korea have historically been receptacles for declining Japanese industries.

Cumings (1984, p. 153) goes on to make the following observation:

> The product cycle is a middle-range explanation for the waxing and waning of industrial sectors, and that it is imbedded in some larger structure — an international division of labor or a world economy.

The FG paradigm has been used also to explain industrialization in the ASEAN-4 economies as they move from labor-intensive to capital-intensive and then to high-tech-intensive production systems. The ASEAN-4 economies, after more than four decades of opening up their economies to FDI — including Japanese FDI — have not moved from labor-intensive type of production. Most of the workers are involved in labor-intensive jobs that need "nimble" fingers to assemble parts and components. Although they may be assembling high-tech parts and components, they are not high-tech workers but unskilled, relatively cheap labor. The process of upgrading the technological level of the ASEAN-4 economies may take a bit longer, maybe several decades or more. Meanwhile, it should be noted that only the labor-intensive type of geese are flying; they have not reached their peak, and the ASEAN-4 economies continue to be dependent on Japanese FDI, the Japanese government, and Japanese business groups.

Shinoda (2013) notes a strong relationship between the surge in Japanese investments in ASEAN after the Plaza Accord and the formation of Japanese industrial clusters in East Asia. According to Shinoda, East Asia has emerged as a region powered by FDI originating from Japanese, South Korean, and overseas Chinese businesses (Shinoda 2013, p. 3):

> This was underpinned by the region's American-led security and triangular trade systems. In other words it was market forces and not political will informed by Asianism, that led to the regionalism that emerged in East Asia in the 1980s and 1990s.

Shinoda contends that ASEAN was more concerned with ISI until the Plaza Accord in 1985. It was only due to the sharp appreciation of the yen that Japanese FDI accelerated in ASEAN, because Japanese manufacturers (especially electronics firms) in wanting to be internationally competitive made major investments in Southeast Asia and moved many of their production facilities into the ASEAN region. Shinoda argues that as ASEAN emerged as a base for export production in the 1990s, Japanese automobile manufacturers together with their parts manufacturers moved their production facilities there. In other words, they set up little Japanese villages with large MNCs and small-scale enterprises supplying parts and equipment. Over time a tight-knit, cost-reducing Japanese production network emerged in ASEAN, paving the way for trade and economic integration without political integration.

TRENDS IN JAPANESE FDI
IN THE ASEAN-4 COUNTRIES, 1987–94

Japanese FDI in the ASEAN-4 economies as a group increased after the Plaza Accord in 1985, as it was cheaper for the Japanese to produce the same goods in the ASEAN-4 economies rather than in Japan. Some of the Japanese FDI that flowed into the ASEAN-4 economies was due also to the outflow of Japanese FDI from the NIEs, where wages were rising and the wage level was higher when compared to the ASEAN-4 economies. Total Japanese FDI inflow into the ASEAN-4 economies increased at a rapid rate between 1987 and 1990, after which it declined marginally in 1991, rose again in 1992, declined in 1993, and rose again in 1994. The average annual growth rate of Japanese FDI to the ASEAN-4 economies between 1987 and 1994 was 26.4 per cent. Among the ASEAN-4 economies, the largest recipient of FDI on a cumulative basis between 1987 and 1994 was Indonesia, followed by Thailand, with Malaysia a close third and the Philippines a distant fourth (see Table 12.1).

TABLE 12.1
Japanese FDI in the ASEAN-4 Economies, 1987–94
(US$ million)

Year	ASEAN-4 Total	Indonesia	Malaysia	Philippines	Thailand
1987	1,030	545	163	72	250
1988	1,966	586	387	134	859
1989	2,782	631	673	202	1,276
1990	3,242	1,105	725	258	1,154
1991	3,083	1,193	880	203	807
1992	3,197	1,676	704	160	657
1993	2,398	813	800	207	578
1994	3,888	1,759	742	668	719
Total	21,586	8,308	5,074	1,904	6,300
Percentage	100	38.48	23.50	8.82	29.18

Source: Bowles, 1997.

The decline in total Japanese FDI in the ASEAN-4 countries in 1991 was small — only about 4 per cent — and was not caused by currency appreciation or a decline in domestic investments in Japan. It was probably caused by the sharp decline in Japanese FDI to Thailand and the Philippines in 1991, perhaps because these two countries were experiencing natural disasters or going through a period of political instability. Or, more important, FDI was moving into China as opposed to the ASEAN-4 economies as labor costs were lower in China. The decline in FDI flows from Japan to the ASEAN-4 countries in 1993 was due largely to the sharp decline of about 52 per cent in FDI flows to Indonesia and the not-so-sharp decline of 12.02 per cent in FDI flows to Thailand the same year. The decline in domestic demand for Japanese-FDI-produced natural resources and products from Indonesia and cars in Thailand may have caused the decline in Japanese FDI in Thailand and Indonesia in 1993.

The decline in Japanese FDI in Indonesia and Thailand was temporary, as between 1993 and 1994 FDI increased by more than 116 per cent in Indonesia and by more than 24 per cent in Thailand. Japanese FDI in Malaysia declined only in two years between 1987 and 1994 — in 1992 and 1994. The decline in 1992 was about 20.5 per cent, while the decline in 1994 was 7.25 per cent. The declining absolute amount of FDI received by the ASEAN-4 economies may also have been due to the attractiveness of China, which offered plentiful supplies of lower-cost labor to foreign investors. The depreciation of the yuan in 1994 further increased China's attractiveness to foreign investors. A related factor in the fluctuations in the inflow of Japanese FDI to ASEAN-4 economies may have been what M. Obstfeld (2008, p. 8) refers to as the "real economy's sharp downturn from 1990–95" and the bursting of the Japanese bubble. Urata (2001, p. 425) has also made the argument that "the sizable fluctuations in the yen-dollar exchange rate in the 1990s had a destabiliz-ing impact on developing East Asian economies, contributing to the currency crisis in 1997". Urata and Kawai (2000), Thursby and Thursby (1987), and Cushman (1988) also found that exchange rate risk inhibited trade and FDI.

JAPANESE FDI FLOWS AFTER THE ASIAN FINANCIAL CRISIS

Japanese FDI flows to the ASEAN-4 countries began to decline after the 1997 Asian Financial Crisis (AFC), especially into three of the four

ASEAN-4 economies affected by the crisis: Indonesia, Malaysia, and Thailand. Only the Philippines continued to receive increased inflows of Japanese FDI one year after the crisis, that is, in 1998, probably because it was not affected by the crisis.

Although the ASEAN-4 currencies appreciated together with the U.S. dollar against the Japanese yen in 1995, Japanese FDI continued to flow into the ASEAN-4 countries in 1996 and 1997. However, there was a sharp fall in Japanese FDI to the ASEAN-4 countries in 1998, probably because the crisis affected ASEAN-4 countries. Indonesia, Malaysia, and Thailand were perceived as risky and not good investment locations, as their economic, financial, and political systems needed restructuring. They were also going through a process of liberalizing and reforming their trade and investment regimes.

Total Japanese FDI to the ASEAN-4 countries declined by more than 28 per cent in 1998 (see Table 12.2). The country most affected in percentage terms was Malaysia, where Japanese FDI inflows declined by more than 55 per cent between 1997 and 1998. The number of new Japanese electronics affiliates in Malaysia declined from 27 per cent in 1996 to 16 per cent in 1997 and to 9 per cent in 1998 (Belderbos and Zou 2006, p. 9). Similarly, the number of new Japanese electronics affiliates in Indonesia declined from 31 per cent in 1996 to 14 per cent in 1997 and to 13 per cent in 1998. In the case of the Philippines, the

TABLE 12.2
Japan's Outward FDI to ASEAN-4 Countries, 1995–2004
(US$ million)

Year	ASEAN-4 Total	Thailand	Indonesia	Malaysia	Philippines
1995	3,312	935	946	371	1,061
1996	3,836	1,337	1,494	522	483
1997	4,954	2,044	1,570	992	349
1998	3,551	1,668	916	445	521
2000	1,684	593	585	–4	510
2001	2,920	1,594	481	570	275
2002	2,166	528	307	257	1,074
2003	773	678	484	–504	114

Source: JETRO, Japanese Trade and Investment Statistics, <http://www.jetro.go.jp/en/reports/statistics/>.

number of new Japanese electronics affiliates declined from 27 per cent in 1996 to 16 per cent in 1997 and to 9 per cent in 1998. In Thailand the number of new Japanese affiliates increased from 13 per cent in 1996 to 16 per cent in 1997 but then declined to 13 per cent in 1998. In the case of attracting new Japanese electronics affiliates, all the ASEAN-4 economies were on the losing end in 1998 when compared to 1996.

The fall in Japanese FDI in the ASEAN-4 countries was much steeper in 1999 than in 1998. As noted earlier, the fall in Japanese FDI flows in 1998 was felt most significantly in the crisis-affected ASEAN-4 countries: Indonesia, Malaysia, and Thailand. In fact, in Thailand and Malaysia there were outflows or divestments of Japanese FDI in 1999, probably because of the unresolved political, economic, and financial crises in these two countries. There was probably a flight of Japanese FDI from these two countries to China to capture lower labor costs and a large domestic market. Not only was the flow of Japanese FDI into China huge, but China had "increased its share of Japanese manufacturing affiliates from less than 10 per cent in 1991 to almost 40 per cent in 2000" (Belderbos and Zou 2006, p. 5). The divestments in Thailand and Malaysia may have been due also to the closure of Japanese MNCs due to increased competitive pressures originating from technological changes by MNCs in Taiwan, Korea, and China (James and Movshuk 2004; Belderbos and Zou 2006, p. 7). Japanese FDI flows to Indonesia did not turn negative but fell by more than 78 per cent in 1999. Only the Philippines experienced a positive increase of FDI in 1999.

However, the FDI inflows from Japan into the ASEAN-4 countries increased in 2000 by more than 369 per cent. The largest increases were recorded in Thailand and Indonesia, followed by the Philippines. But divestments of Japanese FDI from Malaysia continued in 2000. Japanese FDI inflows to Malaysia recovered and became positive only in 2001. In 2001, total Japanese FDI inflows to the ASEAN-4 countries increased by more than 73 per cent. The largest inflow of Japanese FDI in 2001 was to Thailand, followed by Malaysia, Indonesia, and the Philippines. Japanese FDI inflows to Thailand were probably in the auto industry, whereas in the case of Malaysia and the Philippines they were in the electronics industry. In the case of Indonesia, Japanese FDI flowed into the exploitation and extraction of natural resources.

The uptrend in positive Japanese FDI inflows to the ASEAN-4 countries in 2001 was short-lived, as total Japanese FDI to the ASEAN-4 countries declined by more than 25 per cent in 2002 and by more than

64 per cent in 2003. This was probably because China became a member of the WTO in 2001, which made the country more attractive to FDI — there was a commitment on China's part to adhere to the standards, rules, and regulations set by the WTO. As noted earlier, in three of the ASEAN-4 countries — that is, Thailand, Indonesia, and Malaysia — total Japanese FDI inflows declined in 2002. Only the Philippines registered an increase in Japanese FDI inflows in 2002, with nearly half the Japanese FDI inflows to ASEAN-4 in 2003 going to that country.

In 2003, all the countries in ASEAN-4 experienced a fall in the inflow of Japanese FDI. Malaysia was the only country to have experienced a divestment of Japanese investments, as it experienced a negative inflow of FDI from Japan in 2003. FDI inflows into the ASEAN-4 countries in 2003 were only about 15 per cent of the total FDI inflows from Japan into the ASEAN-4 countries in 1997. In Thailand, total Japanese FDI inflow in 2003 was only a third what it had been in 1997; in the case of Indonesia and the Philippines the figures were respectively 30.82 per cent and 32.66 per cent. In the case of Malaysia, total Japanese FDI inflow had declined from US$992 million in 1997 to -US$504 million in 2003. The decline in Malaysia was not isolated, as global FDI flows had declined between 2000 and 2003 (UNCTAD 2005) and China was capturing a larger share of Japanese FDI outflows.

The divestments in the ASEAN-4 countries, especially in Malaysia and Thailand, may have been due to the relocation of electronics firms. They may have also been due to rising labor costs, which made these countries less competitive in relation to countries with surplus labor such as China. A study by Belderbos and Zou found that "divestments are much more frequent in higher labor cost countries and in approximately one-third of cases, are accompanied by relocations to lower wage countries, particularly in China" (Belderbos and Zou 2006, p. 1). There was obviously a strong rivalry between the ASEAN-4 economies and China based on labor costs in attracting Japanese FDI, and some have identified this as one of the reasons for the deterioration in the current account balance of some of the ASEAN-4 countries in the years leading to the AFC in 1997. The rivalry between China and the ASEAN-4 economies can also be seen in the context of divestments from the ASEAN countries between 1999 and 2003. According to Belderbos and Zou (2006, p. 17), "most affiliates or production lines that were relocated to China (12 out of 16) were originally based in one of the ASEAN countries," including Malaysia, Indonesia, and Thailand. Between 1999 and 2003 Malaysia accounted for 25 per cent of all divestments, or nine cases of divestments by Japanese electronics firms (Belderbos and Zou 2006, p. 17).

There was already rising anxiety in the ASEAN-4 countries from the early 1990s that China may displace them as an attractive destination for FDI, including Japanese FDI (Wu and Puah 2002, pp. 45–58). The relocations from the ASEAN-4 economies to China involved labor-intensive and not more technology-intensive production activities (Belderbos and Zou 2006, p. 17).

A related cause of the decline, relocation, and divestment of Japanese FDI in the ASEAN-4 countries after the AFC in 1997 and before 2004 may have been the "Japanese firms' strategy to reconfigure their Asian production networks in response to changing competitiveness, regional integration, and changes in local investment environment" (Belderbos and Zou 2006, p. 1). The international production network of MNCs normally "combines a lead firm, its subsidiaries, affiliates and joint ventures, its suppliers and subcontractors, its distribution channels and VARs as well as its R&D alliances and a variety of cooperative agreements (such as standards consortia)" and might involve "the spread of broader and more systemic forms of international production that cuts across different stages of the value chain" (Ernst 1997, p. 31). Because of the Asian Financial Crisis of 1997 and its significant economic impacts, "MNCs investing in the region have been under great pressure to reconfigure their APN (Asian Production Network), which has involved an increasing number of divestments and relocations" (Belderbos and Zou 2006, p. 3).

Japanese electronics firms have had to restructure their Asian production networks because of the following reasons: (1) pressure due to technological change from analog technologies to digital technologies, where previously the Japanese dominated the market using analog technologies; (2) the Japanese strategy of relying on mass production, quality control, and cost reduction is in contrast to the market for incessant technological change for product differentiation and innovation; and (3) the new open regionalism strategy adopted by the ASEAN countries since the formation of AFTA in 1992 and the reduction in CEPT (Common Effective Preferential Tariffs) to 0.5 per cent in 2002 and the negotiations to create an ASEAN-China Free Trade Area implies that Japan will face increased competition from MNCs from China and other more advanced East Asian countries.

The divestments were necessitated also by the reorientation of the Asian production network of Japanese MNCs. To reduce costs through large-scale production so as to achieve economies of scale, Japanese MNCs have consolidated production in a "single low cost location," where labor costs are also low (Belderbos and Zou 2006, p. 21). For example, Toshiba has moved TV and notebook production to China, whereas previously its production activities were disbursed over China and Indonesia (Belderbos and Zou 2006, p. 21).

The divestments occurred also because Japanese MNCs were concentrating or forming clusters in areas that "provide the highest efficiency, best supporting industries, and cluster advantages" (Belderbos and Zou 2006, p. 21). According to Belderbos and Zou (2006, p. 23), "the ongoing trade and investment liberalization efforts by ASEAN countries and their trade partners have made geographic concentration strategies more attractive." The need to concentrate on key-product markets has also caused a change in the production network strategy of Japanese firms and led to divestments from low-growth areas for their products as they focus on high-technology products in the more advanced countries with a larger and more affluent middle class. Another reason for divestments is that production activities have been increasingly outsourced (Felker 2003, pp. 255–83).

JAPANESE FDI IN THE ASEAN-4 COUNTRIES, 2004–12

Japanese FDI in the ASEAN-4 countries increased by more than 227 per cent in 2004, after the great fall in 2003 (see Table 12.3). The upward trend in Japanese FDI inflows into the ASEAN-4 economies continued in 2005 and 2006, when FDI inflows from Japan increased by more than 68 per cent and 41 per cent respectively. These increases were possibly due to the growing unattractiveness of China as a low-labor-cost center for concentrating MNC activities for assembling electronic components and parts for export to the developed world, especially the United States, Europe, and Japan. The creation of a free trade area in ASEAN with low CEPT and the possibility of concentrating production networks within the free trade region also increased the attractiveness of the ASEAN-4 countries for MNCs to locate or relocate their operations to.

However, the trend of the upward increase in Japanese FDI in the ASEAN-4 economies was short-lived as the Global Financial Crisis (GFC) erupted in 2007 and reduced the demand for electrical and electronic goods, which had dominated Japanese MNC activities in the ASEAN-4 economies. Leaving aside Indonesia, where the focus of Japanese MNCs was on oil and natural resources, the main production activities in the

TABLE 12.3
Japan's Outward FDI by Country, 2003–11
(US$ million)

Year	ASEAN-4 Total	Thailand	Indonesia	Malaysia	Philippines
2003	773	678	484	−504	114
2004	2,534	1,867	498	163	6
2005	4,276	2,125	1,185	524	442
2006	6,038	1,984	744	2,941	369
2007	5,007	2,608	1,030	325	1,045
2008	4,043	2,016	731	591	705
2009	3,540	1,632	483	616	809
2010	4,310	2,248	490	1,058	514
2011	13,204	7,133	3,611	1,441	1,019

Source: JETRO.

other ASEAN-4 economies were concentrated in manufacturing. The manufacturing activities of Japanese MNCs were dominated by the manufacture and assembly of electrical and electronic components for export to Japan, the United States, and Europe.

However, the impact of the GFC did not last beyond 2009 as Japanese FDI flows to the ASEAN-4 economies increased and grew by more than 21 per cent in 2010 and by more than 206 per cent in 2011. This was probably because wages in the manufacturing sector in China had increased by an average of 20 per cent per year between 2005 and 2011 (Nguyen 2013, p. 6). The impact of the territorial dispute between China and Japan and the resulting hostilities Japanese MNCs faced in China may also have contributed to the positive inflows of Japanese FDI into several of the ASEAN-4 economies.

Another factor that may have contributed to the rising FDI inflows into the ASEAN countries was the China+1 strategy adopted by Japan and its MNCs. As noted by Eichengreen and Tong (2005), the activities of affiliates of MNCs in China are complementary to the production activities of affiliates of MNCs in other parts of Asia, including the ASEAN-4 economies, as they are part of an integrated Asian production network. The China+1 strategy initiated by Japan to integrate the production activities of its affiliates in China with one other ASEAN country may have been to take advantage of relatively lower labor costs and also to benefit from the effort to integrate ASEAN by lowering tariffs in a common free trade area as envisaged in the formation of AFTA in 1992. Efforts at improving ASEAN connectivity by improving and updating infrastructure are also attractive to Japanese MNCs that intend to concentrate their investments in ASEAN into a Japanese cluster. The growing middle class also makes the ASEAN-4 economies a valuable market for Japanese MNCs to focus on for the marketing of their key products. Trade and investment liberalization and the growing trend toward open regionalism make ASEAN an attractive alternative for Japanese MNCs to concentrate their production activities to increase efficiency, achieve economies of scale, reduce costs, and take advantage of the relatively cheap supply of labor.

The individual ASEAN-4 economies show a broadly similar trend in the ebb and flow of Japanese FDI into their respective countries, as is shown by the aggregate data for all the ASEAN-4 countries but with the exception perhaps of the Philippines (see Table 12.3). In Thailand, the inflow of Japanese FDI increased in 2004 and 2005 but became negative in 2006, probably because of problems with national security and political stability. In 2007, Japanese FDI inflow into Thailand was positive despite the GFC. However, in 2008 and 2009, as the full impact of the adverse effects on external demand of the GFC was felt, the inflow of Japanese FDI turned negative. In 2010 and 2011, Thailand received the largest inflows of Japanese FDI among the ASEAN-4 economies. These inflows probably went to the auto industry and the manufacturing sector, which was dominated by the assembly of electrical and electronic parts by largely unskilled and relatively low-cost labor.

Japanese FDI inflows into Indonesia exhibited the same features as Japanese FDI inflows into Thailand, as Japanese FDI inflows increased in Indonesia in 2004 and 2005 but not in 2006. As in the case of Thailand, Japanese FDI inflows into Indonesia recovered and were positive in 2007 but declined and were negative in 2008 and 2009. However, as in the case of Thailand, Japanese FDI inflows became positive in 2010 and increased by a huge amount in 2011, probably benefiting from Japanese MNC divestments from China and the China+1 strategy.

In the case of Malaysia, Japanese FDI inflows were negative only in 2007, before and after which they were positive. However, Malaysia did not receive as large an amount of FDI inflows as Thailand and Indonesia in 2011. It received about 20 per cent of the Japanese FDI received by Thailand and only about 40 per cent of the Japanese FDI received by Indonesia in 2011. Clearly Indonesia and Thailand offered better prospects for the concentration of production and the building of Japanese clusters than did Malaysia. Indonesia and Thailand also had larger populations and offered an emerging relatively large, affluent market, where Japanese MNCs could market their key products. Malaysia's relatively small population meant that it could not provide plentiful supplies of low-cost labor and hence may have been unable to compete for MNCs focused on using cheap labor. It was also unable to supply the skilled labor required to attract high-technology-intensive MNCs to get out of the middle income trap in which it has been caught for decades.

The trend of Japanese FDI inflows into the Philippines was more erratic: FDI inflows declined and were negative in 2004, 2006, 2008, and 2010. In 2011, Japanese FDI inflows into the Philippines amounted to only about 14 per cent of the amount that Thailand was able to attract. The Philippines has been unable to attract large amounts of Japanese FDI because of poor infrastructure, especially poor roads and rail networks and "tough restrictions on FDI" (Nguyen 2013, p. 1). The country's endemic corruption and political instability also deter FDI.

CONCLUSION

This paper traced the evolution of Japanese FDI outflows into the ASEAN-4 economies from after World War II until 2011. It is clear that the Japanese were able to reenter the ASEAN-4 economies after World War II due to their ability to provide aid, generate trade, and promote long-term greenfield investments in the ASEAN-4 economies, which was beneficial to the ASEAN-4 economies as they were in need of creating jobs, especially since their major export commodities were subject to wild swings in their terms of trade. The ASEAN-4 economies benefited from facilitating the re-entry of Japanese into the economy because Japanese FDI created much-needed labor-intensive jobs, without which there might have been rising unemployment and political instability in the ASEAN-4 countries.

The big surge in Japanese FDI flows into the ASEAN-4 economies occurred after the 1985 Plaza Accord, when the Japanese yen began to appreciate sharply against the U.S. dollar, making it profitable for Japanese firms to migrate to the ASEAN-4 economies as even wage rates in the NIEs were rising. The surge in Japanese FDI flows to the ASEAN-4 economies took a backseat in the early 1990s as China opened up and offered MNCs worldwide labor at relatively lower costs. China had the added attraction of a huge domestic market. The outflow of Japanese

FDI into China and divestments from some ASEAN-4 economies gained momentum after China devalued the yuan in 1994 and joined the WTO in 2001.

The flow of Japanese investments into the ASEAN-4 economies hit a trough in 2003, after which there was a reversal of Japanese FDI flows into the ASEAN-4 economies from China as Chinese labor was no longer cheap — or even cheaper — and there was a risk associated with concentrating Japanese FDI in China and focusing the Asian production network in clusters there. The Japanese were keen to disperse their network operations in China to one other ASEAN country, and hence the formation of a Japanese production network incorporating both China and the ASEAN-4 economies. Building production ties between China and one other ASEAN-4 country is also known as the China+1 strategy. The impetus for deconcentrating from China and dispersing to the ASEAN-4 countries came also from the recent territorial disputes between China and Japan.

References

Akrasanee, N., and A. Prasert. "The Evolution of ASEAN-Japan Economic Cooperation". In *ASEAN-Japan Cooperation: A Foundation for East Asian Community*, edited by Japan Center for International Exchange. Tokyo: Japan Center for International Exchange, 2003, pp. 63–74.

Arase, D. *Buying Power: The Political Economy of Japan's Foreign Aid*. New York: Lynne Rienner Publishers, 1995.

Asahi Shimbun. 15 January 2013, editorial.

Atarashi, K. "Japan's Economic Cooperation Policy towards the ASEAN Countries". *International Affairs* (Royal Institute of International Affairs 1944) 61, no. 1 (1985, Winter 1984–85): 109–27.

Belderbos, R., and J. Zou. "Foreign Investment, Divestment and Relocation by Japanese Electronics Firms in East Asia". *Asian Economic Journal* 20, no. 1 (2006): 1–27.

Blaise, S. "Japanese Aid as a Prerequisite for FDI: The Case of Southeast Asian Countries". Asia-Pacific Economic Papers, Australia-Japan Research Centre, ANU College of Asia and the Pacific, Crawford School of Economics and Government, no. 385, 2009.

Bowles, P. "ASEAN, AFTA and the 'New Regionalism'". *Pacific Affairs* 70, no. 2 (1997): 219–33.

Chintayarangsan, R., N. Thongpakdee, and P. Nakornchai. "ASEAN Economies: Macro-Economic Perspective". *ASEAN Economic Bulletin* 8, no. 3 (March 1992): 353–75.

Cumings, B. "The Origins and Development of the Northeast Asian Political

Economy: Industrial Sectors, Product Cycles, and Political Consequences." *International Organization* 38 (1984): 149–53.

Cushman, D.O. "Exchange Rate Uncertainty and Foreign Direct Investment in the United States". *Weltwirtschaftliches Archiv* 124 (1988): 322–36.

D. Nguyen, T. *The Great Migration*. Hong Kong: Hong Kong and Shanghai Banking Corporation, 2013.

Doner, R. "Japanese Foreign Investment and the Creation of a Pacific Asian Region". In *Regionalism and Rivalry: Japan and the United States in Pacific Asia*, edited by Jeffrey Frankel and Miles Kahler. Chicago: University of Chicago Press, 1993, pp. 159–216.

Easterly, W. "The Elusive Quest for Growth: Economists' Adventures and Misadventures in the Tropics". Cambridge: MIT Press, 2002.

Eichengreen, B., and H. Tong. "Is China's FDI Coming at the Expense of Other Countries?" NBER Working Paper 1135, Washington D.C., 2005.

Ernst, D. "From Partial to Systemic Globalization: International Production Networks in the Electronics Industry". Berkeley Roundtable on the International Economy, Working Paper no. 98, University of California, Berkeley, 1997.

Felker, G.B. "Southeast Asian Industrialization and the Changing Global Production System". *Third World Quarterly* 24 (2003): 255–83.

Goldberg, L., and M. Klein. "Foreign Direct Investment, Trade and Real Exchange Rate Linkages in Southeast Asia and Latin America". NBER Working Paper 6344, 1997.

———. "Foreign Direct Investment, Trade and Real Exchange Rate Linkages in Developing Countries". In *Managing Capital Flows and Exchange Rates*, edited by R. Glick. Cambridge: Cambridge University Press, 1998, pp. 73–100.

Guisinger, S. "Foreign Direct Investment Flows in East and Southeast Asia: Policy Issues." *ASEAN Economic Bulletin* 8, no. 1 (July 1991): 29–46.

Hansen, G. "Indonesia 1974: A Momentous Year". *Asian Survey* 15, no. 2 (February 1975): 148–56.

Henning, C. Rendall, and I.M. Destler. "From Neglect to Activism: American Politics and the 1985 Plaza Accord". *Journal of Public Policy* 8 (June–December 1988): 317–33.

James, W.E., and O. Movshuk. "Shifting International Competitiveness: An Analysis of Market Share in Manufacturing Industries in Japan, Korea, Taiwan and the USA". *Asian Economic Journal* 18, no. 2 (2004): 121–48.

Malmstrom, A. "Power and Development in Indonesia". In *The Business of Japanese Foreign Aid: Five Case Studies from Asia*, edited by M. Soderberg. London and New York: Routledge, 1996.

Ministry of Foreign Affairs, Japan. "Japan 2005 ODA White Paper". Tokyo: Ministry of Foreign Affairs, 2005.

Nakamura, Shin-Ya, and T. Oyama. "The Determinants of Foreign Direct

Investment from Japan and the United States to East Asian Countries, and the Linkage between FDI and Trade". Working Paper 98–11, Research and Statistics Department, Bank of Japan, 1998.

Obstfeld, M. "The Yen and Japan's Economy, 1985–2007". ESRI/CJEB, Pre-Workshop, Columbia University, 21–22 March 2008.

Orr, R.M. *The Emergence of Japan's Foreign Aid*. New York: Columbia University Press, 1990.

Patrick, H. "Legacies of Change: The Transformative Role of Japan's Official Development Assistance in Its Economic Partnership with Southeast Asia". Discussion Paper no. 54, APEC Study Centre, 2008.

Phongpaichit, P. *The New Wave of Japanese Investment in Asean: Determinants and Prospects*. Singapore: Institute of Southeast Asian Studies, 1990.

Rix, A. "Japan's Foreign Aid Policy: A Capacity for Leadership?". *Pacific Affairs* 62, no. 4 (1990).

Shinoda, O. "Evolution of Institutions and Policies for the Economic Integration in East Asia: History and Prospects". Tokyo: GRIPS, 2013.

Soderberg, M., ed. *The Business of Japanese Foreign Aid: Five Case Studies from Asia*. London: Routledge, 1996.

Suehiro, A. "The Road to Economic Re-entry: Japan's Policy toward Southeast Asian Development in the 1950s and 1960s". *Social Science Japan Journal* (1999): 85–105.

Thorbecke, W., and N. Salike. "Understanding Foreign Direct Investment in Southeast Asia". ADBI Working Paper Series, no. 290, June 2011.

Thursby, J.G., and M.C. Thursby. "Bilateral Trade Flows, the Linder Hypothesis and Exchange Risk". *The Review of Economics and Statistics* 69, no. 3 (1987) 647–56.

UNCTAD. *World Investment Report*. Geneva: UNCTAD, 2005.

Urata, S. "Japanese Foreign Direct Investment and Its Effect on Foreign Trade in Asia". In *Trade and Protectionism*, edited by T. Ito and A. Krueger. Chicago: University of Chicago, 1993, pp. 273–304.

———. "Regionalization and the Formation of Regional Institutions in East Asia". In *Asia and Europe: Beyond Competing Regionalism*, edited by Kiichiro Fukasaku, Fukunari Kimura, and Shijiro Urata. Brighton: Sussex University Press, 1998, pp. 13–44.

———. "Emergence of an FDI-Trade Nexus and Economic Growth in East Asia". In *Rethinking the East Asian Miracle*, edited by J.E. Stiglitz and S. Yusuf. Oxford: Oxford University Press, 2001, pp. 409–59.

Urata, S., and H. Kawai. "The Determinants of the Location of Foreign Direct Investment by Japanese Small and Medium-sized Enterprises". *Small Business Economics* 15, no. 2 (2000): 79–103.

Weinstein, F.B. "Multinational Corporations and the Third World: The Case of Japan and Southeast Asia". *International Organization* 30, no. 3 (June 1976): 373–404.

World Bank. *The East Asian Miracle*. New York: Oxford University Press, 1993.

Wu, F., and K.K. Puah. "Foreign Direct Investment to China and Southeast Asia: Has Asean Been Losing Out?" *Journal of Asian Business* 18 (2002): 45–58.

Young, K., W.C.F. Bussink, and P. Hasan. *Malaysia: Growth and Equity in a Multiracial Society.* Baltimore: John Hopkins University Press, 1980.

Yun, Chunji. "Rise of the Chinese Economy and East Asian FTA: Japan's Strategic Change and Continuity". Institute for World Economics and International Management Universitat Bremen, Germany, 2004.

13

JAPAN'S TRIPLE TSUNAMI

Kishore Mahbubani[1]

INTRODUCTION

Over 20 years ago, in the fall of 1992, I published an article in *Foreign Policy* entitled "Japan Adrift". As a friend of Japan, I warned that the post-Cold War era had created an uncomfortable geopolitical environment for Japan. I urged Japan to engage in fresh thinking and to change course. Sadly, my warnings were not heeded. Now, as a result of the failure to adapt over the past 20 years, Japan faces an even more difficult geopolitical environment. The goal of this essay is simple and clear: to save Japan from another 20 years of geopolitical drift.

In 1992, I began my essay with a Japanese folktale. Let me repeat it here: "A Japanese folktale tells of a young boy who lives in a coastal rice-farming village. One autumn morning, walking alone to work in the fields, he sees, to his horror, an approaching tsunami, which he knows will destroy the village. Knowing that he has no time to run down the hill to warn the villagers, he sets the rice fields on fire, sure that the desire to save their crops will draw all the villagers up the hill. The precious rice fields are sacrificed, but the villagers are saved from the tsunami" (Mahbubani 2005, p. 124). In this essay, I may make some inflammatory comments, but I hope my Japanese friends will understand that my goal is to help Japan.

In 2014, Japan will have to deal with not one tsunami but three. These three different tsunami will collide with one another and aggravate Japan's difficulties. The first tsunami is geopolitical. The new balance of power is working against Japan's interests. The second tsunami is political. At a time when Japan needs unified political leadership to cope with dramatic new challenges, the Japanese political system has never been more divided. The third tsunami is demographic. Japan has one of the fastest ageing populations in the entire world. Hence its relative "weight" in the international system will steadily decline. All these three great challenges will be discussed in detail in this paper.

Nonetheless, the conclusion of this paper is optimistic. Japan is not without options as it tries to steer a course in the 21st century. It can, for example, strengthen its relations with ASEAN and India to lay the foundations for a new Asian community that will in the long run enhance the security of Japan. However, to achieve this optimistic outcome, Japanese policy-makers must radically revise their mind-sets. They must stop being cultural slaves of the West and look at Asians with greater respect. I deliberately make this harsh statement at the beginning as I want to shock the complacent Japanese establishment out of the deep intellectual rut it has fallen into. If I succeed, and Japan looks at the world with a fresh perspective, it can sail into a happier future in the 21st century.

TSUNAMI NUMBER ONE

Twenty years ago, Japan was essentially abandoned as a geopolitical orphan by the United States when the Cold War ended. It went from being geopolitically indispensable to being geopolitically dispensable. Japan's geopolitical irrelevance could not have been made clearer when the then U.S. Secretary of State, James Baker, called for the creation of a new "Western" community "from Vancouver to Vladivostok." The only major American ally dropped out of this charmed "Western" circle was Japan.

This should have been a major wake-up call for Japan to change course. Sadly, Japan did not heed it. It continued on autopilot, even as the geopolitical environment around it changed course significantly. As a result, the geopolitical adjustments that Japan will have to make now will have to be even larger. They can be done. But the sooner Japan makes these changes, the less painful it will be. This is why this paper needs to be read urgently in Japan.

Twenty years ago, no-one even dreamt that China could become the number one economy and the United States the number two economy. Now this is going to happen sooner than expected. According to IMF statistics, in purchasing power parity (PPP) terms, the United States had a 25 per cent share of the world economy in 1980 while China had only

2.2 per cent. By 2017, in barely four years, the United States's share will fall to 17.6 per cent while China's will rise to 18 per cent. China will effectively become the number one economy. Justin Lin (2011, p. 6), the former World Bank chief economist, has predicted that China's GDP could become twice as large as the United States' in PPP terms by 2030.

Let me emphasize one point here: all these changes could have and should have been anticipated. As I pointed out in *The New Asian Hemisphere* (2010), which has fortunately been published in Japanese, from the year 1 to 1820, the two largest economies were always that of China and India. It was only in the last 200 years that Europe and the United States took off. But the last 200 years, when viewed against the past 2,000 years, have truly been a major historical aberration. All historical aberrations come to a natural end. Hence, the era of Western domination of the world is coming to a natural end too.

However, Japan's geopolitical policies — which have been fundamentally based on this major geopolitical aberration — have not come to a natural end. One hundred and fifty years ago, Yukichi Fukuzawa, the great Meiji reformer, gave Japan the right advice: "It is better for us to leave the ranks of Asian nations and cast our lot with civilized nations of the West" (Fukuzawa 1885). At that point in history, it was the right advice. Today, why is there no Japanese reformer as brave as Yukichi Fukuzawa to give Japan this obvious advice: "It is now better for us to leave the ranks of Western nations and cast our lot with the civilized nations of Asia"?

The real irony of Japan's rejoining Asia and taking advantage of the Asian century is that Japan has done more than any other Asian country to spark off the Asian century. As I said in a *Time* magazine essay (2005), if Japan had not succeeded early in the 20th century, Asia's development would have come much later. Asia needs to send Japan a big thank-you note.

To take advantage of the Asian century, the Japanese leaders need to change their fundamental mental maps. They now need to work with the following mental assumptions: Europe represents the past, the United States represents the present, and Asia represents the future. Today, Japan invests most of its diplomatic and political capital into cultivating the past and the present. It invests little in cultivating the future. Surely, this is geopolitical folly of the highest order.

All this does not mean that Japan should immediately end its alliance with the United States. Indeed it should retain it as long as possible.

However, the most durable alliances (and the most durable marriages) are between two parties that respect each other and treat each other as equals. Sadly, Japan has allowed its relationship with the United States to drift into what I have described as the Lone Ranger-Tonto relationship, with the United States being the Lone Ranger and Japan being Tonto. My essay "Japan Adrift" (1992) describes in detail how this happened.

Japan's agreement to serve as the United States' Tonto has not only undermined respect for Japan in American eyes, it has also undermined respect for Japan in the eyes of the rest of the world. One key point I emphasize in my book, *The Great Convergence: Asia, the West, and the Logic of One World* (2013), is that the 88 per cent of the world's population who live outside the West have gone from being passive to active stakeholders of the world order. I noticed this when I served as Singapore's ambassador to the UN from 1984–89 and from 1998–2004. Several UN ambassadors asked me why they should support Japan's campaign for a permanent seat on the UN Security Council (UNSC) when Japan would vote automatically in support of every American position in the UNSC. In their eyes, Japan would not add a new or independent voice in the UNSC.

To understand how much the world has changed, Japan should seriously review its quest to become a permanent member of the UNSC. Japan has been pursuing this goal steadily for more than 45 years, since as early as 1968 (Brewers 1968). Normally, after 45 years of enormous effort, a country should get closer to achieving its goal. Instead, Japan has slid backwards and is now even further from achieving permanent membership in the UNSC. This provides powerful proof that Japan has been pursuing wrong geopolitical policies.

In its effort to become a permanent member of the UNSC, Japan did not work out a new strategy to succeed. Instead it carried on autopilot with its standard foreign policy basket of policies: maintaining a close alliance with the United States (and voting with the U.S. in the UN), emphasizing its strong Western credentials (by highlighting its membership in the G7 and OECD), and using cash, instead of ideas and political conviction, to win over the 150 votes of non-Western UN member states. If a Japanese policy-maker had asked me in 1992 whether this standard basket of policies could work, I would have easily said no.

Twenty years later it is even clearer that these policies will not work. Japan has gone from being the number two world economy to becoming number three. By 2050, according to Goldman Sachs projections, Japan will become number eight (Goldman Sachs Global Economics

Paper No. 134, 2005). As I explain in my book *The Great Convergence* (2013), the UNSC will only allow two Asian permanent members, not three. The two Asian permanent members are likely to be China and India (which will have the number one and number two economies in 2050) and not China and Japan.

In short, Japan's standing in the global order is going to drift steadily downwards. The most urgent priority for Japan is to work out a credible long-term policy that arrests the decline of Japanese influence. Hence, the first decision that the Japanese establishment needs to make in response to Tsunami Number One is to stop going on autopilot. Sadly, Tsunami Number Two will prevent this from happening.

TSUNAMI NUMBER TWO

The second tsunami Japan has to cope with is the potential breakdown of the Japanese political system. There are many reasons why Japan successfully catapulted itself from a badly defeated nation in 1945 to the number two economic power in 1968 (Buchanan 2012). One critical reason was that Japan was essentially ruled by the same political party, the LDP, which pursued a predictable set of policies in the predictable geopolitical environment of the Cold War.

The tragedy for Japan is that when the predictable geopolitical environment of the Cold War fell apart in 1989, the predictable rule of the LDP also fell apart in 1993. Similarly, the cohesive Japanese civil service, which had managed to steer a steady course for Japan even when the Japanese political establishment underwent massive changes, began to fall apart. This cohesive Japanese civil service has also gradually disappeared. According to Hideaka Tanaki of the Tokyo Foundation, the National Personnel Authority, Japan's central personnel administration agency, notes the following problems of the current civil service system: scandals involving senior civil servants (erosion of civil service ethics), mistrust of the administrative capacity of civil servants (administrative failure), sectionalism (closed nature of civil service apparatus and fixation on defending interests of ministries), career system (development of a sense of privilege), retirement management (the practice of retired bureaucrats "parachuting" into lucrative jobs in sectors they formerly regulated), close relations between politicians and bureaucrats (ambiguous demarcation), and the seniority system (emasculation of meritocracy and complacency born of protected status) (McCurry and Kollewe 2011). Gerald Curtis (2012), a professor of political science at Columbia University, observes that "Japan's leadership deficit is not the result of a divided Diet or factional infighting, though they no doubt make governance more difficult. Institutional reforms — abolishing the upper house for example or directly electing the prime minister, to name two ideas that are enjoying some currency in Japan today — would not end deadlock. The roots of Japan's political paralysis unfortunately lie much deeper: in the inability of leaders to define national goals and in the failure of both the DPJ and the LDP to recruit enough qualified politicians." In short, Japan was hit by internal political paralysis at the precise time when the external political environment demanded bold and innovative political responses from Japan.

Virtually all nations that have succeeded have done so because of great leadership. The United States succeeded because it had great founding fathers. Japan succeeded because of the brilliant Meiji reformers as well as the wise prime ministers after Japan's shattering defeat in 1945. China succeeded because of Mao Zedong and Deng Xiaoping. Singapore succeeded because of Lee Kuan Yew, Dr Goh Keng Swee, and S. Rajaratnam. In short, strong and decisive political leadership is a necessary, if not indispensable condition, for political success.

Strong political leadership is precisely what Japan lacks when it needs it most. Let me reinforce this point with two critical historical examples. After India, a country of 300 million people, was effortlessly colonized in the early 19th century by 100,000 Englishmen and after China was humiliated in the Opium War in 1842, the leaders of Japan knew that Japan had to change course. It accomplished this with the Meiji restoration. Similarly, when Japan was spectacularly defeated in 1945, the Japanese political leaders knew that Japan had to change course. They wisely dropped all militant policies and focused on economic development and a close alliance.

In short, at two critical points of Japan's history, when Japan had to change course, it did so successfully. Today, there is an even greater need for Japan to change course. Yet there is virtually zero chance that Japan will change course in the next ten years or so. The collapse of the Japanese political establishment means that Japan will continue on autopilot and plod on straight ahead when history has turned a corner. A similar failure to change course has led to Europe's dire predicament today. To understand where Japan is headed if its political establishment fails to change course, Japan should just look carefully at what has happened to Europe. Europe's present is Japan's future.

TSUNAMI NUMBER THREE

The third tsunami that is already hitting Japan is the rapid ageing of its population. In theory, the real damage of the ageing population will only hit Japan in 2050. According to UN estimates, in 2010, there were 38 elderly dependents for every 100 people working. By 2050, the ratio will rise to 76 retired dependents for every 100 people working. Unless birth rates rise, it is predicted that Japan's total population could decrease from around 127.8 million in 2011 to just 91.3 million in 2100 (United Nations Secretariat Population Division 2010).

Figure 13.1 shows clearly how dramatic the shift will become.

Yet even though the real burden of the ageing population will only hit in 2050, the geopolitical effects are already being felt now. Why? Countries make assessments of the political and economic weight of other countries not only on the basis of their current performance; they also factor in future performance. Hence, for the next 10–20 years, Japan will clearly be perceived as a declining power and China will be perceived as a rising power. Most countries in the world will bet on rising powers and not declining powers.

FIGURE 13.1
Changes in the Population Pyramid

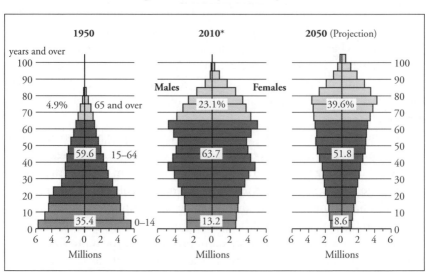

Source: Ministry of Internal Affairs and Communications, Japan. <http://www.stat.go.jp/english/data/handbook/c02cont.htm>.

FIGURE 13.2
Japan's Population by Age Group, 1950–2100
(UN Medium Scenario)

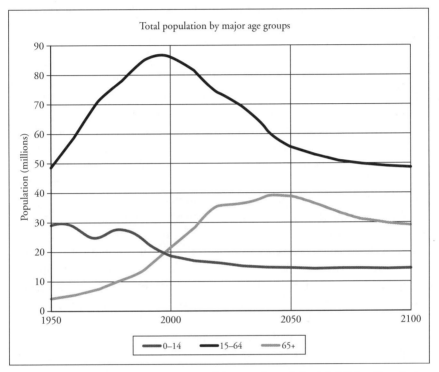

Source: United Nations, Department of Economic and Social Affairs, Population Division (2011).

One important event happened in 2009 that many Japanese are not aware of. They should study this event carefully because they will get a glimpse of Japan's future through it. In that year, Japan, working carefully with Brazil, India, and Germany, came close to tabling a resolution in the UN General Assembly (UNGA) recommending that these four countries be admitted to the UNSC as permanent members. As a result of a fairly concerted campaign, this resolution came close to being passed.

China became very alarmed at the prospect of the UNGA passing a resolution legitimizing Japan's aspirations for permanent membership. Hence, it mounted a ferocious global campaign to lobby against this resolution. One area that China worked hard in was the ASEAN region. In theory, out of the ten ASEAN member states, more should have sympathized with Japan than with China, as Japan had, over the years, given far more aid to the ten ASEAN countries than had China. According to the OECD, Japan has donated a total of almost US$57 billion to ASEAN from 1960–2010, making it the region's largest single donor (World Bank 2011). Hence, in theory, the ten ASEAN countries should have felt closer to Japan than to China.

In practice, they did not. Indeed, out of the ten ASEAN countries, only one supported Japan publicly (Singapore) and only one supported Japan privately (Vietnam). The other eight either kept quiet or supported China. Why did this happen? The answer can be long and complicated as there were many factors at play. But the most critical factor is not difficult to discern: Japan represented a declining power; China represented a rising power. To make matters worse, in the very period of Japan's geopolitical incompetence and impotence, China demonstrated itself to be the most geopolitically competent great power (Mahbubani 2008).

Japan's demographic challenge is therefore not just an "internal" problem for Japan. It is also an "external" problem as it is contributing significantly to Japan's sliding position in the global geopolitical order. Yet, despite the gravity of this challenge, it is truly remarkable that Japanese society and its political establishment are nowhere close to achieving consensus on what needs to be done to reverse this demographic decline. There is no doubt that Japan's political paralysis has also contributed to Japan's inability to deal with this challenge.

Yet, solutions exist. One obvious solution is to allow more immigration. Many nations do this — the United States and Canada, Australia, and Europe are among the countries that welcome immigration. Immigration can affect demographic ratios significantly. Let me cite one dramatic example. In 2011, the population of China was 1.4 billion while that of the United States was 311.5 million. In short, China's population is over four times larger than the United States's. However, by 2100, by current projections, China's population will shrink to 940 million while that of the United States will rise to 478 million (United Nations Secretariat Population Division 2010). In short, China's population will only be twice that of the United States. And China's population will be ageing, while the American population will be young.

I am acutely aware that Japanese society, unlike American society, is relatively closed and insular and does not welcome "foreigners" in its midst. A massive cultural change will be needed in Japanese society before it can begin to allow more foreigners on its soil on a permanent basis. However, before taking this big step toward permanent migration, Japan can take a small interim step forward by allowing temporary migration. In this area, Japan can learn some lessons from Singapore, which is also facing the challenge of a declining and ageing society.

Few Japanese are aware that Singaporeans already live in one of the most densely populated cities in the world. Japan's population density is 335 persons per square kilometer, while that of Singapore is 7,447 persons per square kilometer (United Nations Secretariat Population Division 2010). In short, Singapore is 22 times more densely populated than Japan. Despite this, Singapore allows a remarkable number of "foreigners" on its soil. Of the 5 million people that live in Singapore, only about 3.2 million are Singaporean citizens. Singapore permanent residents number 532,000 and the remaining 1.3 million are foreigners (Singapore Department of Statistics 2013). In short, out of a resident population of 5 million, nearly two-fifths are non-citizens. If Japan were to allow a similar ratio of non-citizens, it could increase its current population from 127.8 million citizens to 175 million people. This would give a huge boost to the Japanese economy.

To assure those in the Japanese public who fear permanent migrants, it is important to emphasize that most of the 1.2 million visitors to Singapore do not stay for long. Out of these 1.2 million, about 400,000 work as foreign domestic workers. Another 300,000 work as construction workers. Most of them leave after a few years. In short, Japan will not be adding to its "permanent" population by letting in a large number of foreign workers. At the same time, they could help Japan to deal with its economic and social problems. A front page *Wall Street Journal* story in August 2012 reported that all three major Japanese electronic companies had suffered serious losses over the past two years (Wakabayashi 2012). More foreign workers might help them to become more competitive. Similarly, Japan's rapidly ageing population could be helped with more imported health workers.

Most of these required changes in Japanese policies towards "foreign" workers will not happen soon. Japan remains, at the end of the day, a deeply conservative society that does not change course easily. Yet, given the triple tsunamis that are hitting Japan, there is also no doubt that Japan will have to consider some radical solutions if it is going to find ways and means of improving its position in the global geopolitical order.

In short, an ageing population is not merely a domestic economic and political challenge. An ageing population is also a major geopolitical liability. It is true that China's population is also ageing. However, China has a far larger population (1.35 billion) compared to Japan. More importantly, China's economy is predicted to become larger and larger while Japan's economy will at best remain stagnant, if not decline, in relative terms, vis-à-vis the rest of the world.

SOME SHORT-TERM SOLUTIONS

Since it will be difficult to make radical changes in some of its long-established attitudes, Japan's policy-makers should make an effort to find short-term solutions for its geopolitical predicament. To find the right solution, Japan has to carry out a comprehensive audit of its geopolitical "assets and liabilities". This audit should be done in a totally frank fashion. All the prevailing "sacred cows" in Japan's geopolitical discussions will have to be slain if Japan is to understand clearly how bad its geopolitical predicament is. To put it bluntly, Japan is one of the geopolitically disadvantaged countries in the world.

To understand this concept of being "geopolitically disadvantaged", Japan should compare itself with its fellow G7 member states, a community of which Japan is extremely proud of being a member. Within the community of seven, Japan is by far the worst off in geopolitical terms. The United States is in a geopolitically advantageous position because it is protected by two large oceans and two weaker neighbors that do not pose a threat, Mexico and Canada. It is also militarily powerful. Canada is also geopolitically blessed because it is a "free rider" on American geopolitical power. No country or neighbor threatens it. Similarly, France, Germany, Italy, and the UK are protected as members of the European Union and NATO.

In contrast to its fellow G7 members, only Japan sits in geopolitical isolation in a relatively "hostile" environment. The term "hostile" may seem a little harsh but Japan is the only G7 member that has difficult relations and unresolved territorial disputes with all of its neighbors. With Russia, it has the long-standing dispute over the Northern Territories/South Kuril Islands, a dispute that was aggravated as recently as July 2012, when Russian Prime Minister Dmitry Medvedev decided to visit the territories. His previous visit was in November 2010 during his presidency, making him the first Russian head of state to visit the islands. With South Korea, Japan is involved in a long-standing dispute over the islands of Takeshima/Dokdo. This was aggravated as recently as August 2012, when South Korean President Lee Myung-bak decided to visit the islands, making him the first Korean president to do so. Former Prime Minister Han Seung-soo had also visited the islands in 2008. In addition, Japan has to deal with a difficult North Korean regime. With China, Japan has the long-standing dispute over the Senkaku/Diaoyu Islands, a dispute that flared up as recently as August 2012 when, in response to an intrusion by a group of Chinese nationalists from Hong Kong, Macau, and mainland China, a group of Japanese parliamentarians decided to visit the disputed islands.

These long-standing territorial disputes illustrate well the geopolitically disadvantaged position that Japan is in. Even more dangerously, the relationships between Japan and China, Russia, and South Korea are marked by high levels of distrust, such that Japan's relations with all three of its neighbors are constantly marked by advances and retreats. These are all highly volatile relationships. Each step forward is often marked by two steps backward a few years later.

The real geopolitical tragedy for Japan is that in the long run, it can only secure its geopolitical security by building an "iron triangle of trust" with its two most important neighbors: China and South Korea. Right now, this may seem like "mission impossible". It will not happen overnight. Yet, it is also clear that unless Japan is able to stabilize and improve its relations with its two key neighbors, it will always remain in a geopolitically disadvantaged position. For the next two decades, Japan can rely on American power to protect it, but by year 2030, when China's economy in PPP terms will be twice the size of the U.S. economy, it would be unwise for Japan to rely solely on American power to protect it. Great powers always put their national interests first, not the interests of previous allies. Nor is there as deep a reservoir of trust and goodwill between the Americans and the Japanese as there is between the British and the Americans.

Given these "hard facts" about Japan's geopolitical environment, Japan should set for itself the clear long-term target of building an "iron triangle of trust" with China and South Korea. It should analyze all the difficulties that stand in the way of a positive relationship with China and South Korea. The bad news is that history is the main obstacle to achieving positive relationships. The good news is that history is the main obstacle to achieving positive relationships.

Let me explain this paradox. A difficult historical record stands in the way between Japan's relations with China and South Korea. This is a problem. Indeed, it is a very big problem. But, at the end of the day, history is history. We cannot change history. We can, however, find creative and innovative ways of dealing with it. There are several positive examples of countries rising above past historical animosities that we can learn from, whether they are from Europe, for example, Germany and France, or from Asia, such as Indonesia and East Timor.

There are a variety of means Japan can use to understand and deal with the painful record of history. These could include joint historical commissions and third-party expert panels. Japan could even follow the South African experience with apartheid and try out unilateral truth-telling commissions. Some historical commissions have been established, such as the 2002 Japan-South Korea Joint History Research Project and the 2006 Japan-China Joint History Research Committee, both still ongoing. Scholars from all three countries have also written a joint East Asian history textbook together (Center for Korean Studies 2005). Dr Heo Seung-hoon (2008) has also explained that the post-World War II Franco-German reconciliation was only able to take place in the midst of deep civil society interaction between the two countries, particularly collaboration in the field of higher learning, in the form of youth exchanges, joint schoolbook commissions, and joint university programs. This contributed to the gradual abatement of historical enmity between the two nations, allowing their political leaders to pursue reconciliation in keeping with both countries' long-term national interests.

There is absolutely no doubt that various atrocities were committed by Japanese forces. These facts cannot be changed. But these facts can also be understood in their historical contexts. In the 19th century and up to World War II, Western armies had carried out atrocities. The infamous British massacre of innocent civilians in Amritsar was carried out in 1919. Terrible acts were carried out by all European colonial authorities throughout the world. If the Europeans have no difficulty admitting the terrible acts carried out by their ancestors, the Japanese people should not hesitate to do the same. Indeed, Japan should take the lead in carrying out a massive global historical study documenting all the horrible acts carried out by all colonial forces. This would be a gift from Japan to the world.

All this will take time. It will take time for Japan to stabilize its relations with China and Korea. No "iron triangle of trust" will be established soon with these two countries. Hence, before trying to do this, Japan should try a "practice session" before attempting the real thing. This "practice session" could take the form of establishing an initial "iron triangle of trust" with ASEAN and India. Fortunately, Japan has enjoyed, overall, relatively good relations with both ASEAN and India. However, neither one of them has been a major foreign policy priority for Japan. Japan has invested tons of its diplomatic and other resources on previous foreign policy priorities such as the G7 and the OECD. Both are clearly sunset organizations now. Despite this, Japan has not rearranged its priorities.

Hence, the first significant foreign policy decision that Japan has to take now to prepare itself for the Asian century is to "practice" on improving its relations with its Asian neighbors by attempting some bold new initiatives with ASEAN and India. Here Japan can clearly learn some lessons from China. In 2000, China shocked Japan by becoming the first country to propose a "bilateral" FTA with ASEAN. This FTA was then negotiated and concluded in record time in 2004. After this Chinese initiative, Japan had to play catch-up by proposing its own FTA with ASEAN in 2003 and concluding it in 2008. In so doing, Japan demonstrated that it was a follower, not a leader, in the new Asian diplomatic game.

Just as China demonstrated its leadership by proposing a "bilateral" FTA with ASEAN, Japan can now demonstrate its leadership by proposing a new "trilateral" FTA with ASEAN and India. This should be a relatively easy process to undertake since all three parties already have bilateral FTAs among themselves. These three bilateral FTAs can be combined and converted into a "trilateral" FTA. Of course, there will be intense negotiations over some aspects of this "trilateral" FTA. But these intense "trilateral" negotiations will provide Japan with a valuable practice run when it eventually tries to negotiate a trilateral FTA with China and South Korea.

Indeed, if Japan's initiative of proposing and concluding a trilateral FTA succeeds, it could have the same positive effect on the region as China's "bilateral" FTA with ASEAN. After China's proposal, several other countries tried to catch up with China's initiatives by proposing similar FTAs with ASEAN. Hence, India (2002), Japan (2003), South Korea (2004), and Australia-New Zealand (2004) did the same. Similarly, if Japan's proposal for a "trilateral" FTA succeeds, other countries will then rush to catch up with this Japanese initiative. In this process, it is conceivable that either China or South Korea would propose a trilateral FTA with Japan too.

In short, Japan should not see this "trilateral" FTA proposal with ASEAN and India in isolation. Its value and significance will not be confined to these three parties. Instead, it could actually change the political chemistry of the region surrounding Japan. This new positive chemistry could in turn provide a comfortable geopolitical environment to replace the current uncomfortable one that Japan is living in. In short,

Japan should not accept its current geopolitical environment as a given. Instead, it should try to shape it and improve it. And it can be done.

There is another powerful "weapon" that Japan has to improve its geopolitical situation: its soft power. Japanese culture in all dimensions is highly regarded throughout the world, especially in Asia. Both its ancient and modern culture are revered. Some of the best contemporary movies that I have seen are Japanese ones — *Tampopo* and *Departures* being two good examples. Similarly, Japanese cuisine is widely admired globally. One way of winning over creative young Asian minds is to organize "summer" culture camps for young people from all over Asia.

These creative young minds could in turn trigger a new perception of Japan in Asian societies. Joseph Nye was right in emphasizing that American soft power has allowed the United States to gain many geopolitical dividends. As Nye (2010) says, "The results [of American soft power] can be dramatic. For example, at the end of the Cold War, Gorbachev's embrace of perestroika and glasnost was influenced by ideas learned in the U.S. by Alexander Yakovlev when he was an exchange student [in the United States]. Although it took two decades to materialize, that was a huge return on a small investment." Certainly, American culture has much to admire, but in "high culture," it is no exaggeration to say that the pool of Japanese culture is deeper and richer. However, given the language difficulties, many in the rest of the world have not been given an opportunity to understand the depth and beauty of Japanese culture. This is why Japan should make a major effort to cultivate cultural elites, especially among the young budding artists in Asia. This talent pool could well provide the best reservoir of pro-Japanese sentiment in Asia.

One reason why I emphasize the point on cultural diplomacy is that when I grew up in Singapore in the 1970s and 1980s, Japan was perceived primarily as an economic animal. The whole world spoke about the economic prowess of the Japanese people. Few spoke about the cultural strengths of Japanese society. I feel that this perception of an "economic animal" may still remain the defining perception of Japan in Asian eyes. If so, more active cultural diplomacy by Japan, especially in Asia, could well make a huge difference and win over more friends for Japan in Asia.

However, to achieve all this, there is one painful step that the Japanese people need to take. The only way to explain this painful step is to explain it in painful terms. Right now, among the Japanese people, especially the established elites, there is a natural psychological reverence for Western cultures and societies and a thinly disguised contempt for Asian cultures and societies. One need only look at the number of Western authors who are translated into Japanese, compared to the number of Asian authors translated into Japanese. The Asian elites are neither stupid nor insensitive. They can clearly sense when they are being treated with genuine respect or with mild condescension.

In short, the Japanese people now need to carry out a massive exercise of educating themselves on the rich cultural heritage of other Asian societies. Evidently they need to understand Chinese and Korean cultures better. Equally importantly, they also need to understand the rich cultural diversity of the ASEAN societies. Since many Japanese go to Europe on cultural pilgrimages, they will be astonished to discover that the cultural diversity of Southeast Asia far exceeds that of Europe.

Even more importantly, to understand the multi-civilizational world that is coming with the end of the era of Western domination of world history, the best microcosm of this new multi-civilizational world is provided by the ASEAN community. The region has almost 600 million people, comprising 300 million Muslims, 80 million Christians, 150 million Hinayana Buddhists, 80 million Mahayana Buddhists, and 5 million Hindus. Some Vietnamese Buddhists also practice Taoism and Confucianism, while being communists. On the ethnic front, there is even greater diversity, and on the political front, ASEAN has the full spectrum of political systems. To understand the future, the Japanese should travel to Southeast Asia and not to Europe.

The conclusion of this essay is therefore a simple one. Japan's future will no longer be determined by Europe or the United States. It will be determined by its capacity to integrate with its Asian neighbors. I am confident that Japan can and will be accepted by members of the Asian community. However, to achieve respect and acceptance from its fellow members, the Japanese people must begin to show sincere respect and admiration for them. If the Japanese people can do this, a great future beckons for Japan. It can become as successful in this century as it was after the Meiji restoration and after World War II. In short, the Japanese people can begin to hope again for a better future.

Notes

[1] Professor Kishore Mahbubani is Dean, Lee Kuan Yew School of Public Policy, NUS, and author of *The Great Convergence: Asia, the West, and the Logic of One World*. Public Affairs: 2013.

References

Brewers, Sam. "Japanese Seeking Full Council Seat; U.N. Delegate Says Tokyo Wants Permanent Role". *New York Times*, 18 October 1968. Available at <http://select.nytimes.com/gst/abstract.html?res=F70E16FF3A54157493CAA 8178BD95F4C8685F9>.

Buchanan, Patrick J. "Land of the Setting Sun". Available at <http://takimag. com/article/land_of_the_setting_sun_patrick_buchanan/print#axzz226LXYkAv> (accessed 12 August 2013).

Center for Korean Studies, University of Hawai'i at Manoa. "History that Opens the Future: A Conference and Planning Meeting Concerning a Multinational East Asian Textbook", October 2007. Available at <http://www.hawaii.edu/ korea/pages/announce/openhist.html> (accessed 13 August 2013).

Curtis, Gerald. "Tokyo Drift". *The Wall Street Journal*, 29 May 2012. Available at <http://online.wsj.com/article/SB100014240527023036740045774338704 86688262.html>.

Fukuzawa, Yukichi (attributed). "Datsu-A Ron"「脱亞論」. Jiji Shimpo, 16 March 1885.

Goldman Sachs Global Economics Paper No. 134, December 2005. Available at <http://www.goldmansachs.com/our-thinking/topics/brics/brics-reports-pdfs/ how-solid.pdf>.

Heo, Seung-hoon. "Reconciling Hereditary Enemy States: Franco-German and South-Korean Japanese Relations in Comparative Perspective". *Journal of International Policy Solutions*, vol. 8, Winter 2008.

Lin, Justin Yifu. "China and the Global Economy", Remarks at the Conference "Asia's Role in the Post-Crisis Global Economy". San Francisco Reserve Bank, 29 November 2011. Available at <http://siteresources.worldbank.org/ DEC/Resources/84797-1104785060319/598886-1104852366603/599473- 1223731755312/JustinLin-China_and_the_Global_Economy-SF-Fed-final.pdf> (accessed 11 August 2013).

Mahbubani, Kishore. *The Great Convergence: Asia, the West, and the Logic of One World*. Public Affairs, 2013.

———.「アジア半球」が世界を動かす [The New Asian Hemisphere]. Japan: Nikkei BP Publishing Centre, Inc., 2010.

———. *The New Asian Hemisphere*. Public Affairs, 2008.

———. *Can Asians Think?* Singapore: Marshall Cavendish Editions, 3rd edition, 2004.

———. "The Making of Modern Asia". *Time*, 15 August 2005. Available at <http://www.time.com/time/world/article/0,8599,2054522,00. html#ixzz225524qVz> (accessed 11 August 2013).

———. "Japan Adrift". *Foreign Policy* No. 88 (Fall 1992): 126–44.

McCurry, Justin and Julia Kollewe. "China overtakes Japan as world's second-largest economy." *The Guardian*, 14 February 2011. Available at <http://

www.guardian.co.uk/business/2011/feb/14/china-second-largest-economy>
(accessed 12 August 2013).

Nye, Joseph S. "Restoring America's Reputation in the World and Why it
Matters". U.S. Congress, House Committee on Foreign Affairs, Sub-
committee on International Organizations, Human Rights and Oversight
Hearing, 4 March 2010.

Singapore Department of Statistics. "Latest Data". Available at <http://www.
singstat.gov.sg/statistics/latest_data.html> (accessed 12 August 2013).

United Nations Secretariat, Population Division of the Department of Economic
and Social Affairs. "World Population Prospects: The 2010 Revision".
Available at <http://esa.un.org/unpd/wpp/index.htm> (accessed 13 August
2013).

Wakabayashi, Daisuke. "How Japan Lost Its Electronics Crown". *The Wall Street
Journal*, U.S. edition, 15 August 2012. Available at <http://online.wsj.com/
article/SB10000872396390444840104577551972061864692.html> (accessed
13 August 2013).

World Bank. "World Databank 2011". <databank.worldbank.org> (accessed
13 August 2013).

14

ASEAN-JAPAN RELATIONS: A SINGAPORE PERSPECTIVE

Tommy Koh

INTRODUCTION

ASEAN and Japan are partners. For a partnership to succeed, it must be grounded on shared interests, common objectives, and mutual trust and confidence. A partnership will not succeed if the partners do not have shared interests or common objectives or if they do not trust each other. In 1977, Prime Minister Takeo Fukuda pledged that Japan would do its best to establish an equal partnership of mutual confidence and trust based on "heart-to-heart" understanding between ASEAN and Japan.

Shared Interests

I will begin this essay by asking whether ASEAN and Japan have shared interests. I will argue that they do. What are their shared interests? They have a shared interest in maintaining peace and stability in East Asia and Asia-Pacific. They have a shared interest in promoting sustainable development and human security. They have a shared interest in promoting regional cooperation and integration.

Common Objectives

ASEAN and Japan have many common objectives. Let me list some of them. They aim to increase trade and investment between them. They aim to facilitate the manufacturing, trading, and servicing activities of the private sector in the two economies. They aim to increase the flow of tourists, students, interns, and talented workers between the two sides. They aim to enhance financial cooperation between them. They aim to augment the connectivity among the ten ASEAN countries and between ASEAN and Japan. They aim to promote human security in ASEAN, through the efficient, productive, and wise use of Japan's official development assistance (ODA). They aim to maintain the freedom of navigation and the security of strategic sea-lanes, such as the Straits of Malacca and Singapore, as well as the Lombok and Sunda Straits. They aim to promote a balance of power in Asia-Pacific and to reduce tension, suspicion, and misunderstanding. They aim to promote greater regional cooperation and integration, bilaterally, as well as through the various regional and sub-regional institutions. They will continue to support the central role that ASEAN plays in those institutions and processes. They also aim to cooperate to promote the green economy and to abide by the ancient Asian ethic that Man must live in harmony with Nature.

Section I: How ASEAN Benefits Japan

For a partnership to thrive, each partner must bring value or benefit to the relationship. What is ASEAN's value proposition for Japan?

First, ASEAN/Southeast Asia is endowed with abundant natural resources. It is a major supplier to Japan of oil, gas, coal, iron ore, palm oil, tin, rubber, etc.

Second, ASEAN has a combined population of close to 600 million. It is a relatively young population, unlike the demographic profiles in Japan and China. With rising educational levels, a strong work ethic, and willingness to learn, the human resource in ASEAN is an economic asset to Japan. Japanese companies in ASEAN employ millions of ASEAN workers and employees.

Third, ASEAN has a market of 600 million consumers with a substantial and growing middle class. ASEAN consumers have a high regard for the quality and reliability of Japanese brands and products. Culturally, ASEAN consumers are favourably disposed to Japanese products and services. There is no or very little anti-Japan sentiment among the people of ASEAN. On the contrary, Japan is much admired by ASEAN citizens.

Fourth, ASEAN sits astride some of the most important sea-lanes of the world, specifically, the Straits of Malacca and Singapore, the Lombok Strait, and the Sunda Strait. Japanese imports and exports have to pass through these sea-lanes. Eighty per cent of Japan's import of oil from the Middle East also goes through these sea-lanes — this has been described as the lifeline of the Japanese economy. The three littoral states, Indonesia, Malaysia, and Singapore, enjoy very good relations with Japan. They have also comported themselves in an exemplary manner by abiding faithfully with international law, including the UN Convention on the Law of the Sea. In a first, the three littoral states have implemented Article 43 of the said Convention by establishing a Cooperative Mechanism that gives Japan and other user states seats at the table, ensuring the safe passage of ships through the Straits and the protection of the marine environment therein.

Fifth, ASEAN hosts US$8.9 billion of foreign direct investment (FDI) by Japan (2010). This is greater than Japan's FDI in China of US$7.3 billion and in India of US$2.9 billion. ASEAN countries continue to welcome investment in their economies by Japanese companies. A priority area is infrastructure development in order to enhance connectivity. According to the U.S. Department of Commerce, investment in ASEAN yields a higher return than in any other developed or developing countries. We understand that the return on Japanese investment in ASEAN is 50 per cent higher than Japan's investment in China. The ASEAN countries are constantly seeking to improve their business environment in order to attract more investment from Japan and other countries.

Sixth, ASEAN/Southeast Asia is the sub-region in Asia with the most positive feelings for Japan. Japan's relationship with China and the Republic of Korea continues to be burdened by the legacy of history. Japan's relationship with South Asia is relatively new and lacks cultural affinity. Japan's relationship with Central Asia is even more remote. The positive feelings for Japan were on full display following the triple disasters in 2011. On 9 April 2011, ASEAN convened a special ASEAN-Japan Ministerial Meeting in Jakarta, as a reflection of ASEAN's solidarity with Japan. In addition, the ASEAN Secretary-General organized an ASEAN Caravan of Goodwill to northeast Japan, from 3–5 June 2011. In April 2012, the ASEAN Economic Ministers took part in an "ASEAN Road Show" in Sendai and Tokyo and visited the areas in Sendai affected by the earthquake. In Singapore, the outpouring of support for Japan by the people of Singapore, from all walks of life and of all ages, was quite overwhelming.

Section II: How Japan Benefits ASEAN/Southeast Asia

Japan has played a very important role in the development of Southeast Asia and of ASEAN. Let me try to enumerate the most important benefits that Japan has brought to Southeast Asia and to ASEAN.

First, Japan's rise from the ashes of war to first world status by the 1960s served as a powerful role model and inspiration for the ASEAN countries. Having emerged from long years of colonial rule, during which they were brainwashed into thinking that they were an inferior people, it was inspiring for them to see that an Asian country has achieved first world status. Japan also played the role of the leader goose in what Dr Saburo Okita has described as the flying-geese pattern of development in Asia. Flying behind Japan were the four newly industrialising economies (NIEs) of Singapore, Hong Kong, South Korea, and Taiwan, which took off in the 1970s. The NIEs were able to tap into Japan's technology and capital, which accelerated their take-off. The rest of ASEAN and China took off in the 1980s. According to Dr Okita, the success of the Asian economies was due, in part, to the effectiveness of the export-oriented industrial development strategies, the expansionary trend of the world economy, and the availability of large pools of inexpensive labor.

Second, ASEAN is the largest recipient of Japan's ODA, totalling US$52 billion or 25 per cent of Japan's total ODA from its establishment in 1967 to 2010. Japan accounts for 40 per cent of the total ODA of US$130 billion received by ASEAN during this period. In recent decades, ODA has come under severe criticism from many quarters. However, in the case of ASEAN, the record suggests that it has done more good than harm. Ambassador Takaaki Kojima (2006) stated that: "Japan improved the economic infrastructure in these countries through ODA and its focus on human resource development assistance, including education to groom a high quality workforce." In addition, Japanese ODA has also focused on improving basic human needs and human security; narrowing the development gap within ASEAN; and strengthening ASEAN through the Japan-ASEAN Integration Fund (JAIF), the ASEAN Cultural Fund, Japan-ASEAN Exchange Projects, the Japan-ASEAN General Exchange Fund, the Japan-ASEAN Solidarity Fund, and the Japan-funded Economic Research Institute for ASEAN and East Asia (ERIA). It would, I think, be fair to say that, in spite of the leakages and other imperfections of Japan's ODA, it has played a positive role in the social and economic development of ASEAN and its people, and in strengthening ASEAN as an institution.

Third, I wish to highlight the role that Japan's private sector has played in the development of ASEAN. Foreign direct investment creates jobs, markets for exports, and transfers of technology and know-how. ASEAN welcomes FDI from all sources. From 1995–2010, ASEAN received FDI totalling US$604 billion, with Japan as the foremost investor, accounting for US$76.2 billion or 12.6 per cent. In the same period, Japan's FDI in Asia totalled US$193 billion, with ASEAN as the number one recipient, accounting for 39.4 per cent or US$76.2 billion. Japanese companies have seized upon the comparative advantages of different ASEAN countries, by locating plants in different countries to make different components. This has spurred intra-company and intra-regional trade. It has also resulted in a new pattern of manufacturing in the region. Two World Bank economists, Indermit Gill and Homi Kharas, wrote a thoughtful book in 2006 entitled *An East Asian Renaissance: Ideas For Economic Growth*, in which they described the emergence of new regional production networks.

Fourth, I wish to focus on trade between Japan and ASEAN. In recent decades, many developing countries have argued that trade is more important than aid. In the World Trade Organization, United Nations Conference on Trade and Development (UNCTAD), and other forums, they have demanded the removal of barriers to trade and a more level playing field. Trade between Japan and ASEAN is booming, amounting to US$247.3 billion in 2011. Japan is ASEAN's third largest trading partner, after China and the EU. ASEAN is Japan's second largest trading partner, after China. The ASEAN-Japan Comprehensive Economic Partnership (AJCEP) came into force on 1 December 2008. Japan has also been a keen supporter of the ASEAN-led Regional Comprehensive Economic Partnership (RCEP), which synergizes the web of ASEAN+1 FTAs. At the 44th ASEAN Economic Ministers' Meeting in Siem Reap in August 2012, Japan confirmed its participation in the launch of RCEP negotiations at the 21st ASEAN Summit in November 2012.

Fifth, tourism is an important sector in all the ASEAN economies. Japan is a major source of tourism for ASEAN, with 3.4 million Japanese visiting ASEAN in 2010. This accounted for 8.7 per cent of all tourists visiting ASEAN, behind the EU, China, and Australia.

Sixth, Japan has been enormously helpful to Indonesia, Malaysia, and Singapore, regarding the safety of navigation through the Straits of Malacca and Singapore. Long before the establishment of the Cooperative Mechanism, Japan had been helping the three littoral states with seismic surveys, the removal of wrecks, etc. Japan has also helped these countries to combat piracy in the Straits. ReCAAP, which is located in Singapore, is a Japanese initiative.

Seventh, Japan is helping ASEAN to fulfill its Connectivity Initiative. Japan was the first ASEAN Dialogue Partner to establish its own Connectivity Task Force to engage with the ASEAN Connectivity Coordinating Committee. Japan has identified 33 projects related to the three ASEAN corridors: the East-West Corridor, the Southern Economic Corridor, and the Maritime Economic Corridor. In October 2011, the Japanese Embassy in Singapore co-organized a workshop with the ASEAN Studies Centre of the Institute of Southeast Asian Studies (ISEAS). The purpose of the workshop was to promote ASEAN Connectivity to the private sector, emphasizing the business opportunities present in the various priority projects under the Master Plan on ASEAN Connectivity (MPAC). At the 14th ASEAN-Japan Summit in November 2011, the ASEAN leaders expressed their appreciation to Japan for its strong commitment to the Connectivity Initiative.

Eighth, there is an English saying "A friend in need is a friend indeed". Japan proved the sincerity of its friendship for ASEAN during the Asian financial crisis of 1997. Japan came to the rescue of all the countries affected by the crisis, namely, Thailand, Indonesia, Philippines, Malaysia, and a non-ASEAN country, South Korea. In addition, Japan proposed the setting up of an Asian Monetary Fund, which was scuttled by the United States and the IMF. Following the crisis, Japan proposed that the finance ministers and central bank governors of ASEAN Plus 3 cooperate more closely. This has come to be known as the Chiang Mai Initiative. What has been achieved so far, by way of the currency swap arrangements, the better coordination of macroeconomic policies and peer review, the development of the Asian bond market, and the establishment of a pool of readily available liquidity in the event of a currency crisis, are modest steps taken in the long journey toward financial cooperation among the ASEAN Plus 3 countries.

Section III: Japan-Singapore Relations

Singapore is the only ASEAN country that has achieved first world status. However, in the years ahead, it is very likely that several ASEAN middle-income countries will achieve a breakthrough and become high-income countries. In view of that prospect, the relationship between Japan and Singapore could be a precursor of things to come.

Japan's relations with Singapore go back to the colonial period. After Singapore's independence, Prime Minister Lee Kuan Yew invested substantial time and effort in activating Singapore-Japan relations. He was able to earn the trust of a succession of Japanese prime ministers. He did this by showing that he had no interest in stoking the embers of the past but in building a new future. He understood the importance to Japan of the freedom of navigation, in general, and specifically, through the Straits of Malacca and Singapore. He warmly welcomed the visits of the then Crown Prince Akihito and Princess Michiko and Prime Minister Eisaku Sato.

In return, Japan helped Singapore's development and industrialization in many ways. Japan established the Japan-Singapore Training Centre, the Computer Software Training Centre, the Japanese Studies department at the National University of Singapore (NUS), and paired the Faculty of Engineering at NUS with a Japanese counterpart. All these activities helped in Singapore's human resource development.

The Japanese private sector also played a major role in Singapore's economic development. The famous Japanese company Seiko was an early investor. The Seiko factory was opened in 1976. In addition to making watches, the factory made precision instruments, industrial robotics, and automation systems. Another important investor was Sumitomo Chemical Corporation. With the support of Prime Ministers Miki, Fukuda, and Nakasone, Sumitomo took the lead in establishing Singapore's first petrochemical project. Many other Japanese companies have also played a vital role in the success of Singapore's industrialization. The Japan Productivity Centre helped Singapore to start its own National Productivity Council and the productivity movement.

In his memoirs *From Third World to First*, Mr Lee Kuan Yew (2000, p. 589) wrote:

> ... I have seen the strength of the Japanese people and the quality of their education. While they may not have encouraged as many entrepreneurs in new start-ups as Americans have done, their young men and women do not lack imagination, creativity and innovative ideas. Within five to ten years, the Japanese will come fighting back.

At independence in 1965, Singapore's per capita income was US$516. Today, Singapore's per capita income is US$52,051 — a hundred-fold increase. The relationship between the two countries has evolved from that between a developed and a developing country to that between two developed countries. The relationship is strong, multi-faceted, and mutually beneficial. Singapore was the first country with which Japan concluded an economic partnership agreement in 2002. The two-way trade is US$42.1 billion and Singapore is Japan's fourth largest trading partner in ASEAN. Japan's cumulative foreign direct investment in Singapore stands at US$42 billion — one notch behind Thailand. Singapore has become an investor in Japan and its cumulative investment in Japan is estimated at US$12.29 billion. Many Japanese tourists visit Singapore and Japan is one of the favourite destinations of Singapore's tourists.

Section IV: Raising ASEAN-Japan Relations to a Higher Peak

The relationship between ASEAN and Japan is substantive, comprehensive, and mutually beneficial. It is a comfortable and trouble-free relationship. There is a high level of mutual trust between ASEAN and Japan. 2013 marks 40 years of dialogue relations between ASEAN and Japan. However, like all old relationships, it is in danger of being taken for granted by both sides. It is, therefore, good for us to review the relationship and ask how we can take it to a higher peak. I have three recommendations.

Japan's Green Power

First, Japan should seek to play the role of thought leader on the environment, green economy, and green philanthropy. Japan is not only Asia's most advanced economy; it is also the greenest economy. Japan's environment is in pristine condition. It leads the world in the efficient use of energy. It is also a world leader in electric and hybrid vehicles. Many Japanese companies are at the cutting edge of innovation in the water industry, energy industry, transport industry, etc. Japan should consider launching a major new initiative with ASEAN, focusing on helping the ASEAN countries to do a good job in the sustainable exploitation of their natural resources, in the more efficient use of water and energy, in coping with climate change, and in their transitions to a low-carbon economy. Japanese ODA, private investment, and public-private partnership can be used to achieve the desired objectives. Japan has not done enough to project its green power to the world.

Japan's Peace Power

Second, Japan can also do more to project itself as a thought leader for peace. The Japanese people do not wish for Japan to be a great military power or a nuclear-armed state. They are dedicated to the cause of peace. Japan has not, however, done enough to promote this mission. There is no institute in Japan like the Stockholm International Peace Research Institute (SIPRI). Japan has not emulated the examples of Norway or Qatar in seeking to mediate international disputes. I would encourage Japan to consider giving its strong support to the ASEAN Institute for Peace and Reconciliation. Japan should seriously consider how it could play the kind of positive roles that countries such as Sweden, Norway, and Qatar have played in the promotion of peace and the peaceful resolution of conflicts in the world.

Japan's Soft Power

According to Professor Joseph Nye, there are three forms of power: coercion (stick), payment (carrot), and soft power. Soft power is derived from culture, political goals or ideology, and foreign policy. Japan is constitutionally unable to resort to coercion. It can use chequebook diplomacy and soft power. The benefit of chequebook diplomacy is often short-lived. This was brought home to me some years ago, when Bangladesh defeated Japan in its bid for a non-permanent seat in the UN Security Council. Countries that were recipients of Japanese ODA were expected to vote for Japan. Instead, they voted for Bangladesh. Chequebook diplomacy is, therefore, an unreliable instrument for influencing the conduct of states.

My third recommendation is for Japan to harness and project its soft power, to ASEAN first, and then to the world. Recently I came across an opinion poll conducted by an Australian think tank, the Lowy Institute, on the attitudes of the Indonesian public toward various countries in the world. I was struck by the fact that Japan was the country that the Indonesian public liked the best. Although I do not have the empirical evidence, my impression is that Japan is also very popular with the people of Singapore.

How did I come to my conclusion? I did so for the following reasons. There are many Singaporeans, both students and adults, who are learning the

Japanese language. Japanese anime and J-pop are very popular with young Singaporeans. Japanese cuisine has been embraced by Singaporeans. Japanese fashion is a hit, with brands such as UNIQLO and Muji proliferating in our shopping malls. Despite its small size, Singapore has become the seventh largest source of tourists to Japan from Asia. The opening of the Japan Creative Centre in 2009 was an important milestone. Japan should consider establishing a similar center in each of the ASEAN countries.

Education, Science, and Technology

Japan is a world player in education, science, and technology. Tokyo University is reputed to be the best in Asia and one of the top ten in the world. Because of the difficulty of learning the Japanese language, Japan does not have as many foreign students as it should. My proposal is for Japan's elite universities to offer graduate degrees in English. Some are already doing so.

Many Japanese scientists have won the Nobel Prize and many Japanese architects have won the Pritzker Prize. I am therefore convinced that Japan has much to offer the world, in general, and ASEAN, in particular, in science and technology, architecture and design, etc. The Okinawa Institute of Science and Technology and the Ritsumeikan Asia Pacific University in Beppu can play a significant role in attracting Asean talent to study in Japan.

I propose that the government of Japan consider setting up the Japanese equivalent of the Fulbright Scholarships for students and professors from Japan and ASEAN. This will achieve two objectives at the same time: enhance human resource development in ASEAN and strengthen the human bridge between us.

CONCLUSION

My report card on the state of ASEAN-Japan relations is a very positive one. The relationship is founded on shared interests, common objectives, and a high level of mutual trust. We should not, however, take each other for granted. We should consider how to upgrade the relationship to a higher peak. I have suggested four ideas that play to Japan's strength — its green power, its peace power, its education power, and its attractive soft power.

References

Kojima, Takaaki. *Japan and ASEAN Partnership for a Stable and Prosperous Future.* Singapore: Institute of Southeast Asian Studies, 2006.

Lee Kuan Yew. *From Third World to First: The Singapore Story: 1965–2000.* Harper Collins, 2000.